# *3D with HOOPS*

## Build Interactive 3D Graphics into Your C++ Applications

Wm Leler and Jim Merry
Autodesk, Inc.

x

▲▲ **ADDISON-WESLEY**

An imprint of Addison Wesley Longman, Inc.

Reading, Massachusetts • Menlo Park, California • New York • Harlow, England
Don Mills, Ontario • Amsterdam • Bonn • Sydney • Singapore
Tokyo • Mexico City • Madrid

The following organizations have granted permission to reprint their artwork:
Plate 1, Cognition Corporation
Plate 2, ICEM Systems
Plate 3, Han Dataport
Plate 4, Tecoplan Informatik
Plate 5, Jandel Scientific
Plates 6–8, Visual Numerics, Inc.
Plate 10, CADCentre
Plate 11, Laboratory of Structural and Continuum Mechanics of the
    Swiss Federal Institute of Technology
Plate 12, Fluent, Inc.
Plate 13, Theratronics
Plate 14, Radiological Oncology Computer Services

**Library of Congress Cataloging-in-Publication Data**
Leler, Wm. (William)
    3D with HOOPS : building interactive 3D graphics into your C++ applications / Wm Leler,
Jim Merry.
        p.   cm.
    Includes bibliographical references and index.
    ISBN 0-201-87025-8
    1. Computer graphics. 2. Three-dimensional display systems. 3. Hoops (Computer file)
I. Merry, Jim. II. Title.
T385.L427   1996
006.6—dc20                                                                95-37454
                                                                               CIP

Autodesk part number: 05200-000000-5100

HOOPS is a registered trademark of Autodesk, Inc.

Published by Addison Wesley Longman, Inc.

1 2 3 4 5 6 7 8 9 10—CRW—0099989796

# Contents

# Preface

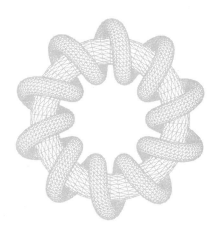

## Intended Audience

This book and accompanying CD-ROM are for software developers who want to write three-dimensional (3D) graphics applications. They will help you to add 3D graphics to an existing application, or to design and implement new 3D graphics applications. In either case, our goal is to help you create commercial-quality applications that are fast, powerful, portable, and easy to extend and maintain. We also want to show you that writing 3D graphics applications does not need to be difficult; it can even be fun. There is nothing like the thrill of generating your first 3D image — seeing your two-dimensional monitor screen become a transparent window onto a 3D world.

Unlike many graphics books, this one is not designed to teach you how to write a 3D graphics library; rather, it shows you how to use a commercial graphics library to write a commercial-quality 3D application. After all, you do not need to know the laws of thermodynamics to learn how to drive a car. Of course, it sometimes helps to know how a car works if you want to drive well, so this book also contains information that you will find helpful about 3D graphics, including

- Graphics principles
- Techniques for structuring your application
- Optimization for maximum performance

All the examples in this book are written in C++ and use the HOOPS® graphics library from Autodesk, Inc (the HOOPS library is included on the CD-ROM). You will find that both C++ and HOOPS make it easy to write 3D graphics applications. Both are high-level languages that let you concentrate on the task of writing your application, rather than on low-level (and often extraneous) details, and both have a proven track record for writing commercial-quality software.

## Prerequisites

This book assumes that you have a knowledge of C++. If you do not, but you are comfortable with the C language, you should be able to learn sufficient C++ by working through the example programs in this book. After all, one of the best ways to learn C++ is by example. If you cannot or do not want to use C++ for your application, you can also use HOOPS from C, FORTRAN, or any other language that can call C subroutines.

There are notes (just like this one) that appear whenever we use a C++ feature that might be unfamiliar to C programmers. If you are already a C++ programmer, you can ignore these notes.

Example programs that use a specific window system are shown for Microsoft Windows (WIN32), the Microsoft Foundation Classes (MFC), X11 (X-Windows) on UNIX, and Motif on X11. If you use some other window system, however, it should be straightforward to adapt the examples to your needs.

This book does not assume that you have any knowledge of the HOOPS graphics library. Familiarity with 3D graphics in general is helpful, but is not required. Chapter 3 covers all the necessary graphics fundamentals.

There are also notes (like this one) scattered throughout this book that provide additional information on the theory of computer graphics, or that go into the inner details of HOOPS or of some other system. These informational notes often assume that you have advanced knowledge of computer systems or of 3D graphics. You do not need to understand (or even to read) these notes to write a 3D graphics application, but sometimes it helps to know what is going on under the hood if you want to get maximum performance out of your graphics application.

## Included Software

The CD-ROM included with this book contains the source code for the example programs in the book, plus a large number of programs not covered in the book.

The CD-ROM also contains the full HOOPS graphics library for practically every computer system available today, including

- Intel architecture (x86) machines running Microsoft Windows or Windows NT

- PowerPC and DEC Alpha running Windows NT or OpenVMS

- Several flavors of UNIX machines (including Sun Microsystems, Hewlett-Packard, Digital Equipment Corp., IBM, and Silicon Graphics) running X11 and Motif

- Apple Macintosh

- A few platforms that have specialized acceleration hardware (GL on SGI, XGL on Sun, Starbase on HP, and OpenGL on NT)

Also included on the CD-ROM is the complete documentation for HOOPS: the reference manual, cookbook, tutorial, installation guide, and release notes. The documentation is in PostScript format, so it can be printed or viewed with any viewer that reads PostScript. There is also a version of the reference manual in Hypertext Markup Language (HTML), in addition to the PostScript version. You can read the HTML reference manual using any World Wide Web (WWW) browser such as Mosaic or Netscape (you do not need Internet access). Hardcopy versions of these manuals can be ordered from Autodesk (contact information is at the end of this section).

To use the HOOPS library to compile the example programs, you will need to provide your own programming environment, including a C++ compiler. See Appendix B or the *HOOPS Installation Guide* on the CD-ROM for information on supported compilers.

You can find information on HOOPS in a WWW page, by using any Web browser with the URL

ftp://ftp.autodesk.com/pub/component_technologies/hoops/www/main.htm

Note that you must access this Web page using the FTP protocol (rather than HTTP, as is normal with Web pages), because it is on the Autodesk FTP server. It will display just like a normal Web page. Alternatively, Tech Soft in Germany maintains a HOOPS page at the URL

http://www.germany.eu.net/shop/techsoft/hoops/main.htm

The HOOPS libraries contained on the CD-ROM previously cost several thousand dollars per developer seat — a development license that included every platform contained on the CD-ROM sold for $65,000. Autodesk has licensed you, the purchaser of this book, to use this software for individual and developmental work. However, you may not distribute any program based on this software without first licensing HOOPS from Autodesk. In addition, free support is limited to the online newsletter — to be added to the newsletter mailing list, contact Autodesk OEM Sales.

Autodesk also offers training courses, consulting services, and other support. For more information, to purchase support, or to license HOOPS for distribution, contact Autodesk OEM Sales at 510/523-5900, or send electronic mail to oem_info@autodesk.com with the words "3D with HOOPS" in the subject line.

## How to Install the Software

How you install the included software will depend on what system you will be using. The *HOOPS Installation Guide* provided on the CD-ROM describes the installation process for every supported platform. Essential installation information also appears in Appendix B of this book.

For most platforms, installation is simple: You either run an installation script from the CD-ROM, or just copy the HOOPS library and other files onto your hard disk.

You will probably also want to copy the HTML reference manual onto your hard disk, to use for online help. The top-level page for the *HOOPS Reference Manual* is in the file cover.htm.

## How to Run the Example Programs

The example programs in this book are designed to be portable, so they can be run, unchanged, on as many of the supported platforms as is possible. Unfortunately, writing truly portable programs is not an easy task. For example, on UNIX, the main entry point to a program is called main; on Microsoft Windows, the main entry point is called WinMain. In addition, on certain platforms (such as Windows), routines such as printf do not work.

We have written the example programs using the symbol main as their entry point, and occasionally using printf to print out information. Thus, they will run unchanged on UNIX platforms, but will not compile on Microsoft Windows. To solve this problem, HOOPS includes a file called w32cmain.c (in the directory demo/win32/unixport) that you can compile and link in with the example programs to make them compile on Windows. This file includes definitions of WinMain and printf. You should include this file when compiling the example programs from this book on Microsoft Windows or Windows NT.

A few of the supported platforms may require changes to the example programs in this book. In particular, on the Apple Macintosh, you will need to make changes such as removing any calls to printf.

## Further Information

If you are interested in the inner workings of 3D graphics libraries, you can look at one of the many good textbooks on the subject. The standard text is

Foley, van Dam, Feiner, and Hughes, *Computer Graphics: Principles and Practice, Second Edition in C*, Addison-Wesley, Reading, MA, 1996, 1112 pages, ISBN #0-201-84840-6.

Starting with the 1996 edition, the example programs in Foley, van Dam, Feiner, and Hughes are written in C (rather than in Pascal, as they were in earlier editions).

There is a more introductory version of the Foley, van Dam, Feiner, and Hughes book; it also has more program examples:

Foley, van Dam, Feiner, Hughes, and Phillips, *Introduction to Computer Graphics*, Addison-Wesley, Reading, MA, 1994, 526 pages, ISBN #0-201-60921-5.

Here are two other books on computer graphics that you might find useful:

Alan Watt, *3D Computer Graphics, Second Edition*, Addison-Wesley, Reading, MA, 1993, 508 pages, ISBN #0-201-63186-5.

John Vince, *3D Computer Animation*, Addison-Wesley, Reading, MA, 1992, 363 pages, ISBN #0-201-62756-6.

Finally, here are several books on C++. The first book, by Bjarne Stroustrup, is the standard reference book that every C++ programmer should own. The book by Winston is a good book for C programmers who want to learn C++. The Lippman book is probably the best guide for new programmers learning C++.

Bjarne Stroustrup, *The C++ Programming Language, Second Edition*, Addison-Wesley, Reading, MA, 1991, 576 pages, ISBN #0-201-53992-6.

Patrick Henry Winston, *On to C++*, Addison-Wesley, Reading, MA, 1994, 297 pages, ISBN #0-201-58043-8.

Stanley Lippman, *C++ Primer, Second Edition*, Addison-Wesley, Reading, MA, 1991, 572 pages, ISBN #0-201-54848-8.

Barton and Nackman, *Scientific and Engineering C++*, Addison-Wesley, Reading, MA, 1994, 704 pages, ISBN #0-201-53393-6.

## Organization of the Book

Chapter 1 is an introduction to 3D graphics and HOOPS. It covers the reasons why you should add 3D graphics to your application, and what the advantages and disadvantages are of using a graphics library such as HOOPS. It then jumps right in and presents several simple HOOPS programs (which include interaction and even simple animation).

Chapter 2 covers how to organize graphics applications; it includes an introduction to the principles of object-oriented programming that apply to graphics applications.

Chapter 3 is an overview of everything that you will need to know about 3D graphics. This information has been placed into a single chapter, so that the other chapters can assume that you are already familiar with the principles of 3D graphics. Depending on your level of expertise, you can either read this chapter in its entirety or refer back to it as necessary.

Chapter 4 discusses the heart of the HOOPS graphics system, including segments, attributes, drivers, and options. There is also a section that describes the features of HOOPS that help you to organize your graphics application.

Chapter 5 covers the different kinds of geometry that HOOPS provides, and the attributes that apply to them. This chapter concludes with an example program that draws every kind of geometry about which HOOPS knows.

Whereas Chapters 4 and 5 describe how to create a HOOPS database, Chapter 6 covers all the different operations that you can perform on the resulting graphics database. You can view the database using a camera, you can print or plot it, and you can create an image of it. You can also save the database into a file, or search it.

Chapter 7 covers how to use HOOPS with a window system. There are sections on using HOOPS as its own window system, and ones on using HOOPS with X11, Motif, Win32, and MFC.

Chapter 8 explains interaction, including how to organize your application to handle user input, what the different kinds of user input are, and how to work with a window system.

Chapter 9 covers color and texture. An important topic in this chapter is how to deal with hardware color maps.

Chapter 10 contains a wealth of tips and techniques that you can use to make your graphics application run faster, and to avoid common problems. This chapter also includes a list of all the example programs included on the CD-ROM.

Appendix A contains a short history of HOOPS, and of the company that built HOOPS.

Appendix B contains directions for installing HOOPS for available platforms.

The book also includes a CD-ROM that contains the HOOPS libraries and documentation, the example programs from the book, and the source code for a complete graphics application called the viewer. See Section 10.5 for more information about the viewer.

## Acknowledgments

This book has truly been a work of collaboration. Wm Leler was the primary author. Most of the words came from his keyboard, and he takes full responsibility for any errors and omissions. Jim Merry brought a unique perspective on the problems programmers face when writing real graphics applications. He wrote the Motif version of the viewer application, and many of our example programs. During the writing of this book, Jim also held the job of marketing manager for HOOPS, and was the principal advocate of the idea of giving away with the book a development copy of HOOPS.

Garry Wiegand was the primary founder of Ithaca Software. He is one of the best programmers we know, and has the gift of taking complex problems and finding simple and elegant solutions. Wiegand's personality and style pervade the design and implementation of HOOPS. And, as one of Wm's housemates, Wiegand was constantly available (whether he liked it or not) to answer millions of questions. He also pitched in to write the MFC version of the viewer application.

Everybody on the HOOPS team played a role in this book, answering questions, fixing bugs, and reviewing chapters. We express sincere gratitude to Michael Butler, Milt Capsimalis, Robert Covey, Robert Fjerstad, Ashu Goel, Subramanya Gupta, Tanvir Hassan, C. Billy Hsu, Azhar Khan, Jeff Kowalsky, Mark Kumler, Brian Mathews, Rob Mazeffa, Erin Porter, Usha Sanagala, Kathleen Schubert, Tim Scully, Scott Sheppard, Natarajan Srinivasan, Jim Stiefel, Eric Wagner, and David Whitehead.

Several friends and colleagues provided timely reviews during the writing of the book. Michael Wilk was especially helpful. We also thank Vicki deMey and Tom Burrows for their reviews.

Addison-Wesley has gone above and beyond the call of duty in their help publishing this book. Peter Gordon was the driving force. Lyn Dupré has to be the most perfectionist copy editor in the business.

Leler also thanks Lisa Martinengo for her support and love.

# 1 A Taste of HOOPS

This chapter discusses the reasons why you might want to add three-dimensional (3D) graphics to your application, why you should use a 3D graphics library rather than writing your own graphics routines, and why you might want to use HOOPS as that graphics library. Then, we plunge right in and write a few 3D graphics programs, to show you how easy it can be.

## 1.1 The Uses of 3D Graphics

*Why use 3D Graphics?*

*Because the world is 3D.*

If you look at the most exciting new applications that are being developed today, you will see that most of them use 3D graphics.

- Computer-aided–design systems for mechanical parts are changing from two-dimensional (2D) drafting-oriented systems to true 3D design systems (Plates 1 through 4).

- Visualization systems allow scientists to see patterns in data, such as pollution flows in air and water, the configuration of the universe seconds after the big bang, or even monetary flows in world markets (Plate 5).

- Computer graphics helps mathematicians to understand complex equations (Plates 6 through 9).

- Engineering-analysis applications help engineers to plan the steps required to manufacture a part, to understand the stress placed on materials, or even to study the air flow around an airborne skier (Plates 10 through 12).

- Medical applications can use computer graphics to help doctors see inside of the human body (Plates 13 and 14).

- Synthetic actors — including toys, cartoon rabbits, realistic dinosaurs, and even humanlike robots that go beyond special effects — are becoming common in motion pictures.

- Computer games are going 3D — there are even 3D screen savers — and these games will eventually appear on our home TV sets with digital interactive TV.

- Architects (and their customers) can do a visual walkthrough of a building, and can make changes before the first nail is driven.

- Professionals can use 3D graphs and charts to display multivariate data in spreadsheets, highlighting trends and exceptions.

- Artists can use 3D graphics to make their art more engaging, and to attract attention to advertisements and posters.

- The term *virtual reality* has grabbed a lot of attention, but it is just a fancy name for an interactive 3D graphical user interface.

You can probably think of other examples, including the next application that you were planning to write. Practically all computer applications can benefit from the use of 3D graphics.

We can expect to see more applications that use 3D graphics as that technology becomes less expensive. When the price of 2D graphics hardware became reasonable, 2D graphical user interfaces took off, resulting in the Macintosh finder, X-Windows and Motif for UNIX, and Microsoft Windows and OS/2 Presentation Manager for the IBM PC. Applications that took advantage of these 2D graphical interfaces soon followed, and they had a significant competitive advantage over their text-based predecessors. Now that 3D graphics hardware is becoming less expensive, we can expect 3D graphics applications to take off.

## 1.2    The Advantages of Using a Graphics Library

In the past, writing 3D graphics applications was difficult. If you wanted to write a graphics application, you had to write your own graphics routines. These routines are tedious to write, prone to subtle errors, and difficult to debug. Writing your own graphics routines required specialized knowledge of geometry and mathematics that typically had little to do with your application. Tools to help you write such routines were either nonexistent or difficult to use. At best, manufacturers would provide a low-level programming interface to their graphics hardware, so the resulting applications were not portable to different systems, or even to the same system with a different display card or a different input device. Writing efficient (fast) graphics programs was especially difficult, and writing efficient graphics programs that were also portable to different systems was nearly impossible.

Today, applications are built using software components. For example, if you were writing an application, you would normally never even consider writing your own user-interface library. Instead, you would use an existing user-interface library, such as MFC or Motif. Using such a library has several advantages:

- You can concentrate on writing your application without wasting time writing user-interface code.

- A program written for a popular user-interface library is much more portable than is a program that depends on specific user-interface hardware.

- An application written using a portable user-interface library will have a common look and feel on all platforms on which it runs, increasing its usability.

- Your program probably even runs faster, because the cost of optimizing a single user-interface library can be amortized over many different applications. In addition, hardware manufacturers will optimize their hardware to a popular library.

A 3D graphics library can be used as the 3D graphics component of your application, and using it will confer the same advantages as would using a 2D user-interface component:

- You can avoid learning how to write 3D graphics routines.

- Your application will be more portable.

- Your application will produce the same 3D output on many different platforms.

- Your application will usually run faster.

## 1.3     The Advantages of Using HOOPS

There are many 3D graphics libraries available today; as a programmer, you will pick the one that is right for your job. In the remainder of this book, you will learn the reasons why you might (or might not) want to use HOOPS as your 3D graphics library. Here, we give only a summary of those reasons.

- *HOOPS is complete.* Rather than being a low-level interface to some graphics hardware, HOOPS is a complete package that includes all the graphics tools that you will need to build an application. For example, many graphics libraries can draw a picture on the screen, but when you want to print that picture, they offer no help at all.

- *HOOPS is easy to use.* HOOPS was built by software engineers who wanted to make writing applications easy; it was not built by a hardware manufacturer or a committee. Among the features that make HOOPS easy to use are its declarative programming interface and structured device interface.

- *HOOPS is portable.* HOOPS gives you the same powerful 3D graphics whether your application runs on a high-powered graphics workstation or an inexpensive personal computer. HOOPS runs on all major personal computers and workstations, and even on many large computer systems. HOOPS is more portable than is any existing user-interface library.

- *HOOPS gives your graphics a consistent look across all platforms.* If a platform lacks hardware to support a capability, HOOPS fills in with software. In the past, you had to buy an expensive graphics workstation to get powerful 3D graphics. HOOPS provides all capabilities on all platforms.

- *HOOPS is fast.* More than a half century of combined work has gone into optimizing HOOPS. And, because HOOPS is used in many commercial applications, hardware manufacturers (including Hewlett-Packard, Sun Microsystems, Silicon Graphics, and Digital Equipment Corp.) have helped to make it run quickly on their systems. In addition, PC display-board manufacturers, such as Matrox and Artist Graphics, have written optimized HOOPS drivers for their 3D graphics cards. You do not need an expensive workstation to enjoy high-speed, interactive 3D graphics.

- *HOOPS works with other standards.* For example, HOOPS is compatible with all major window systems.

## 1.4    A Simple 3D Graphics Program

This section presents an especially simple 3D graphics program to give you a feeling for how easy it can be to use 3D graphics. As is traditional in textbooks on programming, this program will display the text "hello, world!" in a window.

We will start by looking at the program without graphics. Program 1.1 just prints the text "hello, world!" on the console.

```
1   #include <stdio.h>
2   void main() {
3       printf("hello, world!\n");
4   }
```

**Program 1.1**    Display "hello, world!" — using text only.

When you execute Program 1.1, it should display the following text.

```
hello, world!
```

**C++**    C++ programs normally do not use the printf function; instead, they use the C++ streamio (stream input and output) facilities. Because few programs in this book will be printing text output — most will use graphical output instead — we shall stick to the familiar C printf function for those few times that we need to output text to the console.

Program 1.1 may look simple, but it presents problems. For example, it will not run on systems that do not support the concept of console output, such as certain programming systems on Microsoft Windows or the Macintosh, where all input and output must go through a window. On Windows, this program can be compiled with QuickWin. On Microsoft Windows NT, it can be compiled as a console application so that character output can be directed to the console.

Alternatively, for Microsoft Windows and Windows NT, HOOPS provides the file w32cmain.c (found in the directory demo\win32\unixport of the HOOPS distribution) that implements the printf function. This version of printf displays its output in a dialog box, rather than on the console. On these platforms, you can use printf if you compile and link in w32cmain.c.

The file w32cmain.c also defines WinMain, which is defined to call your main function. This function allows the example HOOPS programs in this book to be compiled without change under both UNIX and Windows. On UNIX platforms, you can compile the example programs from the book directly. On Windows, the only change that you need to make is to compile and link in w32cmain.c with the example program.

Make sure that you can compile and run Program 1.1 on your system, before you proceed to use 3D graphics.

### 1.4.1        Our First Graphics Program

Program 1.2 uses HOOPS to display the string "hello, world!" centered in a window.

```
1   #include <hc.h>

2   void main() {
3       HC_Open_Segment("?Picture");
4           HC_Insert_Text(0.0, 0.0, 0.0, "hello, world!");
5       HC_Close_Segment();
6       HC_Pause();
7   }
```

**Program 1.2**     Display "hello, world!" — using HOOPS.

When you execute Program 1.2, the result will look something like Figure 1.1 (depending on your window system).

**Figure 1.1**     Output from Program 1.2.

**6**

Program 1.2 is slightly more complicated than is Program 1.1, but it also does more. HOOPS creates a new window (using the window system that is running on your computer). The text is displayed, centered in this window, and the program pauses until you close the window, or until you send it input, such as a mouse click or a keyboard key press.

Line 1 of Program 1.2 includes the header file for the HOOPS library (in the same way that we included the header file for the library "stdio" in Program 1.1). The names that begin with "HC_" are HOOPS commands. Line 3 opens a HOOPS segment named "?Picture". A *segment* is basically an object that you open, make changes to, then close (in the same way that you can open, read and write, and close a file or directory in a file system). Each segment has a *name;* the name "?Picture" is a special HOOPS name that corresponds to an output display window on your screen.

Line 4 inserts a text string into the current segment (the one that we just opened) at coordinates (0, 0, 0) — in HOOPS, this point is the center of the display and, by default, the string is centered at this location. Since the current segment is "?Picture", this text string will be displayed on the screen. Note that the text string no longer ends with a new-line character (\n). The open segment is closed on line 5. Note the convention of indenting program lines between an HC_Open_Segment and HC_Close_Segment call, to give a visual cue when a segment is open. Like indenting curly braces in C, using this convention helps you to ensure that all HOOPS segments are closed properly.

Finally, the HC_Pause command on line 6 causes the display to be updated, and then waits for an input event before proceeding. Because the output window of an application vanishes when the application terminates, if we did not call HC_Pause, the output would vanish before we got a chance to see anything. After HOOPS receives an input event (a mouse click or key press, for example), the program terminates and the output window vanishes.

| C++ | Program 1.2 will work — exactly as written — in either C or C++. Since HOOPS uses C calling conventions, it can be called from any language that can call C subroutines. |
| --- | --- |

Text output in Program 1.2 is displayed using the HOOPS default font, which on most systems is a (fairly ugly) stroked font (drawn with line segments). You can use the HC_Set_Text_Font command to choose other fonts, including any outline (PostScript or TrueType) fonts on your system. HOOPS also comes with several outline fonts. See the HC_Set_Text_Font command in the *HOOPS Reference Manual* for more information.

### 1.4.2      Use of HOOPS for 2D Graphics

You may wonder why anyone would want to use a 3D graphics library such as HOOPS just to display 2D text in a window. After all, that is what window systems such as X-Windows or Microsoft Windows are for. Although it is true that you would normally use a window system to display 2D graphics, most 3D applications also use some 2D graphics, so HOOPS has a full set of 2D capabilities, including the ability to create windows, to display text, and to handle graphical input.

It is possible to write an interactive graphical program entirely in HOOPS, without making any calls whatsoever to a window system. Writing such a program gives you an advantage over using a window system, in that the program is more portable. For example, Program 1.2 will run unchanged on dozens of different systems, whereas the equivalent program written in X-Windows would not run on Microsoft Windows, and vice versa. HOOPS is also easier to use: The equivalent program written in X-Windows or Microsoft Windows would be considerably more complicated.

### 1.4.3      Compilation and Execution of HOOPS Programs

To compile and run a HOOPS program, you will need several files from the CD-ROM. Be sure to install the correct files for your system.

When you compile your program, you will first need to make sure that the include file "hc.h" is in a directory where the compiler can find it (such as the current directory, or a directory on your include path). Second, you will have to link your program with the HOOPS library (normally called something like "HOOPS.LIB" or "hoops.a"). You may also need to link to the math library for your system (HOOPS uses floating-point computations) and to the library for the window system that you are using (so that HOOPS can create windows).

For example, on most UNIX systems, you would compile Program 1.2 by typing

```
CC -o hello hello.cpp -lhoops -lX11 -lm
```

On Microsoft Windows, you would link with the library "hoops.lib". If you are using Microsoft Visual C++, you should tell the compiler where to find "hc.h" and "hoops.lib". On this system, HOOPS is a dynamically loaded library (DLL), so you need to make sure that the file "hoops.dll" is in a directory in your path.

When you are running the examples in this book on Microsoft Windows or Windows NT, you should compile and link the file "w32cmain.c" (found in the directory demo\win32\unixport of the HOOPS distribution) in your project. This file defines the Windows WinMain function and a version of printf that prints to a window.

See the *HOOPS Installation Guide* on the CD-ROM for further information about how to compile and run HOOPS programs on your system.

## 1.4.4    Environment Variables

There are several HOOPS environment variables that are not strictly necessary to run HOOPS, but that can be useful. On UNIX, you set environment variables with the setenv command. On Microsoft Windows, environment variables are set with the DOS set command, or through the system control-panel applet.

The complete set of HOOPS environment variables will be covered in Sections 4.4.6 and 4.4.7. For now, we shall discuss the ones that you might find most useful: HOOPS_PICTURE, HOOPS_FONT_DIRECTORY, and HOOPS_METAFILE_DIRECTORY,

**1.4.4.1**    **HOOPS_PICTURE.** The HOOPS_PICTURE environment variable tells HOOPS where to send its output. If you do not set this variable, HOOPS will choose a reasonable default output device, but will display a warning message. By setting HOOPS_PICTURE, you not only can avoid the warning message, but also may speed up your graphics output. Many platforms have more than one way to display output graphics, and the default way may not be the most efficient.

For example, on UNIX, the default output is through X-Windows, but, on a Sun workstation, it is more efficient to send the output through the Sun graphics system, called XGL. Likewise, on a Silicon Graphics machine, it is more efficient to use GL output, rather than X11 output. On some Microsoft Windows platforms, you have a choice of sending output through Windows, or through OpenGL (currently, however, OpenGL is significantly slower than Windows).

See the *HOOPS Installation Guide* for more information on the possible settings for HOOPS_PICTURE for your platform.

**1.4.4.2**     **HOOPS_FONT_DIRECTORY.** The HOOPS_FONT_DIRECTORY environment variable tells HOOPS where its fonts are stored. For example, if you installed HOOPS in the directory C:\HOOPS (on Microsoft Windows), then you would set this environment variable to C:\HOOPS\FONTS.

**1.4.4.3**     **HOOPS_METAFILE_DIRECTORY.** The HOOPS_METAFILE_DIRECTORY environment variable tells HOOPS where it can find metafiles. *Metafiles* are HOOPS descriptions of 3D objects. HOOPS comes with several dozen metafiles, including an automobile, various mechanical parts, a cow, a mushroom, a dragon, and the ever popular teapot. For example, if you installed HOOPS in the directory C:\HOOPS (in Microsoft Windows), then you would set this environment variable to C:\HOOPS\DEMO\COMMON\HMF. In the same directory is the source for a program called setmeta that you can use to view these metafiles.

**1.4.5**     **Our First 3D Graphics Program**

We can modify Program 1.2 to make Program 1.3, which displays the text in 3D.

```
 1   #include <hc.h>
 2   void main() {
 3       HC_Open_Segment("?Picture");
 4           HC_Set_Text_Font("transforms");
 5           HC_Insert_Text(0.0, 0.0, 0.0, "hello, world!");
 6           HC_Scale_Object(5.0, 5.0, 5.0);
 7           HC_Rotate_Object(0.0, 60.0, 0.0);
 8       HC_Close_Segment();
 9       HC_Pause();
10   }
```

**Program 1.3**     Display "hello, world!" — in 3D.

When you execute Program 1.3, the output should look like Figure 1.2.

**Figure 1.2**        Output from Program 1.3.

In this version of the program, we have added three HOOPS calls. By default, HOOPS assumes that text is 2D; the HC_Set_Text_Font command on line 4 tells HOOPS that the text is 3D and can be transformed (rotated, translated, and scaled) in three dimensions. The HC_Scale_Object command increases the size of the text by a factor of 5.0 in all three dimensions. We scale the text to make it larger and thus easier to see when it is rotated. Finally, the HC_Rotate_Object command rotates the text 60 degrees about the $y$ (vertical) axis.

## 1.5        Experiments with HOOPS and 3D

The "hello, world!" program is one of the most trivial of graphics programs, but we have already learned enough HOOPS commands to create a few special effects. In this section, we shall experiment with our program. You are encouraged to try other changes.

### 1.5.1        The Declarative Nature of HOOPS

For your first experiment, try rearranging the order of the four HOOPS commands between the HC_Open_Segment and HC_Close_Segment commands (lines 4 through 7) in Program 1.3. Does that make any difference to the displayed image? Can you explain why it does or does not?

Changing the order of the HOOPS commands in this example does not affect the displayed picture. There are two reasons why.

Unless two commands affect the same attribute, the order in which commands are executed in each segment does not matter in HOOPS. In many other graphics systems, the order does matter. In those systems, the rotate command would have to be executed before the text was inserted; otherwise, the text would not be affected. Such a system is said to be *procedural*. In contrast, HOOPS is *declarative*. In HOOPS, attributes affect all geometry in a segment. Thus, attributes can be set in any order, and geometry can be inserted either before or after any attributes.

In this example, however, the commands HC_Rotate_Object and HC_Scale_Object do affect the same attribute; they both modify the transformation applied to the segment. A rotation about the origin and a uniform scale about the origin, however, are independent of each other, so the order of these two particular commands does not matter either. If the HC_Scale_Object had scaled twice as much in the $x$ as in the $y$ direction, or if we had done an HC_Translate_Object, then the order would have been significant.

A HOOPS segment behaves like an object. In an object-oriented language, methods are used to modify the internal state of the object. Likewise, in HOOPS, a segment contains attributes and geometry, and HOOPS commands modify this state. There is no implied procedural ordering of the attributes or geometry of a segment. This lack of ordering makes it easy to modify a segment, because changing an attribute in a segment affects all geometry in that segment (rather than just the geometry that occurs "after" that attribute).

In object-oriented programming, the order in which methods are called on an object matters only when two method invocations change the same internal state. If two methods set the same piece of internal state, then the most recently called method wins. Or, if the two methods modify the same internal state (for example, one multiplies a number by 2, and another adds 5 to the number), then the order in which the methods are called may change the result. The same principle applies to HOOPS.

### 1.5.2      Streaming Mode

Program 1.2 is not the smallest graphics program that we can write using HOOPS. Go back to Program 1.2 and remove lines 3 and 5 (the lines that open and close the segment), leaving Program 1.4.

```
1  #include <hc.h>
2  void main() {
3     HC_Insert_Text(0.0, 0.0, 0.0, "hello, world!");
4     HC_Pause();
5  }
```

**Program 1.4**  HOOPS in streaming mode.

Program 1.4 does exactly the same thing as Program 1.2. When a HOOPS program does not open any segments, HOOPS is placed into streaming mode. In *streaming mode,* HOOPS acts like a procedural graphics system.

If we removed the open and close segment commands from Program 1.3 (lines 3 and 8), then we would also need to rearrange the program so that the rotate and scale commands would be executed procedurally before the text is inserted. In a procedural graphics system, the order in which attributes are set is significant.

Other than letting us see how short a graphics program we can write, streaming mode is not particularly useful. Program 1.4 is the only example of streaming mode in this book.

### 1.5.3  Transformations

Program 1.3 rotates the text about the $y$ (vertical) axis. Modify Program 1.3 to rotate the text about the other two axes — about the $x$ axis to flip it top to bottom, and about the $z$ axis (which is perpendicular to the monitor screen) to twirl it clockwise around the screen. To do these rotations, change the arguments to the HC_Rotate_Object command on line 7. The three arguments specify the amount to rotate about the $x$, $y$, and $z$ axes.

You can also change the size of the text by changing the arguments to the HC_Scale_Object command on line 6. Try scaling the text by different amounts in each dimension. What happens when you change the amount by which the text is scaled in the $z$ dimension? Can you explain why the output image does not change?

### 1.5.4  Interaction

Next, in Program 1.5, we shall modify Program 1.3 to start out with the text unrotated (and looking like the 2D text in Program 1.2). Then, every time you click the mouse, the text rotates 20 degrees about the $y$ axis until it has spun all the way around 360 degrees (back to its original position). The next mouse click will then exit the program.

```
 1   void main(int argc, char * argv[]) {
 2      HC_Open_Segment("?Picture");
 3         HC_Set_Text_Font("transforms");
 4         HC_Insert_Text(0.0, 0.0, 0.0, "hello, world!");
 5         HC_Scale_Object(5.0, 5.0, 5.0);

 6         for (int i = 0; i < 360; i+=20) {
 7             HC_Pause();
 8             HC_Rotate_Object(0.0, 20.0, 0.0);
 9         }

10      HC_Close_Segment();
11      HC_Pause();
12   }
```

**Program 1.5**     Display "hello, world!" — rotating.

---

**C++**

In C++, variables can be defined in the first clause of a "for" statement, such as the integer "i" on line 6 of Program 1.5. C++ encourages you to define variables at the point where you first use them, rather than requiring you to define them at the top of a block of statements (as C does). Defining variables where you first use them makes it easier to ensure that variables are initialized properly.

---

Each execution of the loop on lines 6 through 9 rotates the text by an additional 20 degrees. A common mistake that people make when writing a program like this one is to use the following rotate command, instead of the one on line 8:

```
HC_Rotate_Object(0.0, i, 0.0);
```

This command would rotate the text by 0 degrees the first time through the loop, then by 20 degrees, then by an additional 40 degrees (for a total of 60 degrees), and so on. The effect of HC_Rotate_Object is cumulative. The argument to the HC_Rotate_Object command should be a constant 20 (as on line 8), so that, each time that it is called, it rotates the text by 20 degrees.

The HC_Pause command (on line 7) is placed before the HC_Rotate_Object command, so that the program pauses each time before rotating the text. There is an additional HC_Pause command on line 11 to make the program wait before terminating.

### 1.5.5     Animation

When you call the HC_Pause command, HOOPS updates the display, and then waits for user input (such as a mouse click). You can use the HC_Update_Display command to update the screen without pausing. This command is useful for programs that do animation.

In Program 1.6, the HC_Pause command (on line 7 in Program 1.5) is replaced with an HC_Update_Display command, so the text will rotate continuously, rather than waiting for a mouse click each time.

```
1   void main(int argc, char * argv[]) {
2      HC_Open_Segment("?Picture");
3         HC_Set_Text_Font("transforms");
4         HC_Insert_Text(0.0, 0.0, 0.0, "hello, world!");
5         HC_Scale_Object(5.0, 5.0, 5.0);
6         HC_Pause();

7         for (int i = 0; i < 360; i+=5) {
8             HC_Update_Display();
9             HC_Rotate_Object(0.0, 5.0, 0.0);
10        }
11     HC_Close_Segment();
12     HC_Pause();
13  }
```

**Program 1.6**     Display "hello, world!" — animating.

We also increased the number of iterations (on line 7) to 72 (360 ÷ 5), and decreased the amount by which the text is rotated each iteration (on line 9) to 5.0 degrees, to make the animation smoother.

In Program 1.6, the animation runs freely — as fast as the machine on which it is running can manage. On a fast machine, it may run too fast to be seen. To make an animation run at a constant speed, you can use a HOOPS *timer event*. A simple (but somewhat inaccurate) way to add a timer event is to replace the HC_Update_Display command with HC_Get_Wakeup($t$), where $t$ is a float containing the amount of time (in seconds) to delay before the wakeup for the next frame of the animation. For example, HC_Get_Wakeup(0.1) will delay (approximately) 0.1 second between frames. Timer events are discussed in Chapter 8.

## 1.6    Summary

This chapter has given you a small taste of how easy it can be to write a 3D graphics application using HOOPS. If you have never written a 3D graphics program using another library (such as OpenGL, PEX, or PHIGS), however, you may be wondering what the fuss is all about. Unfortunately, most graphics libraries require you to deal with unnecessary details, such as procedural ordering, hardware capabilities (or lack thereof), device initialization, and window-system interfaces.

If you are comparing HOOPS to some other graphics library, pick an example program and write it using both libraries. The HOOPS version will be easier to write, will definitely be more portable, and in most cases will even run faster.

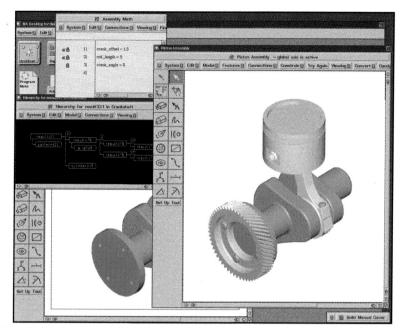

**Plate 1**   Mechanical analysis.

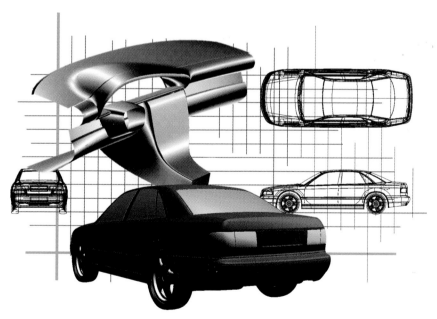

**Plate 2**   Mechanical design.

**Plate 3**   Industrial design.

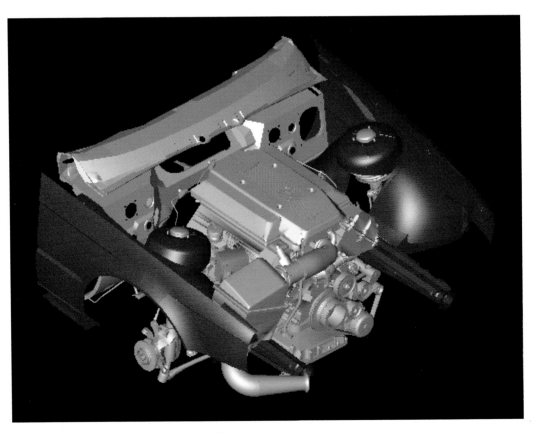

**Plate 4**   Mechanical design and analysis.

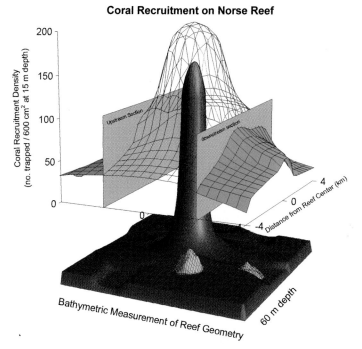

**Plate 5**  Scientific visualization.

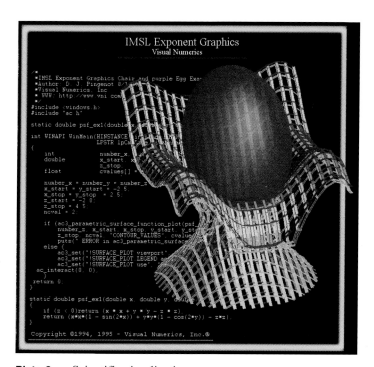

**Plate 6**  Scientific visualization.

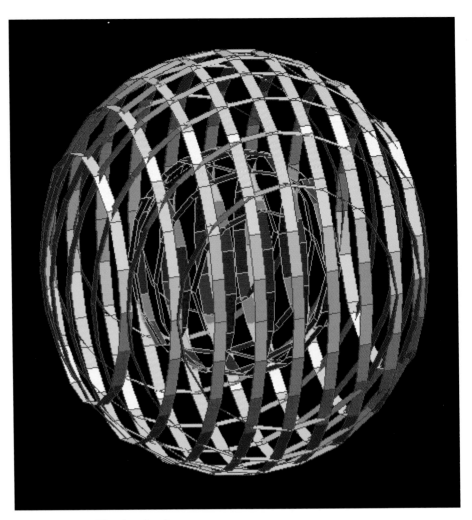

**Plate 7** Scientific visualization.

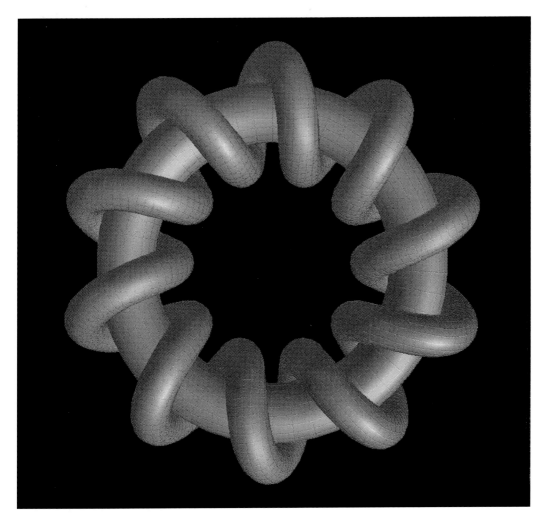

**Plate 8** Scientific visualization.

**Plate 9** Scientific visualization.

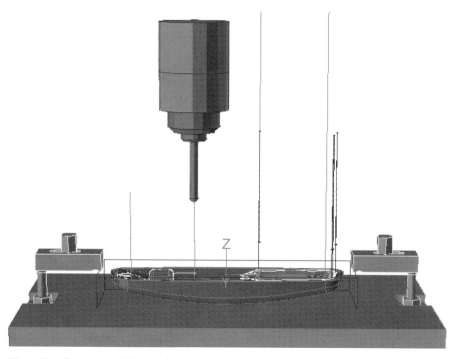

**Plate 10** Computer aided design.

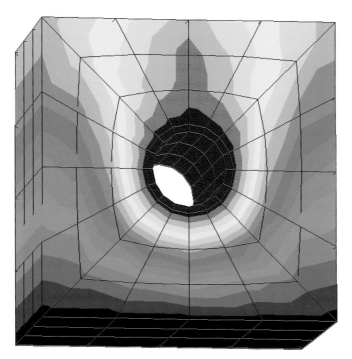

**Plate 11**   Structural analysis.

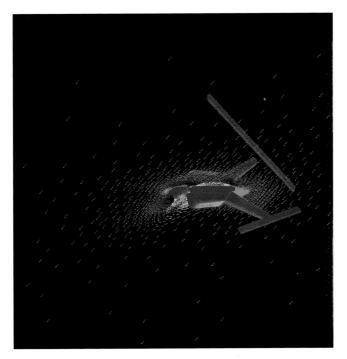

**Plate 12**   Computational fluid dynamics.

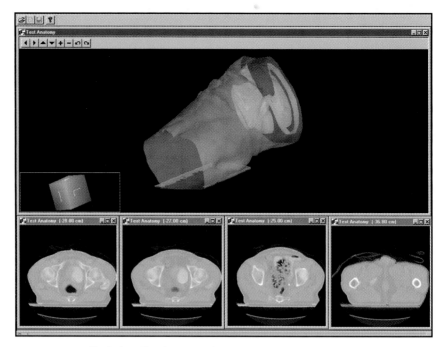

**Plate 13** Medical visualization—surface representaion.

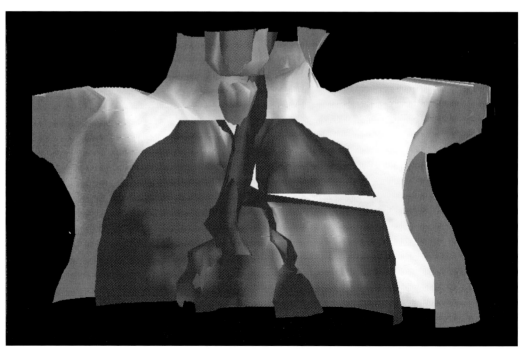

**Plate 14** Medical visualization—image display.

# 2     Design of Graphics Applications

This chapter presents design principles that make it easier to write, debug, and maintain 3D graphics applications. These principles apply whether you are writing a new application from scratch or are adding 3D graphics to an existing application. They are based on object-oriented programming, so this chapter starts with a quick review of object-oriented concepts and terminology.

## 2.1     Object-Oriented Programming

Object-oriented programming and design are rich topics, and many good textbooks have been written about them. Briefly, the aspects of object-oriented programming that are most important to programmers who are building interactive graphics applications are *encapsulation, data hiding,* and *software reuse.*

### 2.1.1     Encapsulation

*Encapsulation* is the practice of associating closely the functions that operate on a data structure with that data structure. The data structure and functions together are called an encapsulated *object.* The data inside an object form the object's *representation,* and the functions that operate on those data are called the object's *methods.* Encapsulation encourages the user to define good interfaces to data structures, so that the data structures are more robust and reusable. It also increases modularity by clustering functionality around key data structures.

Consider an application that contains a number of drawable objects (lines, circles, rectangles, and so on) that can be moved about on the screen. One way to implement the move operation is to write a subroutine that knows how to change the position of every kind of drawable object. In this approach, if a new kind of drawable object is added, or the representation of one of the existing drawable objects is changed, then the move routine will have to be changed. If there are other routines, such as scale or rotate, they will need to be changed as well. Figure 2.1 shows the dependencies between the drawable objects and the operations.

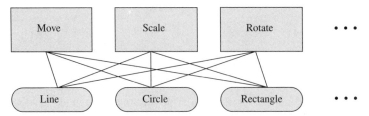

**Figure 2.1**        Traditional organization for drawable objects and operations.

A more object-oriented way to implement the move operation is to associate a separate move method with each kind of drawable object, as shown in Figure 2.2. The move method for an object needs to know about only its single kind of object. Likewise, you would associate a scale method and rotate method with each kind of object. That way, all the information about an object is encapsulated with the object, rather than spread among a data structure and multiple global functions. When a new kind of drawable object is added, the methods for that object are defined with it, and none of the other objects (including their methods) are affected.

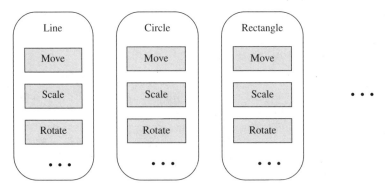

**Figure 2.2**        Object-oriented organization for drawable objects and operations.

## 2.1.2       Data Hiding

*Data hiding* prevents functions other than the methods of an object from accessing the representation of that object. Data hiding forces any use of an object to go through one of that object's methods. When implementing a drawable object (such as line, circle, and rectangle), we would hide the internal variables of the object (its position, orientation, size, and so on), so that the only way a function could access the object would be to go through one of the object's methods (move, scale, rotate, and so on).

If data hiding is not used, then any function can access the internal variables of an object. If the representation of an object is changed, or if we change an algorithm used on an object (for example, to improve efficiency), functions scattered all over the application may be affected, creating a maintenance nightmare.

## 2.1.3       Software Reuse

*Software reuse* is the ability to use code and objects in more than one place. An example of software reuse common to practically all computer languages is the use of subroutines. A subroutine allows a single piece of code to be called from multiple places. By supporting software reuse, subroutines make programming easier.

This section covers the programming principles that encourage software reuse: *good interfaces, sharing, components,* and *design for reusability.*

### 2.1.3.1       Interfaces.

**Interfaces.** Good interfaces are critical to software reuse. For example, consider a routine to return (space-delimited) words from a text string. This routine becomes useful enough that you want to adapt it so that it can be used in multiple places, or even in multiple applications. To make this routine reusable, you must give it a good interface. A good interface uses function arguments (rather than global variables) to pass information to the subroutine, and does not use goto statements to jump into the middle of the subroutine.

Modern computer languages make it easier to reuse subroutines by enforcing type checking on function arguments, encouraging the use of arguments (rather than global variables) to pass information, and discouraging the use of goto statements into the middle of subroutines. Object-oriented programming languages make it easier to reuse objects by encouraging encapsulation and data hiding. Objects with well-defined interfaces are easier to reuse.

**2.1.3.2**      **Sharing.** A second way that object-oriented languages support software reuse (in addition to encouraging good interfaces) is by providing features for software sharing, such as *aggregation*, *inheritance*, or *delegation*. These features allow common functionality to be shared. If you are creating a number of objects that share common functionality, you can create a single object that implements the common functionality, and then have the other objects share that object, by including it as a member (aggregation), by being derived from it (inheritance), or by implementing methods through it (delegation). That way, the common functionality is implemented only once; if the common behavior changes, it needs to be changed in only one place.

In the drawable-object example in Section 2.1.1 (which implements graphical primitives, such as lines and circles, and operations on those primitives, such as move and rotate), the object-oriented organization might have appeared to require extra code, because each primitive needs to have a separate implementation for each operation. However, we can share code among primitives that can use the same method to implement an operation; we thus avoid the redundant code. In a language that supports inheritance (such as C++), we can share code by implementing a base class with default methods for each operation, and overriding the inherited behavior for only those primitives that cannot use the default methods.

**2.1.3.3**      **Components.** Another form of software reuse that is common to both object-oriented and non–object-oriented languages is the construction of applications from components. Such an application may contain a user-interface component (such as Motif or MFC), a 3D graphics component (such as HOOPS), and other components. By taking advantage of existing components, the application programmer can concentrate on the functionality of the application, rather than on rewriting of common utility software. In the future, distributed object-oriented frameworks, such as OLE and CORBA, will make components — and the use of components — even more important.

**2.1.3.4**      **Design for reusability.** A major balancing act in object-oriented programming is designing objects that are general enough to be reused, but are not so overly general that they are useless. An object cannot be reusable if it is not usable. A trap into which programmers — flush with their first taste of objects — often fall is trying to anticipate all possible uses for an object, and then adding large numbers of methods to support those uses. Instead of designing an object according to the use to which you think it might be put — throwing in extra methods to satisfy different kinds of uses — it is better to design the object from the viewpoint of what the object is supposed to do.

Or, put in a different way, *each kind of object should do one job, and should do that one job well.*

## 2.2        Separation of Model and View

One of the most popular and fruitful uses of object-oriented programing is for computer-graphics applications. It is no coincidence that a major strength of Smalltalk (one of the original object-oriented languages) is that language's graphical user interface, or that toolkits for writing interactive graphical user interfaces (such as NeXTStep and the Microsoft Foundation Classes) are invariably object oriented.

An important way that object-oriented programming concepts are applicable to graphics applications is through the use of data hiding and encapsulation to separate the data model of an application from the latter's graphical views. This concept is the focus of the remainder of this chapter.

### 2.2.1        Models and Views

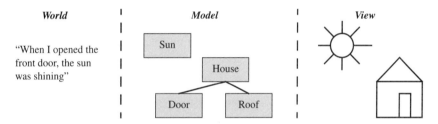

**Figure 2.3**        A statement about the real world, a data model, and a view.

**2.2.1.1**        **The data model.** A *data model* is a set of objects that symbolically reproduce one or more aspects of the real world. For example, in Figure 2.3, the sentence "When I opened the front door, the sun was shining" is a statement about the real world, which contains a house, a door, and the sun. We can create an application that models this aspect of the real world by creating computer objects (data structures and functions) for the real objects (houses and stars). An application will model only those aspects of the real world that are relevant, and will abstract away the rest. It may not be important that my house is only one house out of millions of houses in the world, or that the sun is only one star in billions (and billions) in the universe, so the types for these objects do not contain information to identify which house or which star. A mapping application, however, might need to know which house, and an astronomy application might care which star. The data model may also elaborate on the real world; for example, the data model in Figure 2.3 has added a data structure to represent the roof of the house.

Every application forms such a model. A spreadsheet application forms a model of a real-world accountant's ledger. A word processor forms a model of text on paper, using data structures containing arrays of characters and each character's positions on a page. Likewise, a 3D graphics application, such as a computer-aided–design system, creates data structures representing the geometry of real, physical objects.

**2.2.1.2**          **Views.** A *view* is a representation of the data model that is presented to the user of the application. For example, Figure 2.3 contains a simple stick-figure view of a house and the sun.

A view does not need to be graphical. For example, your bank statement is a printed, textual view of your bank account — or, more precisely, it is a view of the computer model of your bank account — over a period of time. An automated teller machine presents a different view of the same data model — a view that is interactive. An application will often have more than one view of a single data model.

If an application is interactive, then a view includes not only output, but also a way of interpreting user input to make changes to the application's data model. The view helps the user to interact with the application's data model.

**2.2.2**          ## Model–View Separation

As stated in Section 2.1.3.4, a precept of object-oriented programming is that you should design objects that do one job well. Unfortunately, many programmers violate this principle by mixing data for the model and view in a single object. As you might expect, this mixing can cause you to lose some of the advantages of object-oriented programming, such as extensibility and ease of maintenance.

A clean separation between a model and its views allows us to add a new view, or to change an existing one, without affecting the data model. If model and view are mixed, making changes can be more difficult. For example, consider a banking application originally written for a bank account with only a single view — a printed bank statement. If data about the view were mixed with the account information, then adding a new view — such as a view for an automated teller machine — would require modifying the account data structure.

Keeping model and view separate also makes it easier to change the model without affecting existing views. For example, the data model of a bank account may change, perhaps to modify 401K accounts because of a change in tax laws. If model and view data were combined, then this change would unnecessarily affect the views.

In summary, a clean interface between a model and its views makes it easier to change the data model without affecting existing views, and easier to add new views. Unfortunately, mixing model and view is an inviting trap; even books on object-oriented programming occasionally make this mistake. Ask a programmer (even one well versed in object-oriented programming) to design an object to represent a bank account, and the result will probably look something like Program 2.1, with a view (the print method) mixed in as part of the data model.

```
1   class Bank_Account {
2    private:
3      long number;        // account number
4      double balance;
5    public:
6      void open(long n) {
7          number = n;
8          balance = 0.0;
9      }
10     void deposit(double v) {
11         balance += v;
12     }
13     void withdraw(double v) {
14         if (balance < v) error("insufficient funds");
15         else balance -= v;
16     }
17     void print() {
18         printf("Balance for account # %d is %g\n",
19                 number, balance);
20     }
21   };
```

**Program 2.1**    A flawed data model that contains a view.

**C++**

Program 2.1 defines a class; *class* is the C++ name for a type of object. A C++ class is similar to a C struct. In addition to containing data values, however, a class can contain functions, called member functions, which are the methods of the type. A class can also use the public and private labels to separate private members from public members. Member functions support encapsulation, and the ability to specify private members supports data hiding.

In C++, all class names (and struct names) are automatically type names, so there is no need to typedef struct and class definitions.

The // on line 3 is the start of a comment that runs to the end of the line. C++ also understands C comments that begin with /* and end with */.

The print function (on line 17) probably was made a method of the class Bank_Account because it needs to access the private variables number and balance. Printing should be part of a view, however, rather than part of the data model.

Methods that belong in a view can cause problems if they are mixed with the methods in the data model. Because there is no clean interface between the model and the view, changing one will unnecessarily affect the other. What if we wanted to change the way that the printout is formatted — for example, to arrange the numbers in columns, to use different text, or to place commas before every three digits in large numbers? Information about the format of the output has nothing to do with the concept of a bank account and should not be part of the data model.

In addition, what if we are running Program 2.1 on an operating system that uses a graphical user interface, and has no concept of console output? Changing the print method to bring up a dialog box would add to the Bank_Account class complexity that has little to do with a bank account. Finally, if we wanted to add a new view, such as for an automated teller machine, we would have to make even more changes to the data model.

A print method like the one in Program 2.1 should be included only as a debugging aid, and should never be used as part of an application's view of the data. Instead, each view should be a separate object. To allow the views to be separated from the data model, we need to add methods to the data model that can be used by all the views. In Program 2.1, the data model contains two pieces of information that will probably be used by a view. Program 2.2 adds two methods to the data model to give access to this information.

```
 1  class Bank_Account {
 2     // other private and public members
 3     long get_number() {
 4        return number;
 5     }
 6     double get_balance() {
 7        return balance;
 8     }
 9  };
10  void print(Bank_Account ba) {
11     printf("Balance for account # %d is %g\n",
12             ba.get_number(), ba.get_balance());
13  }
```

**Program 2.2**  Access functions and print function to add to Program 2.1.

The print view is no longer part of the class Bank_Account. In this case, the print view is not sufficiently complex to warrant its own class, so we just make it a function.

Each different kind of view can then use the same access functions to access the data model. A specific view may not use all the information in the data model. For example, a summary view that totals all the account balances for the bank would not use the account-number field in the data model.

If you keep the data model separate from the view, then you can change the implementation of the data model (as long as the interface stays the same) without affecting the views. For example, if you change the way that the balance is stored from a single number to two separate numbers — one for principal and one for accrued interest — only the access function get_balance has to change, and all views that use the balance are not affected.

A data model that does not contain any view-specific information is called *view independent*. It is clear why view independence is good from a software-engineering viewpoint. We also claim (without justification other than from experience) that separating view from data model results in a better interface for the users of your application, or (to use the current buzz words) a user interface that is friendly and easy to use.

You (as the writer of an application) are responsible for designing and implementing the data model of your application. You are also responsible for designing and implementing the views that are presented to the user. The role of the graphics system is to help you to implement these views. As we shall see in later chapters, HOOPS has several unique features that make it easy to create views, and to keep those views separate from the data model of your application.

## 2.3     Spreadsheet Example

More than any other application, the computer-based spreadsheet (for example, VisiCalc, Lotus 1-2-3, and many others) was responsible for the success of the personal computer. Interestingly, the spreadsheet did nothing that could not already be done by existing accounting programs. What is significant about a spreadsheet is not its data model — which is just normal accounting data — but the view that it uses to present this data model to the user. The view presented by a spreadsheet is at once familiar, because it resembles an accountant's ledger, and more powerful, in that the numbers update themselves automatically, unlike numbers on a paper ledger. This view allows people to interact with the data in new ways.

In this chapter, we define a data model and several views for a simple version of a spreadsheet application. The main purpose of this example is for you to get a feel for how such an application is organized. The example will implement only the output part of the application, and will not include the input part. Graphical input can also influence the organization of an application, as we shall see in Chapter 8.

### 2.3.1     Declarative Versus Procedural

Another significant aspect of spreadsheets is that they are declarative, whereas previous accounting systems were procedural. In a declarative system, the user states relationships among data, and the system automatically updates the data to keep the relationships true. In a spreadsheet, you need only to declare the relationships among numbers; when you change one number, the other numbers that are related to it are updated. For example, in a spreadsheet, you can define a cell to be the total of a group of other cells, and it is up to the system to update the total cell if one of the other cells changes.

A procedural system updates data values by executing sequences of instructions (procedures), where the order in which the instructions are executed can affect the result. Using a procedural system is like using a calculator: You must execute operations in a specific order to get the right answer.

As we discussed in Chapter 1, HOOPS is declarative. Although a spreadsheet is an application and HOOPS is a library, being declarative is just as significant in HOOPS as it is in a spreadsheet. In HOOPS, the programmer declares what is to be displayed, rather than specifying the procedural details of how to display it. In a spreadsheet, the user declares relationships among numbers. In a graphics application, the relationship to be maintained is the relationship between the application's data model and that model's views. If the data model changes, then any views must be updated to reflect that change; if the user changes a view, then the data model must be updated. The declarative nature of HOOPS makes it easy to keep these relationships valid, as we shall discuss in Chapters 6 and 8.

## 2.3.2  Spreadsheet Data Model

For the sake of example, our spreadsheet is one-dimensional — it is just a column of numbers — and each cell in the spreadsheet has a text label (in a real, 2D spreadsheet, the label would be in a separate cell). Lines 1 through 11 in Program 2.3 contain the C++ class for a cell in the data model of our spreadsheet.

```
1  class Cell {
2   public:
3     Cell() { d_value = 0.0; d_label = (char *) 0; }
4     void set_value(double val) { d_value = val; }
5     void set_label(char * label) { d_label = label; }
6     double get_value() { return d_value; }
7     char * get_label() { return d_label; }
8   private:
9     double d_value;
10     char * d_label;
11  };
```

**Program 2.3**    Data model for a cell in a spreadsheet.

Program 2.3 ignores that it can be dangerous to store pointers to character strings without making a copy of the string. In a real application, the set_label method (line 5) would make a copy of its argument character string.

> ## C++
>
> In C++, class definitions (like the one for class Cell in Program 2.3) are normally placed in a header (.h) file. For a small example such as ours, however, it is fine to place everything — class definitions, member-function definitions, and the main-function definition — in a single file, and to compile them all together.
>
> When functions are defined inside of the class definition (as are the functions inside class Cell), they are compiled inline, so there is no function-call overhead. An *inline function* combines the speed of a macro with the type checking of a real function. You can force member functions defined outside the class definition to be compiled inline by explicitly specifying the inline keyword, just as you would with any other function.
>
> A C++ class can contain special member functions, like the one on line 3, called *constructors*. A constructor has the same name as the class, and no return value. A constructor is called automatically when an object of the class is created. Constructors are used to initialize the object.

Program 2.3 continues with the definition of the C++ class to hold the data model for the spreadsheet. The spreadsheet data model consists of a single array of cells (numbers with labels), and a single total.

```
12  class SpreadSheet {
13  public:
14      SpreadSheet(int size);
15      ~SpreadSheet();          // destructor
16      int get_num_cells() { return d_num_cells; }
17      void set_cell(int i, char * label, double value) {
18          d_cells[i].set_label(label);
19          d_cells[i].set_value(value);
20      }
21      double get_value(int i) {
22          return d_cells[i].get_value();
23      }
24      char * get_label(int i) {
25          return d_cells[i].get_label();
26      }
27      double get_total_value();
```

```
28   private:
29      int d_num_cells;
30      Cell * d_cells;
31   };
```

**C++**

In class SpreadSheet, three member functions (on lines 14, 15, and 27) are *declared* inside the class definition, and then are *defined* outside the class (on lines 32 through 46, which follow). When a member function is defined outside the class definition, its name must be preceded by the class name and the C++ scope operator (two colons, ::). The scope operator defines the class of which this function is a member, and thus the scope of the name.

If the class definitions are placed in a header (.h) file, then any member functions that are not declared inline (that is, those that are not defined inside the class definition, or are not explicitly inline) must be placed in a program (.cpp) file. Again, in this small example, it is reasonable to place all the code into a single file.

```
32   SpreadSheet::SpreadSheet(int size) {
33      d_num_cells = size;
34      d_cells = new Cell[size];   // array of Cells
35   }

36   SpreadSheet::~SpreadSheet() {
37      delete [] d_cells;
38      d_num_cells = 0;
39   }

40   double SpreadSheet::get_total_value() {
41      double sum = 0.0;
42      for (int i = 0; i < d_num_cells; i++) {
43          sum += get_value(i);
44      }
45      return sum;
46   }
```

**Program 2.3 (continued)** Data model for a spreadsheet.

The function with the same name as the class, but with a tilde, ~, prepended, is a destructor function (declared on line 15, and defined on lines 36 to 39). The destructor is called automatically when an object of this class is deallocated. It is normally used to free memory or other resources that were allocated by a constructor function for the class.

On line 34, the C++ new operator is used by the constructor function to allocate an array of class Cell on the heap (the new operator is similar to the C malloc function, but it is type safe). The destructor function ~SpreadSheet uses the C++ delete operator (on line 37) to free the memory that was allocated with the "new" operator. The square brackets, [ ], indicate that an array, rather than just a single value, is being deleted.

Lines 47 through 52 of Program 2.3 create a data model for our spreadsheet.

```
47  SpreadSheet ss(5);    // a spreadsheet with 5 cells
48  ss.set_cell(0, "Monday", 2375);
49  ss.set_cell(1, "Tuesday", 198);
50  ss.set_cell(2, "Wednesday", 482);
51  ss.set_cell(3, "Thursday", 7209);
52  ss.set_cell(4, "Friday", 3002);
```

**Program 2.3 (continued)**   An instance of a spreadsheet data model.

Line 47 creates an instance of class SpreadSheet. The argument to the constructor function for the SpreadSheet specifies that the spreadsheet has five cells.

**C++**     The code on lines 47 through 52 should be placed inside the function in your application that creates the spreadsheet object. For example, it could be placed in the main function of your application.

### 2.3.3     Text View

Our first view of the spreadsheet data model, Program 2.4, does not involve any graphics. It simply prints out a text view of the data model on the output console.

```
1  #include <stdio.h>
2  class Text_View {
```

```
3   public:
4      Text_View(SpreadSheet & ssdm) : d_dm(ssdm) { }
5      void display();

6   private:
7      SpreadSheet & d_dm;       // data model
8   };

9   void Text_View::display() {
10     const int num = d_dm.get_num_cells();
11     for (int i = 0; i < num; i++)
12        printf("%10s %g\n", d_dm.get_label(i),
13              d_dm.get_value(i));
14     printf("          --------\n");
15     printf("     total %g\n", d_dm.get_total_value());
16  }
```

**Program 2.4**     Text view of spreadsheet.

---

**C++**     The variable on line 7, d_dm, is defined to be a *reference* to a spreadsheet. An ampersand, &, declares a reference in the same way that an asterisk, *, declares a pointer in C. Reference variables are passed and stored by reference — only the address of the variable is stored, instead of a copy of the entire object. The argument ssdm to the constructor function on line 4 also is a reference. A reference argument avoids the implicit copy that would be made if the data model were passed by value. In C, all arguments are passed by value, unless a pointer is used explicitly. References in C++ allow functions to pass arguments by reference and to store references to variables without the use of explicit pointers.

---

**C++**     Reference variables and constants must be initialized before they can be used. Therefore, C++ has a special notation (which looks like a function call) that allows reference variables in a class to be initialized by the class constructor. This notation is used in line 4, where the reference variable d_dm is initialized with the value of the parameter ssdm.

This view is output only — it does not make any modifications to the data model. Therefore, we could also have specified both the data-model variable d_dm and the argument ssdm to the constructor as constants.

Lines 17 through 26 show how to take a view of the spreadsheet data model that we created in Program 2.3.

```
17  void main() {
18      SpreadSheet ss(5);    // a spreadsheet with 5 cells
19      ss.set_cell(0, "Monday", 2375);
20      ss.set_cell(1, "Tuesday", 198);
21      ss.set_cell(2, "Wednesday", 482);
22      ss.set_cell(3, "Thursday", 7209);
23      ss.set_cell(4, "Friday", 3002);

24      Text_View tv(ss);
25      tv.display();
26  }
```

**Program 2.4  (continued)**    An instance of a text view.

---

**C++**    On line 24, the variable, ss, containing the spreadsheet data model is passed to the Text_View constructor. Because the argument to the constructor is passed by reference (line 4) and is stored in a reference variable (line 7), after initialization, the member variable d_dm will refer to the same spreadsheet object (that is, the same storage) as the variable ss.

---

The output of Program 2.4 should look something like Figure 2.4.

```
   Monday 2375
  Tuesday 198
Wednesday 482
 Thursday 7209
   Friday 3002
          --------
    total 13266
```

**Figure 2.4**    Output from Program 2.4.

### 2.3.4    Ledger View Using HOOPS

In Program 2.5, we will create a new view of the spreadsheet. This view uses HOOPS to display the cells like a spreadsheet (in a tablelike format similar to an accountant's ledger).

```
1   #include <hc.h>
2   class Ledger_View {
3    public:
4      Ledger_View(SpreadSheet & ssdm) : d_dm(ssdm) { }
5      void display();
6    private:
7      SpreadSheet & d_dm;
8   };
```

**Program 2.5**    Ledger view of spreadsheet.

The class definition for the ledger view (on lines 2 through 8) is almost identical
to the one for the text view (lines 2 through 8 in Program 2.4), but the definition
of the display method (lines 9 through 39) is different.

```
9   void Ledger_View::display() {
10      const float labelpos = 0.0;
11      const float valuepos = 0.8;
12      const int num = d_dm.get_num_cells();
13      const float vspace = (float) (2.0 / (num + 1));
14      float vpos = 1.0;
15      char buf[64];

16      HC_Open_Segment("?Picture/ledger view");
17         HC_Set_Camera_Projection("stretched");
18         HC_Set_Text_Alignment(">*");

19         for (int i = 0; i < num; i++) {
20             sprintf(buf, "cell %d", i);
21             HC_Open_Segment(buf);
22                 HC_Set_Window(-1.0, 1.0,
23                     vpos - vspace, vpos);
24                 vpos -= vspace;
25                 char * lbl = d_dm.get_label(i);
26                 if (lbl) HC_Insert_Text(labelpos,
27                     0.0, 0.0, lbl);
28                 sprintf(buf, "%g", d_dm.get_value(i));
29                 HC_Insert_Text(valuepos, 0.0, 0.0, buf);
30             HC_Close_Segment();
31         }
```

```
32        HC_Open_Segment("total");
33            HC_Set_Window(-1.0, 1.0, -1.0, vpos);
34            HC_Insert_Text(labelpos, 0.0, 0.0, "total");
35            sprintf(buf, "%g", d_dm.get_total_value());
36            HC_Insert_Text(valuepos, 0.0, 0.0, buf);
37        HC_Close_Segment();
38     HC_Close_Segment();
39 }
```

**Program 2.5 (continued)**   Display method for the ledger view of a spreadsheet.

At this point, it is not important that you understand exactly what all the HOOPS commands do (you can look them up in the *HOOPS Reference Manual* on the CD-ROM, if you wish).

Because HOOPS is a 3D graphics library, its treatment of windows is slightly different from that of a 2D window system. In particular, the $x$ and $y$ origin lies in the middle of the window, because that is where you would normally place 3D objects to be drawn. Line 17 sets the camera projection to stretched, which stretches the coordinate system to fit the window exactly. This command places the left and right sides of the window at $x$ coordinates $-1$ and $+1$, and the bottom and top of the window at $y$ coordinates $-1$ and $+1$, respectively. Stretched projections are discussed in Section 6.1.10.

This program vertically divides the application's window into nonoverlapping horizontal subwindows — one for each spreadsheet cell. Line 13 calculates how much vertical space each cell will take up in the overall window by dividing 2.0 (the distance from $-1$ to $+1$) by the number of cells (plus 1 more for the total cell).

Each subwindow is a separate segment (created on lines 21 and 32). The HOOPS segments form a tree structure under the segment named "ledger view", with "?Picture" at the root of this hierarchy, as shown in Figure 2.5. Line 16 opens the "ledger view" segment directly, using a *segment path name* ("?Picture/ledger view"). A path name is a sequence of individual segment names separated by the slash character, /.

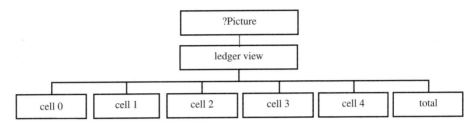

**Figure 2.5**    Segment hierarchy for Program 2.5.

The view creates one HOOPS segment for each C++ object of type Cell in the data model. This organization is common for a graphics application.

The HC_Set_Window commands (on lines 22 and 33) set the size of the subwindow used to display each cell, relative to the outer window. Thus, when you change the size of the application window, the subwindows will change size automatically to match. The HC_Set_Window command also draws a border around each subwindow.

The ledger view is displayed in the same way as the text view is (except that we added an HC_Pause command on line 49, so that we have a chance to see the output). We are now ready to compile and run Program 2.5.

```
40   void main() {
41      SpreadSheet ss(5);    // spreadsheet with five cells
42      ss.set_cell(0, "Monday", 2375);
43      ss.set_cell(1, "Tuesday", 198);
44      ss.set_cell(2, "Wednesday", 482);
45      ss.set_cell(3, "Thursday", 7209);
46      ss.set_cell(4, "Friday", 3002);

47      Ledger_View lv(ss);
48      lv.display();
49      HC_Pause();
50   }
```

**Program 2.5 (continued)**    An instance of a ledger view.

The output should look like Figure 2.6.

| | |
|---|---|
| Monday | 2375 |
| Tuesday | 198 |
| Wednesday | 482 |
| Thursday | 7209 |
| Friday | 3002 |
| total | 13266 |

**Figure 2.6**     Output from Program 2.5.

 If you are using Microsoft Windows or NT, you may have to change the way that you compile and link when you switch from a text-only view to a graphical view. These operating systems treat graphical programs differently from text programs (called *console programs*). See the compilation instructions in Section 1.4.3, or the *HOOPS Installation Guide* on the CD-ROM.

### 2.3.5     Ledger View with Changed Font Size

HOOPS makes it easy for us to make simple changes to the ledger view of our spreadsheet. For example, let us change the size of the font, using the command HC_Set_Text_Font. Program 2.6 contains the new version of the display method for class Ledger_View (the rest of the program is the same as Program 2.5). To change the font size, we need to set it in only a single place: on the segment "?Picture/ledger view" (on line 11 in Program 2.6). Attributes such as text font that are set on a segment affect all that segment's children (unless the children explicitly override the attribute), so the font set on the "ledger view" segment will affect all cells in the spreadsheet display.

```
1   void Ledger_View::display() {
2      const float labelpos = 0.0;
3      const float valuepos = 0.8;
4      const int num = d_dm.get_num_cells();
5      const float vspace = (float) (2.0 / (num + 1));
6      float vpos = 1.0;
7      char buf[64];

8      HC_Open_Segment("?Picture/ledger view");
9         HC_Set_Camera_Projection("stretched");
10        HC_Set_Text_Alignment(">*");
11        HC_Set_Text_Font("size = 0.75 wru");

12        for (int i = 0; i < num; i++) {
13            sprintf(buf, "cell %d", i);
14            HC_Open_Segment(buf);
15                HC_Set_Window(-1.0, 1.0,
16                        vpos - vspace, vpos);
17                vpos -= vspace;
18                HC_Insert_Text(labelpos, 0.0, 0.0,
19                        d_dm.get_cell_label(i));
20                sprintf(buf, "%g",
21                        d_dm.get_cell_value(i));
22                HC_Insert_Text(valuepos, 0.0, 0.0, buf);
23            HC_Close_Segment();
24        }

25        HC_Open_Segment("cell total");
26            HC_Set_Window(-1.0, 1.0, -1.0, vpos);
27            HC_Insert_Text(labelpos, 0.0, 0.0, "total");
28            sprintf(buf, "%g", d_dm.get_total_value());
29            HC_Insert_Text(valuepos, 0.0, 0.0, buf);
30        HC_Close_Segment();

31     HC_Close_Segment();
32     HC_Pause();
33  }
```

**Program 2.6**    Change of the font size in the ledger view.

The specification "size = 0.75 wru" sets the font size in window relative units, so that the font scales automatically when the smallest enclosing subwindow size changes. You can also set the font size in points, in pixels, or relative to the outermost window in your application.

## 2.3.6     Bar-Graph View

To illustrate that a single data model can have multiple views, we create a third view for our spreadsheet in Program 2.7. This view is a bar graph, where each cell in the spreadsheet is a bar in the graph.

```
1   class BarGraph_View {
2    public:
3      BarGraph_View(SpreadSheet & ssdm) : d_dm(ssdm) { }
4      void display();
5    private:
6      SpreadSheet & d_dm;
7      static double scale(double max);
8   };

9   // calculate maximum scale value
10  double BarGraph_View::scale(double max) {
11      double s = 1.0;
12      while (max > 10.0) { s *= 10.0; max /= 10.0; }
13      while (max < 1.0) { s /= 10.0; max *= 10.0; }
14      s *= (double) (1 + (int) max);
15      return s;
16  }
```

**Program 2.7**     Bar-graph view of spreadsheet.

We use the function BarGraph_View::scale (declared on line 7, and defined on lines 9 through 16) to calculate the maximum $y$ coordinate for the bar graph.

> **C++**     The scale function is declared to be a static function (on line 7). A static member function does not depend on any instance variables, so it can be called without a specific instance of a BarGraph_View.

```
17  struct Point { float x, y, z; };
18  void BarGraph_View::display() {
19      const float labelpos = -0.25;
```

```
20      const float valuepos = -0.1;
21      const int num = d_dm.get_num_cells();
22      const float hspace = (float) (2.0 / (num + 1));
23      const float barwidth = hspace / 4.0;
24      float hpos = hspace / 2.0 - 1.0;
25      const double total = d_dm.get_total_value();
26      const float ymax = (float) scale(total);
27      char buf[64];
28      Point rect[4] = { {0,0,0}, {0,0,0},
29                        {0,0,0}, {0,0,0} };

30      HC_Open_Segment("?Picture/bar graph view");
31          HC_Set_Camera_Projection("stretched");
32          HC_Set_Color(
33              "lines=edges=text=black, faces=light blue");

34          for (int i = 0; i < num; i++) {
35              sprintf(buf, "cell %d", i);
36              HC_Open_Segment(buf);
37                  float value = (float) d_dm.get_value(i);
38                  char * lbl = d_dm.get_label(i);
39                  if (lbl) HC_Insert_Text(hpos,
40                      labelpos, 0.0, lbl);
41                  sprintf(buf, "%g", value);
42                  HC_Insert_Text(hpos, valuepos, 0.0, buf);
43                  rect[0].x = rect[3].x = hpos - barwidth;
44                  rect[1].x = rect[2].x = hpos + barwidth;
45                  rect[2].y = rect[3].y = 0.95 *
46                      value / ymax;
47                  HC_Insert_Polygon(4, rect);
48                  hpos += hspace;
49              HC_Close_Segment();
50          }

51      HC_Open_Segment("total");
52          HC_Insert_Text(hpos, labelpos, 0.0, "total");
53          sprintf(buf, "%g", total);
54          HC_Insert_Text(hpos, valuepos, 0.0, buf);
55          rect[0].x = rect[3].x = hpos - barwidth;
56          rect[1].x = rect[2].x = hpos + barwidth;
57          rect[2].y = rect[3].y = (float)
58              (0.95 * total / ymax);
```

```
59              HC_Insert_Polygon(4, rect);
60          HC_Close_Segment();

61      HC_Close_Segment();
62  }
```

**Program 2.7 (continued)**   The display member function of the bar-graph view.

The bar-graph view is similar to the ledger view. Unlike in the ledger view, however, each cell in the bar-graph view is not a separate subwindow, but is still a separate segment. The array of points, called rect (defined on line 28) is used to draw each bar in the bar graph.

Program 2.7 displays a bar-graph view similar to the way Program 2.5 displays a ledger view and Program 2.4 displays a text view: by creating an instance of a BarGraph_View object initialized with a spreadsheet data model (on line 70), and calling the view's display method (on line 71).

```
63  void main() {
64      SpreadSheet ss(5);    // spreadsheet with five cells
65      ss.set_cell(0, "Monday", 2375);
66      ss.set_cell(1, "Tuesday", 198);
67      ss.set_cell(2, "Wednesday", 482);
68      ss.set_cell(3, "Thursday", 7209);
69      ss.set_cell(4, "Friday", 3002);

70      BarGraph_View bgv(ss);
71      bgv.display();
72      HC_Pause();
73  }
```

**Program 2.7 (continued)**   An instance of a bar-graph view.

The output is a simple bar graph, as shown in Figure 2.7.

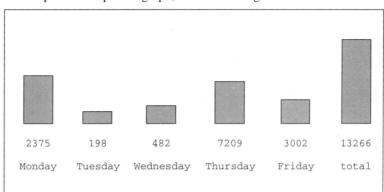

**Figure 2.7**    Output from Program 2.7.

## 2.3.7    A More Informative Bar Graph

In Program 2.8, we shall make a few simple changes to the bar-graph view of our spreadsheet to make the view more informative. The biggest change is the addition of axes: a baseline across the bottom of the bars, and a vertical axis, with the scale factor for the graph at the top of the vertical axis. In addition, we shall change the face pattern of any bar in the graph whose height is less than that of the bar to the left of it, to highlight days when the value went down.

Program 2.8 contains only the display method of class BarGraph_View; the rest of the program is the same as Program 2.7. To make room for the axes, we change the variables hspace and hpos (lines 5 and 7) to shift the graph to the right (these variables were defined on lines 22 and 24 in Program 2.7).

```
1   void BarGraph_View::display() {
2       const float labelpos = -0.25;
3       const float valuepos = -0.1;
4       const int num = d_dm.get_num_cells();
5       const float hspace = (float) (2.0 / (num + 1.5));
6       const float barwidth = hspace / 4.0;
7       float hpos = hspace - 1.0;
8       const double total = d_dm.get_total_value();
9       const float ymax = (float) scale(total);
10      char buf[64];
```

```
11        Point rect[4] = { {0,0,0}, {0,0,0},
12                          {0,0,0}, {0,0,0} };
13        float last = 0.0;

14        HC_Open_Segment("?Picture/bar graph view");
15           HC_Set_Camera_Projection("stretched");
16           HC_Set_Color(
17               "lines=edges=text=black, faces=light blue");

18           HC_Open_Segment("axes");
19               HC_Set_Text_Alignment(">*");

20               // calculate x origin
21               float xorg = (hspace / 2.0) - 1.0;
22               sprintf(buf, "%g ", ymax);
23               HC_Insert_Text(xorg, 0.95, 0.0, buf);
24               HC_Insert_Text(xorg, 0.0, 0.0, "0 ");

25               // draw x axis
26               HC_Insert_Line(xorg, 0.0,
27                     0.0, 0.95, 0.0, 0.0);

28               // draw y axis
29               HC_Insert_Line(xorg, 0.0,
30                     0.0, xor, 0.95, 0.0);
31           HC_Close_Segment();
```

**Program 2.8**     Axes in the bar-graph view.

The segment containing the axes (lines 18 to 31) changes the text alignment (line 19) so that text is right justified. Notice that this change does not affect the text alignment in any sibling segments, which continue to inherit the default text alignment from their parent.

The rest of the display function is the same, except for the addition of lines 13, and 37 through 39, which change the face of the bar to a crosshatch pattern if the previous cell was larger than the current cell.

```
32            for (int i = 0; i < num; i++) {
33                sprintf(buf, "cell %d", i);
34                HC_Open_Segment(buf);
35                    float value = (float)
36                        d_dm.get_cell_value(i);
37                    if (value < last)
38                        HC_Set_Face_Pattern("##");
39                    last = value;
40                    HC_Insert_Text(hpos, labelpos, 0.0,
41                        d_dm.get_cell_label(i));
42                    sprintf(buf, "%g", value);
43                    HC_Insert_Text(hpos, valuepos, 0.0, buf);
44                    rect[0].x = rect[3].x = hpos - barwidth;
45                    rect[1].x = rect[2].x = hpos + barwidth;
46                    rect[2].y = rect[3].y = 0.95 *
47                        value / ymax;
48                    HC_Insert_Polygon(4, rect);
49                    hpos += hspace;
50                HC_Close_Segment();
51            }
52        HC_Open_Segment("total");
53            HC_Insert_Text(hpos, labelpos, 0.0, "total");
54            sprintf(buf, "%g", total);
55            HC_Insert_Text(hpos, valuepos, 0.0, buf);
56            rect[0].x = rect[3].x = hpos - barwidth;
57            rect[1].x = rect[2].x = hpos + barwidth;
58            rect[2].y = rect[3].y = (float)
59                (0.95 * total / ymax);
60            HC_Insert_Polygon(4, rect);
61        HC_Close_Segment();
62    HC_Close_Segment();
63    HC_Pause();
64 }
```

**Program 2.8 (continued)**   Change of face pattern in the bar-graph view.

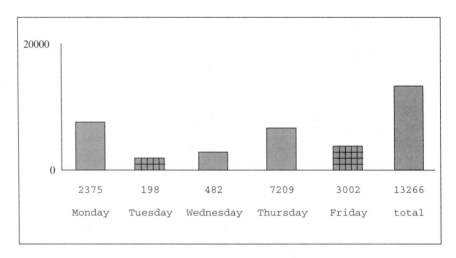

**Figure 2.8**        Output from Program 2.8.


## 2.4        Control Issues

In this section, we discuss several design decisions that you will make when you use object-oriented programming techniques to separate model from view in a graphics application.

### 2.4.1        Model in Control Versus View in Control

Whenever we divide a program into cooperating parts, such as when we separate model from view, we must determine who is in charge. In our example programs so far, the view was used to draw the model, but a reasonable alternative is for the model to use a view to draw itself. In the following sections, we shall consider the alternatives.

**2.4.1.1**        **View in charge.** So far, in our spreadsheet example, the view has been in charge. We passed the model (as an argument) to a view object, and the view made inquiries of the model for whatever information it needed (Figure 2.9).

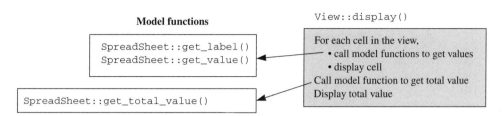

**Figure 2.9**     Control flow with view in charge.

**2.4.1.2**          **Model in charge.** In certain applications, it is appropriate for the model to be in charge. To put the model in charge, we need to turn the view on its head. Instead of a single function that calls model functions for information, the view becomes a set of smaller functions that the model calls to create a view of itself. For example, a ledger view of our simple spreadsheet example would contain a function to view a cell, and a function to view the total (Figure 2.10). The model contains a method called view, which takes the currently active view as an argument. For each cell in the model, the Model::view method calls the View::show_cell routine, and then calls the View::show_total routine to view the total.

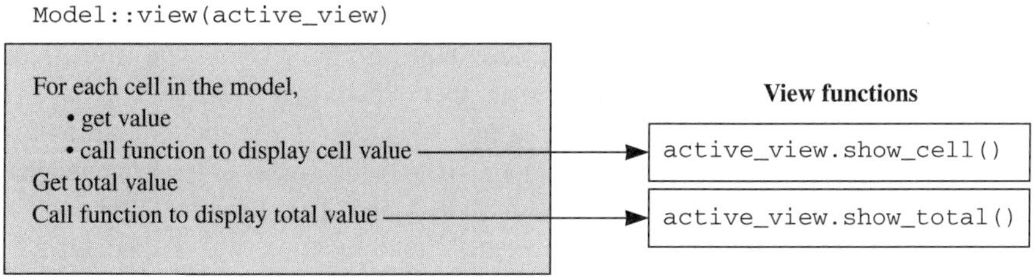

`Model::view(active_view)`

For each cell in the model,
  • get value
  • call function to display cell value ————→ **View functions**
Get total value                                      `active_view.show_cell()`
Call function to display total value ————→ `active_view.show_total()`

**Figure 2.10**     Control flow with model in charge.

It is more common to place the view in charge, because the view is doing the drawing and it knows what information it needs from the model. Consider a summary view, which displays only the total of the spreadsheet, and none of the individual cells. If the view is in charge, then it needs to call only the model's get_total_value routine and to display the result. If the model is in charge, it does not know that the individual cells will not be displayed, so it will call a view routine for each cell. Of course, we can simply make this routine do nothing, but having the model iterate over all cells is still a waste of time.

There are many different ways to put the model in charge in our spreadsheet example: Program 2.9 shows just one of them. We implement only the ledger view of the spreadsheet in this example program.

```
1  class View {
2   public:
3     View() : d_labelpos(0.0), d_valuepos(0.8) { }
4     int init(int cells, int totals);
5     void show_cell(double value, char * text);
6     void show_total(double value);
7     void done() { HC_Pause(); }
8   private:
9     float d_vspace;
10    float d_vpos;
11    int d_cellid;
12    const float d_labelpos;
13    const float d_valuepos;
14  };
```

**Program 2.9**    View when the model is in charge.

The class View now consists of several different functions for displaying individual parts of the data model. The init function (line 4) performs initial size computations and other initialization activities. Its arguments are the number of regular cells in the spreadsheet and the number of cells that will display totals (for our current data model, there is only a single total cell). This function returns 1 if the individual cells are to be displayed, or 0 if only the total is to be displayed in this view (for example, if this view is a summary view). The show_cell function (line 5) displays an individual cell, and the show_total function (line 6) displays the total. The done function (line 7) is called when the data model has finished sending data.

```
15  int View::init(int cells, int totals) {
16    d_vspace = (float) (2.0 / (cells + totals));
17    d_vpos = 1.0;
18    d_cellid = 0;
19    HC_Open_Segment("?Picture/view");
20      HC_Set_Camera_Projection("stretched");
21      HC_Set_Text_Alignment(">*");
22      HC_Set_Text_Font("size = 0.75 wru");
23    HC_Close_Segment();
24    return 1;
25  }
```

```
26  void View::show_cell(double value, char * text) {
27      char buf[64];
28      sprintf(buf, "?Picture/view/cell %d", d_cellid++);
29      HC_Open_Segment(buf);
30          HC_Set_Window(-1.0, 1.0,
31                  d_vpos - d_vspace, d_vpos);
32          HC_Insert_Text(d_labelpos, 0.0, 0.0, text);
33          sprintf(buf, "%g", value);
34          HC_Insert_Text(d_valuepos, 0.0, 0.0, buf);
35          d_vpos -= d_vspace;
36      HC_Close_Segment();
37  }

38  void View::show_total(double value) {
39      char buf[64];
40      HC_Open_Segment("?Picture/view/total");
41          HC_Set_Window(-1.0, 1.0, -1.0, d_vpos);
42          HC_Insert_Text(d_labelpos, 0.0, 0.0, "total");
43          sprintf(buf, "%g", value);
44          HC_Insert_Text(d_valuepos, 0.0, 0.0, buf);
45      HC_Close_Segment();
46  }
```

**Program 2.9 (continued)** Definition of view member functions.

The only change to the data model is the addition of a view function to class SpreadSheet. The rest of the data model is the same as in Program 2.3.

```
47  void SpreadSheet::view(View & v) {
48      int num = get_num_cells();
49      if (v.init(num, 1)) for (int i = 0; i < num; i++) {
50          v.show_cell(get_cell_value(i),
51                      get_cell_label(i));
52      }
53      v.show_total(get_total_value());
54      v.done();
55  }
```

**Program 2.9 (continued)** View function of spreadsheet data model.

The main function of our example program (lines 56 through 64) creates a data model (line 57) and displays a view of it (line 63).

```
56  void main() {
57      SpreadSheet ss(5);    // a spreadsheet with 5 cells
58      ss.set_cell(0, "Monday", 2375);
59      ss.set_cell(1, "Tuesday", 198);
60      ss.set_cell(2, "Wednesday", 482);
61      ss.set_cell(3, "Thursday", 7209);
62      ss.set_cell(4, "Friday", 3002);

63      ss.view(View());
64  }
```

**Program 2.9  (continued)**   Spreadsheet with data model in charge.

In Program 2.9, we defined only a single view class — a ledger view. To allow other kinds of views to be defined, we should treat the View class as a base class, from which we derive the text, ledger, and bar-graph views. Program 2.12, at the end of this chapter, shows how to define multiple view classes.

## 2.4.2      Automatic View Update

Because the model and the view are separate from each other, they can get out of sync. If the data model changes, the view must be updated (redrawn) to reflect those changes. Regardless of whether the model or the view is in charge, you must decide whether updates of the view will be initiated explicitly or automatically. In most of the programs, where the view was in charge, the view was updated when the application called the View::display function. In Program 2.9, where the data model was in charge, the view was updated when the SpreadSheet::view function was called. In both cases, the view was updated explicitly by the application.

Alternatively, the view can be updated automatically whenever the data model changes. In this case, the data model must have access to a list of those views that are currently active. Then, any function that changes the data model calls the display function for each active view. If the model is in charge, then the model's view function will be called for each active view.

If we implement automatic update for the spreadsheet example program, then, any time that the set_cell function (or any other function that changes the data model) is called, the view should be updated immediately. Figure 2.11 shows how we would add a list of active views to the spreadsheet data model (defined in Program 2.3), and how we would modify the set_cell function to update the active views.

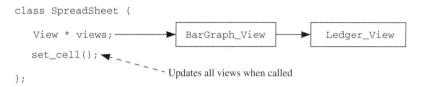

```
class SpreadSheet {

    View * views;                    BarGraph_View        Ledger_View

    set_cell();

                                          Updates all views when called
};
```

**Figure 2.11**    Organization of the spreadsheet data model for automatic update.

The main advantage of automatic view update is that the application does not need to worry about whether the views are up to date, or which parts of the data model are being viewed. The data model keeps track of which views are active, and makes sure that they are updated whenever the data to be viewed change. The main disadvantage is that the view may be updated unnecessarily or excessively if we make many small changes to the data model. We want the view to be updated only after we finish all the changes to the data model.

One way to avoid the problem of excessive view updates is to have changes to the data model schedule a view update, rather than perform it. As each change is made to the data model, a flag is set in the view that says that the view is out of date and needs to be updated. Of course, the view must have a way to know when we are done making changes to the data model, so that it can then update the display. We would rather not have to tell the view when to update itself, however, because updating the view explicitly is what we were trying to avoid in the first place!

Luckily, HOOPS is designed to help us with this dilemma. When we call a HOOPS function, such as HC_Insert_Text or HC_Set_Color, HOOPS stores the change, but does not immediately update the display. Thus, the application can make many small changes to the data model, each time updating the view via HOOPS. Then, when all changes are complete, HOOPS will update the display once.

HOOPS delays display update until the program pauses for user input. In the spreadsheet example, the view is updated when we call HC_Pause. We can also update the display explicitly (without waiting for user input) with the HC_Update_Display command.

### 2.4.3     Spreadsheet with Automatic Update

So far, none of our spreadsheet example programs ever updated their data model. In these simple examples, the spreadsheet was created once, and then was displayed. To demonstrate automatic update, we add to our data model several member functions that update the model. We also add a member variable to hold a pointer to the active view (for the sake of example, we shall allow only a single view, rather than a list of active views, and shall allow only a ledger view).

Our modified data model is given in Program 2.10 (the Cell class and the implementation of any SpreadSheet member functions not shown did not change from Program 2.3).

```
1   class SpreadSheet {
2   public:
3       SpreadSheet(int size);
4       ~SpreadSheet();           // destructor

5       int get_num_cells() { return d_num_cells; }

6       void set_cell(int i, char * label, double value) {
7           d_cells[i].set_label(label);
8           d_cells[i].set_value(value);
9           changed(i);
10      }

11      void set_label(int i, char * label) {
12          d_cells[i].set_label(label);
13          changed(i);
14      }

15      void set_value(int i, double value) {
16          d_cells[i].set_value(value);
17          changed(i);
18      }

19      double get_value(int i) {
20          return d_cells[i].get_value();
21      }
22      char * get_label(int i) {
23          return d_cells[i].get_label();
24      }
25      double get_total_value();
```

```
26   private:
27     void changed(int cellnum);

28     int d_num_cells;
29     Cell * d_cells;
30     Ledger_View * d_viewp;
31   };

32   SpreadSheet::SpreadSheet(int size) {
33     d_num_cells = size;
34     d_cells = new Cell[size];// allocate array of Cells
35     d_viewp = new Ledger_View(*this);
36   }

37   SpreadSheet::~SpreadSheet() {
38     delete [] d_cells;
39     d_num_cells = 0;
40     delete d_viewp;
41   }

42   void SpreadSheet::changed(int) {
43     d_viewp->display();
44   }
```

**Program 2.10**    Spreadsheet data model with automatic update.

The main change in Program 2.10 is that we added a new data member, d_viewp (line 30), which is the pointer to the active ledger view. The constructor initializes this data member (on line 35) by creating a new ledger view. The destructor frees this view on line 40. We also added two functions, set_label and set_value (lines 11 through 18), that update the data model. Any function that modifies the data model (the two added functions set_label and set_value, plus the set_cell function) calls a new function, called changed (declared on line 27, defined on lines 42 through 44), which is passed the number of the cell that was changed. For now, the changed function will ignore its argument and will simply call the display function for the view.

There is a problem. We are now calling the view's display function (on line 43) each time that we change the data model, and this function does not delete any of the old geometry from the HOOPS database. So, each time that the view is updated, new text is added (via HC_Insert_Text) right on top of the old text, leading to a mess. So, we need to remove all old geometry (such as text) when we update a view.

To solve this problem, we modify the Ledger_View::display function.

```
45  void Ledger_View::display() {
46      const float labelpos = 0.0;
47      const float valuepos = 0.8;
48      const int num = d_dm.get_num_cells();
49      const float vspace = (float) (2.0 / (num + 1));
50      float vpos = 1.0;
51      char buf[64];

52      HC_Open_Segment("?Picture/ledger view");
53          HC_Set_Camera_Projection("stretched");
54          HC_Set_Text_Alignment(">*");

55          for (int i = 0; i < num; i++) {
56              sprintf(buf, "cell %d", i);
57              HC_Open_Segment(buf);
58                  HC_Flush_Contents(".", "everything");
59                  HC_Set_Window(-1.0, 1.0,
60                          vpos - vspace, vpos);
61                  vpos -= vspace;
62                  char * lbl = d_dm.get_label(i);
63                  if (lbl) HC_Insert_Text(labelpos,
64                                          0.0, 0.0, lbl);
65                  sprintf(buf, "%g", d_dm.get_value(i));
66                  HC_Insert_Text(valuepos, 0.0, 0.0, buf);
67              HC_Close_Segment();
68          }

69          HC_Open_Segment("total");
70              HC_Flush_Contents(".", "everything");
71              HC_Set_Window(-1.0, 1.0, -1.0, vpos);
72              HC_Insert_Text(labelpos, 0.0, 0.0, "total");
73              sprintf(buf, "%g", d_dm.get_total_value());
74              HC_Insert_Text(valuepos, 0.0, 0.0, buf);
75          HC_Close_Segment();

76      HC_Close_Segment();
77  }
```

**Program 2.10  (continued)** Spreadsheet ledger view with automatic update.

The only change to the Ledger_View::display function (compared to the same function in Program 2.9) is the addition of the HC_Flush_Contents commands on lines 58 and 70.

 The first argument to the HC_Flush_Contents command specifies the name of the segment to flush. The name "." (a single period) denotes the current segment. The second argument specifies the kinds of objects in the HOOPS database to flush — in this case, "everything" (all geometry, attributes, subsegments, and so on).

Lines 78 through 92 contain an example main function; it sets up a spreadsheet, and then makes two changes to that spreadsheet (pausing after each change).

```
78  void main() {
79      SpreadSheet ss(5);
80      ss.set_cell(0, "Monday", 2375);
81      ss.set_cell(1, "Tuesday", 198);
82      ss.set_cell(2, "Wednesday", 482);
83      ss.set_cell(3, "Thursday", 7209);
84      ss.set_cell(4, "Friday", 3002);
85      // the view is created by the spreadsheet

86      HC_Pause();

87      ss.set_value(2, 250);
88      HC_Pause();

89      ss.set_value(2, 500);
90      ss.set_value(4, 2500);
91      HC_Pause();
92  }
```

**Program 2.10 (continued)** Spreadsheet example with automatic update.

## 2.4.4 Spreadsheet with Incremental Updates

Even though HOOPS does not update the screen until HC_Pause is called, each change to the spreadsheet data model calls the Ledger_View::display function, which recreates the entire view from scratch (flushing all geometry and reinserting it), even if only a single cell was changed. HOOPS is a graphics database system, so it has commands to make incremental changes to the database. If only a single cell in the data model changes, we can use these commands to update only that single cell in the view. This technique is primarily a speed optimization, but it also provides a better organization for the view.

In Program 2.11, we reorganize the actions of the view into two parts: those actions that must be done once when the view is created (typically done by the constructor), and those actions that depend on values in the data model, and so must be called when the view is updated.

```
1  class Ledger_View {
2   public:
3      Ledger_View(SpreadSheet & ssdm);
4      void update(int cellnum);
5   private:
6      SpreadSheet & d_dm;
7  };
```

**Program 2.11**    Ledger view class with incremental updates.

The class definition has one new method, called update (line 4), which takes the index of the cell to update. The display method has been removed. The old functionality of the display method is split between the new update function and the constructor (line 3).

The constructor makes any HOOPS calls that affect the display of all cells, such as those calls that set attributes. It also initializes the HOOPS subwindows used to display each cell. Basically, the constructor (lines 8 through 29 in Program 2.11) looks like the old display function (lines 45 through 77 in Program 2.10), minus any variables and commands used to display the text in the cells.

```
8  Ledger_View::Ledger_View(SpreadSheet & ssdm)
9              : d_dm(ssdm) {
10     const int num = d_dm.get_num_cells();
11     const float vspace = (float) (2.0 / (num + 1));
12     float vpos = 1.0;
13     char buf[64];

14     HC_Open_Segment("?Picture/ledger view");
15         HC_Set_Camera_Projection("stretched");
16         HC_Set_Text_Alignment(">*");

17         for (int i = 0; i < num; i++) {
18             sprintf(buf, "cell %d", i);
19             HC_Open_Segment(buf);
```

```
20              HC_Set_Window(-1.0, 1.0,
21                      vpos - vspace, vpos);
22              vpos -= vspace;
23          HC_Close_Segment();
24        }

25      HC_Open_Segment("total");
26          HC_Set_Window(-1.0, 1.0, -1.0, vpos);
27      HC_Close_Segment();

28    HC_Close_Segment();
29  }
```

**Program 2.11 (continued)** Constructor for incremental ledger view.

The update function (lines 30 through 52) updates the cell that was modified in the data model. We update a cell by flushing the current text (if any) and inserting new text (lines 38 through 43). Notice that we always have to update the total cell (lines 45 through 50), because changing the value of any cell changes the total.

```
30  void Ledger_View::update(int cellnum) {
31      const float labelpos = 0.0;
32      const float valuepos = 0.8;
33      const int num = d_dm.get_num_cells();
34      char buf[64];

35      HC_Open_Segment("?Picture/ledger view");

36          sprintf(buf, "cell %d", cellnum);
37          HC_Open_Segment(buf);
38              HC_Flush_Contents(".", "text");
39              char * lbl = d_dm.get_label(cellnum);
40              if (lbl) HC_Insert_Text(labelpos,
41                                      0.0, 0.0, lbl);
42              sprintf(buf, "%g", d_dm.get_value(cellnum));
43              HC_Insert_Text(valuepos, 0.0, 0.0, buf);
44          HC_Close_Segment();

45          HC_Open_Segment("total");
46              HC_Flush_Contents(".", "text");
47              HC_Insert_Text(labelpos, 0.0, 0.0, "total");
48              sprintf(buf, "%g", d_dm.get_total_value());
49              HC_Insert_Text(valuepos, 0.0, 0.0, buf);
```

**55**

```
50          HC_Close_Segment();

51      HC_Close_Segment();
52  }
```

**Program 2.11 (continued)** Ledger view update function with incremental update.

The HC_Flush_Contents commands on lines 38 and 46 were changed to flush "text" instead of "everything", because we do not want to remove the attributes set on the segment (in this case, the window attribute, set on line 26). Equivalently, we could have said to flush all "geometry" instead, since text is a kind of geometry in HOOPS.

Finally, on lines 53 through 55, we change the definition of the changed function in the data model to update only what has changed, instead of redisplaying the whole model (as in Program 2.10, lines 42 through 44).

```
53  void SpreadSheet::changed(int cellnum) {
54      d_viewp->update(cellnum);
55  }
```

**Program 2.11 (continued)** The changed function with incremental update.

Note that this optimization of sending only changes would work in the bar-graph view, but would not save any time, because changing any cell can change the scale of the bar graph, which would require all cells in the graph to be updated anyway.

**2.4.4.1**      **Handling of more than one kind of view.** In this section, we modify Program 2.11 such that it can be used with any view, rather than with only a ledger view. We define two views — bar graph and ledger — for the spreadsheet. These views are derived from a common base class, called View, which has a virtual function named update.

> **C++**
>
> Virtual functions in C++ allow a group of classes that have the same base class to be manipulated through a pointer to their base class. For example, in Program 2.12, we will derive the three view classes (text, ledger, and bar-graph) from a single base class, called View. In Program 2.10, the spreadsheet data model contained a pointer to a ledger view named d_viewp (on line 30). We can change d_viewp to be a pointer to the base View class, and store a pointer to any of the derived view classes in it.
>
> When the data model calls the update function through the d_viewp pointer, we do not want to call the View::update function — we want to call the update function for whatever kind of view is stored in d_viewp. By declaring the update function to be a virtual function, we ensure that the proper derived-class update function will be called. For example, if we store a pointer to a Ledger_View in d_viewp, when we call
>
> ```
> d_viewp->update();
> ```
>
> the update function for the ledger view will be called, even though d_viewp was declared to be a pointer to a View.
>
> By using virtual functions, we can add new kinds of views to our application without changing the data model.

We will add a method to class SpreadSheet that sets the current view. In this simple example, we shall allow only a single view to be active at a time (in Chapter 7, we shall learn how to create multiple windows, so that we can have multiple views, each with its own output window). When one view is replaced by another view, we shall delete the old view from HOOPS using the HC_Delete_Segment command.

> **C++**
>
> Program 2.12 uses advanced features of C++, including virtual functions and protected members. Even if your knowledge of C++ is weak, read the example to get a feel for how an application with multiple views might be organized.

Rather than showing only the parts of Program 2.12 that are changed relative to earlier example programs, we include the entire source.

```
1  #include <stdio.h>
2  #include <hc.h>

3  class Cell {
4   public:
5     Cell { d_value = 0.0; d_label = (char *) 0; }
```

```
 6       void set_value(double val) { d_value = val; }
 7       void set_label(char * label) { d_label = label; }
 8       double get_value() { return d_value; }
 9       char * get_label() { return d_label; }
10     private:
11       double d_value;
12       char * d_label;
13     };
```

**Program 2.12**    Data model for a cell.

A forward reference for class View (line 14) is required because class
SpreadSheet contains a pointer to a View (line 45), but class View also contains a
pointer to a SpreadSheet (line 54).

The data model contains a pointer to the current view (line 45), so the view can
be updated automatically whenever the model is changed. The current view is set
by the set_view function (declared on line 19), which takes a reference to a view.

```
14   class View;    // forward reference

15   class SpreadSheet {
16    public:
17       SpreadSheet(int size);
18       ~SpreadSheet();// destructor
19       void set_view(View & view);
20       int get_num_cells() { return d_num_cells; }

21       void set_cell(int i, char * label, double value) {
22          d_cells[i].set_label(label);
23          d_cells[i].set_value(value);
24          changed(i);
25       }
26       void set_label(int i, char * label) {
27          d_cells[i].set_label(label);
28          changed(i);
29       }
30       void set_value(int i, double value) {
31          d_cells[i].set_value(value);
32          changed(i);
33       }
34       double get_value(int i) {
```

```
35        return d_cells[i].get_value();
36    }
37    char * get_label(int i) {
38        return d_cells[i].get_label();
39    }
40    double get_total_value();
41  private:
42    void changed(int cellnum);
43    int d_num_cells;
44    Cell * d_cells;
45    View * d_viewp;
46  };
```

**Program 2.12 (continued)** Data model for spreadsheet with multiple views.

Class View defines three virtual functions. The setup function (line 50) is called to attach a view to a data model. It is called by the SpreadSheet::set_view function (on line 90), and is similar to the constructor for the view in Program 2.11 (lines 8 through 29). The update function (line 51) is basically the same as the update function in Program 2.11 (lines 30 through 52). The cleanup function (line 52) is used to clean up the old view when a new view is attached to the data model (remember that, in this example, we allow only one active view at a time).

**C++**  Class View is a *pure virtual class*: It is used only for deriving new classes. You never create an instance of class View. All its member functions, except the constructor, have been set to null functions (lines 50 through 52).

```
47  class View {    // pure virtual
48    public:
49      View() : d_dmp(0) { }
50      virtual void setup(SpreadSheet * ssdm) = 0;
51      virtual void update(int cellnum) = 0;
52      virtual void cleanup() = 0;
53    protected:
54      SpreadSheet * d_dmp;
55  };
```

**Program 2.12 (continued)** Base view class for multiple views.

> **C++**
>
> The SpreadSheet pointer d_dmp (line 54) is a protected member variable. A *protected member* is the same as a private member, except that it can be accessed by member functions of derived classes.

Ledger_View is derived from class View. Unlike the constructor in Program 2.11 (lines 8 through 29), the constructor in Program 2.12 (line 58) only initializes the model for this view to null, by calling the constructor for class View (line 49).

```
56  class Ledger_View : public View {
57   public:
58      Ledger_View() : View() { }
59      void setup(SpreadSheet * ssdm);
60      void update(int cellnum);
61      void cleanup();

62   private:
63      static const float labelpos;
64      static const float valuepos;
65  };
```

**Program 2.12 (continued)** Derived ledger view class.

We have changed the labelpos and valuepos constants, which were defined as local variables of the update function on lines 31 and 32 in Program 2.12, to be static class constants (on lines 63 and 64). Static class constants are local to the class, but are global to all member functions in the class; this change allows the same constants to be used by both the setup and update functions of this class. Static class constants must be initialized outside of the class definition (on lines 104 and 105).

> **C++**
>
> Class BarGraph_View also defines static constants for labelpos and valuepos. These values are different from those in a ledger view. By using class variables, rather than global constants (or a preprocessor #define) to define these constants, we allow each kind of view to have different values for the constants, while keeping the same names. Note that the names are local to the class (they have class scope). If they were not private variables, then we could access them from outside of class scope using the Ledger_View::labelpos notation.

```
66  class BarGraph_View : public View {
67   public:
68      BarGraph_View() : View() { }
69      void setup(SpreadSheet * ssdm);
70      void update(int cellnum);
71      void cleanup();
72   private:
73      static double scale(double max);
74      static const float labelpos;
75      static const float valuepos;
76  };
```

**Program 2.12 (continued)** Derived bar-graph view class.

---

**C++**

If we were dividing Program 2.12 into multiple source files, lines 1 through 76 would go into one or more header (.h) file, and everything else (line 77 through the end) would go into multiple program (.cpp) files.

---

The set_view function (line 88) first checks to see whether we already have a current view. If we do, it cleans up that view. It then sets the current view to the value of the argument, and calls setup on the new view, passing the new view a pointer to the spreadsheet data model.

The changed function (line 93) checks to make sure that we have a current view before it calls the update function for the view.

```
77  // members of SpreadSheet
78  SpreadSheet::SpreadSheet(int size) {
79      d_num_cells = size;
80      // allocate array of Cells
81      d_cells = new Cell[size];
82      d_viewp = 0;
83  }

84  SpreadSheet::~SpreadSheet() {
85      delete [] d_cells;
86      d_num_cells = 0;
87  }
```

```
88  void SpreadSheet::set_view(View & view) {
89      if (d_viewp) d_viewp->cleanup();
90      d_viewp = &view;
91      d_viewp->setup(this);
92  }

93  void SpreadSheet::changed(int cellnum) {
94      if (d_viewp) d_viewp->update(cellnum);
95  }

96  double SpreadSheet::get_total_value() {
97      double sum = 0.0;
98      for (int i = 0; i < d_num_cells; i++) {
99          sum += get_value(i);
100     }
101     return sum;
102 }
```

**Program 2.12 (continued)** Member functions of data model.

Note that the setup function (lines 106 through 135) draws the data model, unlike the constructor function in Program 2.11 (lines 8 through 29), because we want the view to be drawn when we switch views. (That is why we changed labelpos and valuepos to class constants — so that we could access them from both the setup and update member functions.) The setup function also sets the pointer to the data model d_dmp on line 107. Other than that, setup is similar to the constructor function for the ledger view in Program 2.11.

The update function (lines 136 through 157) is the same as in Program 2.11 (lines 30 through 52).

The cleanup function (lines 158 through 160) deletes the entire segment (and all that segment's children) from the HOOPS database. Note that it is not a good idea to do this deletion by flushing the contents of "?Picture", because "?Picture" might contain other attributes that you do not want to delete.

```
103 // members of Ledger_View

104 const float Ledger_View::labelpos = 0.0;
105 const float Ledger_View::valuepos = 0.8;

106 void Ledger_View::setup(SpreadSheet * ssdmp) {
107     d_dmp = ssdmp;// set data model for view
108     const int num = d_dmp->get_num_cells();
```

```
109     const float vspace = (float) (2.0 / (num + 1));
110     float vpos = 1.0;
111     char buf[64];

112     HC_Open_Segment("?Picture/ledger view");
113         HC_Set_Camera_Projection("stretched");
114         HC_Set_Text_Alignment(">*");

115         for (int i = 0; i < num; i++) {
116             sprintf(buf, "cell %d", i);
117             HC_Open_Segment(buf);
118                 HC_Set_Window(-1.0, 1.0,
119                                 vpos - vspace, vpos);
120                 vpos -= vspace;
121                 char * lbl = d_dmp->get_label(i);
122                 if (lbl) HC_Insert_Text(labelpos,
123                                         0.0, 0.0, lbl);
124                 sprintf(buf, "%g", d_dmp->get_value(i));
125                 HC_Insert_Text(valuepos, 0.0, 0.0, buf);
126             HC_Close_Segment();
127         }

128         HC_Open_Segment("total");
129             HC_Set_Window(-1.0, 1.0, -1.0, vpos);
130             HC_Insert_Text(labelpos, 0.0, 0.0, "total");
131             sprintf(buf, "%g", d_dmp->get_total_value());
132             HC_Insert_Text(valuepos, 0.0, 0.0, buf);
133         HC_Close_Segment();

134     HC_Close_Segment();
135 }

136 void Ledger_View::update(int cellnum) {
137     const int num = d_dmp->get_num_cells();
138     char buf[64];

139     HC_Open_Segment("?Picture/ledger view");

140         sprintf(buf, "cell %d", cellnum);
141         HC_Open_Segment(buf);
142             HC_Flush_Contents(".", "text");
143             char * lbl = d_dmp->get_label(cellnum);
144             if (lbl) HC_Insert_Text(labelpos,
145                                     0.0, 0.0, lbl);
```

```
146          sprintf(buf, "%g",
147                  d_dmp->get_value(cellnum));
148          HC_Insert_Text(valuepos, 0.0, 0.0, buf);
149       HC_Close_Segment();

150       HC_Open_Segment("total");
151          HC_Flush_Contents(".", "text");
152          HC_Insert_Text(labelpos, 0.0, 0.0, "total");
153          sprintf(buf, "%g", d_dmp->get_total_value());
154          HC_Insert_Text(valuepos, 0.0, 0.0, buf);
155       HC_Close_Segment();

156    HC_Close_Segment();
157 }

158 void Ledger_View::cleanup() {
159    HC_Delete_Segment("?Picture/ledger view");
160 }
```

**Program 2.12 (continued)** Member functions of the ledger view.

In a bar-graph view, incremental update does not gain us much efficiency (changing a single bar often causes all bars to be redrawn, because the scale factor changes). Consequently, we use the same function for both setup and update, and simply call update with an argument of 0 from the setup function (line 180). The setup function also sets the data model pointer d_dmp (line 179), of course.

The update function for the bar-graph view includes the axes from Program 2.8 (but does not include the different-patterned bars; you can add those if you wish).

```
161 // members of BarGraph_View

162 const float BarGraph_View::labelpos = (float) -0.25;
163 const float BarGraph_View::valuepos = (float) -0.1;

164 double BarGraph_View::scale(double max) {
165    double s = 1.0;
166    while (max > 10.0) {
167       s *= 10.0;
168       max /= 10.0;
169    }
170    while (max < 1.0) {
171       s /= 10.0;
```

```
172      max *= 10.0;
173    }
174    s *= (double) (1 + (int) max);
175    return s;
176 }

177 struct Point {float x, y, z;};

178 void BarGraph_View::setup(SpreadSheet * ssdmp) {
179    d_dmp = ssdmp;      // set data model for view
180    update(0);
181 }

182 void BarGraph_View::update(int) {
183    int num = d_dmp->get_num_cells();
184    float hspace = (float) (2.0 / (num + 1.5));
185    float barwidth = (float) (hspace / 4.0);
186    float hpos = (float) (hspace - 1.0);
187    double total = d_dmp->get_total_value();
188    float ymax = (float) scale(total);
189    char buf[64];
190    Point points[4] = { {0,0,0}, {0,0,0},
191                        {0,0,0}, {0,0,0} };

192    HC_Open_Segment("?Picture/bar graph view");
193       HC_Set_Camera_Projection("stretched");
194       HC_Set_Color(
195           "lines=edges=text=black, faces=light blue");

196       HC_Open_Segment("axes");
197          HC_Flush_Contents(".", "geometry");
198          HC_Set_Text_Alignment(">*");
199          float xor = (hspace / 2.0) - 1.0;
200          sprintf(buf, "%g ", ymax);
201          HC_Insert_Text(xor, 0.95, 0.0, buf);
202          HC_Insert_Text(xor, 0.0, 0.0, "0 ");
203          HC_Insert_Line(xor, 0.0,
204                 0.0, 0.95, 0.0, 0.0);   // x
205          HC_Insert_Line(xor, 0.0,
206                 0.0, xor, 0.95, 0.0);   // y
207       HC_Close_Segment();

208       for (int i = 0; i < num; i++) {
```

```
209              sprintf(buf, "cell %d", i);
210              HC_Open_Segment(buf);
211                  HC_Flush_Contents(".", "geometry");
212                  float value = (float) d_dmp->get_value(i);
213                  char * lbl = d_dmp->get_label(i);
214                  if (lbl) HC_Insert_Text(hpos,
215                                          labelpos, 0.0, lbl);
216                  sprintf(buf, "%g", value);
217                  HC_Insert_Text(hpos, valuepos, 0.0, buf);
218                  points[0].x = points[3].x =
219                      hpos - barwidth;
220                  points[1].x = points[2].x =
221                      hpos + barwidth;
222                  points[2].y = points[3].y =
223                      0.95 * value / ymax;
224                  HC_Insert_Polygon(4, points);
225                  hpos += hspace;
226              HC_Close_Segment();
227          }

228      HC_Open_Segment("total");
229          HC_Flush_Contents(".", "geometry");
230          HC_Insert_Text(hpos, labelpos, 0.0, "total");
231          sprintf(buf, "%g", total);
232          HC_Insert_Text(hpos, valuepos, 0.0, buf);
233          points[0].x = points[3].x = hpos - barwidth;
234          points[1].x = points[2].x = hpos + barwidth;
235          points[2].y = points[3].y =
236              0.95 * total / ymax;
237          HC_Insert_Polygon(4, points);
238      HC_Close_Segment();

239   HC_Close_Segment();
240 }

241 void BarGraph_View::cleanup() {
242     HC_Delete_Segment("?Picture/bar graph view");
243 }
```

**Program 2.12 (continued)** Member functions for the bar-graph view.

The main function (lines 244 through 267) creates a data model and two views, and changes values in the data model to show that each view is updated properly.

```
244  void main() {
245      // data model
246      SpreadSheet ss(5);
247      ss.set_cell(0, "Monday", 2375);
248      ss.set_cell(1, "Tuesday", 198);
249      ss.set_cell(2, "Wednesday", 482);
250      ss.set_cell(3, "Thursday", 7209);
251      ss.set_cell(4, "Friday", 3002);

252      // first view
253      Ledger_View lv;
254      ss.set_view(lv);
255      HC_Pause();

256      ss.set_value(2, 500);
257      ss.set_value(4, 2500);
258      HC_Pause();

259      // second view
260      BarGraph_View bgv;
261      ss.set_view(bgv);
262      HC_Pause();

263      ss.set_value(3, 1000);
264      HC_Pause();

265      ss.set_value(2, 4321);
266      HC_Pause();
267  }
```

**Program 2.12 (continued)** Spreadsheet with multiple views.

### 2.4.5    Model–View–Controller

Another way to organize graphics applications is to introduce a third class (in addition to the model and view), called a *controller* (Figure 2.12). This organization is named model–view–controller (MVC), and is the basis of the Smalltalk environment. It solves the problem of whether the model or the view is in charge, by creating a new component whose primary purpose is to be in charge. The controller (1) receives input events, (2) figures out what those events mean by calling routines in the view and (3) updates the model appropriately. When the model is updated, it then (4) updates the view.

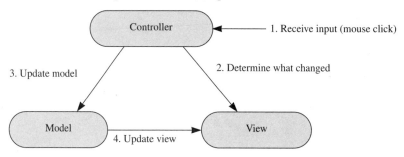

**Figure 2.12**    Model–View–Controller.

Like the programs in the previous few sections, a program that uses the MVC paradigm updates its views automatically whenever the model changes. Thus, when the controller updates the model, the view is updated as well (step 4 in Figure 2.12). In certain cases, however, an input event can affect a view without making any changes to the model. For example, if the user clicks on a scroll bar, this event changes the view but probably does not affect the data model. In this case, the controller calls the view directly to update the view.

The advantages and disadvantages of the MVC paradigm have been debated in the object-oriented programming community. One problem is that the view and the controller both contain information about how to view the model. This division of information creates unwanted interactions between the controller and the view, because modifications to one of them almost always necessitate modifications to the other. It is difficult to build a good interface between the controller and the view, and controllers are not easily reused. It is difficult to create a new view without also creating an entirely new controller.

## 2.4.6    Sharing of Control

There are further solutions to the problem of deciding who is in charge. One technique (which is difficult to implement in practice) is to make the controller part of the view, but to have it be executed by the model. In this paradigm, the model is in control, but it in essence asks the view what it should do. The view answers by returning a controller (in other words, a code fragment) that the model uses to create a view of itself. The advantage of this technique is that it puts the model in charge but calls only those functions needed by the current view. For example, if the current view is a summary view that displays only the total, the update function for the individual cells will not be called.

Building such a system is beyond the scope of this book. In general, this technique works better with a language more dynamic than C++ (such as Smalltalk or LISP). We can use this technique for our simple spreadsheet example, however, by changing the view into a list of pointers to view functions — one for each element of the model — that the model calls to update the view. When our application makes a change to the model, the element that changed would call any associated view functions. For example, a summary view would have only a single view function to call; this function would be called whenever the total cell in the data model changed.

## 2.5 Extensibility

Another important topic is how to make both the model and the view *extensible*. In certain applications, we want the user to be able to add new data types to the data model, and also to be able to add new kinds of views, but these two kinds of extensibility can create a conflict.

- *Data-model extensibility.* To add a new type of object to the data model, we need to be able to define all functions that are required of that type. In particular, we must be able to view that type, so each object in the data model must support all functions required by all views.

- *View extensibility.* To add a new view, we must ensure that the view knows about all types of objects to be viewed. In our spreadsheet, each new view would need to know how to view a regular cell, and how to view the total cell.

- *Both data-model and view extensibility.* If the user is able to add new object types to the data model, it is impossible for new views to know about all possible object types (because new objects types can be added later). If the user is able to add new views, it is impossible for data types to define all functions required of all possible views (because new views might be added later that require new functions to be defined).

Our spreadsheet example is written such that it is easy to add new views but is not so easy to add new kinds of objects to the data model. Say that we want to add a new object type: a new kind of cell that contains a text string, so that we can add comments and labels to our spreadsheet. Then, all views (text, ledger, and bar graph) must know about that kind of cell, so that they can display it. As the spreadsheet example is currently written, there is no way to let the views know about a new object type in the data model without rewriting all of them.

To allow new types of objects to be added to the data model, we could have each type of object have member functions to view itself, and could have the view call the appropriate function for each cell in the data model. For example, each type of cell would have a function to view itself in a text view, another function to view itself in a ledger view, and a third function for a bar-graph view. In this case, of course, each object in the data model would have to know about all views, so, although it would be easy to add new kinds of objects to the data model, it would then be virtually impossible to add new kinds of views (unless we could implement the new view using only the view methods that the data-model objects already provide — for example, a summary view).

Most applications simply choose which is more important — the ability for the user to add new object types or to add new views — and implement one or the other. The first possibility makes the data model extensible, but the views are fixed by the system implementor. The second possibility allows the user to add new views, but the data model is not extensible.

It is possible to create applications where both the data model and the views are extensible, but doing so is difficult (and is far beyond the scope of this book). Such systems usually make assumptions about the kinds of new data-model object types and views that can be added. In such systems, each new data type must have functions to provide all the information that any new view might ever need, and any new view must contain all the functionality it might need to draw any new data type.

The same extensibility problem afflicts graphics libraries such as HOOPS. We want the user to be able to add new kinds of graphics primitives (such as solids, bitmaps, volume data, surface patches), and we want the user to be able to add new kinds of renderers (for example, with antialiasing or motion blur). However, each renderer must know about each graphic primitive, and each primitive must know about each renderer, so there is a conflict.

The developers of HOOPS chose to make the data model, but not the renderers, extensible. Programmers of graphics applications always want to be able to define new types of primitives, but there are typically only a few interesting kinds of renderers. HOOPS already includes a variety of renderers, and it is possible for new renderers to be added to HOOPS — provided that they are not new kinds of renderers that require information that the primitives do not already provide.

# 3     Computer Graphics

This chapter presents an overview of how computer-graphics systems work, with an emphasis on how you can select and use existing graphics systems. There are entire books written about graphics systems; our goal here is to help you build graphics applications, rather than graphics libraries, so we purposely skip unnecessary details. For more information on graphics systems — including on how to build them — see the references in the Preface.

## 3.1     The Graphics System

This section discusses the function and organization of a modern graphics system.

### 3.1.1     Graphics Primitives

When an application wants to draw a picture, it sends scene information to the graphics system as a collection of *graphics primitives*. Examples of graphics primitives are points, lines, circles, text, rectangles, polygons, and surfaces. Each graphics primitive consists of two parts:

1. Geometry

2. Attributes

For example, the geometry of a line is typically represented by the two endpoints of the line, and the attributes are properties such as line thickness, color, pattern, and so on. In Figure 3.1, the geometry is a line from (10, 2) to (4, 8) and the attributes are thin, red, and dashed.

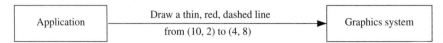

**Figure 3.1**        A line primitive made up of geometry and attributes.

This particular line — a thin, red, dashed line from (10, 2) to (4, 8) — is an *instance* of the line primitive.

### 3.1.2        Rendering

To be displayed, graphics primitives must be converted into an image. Some devices, such as pen plotters, do this conversion directly by drawing on paper. Most display devices, however — including CRT (cathode-ray tube) monitors, flat-panel displays, laser printers, and ink jet printers — display an image as a fine grid of individual picture elements, called *pixels*. For example, Figure 3.2 shows a line segment rendered as a sequence of pixels. The process of converting graphics primitives into an image is called *rendering*.

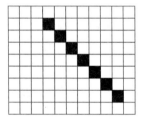

**Figure 3.2**        A rendering of a line segment as a sequence of pixels.

### 3.1.3        Frame Buffers

For an image to be displayed long enough for a human to perceive it, it must be stored somewhere. Hardcopy devices such as printers and plotters store the image as colored inks or pigments on paper. For a CRT or flat-panel display, the image is stored in computer memory and is redrawn over and over fast enough that it appears to be a fixed image.

For display on a typical monitor, a 2D array of pixels is stored in a large memory called a *frame buffer*. The frame buffer contains one word of memory per pixel, which holds the color value of the pixel. This memory word can be as small as a single bit per pixel for systems that display only full black or white, or as large as 24 bits per pixel — 8 bits for each of red, green, and blue, sometimes called *true color*. Certain specialized frame buffers have even more bits per color, or have an *alpha channel* used for mixing images from multiple sources. The alpha channel is typically the same number of bits as one of the color channels. A common configuration is 32 bits per pixel — 8 bits each for red, green, blue, and alpha.

You can use the HC_Show_Device_Info command to determine the size of your frame buffer.

```
char buff[32];
HC_Show_Device_Info("?Picture", "max pixels", buff);
printf("width and height = %s\n",
        buff);

HC_Show_Device_Info("?Picture", "planes", buff);
printf("bits per pixel = %s\n",
        buff);
```

The image to be displayed is read out of frame-buffer memory sequentially, one line at a time — as a *raster*. It is then converted into an analog voltage by a digital-to-analog converter (DAC), and is sent to the display (as in Figure 3.3).

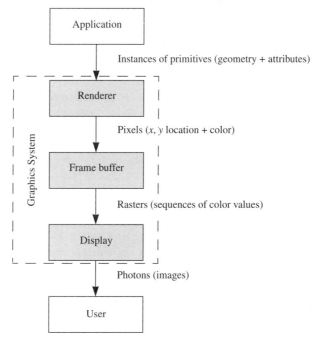

**Figure 3.3**        The graphics-system pipeline.

A frame buffer can contain a considerable amount of memory. For example, a typical graphics card used in a CAD system can display an image that measures 1280 by 1024 pixels, with 24 bits per pixel. That is 4 megabytes of memory just for the display. And this memory must be fast. Screen refresh requires the entire memory to be read out over and over, up to 80 (or more) times per second, or faster than 10 nanoseconds per pixel. In addition, there must be some memory cycles left over to write the image to be displayed into the frame-buffer memory.

Typical computer memory is dynamic random-access memory (DRAM), which has a cycle time of between 60 and 120 nanoseconds, so most frame buffers use special memory chips called video random-access memory (VRAM). VRAM can read out sequential locations in memory (rasters) quickly, while still allowing (somewhat slower) random access by the computer. The decreasing price of VRAM has been a primary gating factor in the change from character-oriented user interfaces (such as DOS and UNIX command-line interfaces) to graphical interfaces (such as Windows and X11). Some less expensive display boards use DRAM anyway and read multiple pixels in parallel, but that does not leave much time for writing the image, so such boards are usually much slower than are VRAM-based boards.

### 3.1.4     Double Buffering

To draw a new image into the frame buffer, the graphics system must first erase the old image by clearing the frame buffer. If you are doing animation, this process makes the image appear to flash on and off, rather than to change smoothly. A common way to solve this problem is to *double buffer* — that is, to use two frame buffers (with twice as much memory). In this scheme, one frame buffer is used to refresh the display, while the other frame buffer is being drawn into. When the graphics system is done drawing a new image, it *swaps* the frame buffers, so the image just drawn is now sent to the display. The graphics system can then clear the other frame buffer and start drawing into it.

An alternative form of double buffering uses only one frame buffer, but never draws directly into it. Instead, a new image is first drawn into some other memory (which can be DRAM on the display card, or even regular system memory). When the graphics system is done drawing the new image, the new image is *copied* quickly into the frame buffer (perhaps via special hardware). This kind of double buffering is often used with a window system, since only the contents of the window being drawn into need to be copied into the frame-buffer memory.

## 3.1.5      Display Lists

In addition to storing the output image from the renderer in the frame buffer, some graphics systems also store the input to the renderer — the graphics primitives. The memory used to retain the graphics primitives is called a *display list* or *graphics database*.

Figure 3.4 categorizes graphics systems by whether and how they use a display list.

- Graphics systems that render primitives immediately, without storing the primitives in a display list, are called *immediate-mode* systems. They are represented by the top diagram of Figure 3.4.

- Graphics systems that retain the primitives in a display list or graphics database are called *retained-mode* systems. They are represented by the bottom two diagrams of Figure 3.4.

- The difference between a simple display list and a graphics database is that a graphics database is a display list that can be modified in place. For example, for a scene containing several dozen primitives, a graphics database would allow you to change the primitives individually (either their geometry or attributes), whereas a simple display list would require you to resend the entire display list to change one primitive.

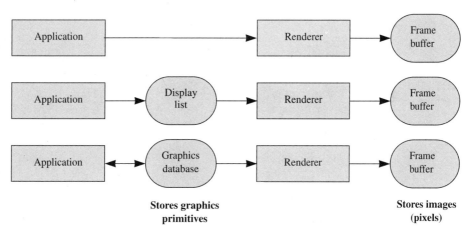

**Figure 3.4**      Immediate-mode, display-list, and database graphics systems.

## 3.1.6     Immediate-Mode Graphics Systems

The simplest graphics systems are immediate-mode graphics libraries. *Immediate* means that, when a graphics command is executed, its output appears immediately. For example, if the graphics-system command to draw a line is executed, the line appears on the display.

The earliest immediate-mode graphics libraries started out as simple interface libraries to the graphics hardware. Graphics-library commands executed direct calls to the graphics hardware — many commands set individual registers in the hardware. Portability was not a consideration; different graphics hardware, even from the same manufacturer, would often have completely different software interfaces. The primary consideration was speed, and anything that appeared to get in the way of that speed was unacceptable. These libraries were the assembly languages of graphics, and they were exceedingly difficult to use.

Nevertheless, many applications were written with these systems. Because software had to be written for specific graphics hardware, applications typically were sold as part of a bundled system, called a *turn-key system,* complete with the computer, graphics hardware, and any other necessary peripherals. As new graphics hardware became available, the application writers would port the application to the new hardware, and would sell a new turn-key system.

As graphics hardware became more widespread, computer manufacturers attempted to standardize their individual graphics libraries so that the same application could run on more than one type of machine. Of course, every manufacturer had its own standard interface: GL from Silicon Graphics, XGL from Sun Microsystems, Starbase from Hewlett-Packard, and so on.

By standardizing their own graphics libraries, hardware manufacturers avoided the problems and expense of rewriting low-level graphics codes for each new graphics hardware device. These standard graphics libraries allowed an application written for a Sun system to run on any Sun (with any Sun graphics hardware), but not on any other manufacturer's system — giving a small degree of portability. Of course, the cost of a software layer that isolated applications from the graphics hardware was a small loss of performance. The fact that manufacturers were willing to pay this cost reflected the changing relationship between hardware and software: instead of designing the hardware first, and then writing software as a thin layer on top of it, for the first time they were building hardware to support a specific software interface.

The main advantage of immediate-mode graphics systems is that (like assembly languages) they are close to the hardware, so, with effort, it is possible to write a fast graphics application. Even if you do not use an immediate-mode graphics system, it is a good idea to understand how these systems work. After all, a retained-mode graphics system is essentially a display list layered on top of an immediate-mode hardware interface.

### 3.1.7    Retained-Mode Graphics Systems

Retaining the graphics primitives in a display list provides the following advantages: the opportunity to optimize rendering, fast selections, support for window systems, and the ability to use global rendering algorithms.

**3.1.7.1**    **Optimizations.** If the graphics system retains a copy of all the primitives, it can perform optimizations to render the scene faster. For example, the graphics system can calculate *bounding volumes*. A bounding volume stores the location and a rough measure of the extent of a set of primitives. During rendering, many primitives will end up completely above, below, or to the left or right of the screen. Bounding volumes allow the system to determine quickly whether a group of primitives is onscreen, so that only visible graphics primitives will be sent to the display hardware to be rendered.

**3.1.7.2**    **Fast selections.** An important function of a graphics system is determining at which graphic primitive the user is pointing with the cursor, so the user can select objects (this function is also called *picking*). Without a display list, the only way for the graphics system to perform a selection is to have the application resend all the primitives (since they were not retained by the graphics system). A display list allows the graphics system to perform selection much faster — typically, an order of magnitude faster.

**3.1.7.3**    **Window-system support.** In a computer with a window system, if a window containing a scene is partially obscured by another window and then is brought to the front, the newly exposed areas of the window need to be redrawn. If the graphics system stores the primitives in a display list, then it can redraw the window without going back to the application.

**3.1.7.4**    **Global rendering algorithms.** Many kinds of renderers require a copy of all the graphics primitives. For example, in ray tracing and radiosity, the color of an object is affected by other objects, so the renderer requires data on all the primitives before it can start drawing any of them. Such advanced rendering algorithms require the use of a display list to store the primitives.

The only common rendering algorithm that does not need a copy of all the graphics primitives is the Z-buffer hidden-surface algorithm, described in Section 3.3.3.5. Graphics systems that do not store graphics primitives are limited to using the Z-buffer or related algorithms.

### 3.1.8    Graphics Databases

Any time that graphics data are stored somewhere, we can interact with those data to modify the displayed scene. If we want to make incremental changes to the primitives in a display list, however, the graphics system must provide commands to insert, delete, and modify individual instances of graphics primitives. A display list that has editing capabilities is called a *graphics database* (because it serves as a modifiable database for the graphics primitives).

Whether or not a graphics system has a graphics database strongly affects how the application interacts with the graphics system; put another way, it affects how your application's data model interacts with its views. In an immediate-mode graphics system, the only way for a view to be modified is for the application to recreate the entire view and to send it to the renderer, even if only a small part of the view changed. In a database graphics system, changes to the data model can be reflected in the view by sending only the changes to the view. Which technique is preferable depends on how much of the data model changes at a time. If the entire data model changes often, then it might be just as easy to resend the entire view each time that the data model changes. If the data model normally changes incrementally, then a retained graphics system can be much faster.

For a graphics database, another consideration is whether the editing commands provided by the graphics system are powerful enough to make the changes to the graphics database that your application requires. If they are not, then it might be easier for the application to store the primitives itself.

Indeed, in most graphics applications, the graphics primitives must be stored somewhere. The main issue is whether they are stored by the graphics system or by the application. If the graphics primitives are stored by the application, then the application writer is responsible for writing the routines to hold and manipulate the geometry and attributes. Using a graphics database to store the primitives can save the application writer time and effort. Like using any component, however, using a graphics database will save time only if the graphics database matches the needs of the application and is easy to use.

HOOPS is a retained-mode graphics system; however, for the reasons stated in this section, there will always be applications that are better off not storing their primitives in a graphics database. To provide the advantages of both kinds of systems, HOOPS has an advanced feature, called *HOOPS Intermediate Mode (I.M.)*, that allows an application to store its own primitives. HOOPS I.M. is not covered in this book. For more information, see Section 3.1.8.

## 3.1.9  Immediate Versus Retained Mode

Whether or not graphics primitives are retained in a display list has been a recurring theme in computer graphics. It has influenced almost every aspect of computer graphics, originally affecting graphics hardware, then affecting graphics software, and even affecting graphics applications.

### 3.1.9.1

**Hardware display lists.** Before frame buffers became inexpensive enough to be practical, graphics primitives were stored in hardware display lists. Rather than an image being displayed as a raster, one scan line at a time, each primitive was drawn directly. For example, the graphics system would draw a line by moving the electron beam of the CRT to one endpoint of the line, turning on the beam, then moving the beam to trace out the line. Because the image on a CRT fades out quickly, the line had to be redrawn over and over, dozens of times per second. Hardware constraints limited such systems to drawing lines and simple curves.

Redrawing all the primitives over and over required fast hardware that was expensive, and produced images that were not realistic. These displays have now been replaced by frame buffers, but there were a few advantages to the old type of system. Because the scene was stored in a display list and redrawn repeatedly, the application could change the image by making small modifications to the display list. Thus, animation was possible without a fast renderer — in fact, such graphics systems were called *dynamic vector-graphics displays* (Figure 3.5).

**Figure 3.5**     A dynamic vector-graphics system.

**3.1.9.2** **Painting and drawing.** The difference between storing images and storing graphics primitives is exemplified by the two main categories of sketching applications on personal computers: *painting* programs that store the drawing as an image (in memory like a frame buffer), and *drawing* programs that store the drawing as individual primitives (in memory like a display list). Prime examples of these two categories are the two graphics applications that came with the original Apple Macintosh — MacPaint and MacDraw, shown in Figure 3.6 (similar programs such as Paintbrush and Coreldraw are available for IBM PC and its clones). A significant advantage of drawing programs is that the primitives are retained, so you can edit the drawing by modifying or deleting individual graphics primitives. In a paint program, the primitives are not remembered, so the only way to make changes is to change individual pixels in the image.

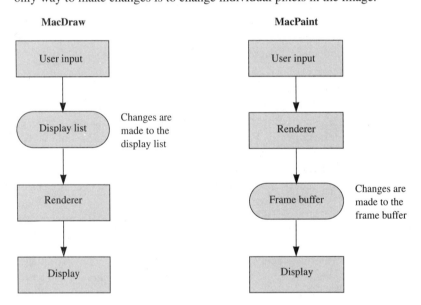

**Figure 3.6** Drawing (object-based) versus painting (image-based) graphics.

**3.1.9.3** **Computer animation.** Computer animation provides another example of the difference between storing images and storing primitives. An animation can be created as a sequence of images that are played back one after another, or each frame can be rendered in real time from a set of dynamically changing primitives. With a sequence of images, you are limited to a single fixed animation, like a movie. Generating the images on the fly from primitives stored in a display list requires a fast renderer, but the user can interact with and control the animation; this kind of interaction is required for applications such as virtual reality.

**3.1.9.4**     **Speed considerations.** Immediate-mode graphics systems are low level, like assembly languages, whereas database graphics systems are high level, like high-level programming languages. Given that programs written in high-level languages are usually slower than programs written in assembly languages, are retained-mode graphics systems necessarily slower than immediate-mode systems? Absolutely not! In many cases, a retained-mode system can be faster than an immediate-mode system. There are several reasons why:

- Whereas high-level languages, such as C, typically have much more overhead than do assembly languages (often by a factor of 2 or more), the overhead from a graphics database is much smaller. It is smaller because a typical graphics command (such as drawing a polygon) takes orders of magnitude longer to execute than does a typical assembly-language instruction (such as adding two numbers). The overhead from using the graphics database is far less significant (as a percentage of total execution time) than is the overhead from using a high-level language.

- Because graphics commands are relatively expensive to execute, any optimizations that can be done to reduce the number of graphics primitives executed can speed up performance significantly. For example, storing bounding volumes can improve rendering speed dramatically.

  Of course, an application using an immediate-mode graphics system can implement its own optimizations. Such an application could calculate and store bounding volumes, for example, but then the application would simply be implementing its own display list, rather than using one provided by a retained-mode graphics system.

- If a graphics application is optimized for a particular system, porting it to a new system can take considerable work. Unless you need that final ounce of graphics performance and are willing to work long and hard for it, you will get better performance if you use a high-level graphics system that has been optimized for multiple platforms. Note that even a change as simple as using a new graphics card can require reoptimization. With a high-level graphics system, this optimization is typically done for you by the card manufacturer or by the graphics-system vendor.

In summary, immediate-mode graphics systems suffer from a number of limitations compared to retained-mode graphics systems:

- They are low-level interfaces and are difficult to use.

- The application writer is responsible for writing all the routines to store and manipulate the graphics primitives.

- Although it is possible for the application programmer to write routines to perform the same optimizations that display-list graphics systems do (such as bounding volumes), writing them is often too much trouble. A retained-mode graphics system can spread the cost of implementing these optimizations across many applications.

- Because they do not store the graphics primitives, immediate-mode systems are limited to certain rendering algorithms — typically a Z-buffer or similar algorithm.

- User interaction is typically slower, because selection is more difficult to perform without a display list.

- Because immediate-mode systems are designed to be low level, it is difficult to make them portable. Trying to make an immediate-mode graphics system portable is like trying to define a portable assembly language — it will always run slower than would a dedicated assembly language running on the hardware for which that language was designed. Because speed is the primary advantage of immediate-mode graphics, a slow immediate-mode system seems pointless.

An immediate-mode graphics system is not necessarily faster than a retained-mode system, and it has several disadvantages. Why, then, would anyone ever use an immediate-mode graphics system? There are a few situations in which doing so makes sense.

- Your computer comes with a free immediate-mode graphics library. In addition, you are writing an application that uses graphics that are simple enough for you to write without the help of a high-level graphics system; also, your application will never be ported to another platform.

- You are writing an animation application where the entire scene changes from frame to frame. Thus, you have no need to make incremental changes to the scene, so the overhead from a display list is unnecessary.

- Your application has to store the graphics primitives anyway (it needs direct access to them for some reason), so using a display list would use extra memory. In addition, you do not need any of the optimizations that can be performed by a retained-mode graphics system, or you are willing to write them yourself.

- The primitives provided by any retained-mode graphics system do not match the primitives that you need in your application, so you have to write a special renderer anyway. Of course, the renderer that you write may have a display list.

## 3.2    Graphics Procedures

So far, this chapter has assumed that graphic primitives are stored as data — for example, in an array, linked list, or tree structure. Sometimes, however, graphical data can be stored more efficiently as a procedure. Consider a sheet of graph paper with 10 squares to the inch. If the paper is 8.5 inches by 11 inches, it can be stored as 195 separate lines, each taking up one graphic primitive.

Alternatively, this graph paper can be described by a simple program containing two loops; one to draw the horizontal lines, and one to draw the vertical lines (Program 3.1).

```
1   for (float x = 0.0; x <= 8.5; x += 0.1)
2          draw_2d_line(x, 0.0, x, 11.0);
3   for (float y = 0.0; y <= 11.0; y += 0.1)
4          draw_2d_line(0.0, y, 8.5, y);
```

**Program 3.1**    Procedure to draw fixed graph paper.

There are two main advantages to storing graphics in a procedure. The most obvious is that a procedural description can take up much less space. A second advantage is that a procedural description can be reusable. If the primitives are stored as data, they describe only a single scene. If the primitives are stored in a procedure, they can be made into a subroutine that can be reused in many different situations. For example, we can change Program 3.1 into a subroutine that can draw graph paper on any size paper, with any desired grid spacing (Program 3.2).

```
1  void graph_paper(float width, float height,
2                        float grid_size) {
3    for (float x = 0.0; x <= width; x += grid_size)
4          draw_2d_line(x, 0.0, x, height);
5    for (float y = 0.0; y <= height; y += grid_size)
6          draw_2d_line(0.0, y, width, y);
7  }
```

**Program 3.2**    Subroutine to draw arbitrary graph paper.

A third advantage is that storing graphics primitives in a procedure is more dynamic than is storing them as data. Storing primitives as data is static and fixed, whereas a procedure can give a different result each time that it is executed. For example, a procedure can be used

- In an animation to draw an object that is moving across the screen (so that the object's position changes as a function of time)

- To express a functional (one-way) relationship between objects; to define an object whose position or appearance is related to that of some other object

- To describe an object whose appearance changes over time, such as a blinking cursor

Finally, a procedure can be used to store primitives that do not have a convenient fixed format. To store a primitive as data, you must choose a fixed data format. Consider all the different ways that a 3D circle can be represented — and even a point can be represented in rectangular or polar coordinates. Most of the time, the fact that graphics systems must choose a single format to represent objects is not a problem, because it is easy to convert from one format to another.

One primitive that is useful in the design industry is a nonuniform, rational B-spline (NURBS), used to describe curves and surfaces. For example, we can use a NURBS curve to define the outline of a plastic bottle for dishwashing liquid, and NURBS surfaces are commonly used to describe the panels on the body of an automobile. Unfortunately, a NURBS can be stored in many different formats, and it is difficult to convert between formats. Different formats allow the user to interact with the NURBS in different ways, so design applications use particular formats depending on why they are using NURBS. Thus, a graphics database system would find it difficult to provide a NURBS primitive that would be useful to more than a small minority of application writers.

Instead, most applications that use NURBS tessellate the NURBS curve or surface into some other primitive. For example, a NURBS curve can be broken up into small line segments, and a NURBS surface can be broken up into polygonal surface patches. Since the tessellator is a procedure that converts a description of a NURBS into a set of primitives about which the graphics system already knows, a good way to store a NURBS is as a procedure.

The problem inherent in choosing a data format for NURBS curves and surfaces is one reason why HOOPS does not have a NURBS primitive and instead requires NURBS to be defined procedurally and tessellated into a polyline or a triangle-strip surface. Few general-purpose graphics systems supply a NURBS primitive, and those that do implement it as an executable procedure known as a *rational evaluator*. Since HOOPS has the ability to define arbitrary procedures using I.M., it is not necessary to include a special-purpose procedure just for NURBS.

A disadvantage of storing graphics data in a procedure is that doing so can make it harder to optimize the drawing of a scene. For example, it is difficult to determine the bounding box of a primitive defined procedurally, because the bounding box will probably change for different invocations of the procedure. It is also difficult to know the state of the graphics hardware after a procedure has been executed, so typically all attributes are saved before a procedure that can change any attributes is executed. After the procedure finishes executing, the state of all attributes is restored.

Using an immediate-mode graphics system is essentially the same as storing all the graphics data in a single procedure. This procedure is your application, and all graphics data must be stored in it regardless of whether or not they would be better stored in a graphics database. Indeed, graphics procedures are hard to optimize for the same reasons that immediate-mode graphics systems are hard to optimize.

### 3.2.1 Storage of Procedures in the Graphics Database

In an immediate-mode graphics system, all graphics information is stored procedurally; in a database graphics system, all graphics information is stored as data in the graphics database. Obviously, these options are extremes of what should be a continuum. To get the benefits of both kinds of systems, we can build a graphics database that allows procedures to be stored in the database. That way, most graphics information is stored as data in the database (so it can be optimized), and procedures can be used as needed.

There are basically two ways that procedures can be stored in a graphics database: using callbacks and using customization.

**3.2.1.1**     **Callbacks.** A callback allows the user to place pointers to user-defined procedures in the graphics database. When the database is traversed (during rendering), these procedures are called when they are encountered. These user-defined procedures are allowed to draw primitives, to read and set attributes, or to perform other actions. In addition to storing the pointer to the procedure, the user must be able to store other data in the graphics database, to be passed as arguments to the procedure. For example, the user can place a pointer to a NURBS evaluator procedure into the graphics database, with the parameters for the NURBS curve to be drawn.

**3.2.1.2**     **Customization.** In customization, the user creates a new kind of data type to place into the graphics database. This type contains user-defined data, and overrides some of the member functions for the normal database-element type. For example, if we have a graphics database written in C++ and the base class of a database element is called DatabaseNode with a virtual function called "render", then the user can use inheritance to derive a new class from DatabaseNode and override the definition of the virtual render method. The derived class also holds any data needed by the render method. You can also do customization using delegation, which in C++ is similar to using a callback (C++ does not have direct language support for delegation).

HOOPS allows procedures to be stored in its graphics database via callbacks. The user can also store user-defined data (typically a pointer to a user-defined structure) in the database.

**3.2.2**     **Procedural Terminology**

Note that the common usage of the words *procedure* and *procedural* can be confusing. In earlier chapters, we said that HOOPS is a declarative graphics system, and that other graphics systems are procedural. In a procedural graphics system, the order in which geometry and attributes occur in the graphics database can affect the resulting scene.

In this chapter, we are describing the use of an executable routine, typically (and unfortunately) called a procedure, to define a set of graphics primitives. The ability to define graphics primitives using a procedure is independent of whether a graphics system is procedural or declarative. You can, for example, use a nonprocedural language to define a procedure.

Being procedural is bad because it is hard for the application to make changes to the database, and it is difficult to optimize the database for greater speed. Having procedures is good, because it lets you represent graphics objects compactly and flexibly.

The fact that HOOPS is a declarative (nonprocedural) graphics system actually makes it easier to define primitives procedurally. In a procedural graphics system, changing an attribute affects every primitive that comes after that attribute in the database. So, if a procedure changes an attribute, that can affect primitives defined after the procedure. In HOOPS, attributes affect primitives in only the same segment, even if the attributes are defined as part of a procedure.

## 3.3    Renderers

As we discussed in Section 3.1.2, a renderer converts graphics primitives into an array of pixels to be stored in the frame buffer. The renderer itself consists of several parts. In just about every graphics system, these parts are arranged (more or less) into an assembly line called the *graphics pipeline*. The stages of this pipeline can be implemented in software, in hardware (for speed), or, more commonly, in a mixture of hardware and software.

The stages of the rendering pipeline (shown in Figure 3.7) are *transformation*, *clipping*, *hidden-surface removal*, and *shading*. The following sections discuss each of these stages in turn.

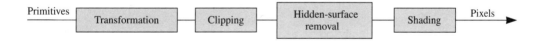

**Figure 3.7**    Stages of the rendering pipeline.

### 3.3.1    Transformation

A *transformation* defines a mapping between one coordinate space and another. A *coordinate space* is defined by an *origin* (where all coordinates are zero) and by two or more *axes* — one for each dimension. In computer graphics, we are mainly concerned with 2D or 3D coordinate systems with axes that are mutually perpendicular.

The most common transformations are *translate* (change position), *rotate* (change orientation), and *scale* (change size). There are many others, including projections (*perspective*, *orthographic*) used to draw 3D objects in a 2D coordinate system, and less common ones such as *skewing* (used in oblique projections), which is useful for transforming a single view into a stereo pair of views, each skewed slightly left or right to the position of an eye.

The coordinates of the output image are called *device coordinates*. For a display monitor, the device-coordinate space is typically in units of pixels and has its origin at the upper-left corner of the display, with the *x* coordinates increasing toward the right, and the *y* coordinates increasing toward the bottom of the display. Figure 3.8 shows the device-coordinate space for a display with a resolution of 1280 by 1024 pixels.

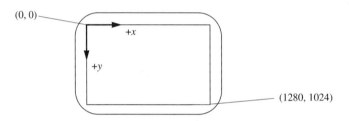

**Figure 3.8**      Device coordinates.

In a window system, each window has its own coordinates, called *window coordinates*. The coordinates of a window are measured in pixels like those of the display, but each window has its own origin. Note that, if a window has a border (also called a frame), then it may have more than one origin. For now, we are concerned with the origin of only the area in to which we are allowed to draw (sometimes called the *client area*), which excludes the border (as shown in Figure 3.9).

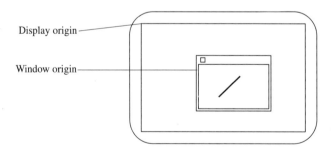

**Figure 3.9**      Window coordinates, using the origin of the client area.

The display understands only device coordinates; it does not understand window coordinates. To draw a line in a window, the system must transform the coordinates of the line (which are specified in window coordinates) into device coordinates. In this case, the transformation consists of adding the origin of the window (in device coordinates) to the coordinates of the line (in window coordinates). This transformation is a translation. For example, if we want to draw a line from (400, 200) to (500, 300) in a window whose origin is at (200, 100), we would add the origin of the window to the endpoints of the line, and draw a line on the display from (600, 300) to (700, 400).

**3.3.1.1**    **Viewing transformations.** In a 3D graphics system, objects are defined in a 3D coordinate system called *world coordinates* or *user coordinates* (Figure 3.10). Often, world coordinates correspond to some real-world measurement. For example, a design application may use a coordinate system defined in centimeters, a mapping application may define coordinates in miles, and a molecular-modeling application may define coordinates in nanometers. World coordinates are normally stored as floating-point numbers.

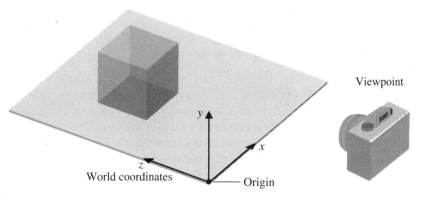

**Figure 3.10**    World-coordinate space.

For the scene to be rendered, the 3D floating-point world coordinate system must be transformed into a 2D device coordinate system. This transformation is called a *viewing transformation.*

A 3D scene is viewed from a location called the *viewpoint, camera,* or *eye position,* with the eye looking toward a location called the *target.* The viewing transformation transforms world coordinates into a coordinate system where the origin is located at the target, with *x* coordinates horizontal, *y* coordinates vertical (in the up direction) and positive *z* going the way the eye is looking (Figure 3.11).

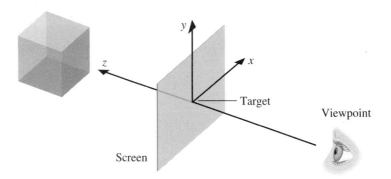

**Figure 3.11**     Conversion from world to device coordinates.

 The 3D coordinate space shown in Figure 3.11 is called a *left-handed coordinate system*, because, if you hold your left hand with your thumb pointing in the positive *x* direction and your fingers pointing in the positive *y* direction, then your palm faces toward the positive *z* direction. For historical reasons, computer graphics normally uses a left-handed coordinate system, whereas almost every other field of science uses a right-handed coordinate system, with positive *z* going toward the viewpoint. HOOPS has the ability to use either a left- or a right-handed coordinate system (for more information, see the HC_Set_Handedness command).

Next, the 3D coordinates are transformed into 2D coordinates via a *projection*. Note that the third coordinate is not thrown away, since it represents a depth value that will be used by hidden-surface calculations. The most common projections are *orthographic*, which simply ignores the *z* coordinate (often used in drafting systems), and *perspective*, which scales the *x* and *y* coordinates to make the object appear smaller the farther away it is from the eye (used for realistic viewing, since it mimics the perception of a real eye).

After the projection, the resulting 2D coordinate space is a flat rectangle called the *screen* (not to be confused with the screen of the display monitor). The screen defines a *screen coordinate system*. In HOOPS, the screen coordinate system is centered at the target, with the lower-left corner at coordinate (–1.0, –1.0) and the upper-right corner at (1.0, 1.0). The screen rectangle represents the extent of what (in world space) can be seen by the eye. Screen coordinates are floating-point numbers, and are independent of the actual display device.

Finally, the resulting 2D coordinates are transformed into the device coordinates of the window. In window coordinates, the origin is at a corner of the screen window, as discussed previously. The different coordinate spaces and transformations that make up a viewing transformation will be discussed further in Section 6.1.

### 3.3.1.2

**Modeling transformations.** To define a graphics primitive, we must assign *coordinates* to its geometry. For example, to draw a line, we specify its endpoints in a coordinate space. Rather than define all the objects in a scene using a single world-coordinate system, we can more conveniently allow each object in a scene to have its own *local coordinate system*, in the same way each window in a window system has a local coordinate system. Thus, we can define an object using coordinates that are independent of the position of the object in the scene, just as a windowing system allows us to define the position of objects in a window using coordinates that are independent of the position of the window on the screen.

For example, consider a furniture-layout application for an office building. Each piece of furniture is represented by its top view, defined in its own local coordinate system. Program 3.3 contains the definition of a desk.

```
1    HC_Open_Segment("desk");
2        HC_Insert_Line(0.0, 0.0, 0.0, 6.0, 0.0, 0.0);
3        HC_Insert_Line(6.0, 0.0, 0.0, 6.0, 2.5, 0.0);
4        HC_Insert_Line(6.0, 2.5, 0.0, 0.0, 2.5, 0.0);
5        HC_Insert_Line(0.0, 2.5, 0.0, 0.0, 0.0, 0.0);
6    HC_Close_Segment();
```

**Program 3.3**    Definition of the top view of a desk.

 Note that, in HOOPS, we specify 2D objects using three coordinates, but with all the $z$ coordinates set to zero. HOOPS automatically detects objects that have no depth, and treats them as 2D objects. Thus, HOOPS uses the same commands to define 2D objects, as well as 3D ones.

Figure 3.12 shows what the desk looks like from above (with coordinates displayed).

**Figure 3.12**     The desk from above, in local coordinates.

Note that we put the origin of the desk in the front left corner, but we could have placed it anywhere: another corner, the front middle of the desk, the center of the desk, or even completely outside the desk. Because we can move the origin using a simple translation of the coordinate systems, the only significant aspect of coordinates is the relationships among them; their absolute values are unimportant.

We are also assuming that the coordinates represent feet, so this desk is 6 feet wide and 2.5 feet deep, but they could also represent inches, meters, or any arbitrary measurement. Because we can easily transform between coordinate systems, it is purely a matter of convenience what measurement system we use to define individual objects.

Local coordinate systems can be nested. Each office has its own coordinate system, so we translate and rotate each piece of furniture to arrange it in position in an office. Then, we place multiple offices into each floor of the building, and place multiple floors one on top of one another, forming the whole building. At each stage, there are transformations — each one made up of a translation, rotation, and possibly a scale — that define the relationship between a coordinate system and its parent. Figure 3.13 shows a possible relationship among the different coordinate systems in a building.

Each coordinate space is related to its parent coordinate space by a transformation, called a *modeling transformation*.

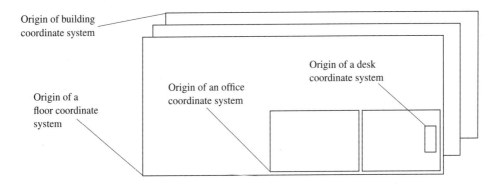

**Figure 3.13** An office building and its coordinate systems.

**3.3.1.3** **Concatenation of transformations.** For each object in the scene, there will be a viewing transformation, and one or more modeling transformations. Rather than apply all the transformations one at a time to each object (moving, rotating, scaling, projecting, and so on, until the object's coordinates fall properly on the screen), we can concatenate all the transformations into a single transformation. The result is a single transformation, called the *net transformation*, that converts the coordinates in the graphics primitives all the way into screen coordinates.

Mathematically, each transformation can be represented by a matrix. A 3D transformation can be represented by a 4 by 4 matrix (the use of 4 by 4 matrices for transformations is called *homogeneous coordinates* — refer to any graphics text if you want to understand the mathematics). We multiply the $x$, $y$, and $z$ coordinates of an object (with a fourth coordinate of 1) by this matrix to produce the transformed coordinates. Since matrix multiplication is associative, instead of multiplying these matrices one after another against each coordinate, we can multiply together all the transformation matrices, and then multiply the resulting single matrix (representing the net transformation) against each coordinate in an object. Thus, each coordinate needs to be multiplied by only a single matrix, rather than by multiple matrices — one for each nested modeling transformation.

The transformation stage of the renderer takes the net transformation and one or more graphics primitives, and transforms their coordinates from the local modeling coordinate space into screen coordinate space.

**3.3.1.4**        **Nested transformations.** Each object in a scene can potentially have a different modeling transform, and calculating the net transform for each object can involve concatenating many transformations. To solve this problem, most graphics systems take advantage of the fact that the transformation for each object differs by a single modeling transformation from that of the object's parent object. The modeling transformations for an entire scene, along with the viewing transform, form a tree (Figure 3.14), with device coordinates at the root of the tree. We can walk this tree (depth first) to calculate the net transformation for each object in the scene.

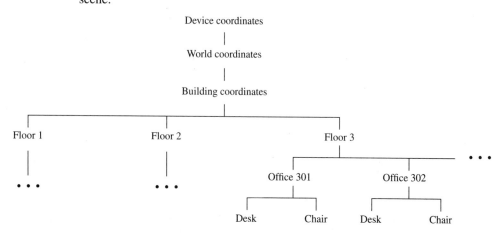

**Figure 3.14**        A hierarchy of transformations.

Most graphics systems support this kind of calculation of transformations by providing a way to stack transformations — that is, to save transformations for reuse later. In our furniture-layout example, we would start with the viewing transformation on the top of the stack. The modeling transformation for the building is multiplied by the transformation on the top of the stack, giving the total transformation for the building. The resulting transformation is pushed onto the stack. Next, we multiply the modeling transformation for the first floor with the top of the stack, and push it; then, we multiply the modeling transformation for the first office on the first floor with the top of the stack, and push it. Finally, we multiply the modeling transformation for the first piece of furniture in the office against the top of the stack, push it, and send that piece of furniture down the rendering pipeline. When we are done rendering that piece of furniture, we pop the stack (back to the total transformation for the office), concatenate on the modeling transformation for the next piece of furniture, and render that piece.

When we are done with all the furniture in the office, we pop the stack twice, concatenate the modeling transform for the next office, and so on.

The transformation stage of a typical renderer understands the following commands:

- Clear the stack and load a new transformation.

- Multiply a transformation against the transformation on the top of the stack, and push the result onto the stack.

- Pop the stack (restore a saved transformation).

- Transform the coordinates of a primitive by the transformation on the top of the stack.

### 3.3.2     Clipping

The clipping stage removes those parts of the scene that fall outside the current view. If you consider the display screen to be a window through which the current view is looking to the scene, then some parts of the scene will not be visible (they will fall outside this window).

First, we simply throw away primitives that fall completely outside the boundaries of the display screen. For example, the triangle labeled *e* in Figure 3.15 is discarded.

Second, we modify primitives that fall on the boundaries of the display to remove those parts that fall outside the display. This step might change the geometry of a primitive; for example, a triangle might be clipped to become a quadrilateral.

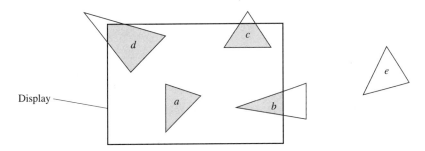

**Figure 3.15**     Clipping of triangles to the display.

In Figure 3.15, the triangle labeled *a* is unmodified. Triangle *b* is clipped to become a smaller triangle. Triangle *c* becomes a quadrilateral, and *d* becomes a pentagon. It is possible for a triangle that is clipped by the display to become a polygon with seven sides. Can you imagine such a triangle? (Hint: Three of the sides come from the original triangle, and the other four sides come from the four sides of the screen.)

Another function of the clipping stage is to clip objects that fall behind the camera. This function is important because, if we convert 3D objects into 2D objects by simply removing all the *z* coordinates (as in an orthographic projection, or after some other projection has been applied by the transformation stage), then objects that are behind the viewpoint will be rendered just as though they were in front of the viewpoint. An object that falls partly behind and partly in front of the camera must be clipped so that only the part in front of the camera is displayed.

In addition, we can also clip objects that are in front of the camera, but are too close to it. This action is called clipping against a *hither plane*. Hither-plane clipping serves two purposes. First, if an object is close to the camera, it probably blocks the entire view, which is usually not interesting to look at. Second, we can use the hither plane like an invisible knife, to cut away parts of a scene to look inside of something. For example, we can use a hither plane to make a cutaway view of the inside of an engine.

Finally, we can also clip objects that are far away from the camera position. This action is called clipping against a *yon plane*. Yon-plane clipping can speed up rendering by removing objects that are too far away to be interesting.

## 3.3.3     Hidden-Surface Removal

In hidden-surface removal, objects (or parts of objects) that are hidden from the viewpoint by other objects are removed, and the pixels that make up each graphics primitive are calculated. Conceptually, these two functions are separate stages; for efficiency, however, they are often combined into a single stage, because they perform similar calculations (depending on the algorithm used).

The hidden-surface–removal stage is considered the heart of the renderer, and often takes the most execution time. In HOOPS, you can choose from a number of hidden-surface–removal algorithms. Which one is best (executes fastest, and gives the most realistic images) will depend on the hardware you have, on your application, and even on the individual scene. Some computers have built-in hardware to support a particular hidden-surface–removal algorithm, in which case that algorithm will probably — but not always — be the fastest. Common hidden-surface–removal algorithms include wireframe, painter's, Z-sort, priority, and Z-buffer.

**3.3.3.1**     **Wireframe.** In the wireframe algorithm, surfaces are not shown; only the edges of polygons are displayed. Wireframe is typically the fastest way to display a scene, but it is not particularly realistic. Wireframe images can be displayed either with or without hidden lines removed.

**3.3.3.2**     **Painter's.** The painter's algorithm is so named because it works like opaque paint — objects painted later cover up earlier objects. All the objects in a scene are sorted in order of their distance from the viewpoint, with the farthest object first. Then, they are rendered in depth order. As each object is rendered, it covers up any object that is farther away.

The painter's algorithm has a problem in that it assumes that each object has a single distance from the viewpoint. If an object is not parallel to the screen, then its distance from the screen is actually a range of values. It is possible for several objects to overlap such that there is no ordering that will result in them being rendered properly (as shown in Figure 3.16). In this case, it is necessary to split one or more of the objects into smaller pieces.

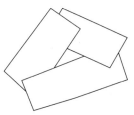

**Figure 3.16**     Three objects that overlap in depth.

**3.3.3.3**     **Z-sort.** The Z-sort algorithm is a faster variation of the painter's algorithm. It assumes that objects never overlap in depth, so they never have to be split. Z-sort is useful when high rendering speed is more important than is an occasional mistake in hidden-surface removal. Z-sort is also used for (so called) 2.5-dimensional scenes, where the objects are all flat and are arranged in separate layers. For example, consider a mapping application. The back layer is the background; the next layer, slightly in front, contains any features such as cities; the next layer in front contains the roads; and the front layer displays the route numbers of the roads. No object is in more than one layer, so we can do a simple sort by depth (layer), and then render the layers from back to front.

**3.3.3.4**       **Priority.** Priority ordering is similar to the Z-sort algorithm, but, instead of drawing the objects according to their depth in $z$, we draw them according to a fixed priority. This priority can be assigned by the programmer, or can be assigned implicitly (for example, according to the order in which the objects were placed into the graphics database). In a mapping application, roads could be assigned a higher priority than cities, and road signs a still higher priority. Objects with the highest priority are drawn in front. Priority ordering can be used in combination with other rendering algorithms — for example to make sure that a background grid stays in back of a rendered object, or that annotation text stays in front.

**3.3.3.5**       **Z-buffer.** The Z-buffer algorithm uses a large block of memory consisting of one word for every pixel in the frame buffer. This memory is initialized with a number larger than the largest $z$ value of any object to be drawn. To render an object, we calculate the pixels that make up the object. Before each pixel is written into the frame buffer, the depth (distance from the viewpoint) of that pixel is compared against the current value for that pixel in the Z-buffer. If the new pixel is closer, its color value is written into the frame buffer, and its depth is written into the Z-buffer. That way, we write only those pixels that are closer than any object already written into the frame buffer.

The main advantage of the Z-buffer algorithm is speed, especially when the algorithm is implemented in hardware. A secondary advantage is this algorithm can handle curved surfaces, such as NURBS patches. In the curved surface shown in Figure 3.17, the same pixel (indicated by the small square) intersects the surface three times. In the painter's algorithm, we would have to subdivide the surface into three pieces; that subdivistion is difficult to do (and is computationally

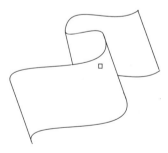

**Figure 3.17**     A curved surface hiding itself.

expensive). The Z-buffer algorithm just renders all the pixels of the surface, and the closest surface at each pixel will be displayed.

The main disadvantage of the Z-buffer is that it is not accurate. Because the Z-buffer contains one word for every pixel in the frame buffer, the cost of the Z-buffer is proportional to the size of the word. A typical Z-buffer holds depth information as an integer with a fixed number of bits. The number of bits used per pixel is almost always 16, although more bits could be used if cost were no object. Regardless of the number of bits used to hold depth information, if two objects are very close together, they can have the same depth value in the Z-buffer. If so, then the object that is rendered first will be visible, even if it is slightly farther away. Imagine two polygons, one red and one green, that are parallel to each other and close enough together to have the same depth value. If they are parallel to the screen and the one that is slightly farther away is drawn first, then it will be displayed in front. If we move the viewpoint back slightly until the two polygons have different depth values in the Z-buffer, the front polygon will pop in front. This switch can be disconcerting in an animation. Further, if the two polygons are slightly angled with respect to the screen, they will appear to be striped red and green.

A second disadvantage of the Z-buffer is that it uses a large amount of memory. A Z-buffer must have the same resolution as the frame buffer, and is commonly 16 bits per pixel deep. Many graphics workstations and some high-end graphics cards for PCs implement the Z-buffer algorithm in hardware using a dedicated block of memory, along with hardware to do the depth comparisons. This memory makes these systems fairly expensive. Otherwise, the Z-buffer must be stored in the computer's main memory.

---

You can ask HOOPS for the size of a hardware Z-buffer using the HC_Show_Device_Info command. For example,

```
char pixels[32], depth[32];
HC_Show_Device_Info("?Picture",
                    "max pixels", pixels);
HC_Show_Device_Info("?Picture",
                    "Z buffer depth", depth);
printf("Z-buffer is %s bits deep\n", depth);
printf("width and height = %s\n", pixels);
```

If the Z-buffer is 0 bits deep, then hidden-surface removal must be done in software.

As memory costs have come down, the Z-buffer algorithm has become the algorithm of choice for hidden-surface–removal, especially for systems where speed is of paramount importance. The major exceptions to this rule are low-end systems, where the memory cost is still too high, or applications that need an advanced rendering algorithm, such as radiosity or ray tracing.

**3.3.3.6**    **Backplane culling.** One additional function that you can use to speed up hidden-surface removal is *backplane culling*. Flat objects such as polygons can be considered to have two sides: a front side and a back side. If a scene is made up of closed polyhedra (closed surfaces with no holes), then the back sides of the polygons can never be visible, because they are all on the inside of the surfaces and will always be hidden by a front-facing polygon. If backplane culling is turned on, then any polygon (or other flat surface) whose front side is facing away from the camera is not sent to the renderer. This function can typically remove one-half of the polygons in such a scene, greatly speeding up rendering.

The side of the polygon that is considered to be the front can be defined in one of two ways. For closed polyhedra, the choice is simple — the front is defined to be the side of the polygon on the outside of the solid object. For other polygons, we define the front side using *polygon handedness*. For example, consider a triangle described using three points, A, B, and C, in that order. If you are using *left-handed* polygons, imagine wrapping your left hand around the edges of the triangle, with your wrist at point A, your knuckles at point B, and your fingertips at point C. Then, extend your thumb out to the side — your thumb is pointing out from the front of the polygon.

If your scene contains only solid objects, then backplane culling should be on to speed up rendering. If your scene contains polygons that are visible from both sides, such as single polygons not connected to other polygons, or objects that have holes or are missing sides, then backplane culling should be off. For example, if you are building a drinking glass and you use only a single layer of polygons to model the glass (so the walls of the glass have no thickness), then you probably will want backplane culling to be off, so that you can see the inside of the glass. But if you use two layers of polygons to model the glass, so that it has both an inside surface and an outside surface and there are no holes where you can see between these two layers, then you will have more polygons in your scene, but you can use backplane culling to speed up rendering to make up for the added polygons.

In Section 3.3.3.5, we discussed a problem with the Z-buffer algorithm where, if two polygons are parallel and are close together, then the farther polygon can sometimes peek in front due to the finite resolution of the Z-buffer. This problem will often occur when you are using two polygons to define the front and back of a thin planar object. Use of backplane culling can help you to avoid this problem.

In HOOPS, you can turn on backplane culling with the command

```
HC_Set_Heuristics("backplane cull");
```

For backplane culling to work, you also need to specify what kind of polygon handedness you are using. For example,

```
HC_Set_Heuristics(
        "backplane cull, polygon handedness = left");
```

**3.3.3.7**     **Object-space algorithms.** Hidden-surface algorithms can be divided into two groups: *image-space algorithms,* which decide the color of each pixel, and *object-space algorithms,* which decide which objects are visible. Image-space algorithms — such as the painter's and Z-buffer algorithms — work at the pixel level; they input a set of primitives and output a set of pixels. Instead, object-space algorithms work at the object level; that is, they input a series of graphics primitives and output a new set of primitives that contains only those primitives, or parts of primitives, that are visible from the viewpoint.

Image-space algorithms tend to be simpler than object-space algorithms, but they require the use of a frame buffer. Object-space algorithms are mainly used when the output of the renderer is being sent to an output device that draws objects rather than pixels — for example, a pen plotter. They can also be used in cases where a frame buffer would be too expensive, such as a high-resolution printer.

When an object-space algorithm is used, the output of the hidden-surface computation is a set of primitives, rather than a set of pixels. In the case of a pen plotter, of course, the primitives are never converted into pixels; they are drawn directly. For a raster device — such as a CRT, flat-panel display, ink-jet plotter, or laser printer — these primitives must be rasterized into pixels in a separate rasterization step. Thus, one advantage of object-space algorithms is that they determine which objects are visible independently of the resolution of the display. The output primitives from an object-space algorithm can be saved (in a display list), and then zoomed in and out on the display, or even redrawn on a display with a different resolution, whereas an image-space algorithm requires recalculation of the visible surfaces for any change of resolution.

Although object-space algorithms are generally more difficult to implement than are image-space algorithms, they tend to give more accurate images. Which type of algorithm is faster depends strongly on the scene to be rendered — in particular, on the ratio of the primitives to be rendered to the pixels that are output. If you have only a few objects that are each fairly large, then an object-space algorithm tends to be faster; for a large number of small objects, an image-space algorithm (especially the Z-buffer) will be fastest. A well-tuned object-space algorithm can be extremely fast.

**3.3.3.8**    **Antialiasing.** Another advantage of object-space algorithms is that the color of a pixel can be determined at finer-than-pixel resolution — a technique commonly called *antialiasing*. For example, on any raster display, lines and polygon edges will contain aliasing artifacts — an effect commonly called *stair-stepping*. (Figure 3.18)

Magnified view

**Figure 3.18**    Aliasing artifacts (stair-stepping).

One way to avoid these unwanted artifacts is to substitute color depth for resolution. For any pixel that falls on the edge of a polygon, we change its color depending on what percentage of the pixel is covered by the polygon. Thus, pixels on the edge of a black polygon (in front of a white background) will be colored various shades of gray, depending on how much of a given pixel is covered by the black polygon (Figure 3.19).

**102**

Anti-aliased edge

**Figure 3.19**    Antialiasing.

Antialiasing increases the effective resolution of a display, and results in more pleasing images — without stair-steps or other rasterization artifacts.

 You can do antialiasing with certain image-space algorithms by running the algorithm at a higher resolution. For example, on a display with 100 pixel-per-inch resolution, you might run the image-space algorithm at 400 pixels-per-inch. Thus, each pixel on the output display is subdivided into 16 subpixels. After rendering, each display pixel is assigned the average color of its subpixels. This technique is called *super-sampling*. Of course, for a Z-buffer algorithm, this trick would require 16 times as much memory for the Z-buffer (and for the frame buffer, too), so it is usually not practical (unless the renderer renders only one-sixteenth of the image at a time, and makes 16 passes through the primitives).

### 3.3.4    Shading and Lighting

In this book, we use the term *shading* in its general sense, including all calculations that affect the color of a pixel (other than to what object the pixel belongs).

The shading stage calculates the color of each pixel in an object. Shading can be simple — for example, to draw a red line, we simply make each pixel in the line red — or it can be complex. An example of complex shading is a polygon that has a texture applied to it, is lit by multiple lights of different colors, and is shiny, so it has highlights that are a slightly blurry reflection of its surrounding objects.

Depending on what hidden-surface–removal algorithm and what kind of shading are used, shading may be part of the same stage as hidden-surface removal, or it may be a separate stage. Shading itself can consist of several calculations, depending on the sophistication of the algorithm used and amount of realism desired. Different component calculations of shading include

- *Lighting*: interaction between objects in the scene and light sources

- *Smooth shading*: whether objects are faceted or smoothly curved

- *Global illumination*: reflections and other interactions among objects

- *Textures*

- *Transparency*

- *Shadows*

Note that truly realistic lighting is extremely complicated and is computationally almost intractable. Computer graphics uses approximations that look reasonable, but are less expensive to compute (in other words, we cheat).

**3.3.4.1**     **Flat lighting.** If there are no light sources in a scene, then no lighting calculations are done. Each object has a fixed color associated with it, and that color is given to each pixel that makes up the object when that object is rendered. Flat lighting is fast, and is commonly used for rendering scenes that are not meant to look realistic, such as a bar graph or a road map. For realistic scenes, flat lighting causes problems. For example, consider a sphere rendered with flat lighting. Since the entire sphere is the same color, it cannot be distinguished from a flat disk of the same diameter. To make the sphere look spherical, we need to add one or more lights to the scene.

**3.3.4.2**     **Diffuse and ambient lighting.** Diffuse lighting is the simplest form of lighting. Diffuse lighting changes the lightness or darkness of a surface depending on how directly the surface is illuminated by a light source. Note that there can be more than one light source.

If the surface is facing away from the light source, then it receives no illumination from that source. If a surface is directly facing a light source, then it is maximally illuminated by that light source. Otherwise, the illumination of the surface is proportional to the cosine of the angle between the surface normal and the light source (a surface normal is a vector that points out from the front of, and is perpendicular to, the surface). Diffuse lighting is similar to the effect of the angle of the sun in the sky (Figure 3.20). When the sun is directly overhead, the ground is brightly lit; in morning or evening, it is less bright; and at night, everything is dark.

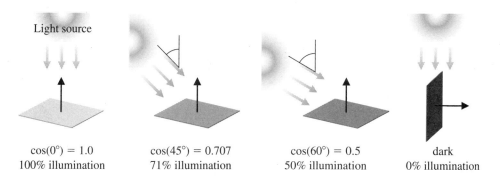

**Figure 3.20**   Diffuse-lighting illumination angles.

One problem with diffuse lighting is that any surface that is not facing a light source will be completely dark, producing a harshly lit, high-contrast scene. In reality, air molecules tend to scatter light, so that even the dark sides of objects have some illumination. For this reason, it is common to add in a constant *ambient* light value to each surface, so that even dark surfaces are slightly lit. Ambient lighting is different from flat lighting in that ambient light can have a color associated with it.

3.3.4.3   **Specular lighting.** Diffuse lighting is reasonable for objects that have matte surfaces, but most objects have a small amount of shininess, which manifests itself as a specular highlight (for example, the gleam in someone's eye, or the shiny spot on an apple). The specular highlight is basically the mirrorlike reflection of a light source by the object (Figure 3.21). Specular lighting depends on three variables: the position of the light source, the position of the object, and the position of the eye (unlike diffuse lighting, which depends on only the position of the light source and the object, and is independent of the position of the eye). In other words, when the viewpoint moves, the specular highlights change.

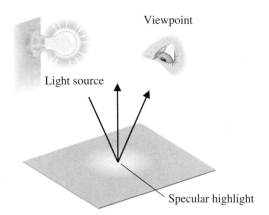

**Figure 3.21**     Specular lighting.

When the angle between the surface normal and a vector pointing toward the light source is equal to the angle between the surface normal and a vector pointing toward the viewpoint, the specular reflection is greatest, and it falls off quickly to either side. This reflection characteristic is typically modeled as

$$(\cos\alpha)^n$$

where $\alpha$ is the difference between the two angles, and $n$ is a constant that depends on the glossiness of the surface material. Dull surfaces have a low value of $n$, and give a large, broad highlight. Glossy, shiny surfaces have a large value of $n$, and give a small, sharp, bright, mirrorlike highlight. A typical value is between 3 and 30. Figure 3.22 shows an object rendered with two different gloss values.

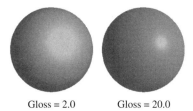

Gloss = 2.0          Gloss = 20.0

**Figure 3.22**     Gloss.

Note that the color of a specular highlight is normally not the same as the diffuse color of the object (the shiny spot on a red apple lit by a white light is white, rather than red). For some kinds of surfaces (for example, plastics), the color of the highlight is the color of the reflected light source. For other kinds of surfaces (for example, metals), the highlight color depends on the material. The highlight color of a material is called its *specular color.*

The specular lighting model discussed in this section is also called Phong lighting (not to be confused with Phong shading, discussed in Section 3.3.4.5). Phong lighting tends to produce objects with smooth diffuse lighting and uniform highlights, like plastic (the next time that you see a movie with computer-generated dinosaurs, notice how their skin looks like vinyl).

The search for better lighting models yielding ever-more-realistic-looking images has been a topic of continuous research, producing increasingly complicated lighting models too numerous to mention here.

**3.3.4.4**    **Light sources.** In computer graphics, there are five common sources of light in a scene, given here in order of increasing complexity:

1. *Ambient light,* discussed in Section 3.3.4.2, is light that is "everywhere" and lights everything. It is the light that keeps objects from turning completely black when they do not have a light shining on them.

2. *Distant lights* are lights like the sun that are so far away that we can assume that the light rays are all traveling in the same direction.

3. *Local lights* are point lights that radiate light equally in all directions. They have a specific position, which may even be inside the scene.

4. *Directional lights* are point lights that radiate light in a specific direction, like a spot light. Directional lights have a position and a direction, and often have other attributes, such as an illumination angle (spot versus flood).

5. *Area lights* are lights that radiate from a surface — for example, a lampshade, or a ceiling diffusion panel in a florescent-light fixture.

To add simple lighting to a scene, we normally use distant lights, along with ambient light. Local lights and spotlights are typically used only if there is a light source inside the scene. Area lights are the most complicated to compute, and are used only with radiosity (described in Section 3.3.4.7).

**3.3.4.5**    **Smooth shading.** One problem with modeling smooth objects (such as spheres or car bodies) with polygons is that the resulting objects do not look smooth; instead, they look faceted. One solution is to increase the number of polygons used to model a surface, but this approach gets expensive quickly and just results in smaller facets. The eye is particularly sensitive to discontinuities in the color of an object, such as the change in color between two facets. (Such discontinuities produce visual artifacts called *Mach bands*). A better solution is to smooth out the shading, so that the lighting changes evenly across the surface — a technique called *smooth shading*.

Smooth shading does not apply to individual primitives such as lines and polygons; it applies to polygonal surfaces — called *shells* and *meshes* — that approximate smooth surfaces using connected polygons. A shell is an arbitrary surface made up of polygons. It can even consist of more than one disconnected part, or can contain holes. A mesh, however, is always a single rectangular array of four-sided polygons (like the one in Figure 3.23).

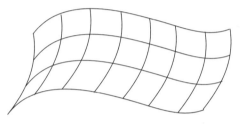

**Figure 3.23**     A mesh (suitable for smooth shading).

There are two principal types of smooth shading: *Gouraud shading* and *Phong shading* (also called *color interpolation* and *normal interpolation*).

Consider a mesh surface like the one in Figure 3.23, made up of regularly connected quadrilaterals, like a wire screen that has been bent into a curved surface. To do smooth shading, we need a normal vector for each vertex in the mesh surface (Figure 3.24). These normal vectors, taken together, approximate the normals for the surface that this mesh represents.

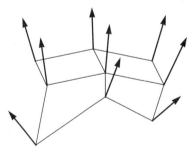

**Figure 3.24**     A mesh with a normal vector at each vertex.

The normal vectors can be specified explicitly by the application if they are known. Specifying normals explicitly is easy to do when the surface is represented by a mathematical formula. For example, if we are creating an approximation of a sphere, the normal vectors are easy to calculate (they are all pointing away from the center of the sphere).

Alternatively, if no normal vectors are supplied by the application, the graphics system can approximate them by averaging the normal vectors for the polygons connected to each vertex. This approximation, in turn, may involve calculating the normal vectors for each polygon in the mesh. In Figure 3.24, the normal vector in the middle of the mesh would be the average of the normals for all four polygons in the mesh, the normals at the four corners would each be the same as the one polygon to which they are attached, and the remaining four normals (in the center of each side) would be the average of the two adjacent polygons.

If your application knows the normal vectors, or can calculate them, it is always better to supply them explicitly (in HOOPS, you supply them with the HC_Set_Normal or HC_MSet_Vertex_Normals command). The real normals are not only more accurate (approximating the polygon normals can cause uneven lighting), but also much faster, because the graphics system does not have to calculate approximations.

For Gouraud shading, we do a lighting calculation for diffuse and (optionally) for specular lighting at each vertex using the normal vector for that vertex. This calculation results in a color value for each vertex in the surface. We then find the color values along each polygon edge by linearly interpolating the vertex colors along the edge. Finally, we determine the color of each pixel in the polygon by taking a line in the plane of the polygon that passes through the pixel — usually the horizontal scan line on which the pixel lies — and linearly interpolating the two color values taken from where this line intersects the edges of the polygon.

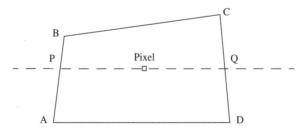

**Figure 3.25**    Linear interpolation of pixel colors.

For example, to find the color of the pixel in the Figure 3.25, given the colors at the four vertices A, B, C, and D, we first linearly interpolate the colors at A and B to find the color at point P. If P is two-thirds of the way between A and B, then the color of P is one-third the color of A and two-thirds the color of B. Next, we linearly interpolate the colors at C and D to find the color at point Q; finally, we linearly interpolate the colors at P and Q to find the color of the pixel. We do this interpolation for every pixel on the scan line between P and Q, then move the line to the next row of pixels and repeat.

Note that the orientation of the scan line relative to the polygon can affect the pixel color. It can do so because, in a polygon with more than three vertices, some orientations of the line will intersect two adjacent edges, and so will ignore the color value of the opposite vertex. If the surface is rotated, then the polygons can change color. This problem can be avoided if the renderer subdivides all polygons into triangles before doing shading.

If colors are linearly interpolated in screen coordinates (pixels) on polygons that have had a perspective transformation applied to them, then some color errors can occur. Consider a long, thin polygon with one end much closer to the viewpoint than the other. The far end of the polygon will appear small due to the perspective transformation, and so will not cover many pixels, whereas the near end will appear large and will cover many pixels. Linear interpolation halfway between the near and far ends of the polygon in screen space (rather than in world space) actually corresponds to a point much closer to the near end of the polygon, so the pixel should be more affected by the color of the near vertices. We can correct for this error by interpolating in world (user) coordinates, or equivalently, by correcting the pixel coordinates for the perspective transformation. In HOOPS, you can specify this correction with the command

```
HC_Set_Rendering_Options("perspective correction");
```

Phong shading is similar to Gouraud shading, but instead of linearly interpolating the colors at each vertex, we linearly interpolate the normal vectors to find a normal vector for each pixel in the surface. Then, we do a full lighting calculation — diffuse and (optionally) specular — at each pixel to calculate the color of the pixel.

Phong shading is (not surprisingly) more expensive to calculate than is Gouraud shading (Phong shading requires a full lighting calculation at each pixel), but it is much more accurate. Consider a specular highlight that falls entirely within one of the polygons in a mesh. Since Gouraud shading does a lighting calculation only at each vertex, and the highlight falls entirely inside the edges of a polygon, the highlight will not affect any vertex in the polygon. Because the color of each pixel is just a linear interpolation of the vertex colors, no highlight will be drawn. If we rotate the mesh slightly in space such that the highlight falls directly over a vertex, then the color of that vertex will be the color of the highlight. If we use linear color interpolation, the four adjacent polygons will be affected, with the highlight falling off linearly across each polygon, and thus the new highlight will be much larger than the original highlight. Thus, using color-interpolation (Gouraud) shading with specular lighting can cause a rotating mesh to flash like a faceted object, rather than appear smooth. Phong shading does not have this problem. In fact, as its name suggests, Phong shading (normal interpolation) was developed at the same time as Phong lighting (specular highlights) to avoid the problem that Gouraud shading has with specular highlights.

Most high-end display systems include hardware to perform linear color interpolation; it is possible to use this hardware to make Gouraud shading even faster. So, despite the advantages of Phong shading, most systems today use Gouraud shading. If the polygon size is kept small enough — in particular, smaller than the highlight size — Gouraud shading can be almost as accurate as Phong shading. Phong shading is typically used only when accurate images are required regardless of computational expense. Since Phong shading was developed mainly to support Phong lighting, if you do not need specular highlights, then Phong shading is almost certainly not worth the added expense (although it does produce more even diffuse lighting with less Mach banding).

3.3.4.6      **Ray tracing.** Ray tracing was originally developed as a way to render scenes that contain reflective objects. Ray tracing follows (or *traces*) each ray of light as the ray bounces around a scene (Figure 3.26). Because we care about only the light that ultimately makes it to the viewpoint, we trace the light rays backward, starting at the viewpoint and going in a straight line through a pixel. We follow the ray until it hits some object in the scene. If the object is reflective, the ray bounces, and we follow the reflected ray until it hits another object. If the object is transparent, we (optionally) bend the light ray slightly to model refraction. Finally, the ray may hit some light source, but even if it does not, we assume some ambient light. We calculate the color of the pixel (the one through which this ray originally passed) by summing the contributions from each object that the ray hit while it was bouncing around the scene.

**111**

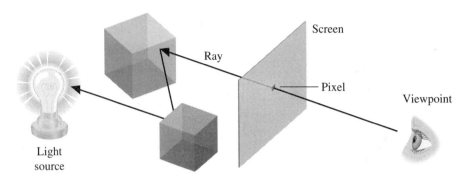

**Figure 3.26**    Ray tracing.

Ray tracing is computationally expensive, because it must compare each ray with each object to see whether they intersect. Many techniques have been used to speed up ray tracing; most of them use some spatial-organization scheme to speed up the intersection tests. (One such scheme uses a data structure called an *oct-tree,* so called because it recursively divides up space into eight octants, and sorts the objects by where they fall in the resulting tree of octants.)

3.3.4.7    **Radiosity.** Although ray tracing is good for viewing shiny, reflective objects, most objects in the real world are not particularly shiny — they are matte. Such *diffuse surfaces* reflect light, but they scatter it evenly in all directions. Consider a white lampshade — light bounces off of it, but is diffused (that is one reason that lamps have lampshades — so the light will be distributed evenly and so be less harsh). Every surface, unless it is a perfect black body, reflects some diffuse light. By modeling this diffuse reflection, we can make the resulting images look much more realistic. Such computations are extremely complex, however, since they need to take into account all light coming off of each surface and reflecting off of every other surface. Algorithms such as radiosity that consider all the sources of light in a scene are called *global-illumination* algorithms.

Basically, a radiosity algorithm has to do the equivalent of a complete hidden-surface calculation for each surface to determine which other surfaces will be lit by this surface. Because the light coming from this surface is just a diffuse reflection of the light falling on it from the other surfaces (which in turn are illuminated by this surface), we must do the calculations for all surfaces simultaneously, and that requires solving a huge set of simultaneous equations (the number of equations is of the order of the number of objects in the scene).

Luckily, radiosity calculations are not dependent on the viewpoint (unlike ray-tracing calculations); so, once we have calculated the diffuse light coming off of each surface, the viewpoint can be moved around the scene with no change to the lighting, as long as nothing that generates or reflects light moves in the scene.

Furthermore, whereas ray tracing also determines which objects are visible from the viewpoint, radiosity calculates only the lighting and color of each surface. Normally, radiosity is used as a first pass, followed by a conventional hidden-surface–removal calculation (for example, Z-buffer) once the viewpoint is specified. For a relatively complex scene, the radiosity calculation may take hours, or even days, but once it is done, we can move around the scene quickly (even in real time on a reasonably powerful system).

Radiosity does a good job of rendering scenes with matte surfaces, but it does not handle reflective surfaces. Some systems combine ray tracing as a separate pass after radiosity, for a truly time-consuming calculation. HOOPS has a optional rendering package, called A.I.R. (Advanced Interactive Rendering) that includes radiosity and ray tracing (with the option of doing both).

**3.3.4.8**  **Textures.** So far, all our calculations have approximated only the effect of light sources on objects; the surfaces themselves are completely plain (each surface has a diffuse color, a specular color, and a glossiness factor). In real life, most surfaces are not so boring. Walls are made from brick or board, wood has grain patterns, curtains and carpets have patterns and texture, metal is anodized or burnished. Rather than model a brick wall by treating each brick as a separate object, a faster approach is to treat the wall as a single large polygon, and to paint the image of a brick wall on it. This approach is not as accurate, since — like faux architecture — the wall is still a flat surface and not rough brick, but it is much faster to calculate. Textures can be painted on any surface, including curved surfaces.

The image to be painted on a surface is called a *texture map*. A scene with just a few dozen surfaces with texture maps can be more realistic looking than a scene with thousands of polygons, and is much faster to render. A texture map can either be stored as a raster (image), or can be defined procedurally (for example, a graph-paper texture). During shading, the appropriate value from the texture map is determined for each pixel in the surface.

It is even possible to use the output of the renderer as a texture map. For example, we can render a scene and use the resulting image as a texture map for a picture on the wall of another scene. Alternatively, consider a shiny metal surface (like a mirror) that reflects its surroundings. One way to render this object that is much less expensive than ray tracing is to use the graphics system to produce a texture map that is a rendering of the scene from the viewpoint of the reflective object. Such a texture map, called an *environment map*, is then painted onto the surface of the object, to approximate the reflection of the scene. This technique can be modified to work for reflective objects of any shape — including spheres, cylinders, and shiny car bodies — rather than for only flat mirrors.

**3.3.4.9**     **Transparency.** Transparency is used for two different purposes. The obvious one is for realism — for example, to model light passing through windows or transparent containers. Transparency is also used for illustrations — for example, to show the pistons inside of a car engine while still showing a transparent ghost image of the outside of the engine.

Realistic transparency is complicated and expensive to compute, because it involves refraction and other effects that can change the color and even the apparent position of objects.

Even ignoring refraction, simply calculating how colors are modified as they pass through transparent objects is virtually impossible in a typical computer-graphics system. The difficulty arises because computer graphics specifies colors using three primaries (red, green, and blue), whereas color is actually a continuous spectrum of energy, typically drawn as a graph (see Section 3.3.5 on color). A transparent object filters the spectral-energy distribution of any incident light. Modeling this filtering by multiplying two RGB triples together almost never gives the right answer. Consider a filter that passes all light with a wavelength less than 550 nanometers, with a monochromatic (single-wavelength) laser light at 560 nanometers shining through it. The blue–green filter has an RGB value of (0.0, 1.0, 1.0), and the green light has a value of (0.0, 1.0, 0.0), so the result (calculated using RGB triples) is that the light is passed entirely. In reality, however, the light is blocked completely.

For illustrations, instead of true transparency, a technique called *blending* is normally used. Blending not only is less expensive to compute, but also gives images better suited to the purposes of illustration. In blending, the light transmission of a surface is specified as a number between 0 and 1, with 0 being an opaque surface and 1 being a completely transparent surface. Consider a scene with a blue transparent object with a transmission coefficient of 0.7, in front of a red opaque object. The transmission coefficient is multiplied by the color of the back object (0.7 × red), and the result is added to 1 minus the coefficient multiplied by the color of the front object (0.3 × blue), so any pixel where the back object shows through the front object will be reddish magenta (0.7 red + 0.3

blue). It is also possible to specify the transmission coefficient as three numbers, one for each primary (red, green, and blue).

Some graphics hardware supports another form of simulated transparency with a technique called *screen-door transparency.* This technique is extremely simple to compute, and works well for simple transparent objects. For screen-door transparency, any objects in the back are rendered normally; then, the transparent objects are rendered, but only some of the pixels are painted. For an object that is 50 percent transparent, we draw only every other pixel. This technique is popular in video games — for example, to draw a scene containing a water fountain, flames, or a ghost.

3.3.4.10    **Atmospheric attenuation.** In real life, objects appear less distinct as they move further from our eye. They fade because the atmosphere randomly mixes up light waves. This effect is especially apparent when there is excess water vapor (fog) in the air. Although the effect of atmospheric attenuation might seem relatively unimportant, it is actually useful in engineering drawings as a way to help the user tell the depth of objects; that is, it provides *depth cueing.* It is also useful in other graphics applications as a way to set off the foreground objects against background objects that are farther away.

Atmospheric attenuation is especially useful when a hidden-surface algorithm is not used. For example, in wireframe drawings, it can be difficult to tell which objects are in front. Atmospheric attenuation can make such drawings much easier to interpret, and is much less expensive than is a hidden-surface calculation.

We typically calculate atmospheric attenuation using a simple approximation. We choose two distances from the viewpoint, called the *hither* and *yon* points. These points are normally chosen such that the objects to be rendered generally fall between these points. Any object that is more distant than the yon point is drawn in the background color. Any object that is closer than the hither point is drawn normally. Between the hither and yon points, the color is linearly interpolated between the color of the object and the background color. The hither and yon points used for atmospheric attenuation are not necessarily the same as the hither and yon points (or planes) used for clipping or for Z-buffer calculations.

3.3.4.11    **Shadows.** Shadows not only add realism to a scene, but also make it easier to determine spatial relationships among objects. For example, we can tell whether a piece of furniture is touching the wall behind it by looking at the furniture's shadow on the wall. Shadows are also used on text — an effect called a *drop shadow* — to make text look as though it is floating slightly above the background.

Ray tracing and radiosity automatically calculate shadows. If we are using another hidden-surface algorithm, however, we can do shadow calculations by doing the equivalent of a hidden-surface calculation from the viewpoint of the light. This calculation determines which surfaces are "visible" to the light, and thus are not in shadow. We then apply the resulting *shadow map* onto the surfaces in the scene, just as we apply a texture map.

### 3.3.5      Color

In computer graphics, the representation of color is a compromise among the capabilities of the graphics hardware, the physical nature of light, and human perception of color.

**3.3.5.1**      **Spectral color.** Physically, light is a continuous spectrum of frequencies, with different frequencies corresponding to different colors in the spectrum (Figure 3.27). The frequency of light is measured as a wavelength in nanometers — the shorter the wavelength, the higher the frequency. Real light (except for monochromatic light, such as from a laser) is made up of many different frequencies, in the same way that music is made up of many different frequencies (pitches).

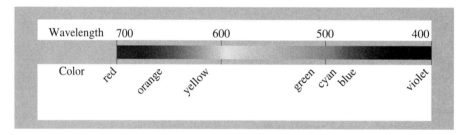

**Figure 3.27**      The spectrum of visible light.

**3.3.5.2**      **Tristimulus color.** Our eyes are sensitive to only three ranges of light frequencies, which we perceive as red, green, and blue (RGB). Thus, we can represent colors as three numbers; this representation is much more compact than a representation of a continuous spectrum. Note, however, that the three numbers are just a sample, so the method is subject to the same problems as those that plague any sampling. For example, there are colors — including common ones such as turquoise, deep brown, or rich indigo — that are not represented satisfactorily in this way. In addition, we cannot accurately predict the effects of mixing or filtering colors by adding or subtracting the colors' R, G, and B values. Despite these problems, computer graphics uses RGB color triples to represent colors, and doing so works most of the time.

The next issue is how many color levels the eye can sense. Most computer-graphics systems use 8 bits to represent each primary, giving 256 levels per color, and 24 bits to represent a color. This number of bits gives us 16,777,216 possible colors. That might seem to be many colors, but when we are doing smooth shading, we need minute variations of each color to avoid color banding and other artifacts. Some specialized frame buffers used for high-quality reproduction even store 12 bits per primary, giving over *68 billion* colors.

It is possible to use fewer levels. For example, the eye is less sensitive to levels of blue and red than to levels of green, so we could use 7 bits for green, 5 bits for red, and 4 bits for blue, for a total of 16 bits to represent a color, yielding 65,536 different colors. This approach causes some color artifacts, but it works well most of the time.

**3.3.5.3**    **RGB color space.** Graphically, we can think of the RGB color space as a unit cube, with black at the origin, white at (1.0, 1.0, 1.0), the three additive primary colors (red, green, and blue) at the three corners closest to the origin, and the three subtractive primary colors (magenta, cyan, and yellow) at the remaining three corners (Figure 3.28).

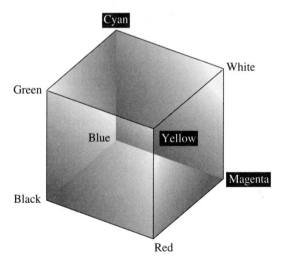

**Figure 3.28**    The RGB color space.

We can locate any color in the RGB space using its three color coordinates.

The red, green, and blue primaries are called the *additive primaries* because we can produce any color of light in the space by adding red, green, and blue light. For example, the color phosphor dots on a color monitor are red, green, and blue; our eye blends the light from these dots to get any color of light.

The magenta, cyan, and yellow primaries are called the *subtractive primaries*, because we can produce any color by subtracting magenta, cyan, or yellow from white light. Each subtractive primary removes light of the additive primary that is on the opposite corner of the RGB color cube; cyan removes red (but passes green and blue), magenta removes green (but passes red and blue), and yellow removes blue (but passes red and green). For example, color transparencies (slides) use magenta, cyan, and yellow pigments. When white light is passed through a color transparency, the correct colors are subtracted by each pigment to form a full-color image. The same process works for photographs and printed color images, with the correct colors subtracted by each pigment as the light reflects off the surface.

**3.3.5.4**     **Hue-based color spaces.** Humans do not naturally think of color in terms of adding or subtracting primaries, so even though computer-graphics systems specify colors internally in an RGB color space, other color spaces have been developed that are more natural for humans. Most of these color spaces specify a color using three numbers: the dominant *hue* (for example, yellow versus purple); the amount of *tint*, also called *saturation* or *chromaticity* (for example, red versus pink); and a *lightness* or *intensity* value (for example, orange versus brown). Note that, technically, the term *lightness* is used for reflecting objects, and *intensity* is used for light sources; however, the terms are often confused in computer graphics.

An example of a hue-based color space is the color space used by a typical color TV set. The controls to adjust the colors on a TV set have names such as *hue*, *saturation*, and *brightness* (even though the CRT of the television set displays colors using red, green, and blue phosphors).

In computer graphics, hue is specified as an angle between 0 and 360 degrees, like an artist's color wheel, with red at 0°, green at 120°, and blue at 240°. The amount of tint is specified with a number between 0 and 1.0, with 1.0 specifying a fully saturated color, and 0 specifying the absence of color. For example, pink can be thought of as having a hue of 0° (red) and a tint of 0.5. The lightness or intensity value is also specified as a number between 0 and 1.0, with black at 0 and white at 1.0, with shades of gray in between.

Three commonly used hue-based color spaces are shown in Figure 3.29.

- *Hue, lightness, and saturation (HLS).* The HLS color space can be thought of as a double-ended cone, with black and white at the tips and the fully saturated colors around the circle at the widest part where the two cones meet. If you take the RGB color cube and tip it up on one vertex so that black is at the bottom and white is at the top, it looks almost like the HLS color space. One problem with the HLS color space is that the fully saturated colors all have a lightness value of 0.5.

- *Hue, saturation, and value (HSV).* The HSV color space can be thought of as a single cone standing on its apex. Black is at the apex, the fully saturated colors are around the base of the cone, and white is at the center of the base of the cone.

- *Hue, intensity, and chromaticity (HIC).* The HIC color space is similar to the HLS color space, except that, instead of being a double-ended cone, it is a cylinder. In the HIC color space, black and white are not single points — they are the entire bottom and top ends of the cylinder, respectively.

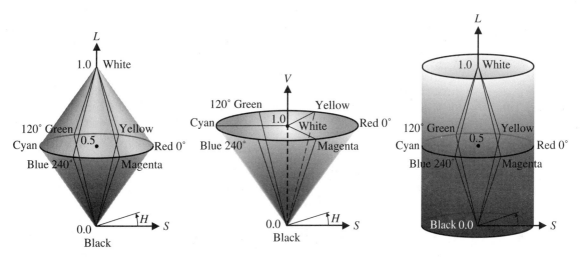

**Figure 3.29**    Hue-based color spaces.

It is possible to write a program to convert from one space to another. One disadvantage of hue-based color spaces is that it is possible to specify a color in one space that does not correspond to a valid color in another space. For example, there are valid colors in RGB space that cannot be specified in a hue-based space, and there are valid colors in the hue-based colors spaces that do not correspond to a valid RGB color.

 You can use the HOOPS command HC_Compute_Color_By_Value to convert a color value from one color space to another for HLS, HSC, HIC, or RGB.

**3.3.5.5**     **Named-color systems.** Even hue-based color spaces are awkward for humans to use (quick, what color is HIC 180°, 0.5, 0.5?). Instead, humans normally specify color by name. The problem with using names is that color names are subjective (is a manila envelope brown or yellow?), and can even be ambiguous (for example, different people may associate different colors with the names *sky blue, sea green,* and *brick red*). To avoid these problems, we can create a well-defined grammar for color names, with precise and unambiguous values for each name.

The first step is to choose a set of standard color names and to assign values to each name (using any convenient color space). For example, red is RGB value (1.0, 0.0, 0.0), blue is HLS value (240°, 0.5, 1.0), and moose brown is HIC value (12°, 0.63, 0.89).

The second step is to define a set of rules for combining colors to form new colors. For example, two color names separated by a dash denote a color halfway between the two colors. What *halfway* means will depend on what color space we use to combine colors. For example, if we choose RGB space to combine colors, then red–blue would be a dark magenta with RGB value (0.5, 0.0, 0.5). If, instead, we choose a hue-based space for combining colors (such as HIC), then red–blue would be a fully saturated magenta with HIC value (300°, 0.5, 1.0). Using RGB space to combine colors is more physically accurate (it corresponds roughly to what would happen if we mix two colors together), but using a hue-based color space to mix colors has the advantage that, when we mix two fully saturated colors together, we end up with a fully saturated color.

Optionally, we can define degrees of color for mixing colors. For example, the term *reddish blue* might mean a color that is 20 percent red and 80 percent blue, and *darker red* might mean a color that is 35 percent black and 65 percent red.

**120**

The combined colors can themselves be combined — for example, *greenish redder dark moose brown.*

The HC_Compute_Color command can provide the RGB (or other color-space) value of a color name.

```
struct RGBColor { float r, g, b; };
RGBColor rgb;
char name[] = "greenish redder dark moose brown";
if (HC_Compute_Color(name, "RGB", &rgb))
    printf("RGB = (%g, %g, %g)\n",
            rgb.r, rgb.g, rgb.b);
else printf("color %s is invalid\n", name);
```

**3.3.5.6**   **Specification of colors.** What is the best color space to use to specify colors? No single color space is superior to any other. Different users will prefer to use different color spaces, and, in different situations, a single user might prefer one color space over another. As an application writer, your best bet is to let the user decide what color space to use. In some cases, it might be appropriate to let the user specify colors by name. In other cases, it is better to let the user indicate a numeric color value (in a space such as RGB or HSV) — for example, by having the user specify each component using an interactive slider. In still other cases, it is better to display a palette of colors, and to let the user pick one (and then possibly to let the user modify it).

**3.3.5.7**   **Mapped color.** We could argue that many applications do not need 24 bits (or even 16 bits) to represent each color. Indeed, we do not have 16 million separate pixels on the screen, so we could never display 16 million different colors at the same time. *Mapped-color* systems use a smaller number of bits per pixel in the frame buffer, and then use a hardware *color map* to map these values into real colors (Figure 3.30). The value in the frame buffer is used as an index, called a *color index*, into the color map. For example, many systems store 8 bits for each pixel, and that allows only 256 different colors at the same time. The color map contains 256 entries, one for each possible value, and each entry is typically 24 bits (or more) long (8 bits for each primary).

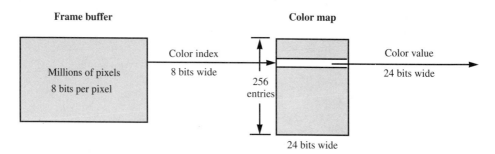

**Figure 3.30**　　A color map.

 You can use the HC_Show_Device_Info command to tell you the number of bits in each pixel in the frame buffer.

```
char bits[32];
HC_Show_Device_Info("?Picture", "planes", bits);
printf("number of bits per pixel = %s\n", bits);
```

You can also use HC_Show_Device_Info to determine the resolution of the frame buffer.

Using a color map reduces memory requirements — an 8-bit frame buffer is one-third the size of a 24-bit frame buffer for the same resolution. Some frame buffers support multiple resolutions with the same amount of memory; for example, they may provide 24 bits of color at a resolution of 640 by 480, and only 8 bits at 1280 by 1024 (using mapped color for the higher resolution).

**3.3.5.8**　　**Continuous color versus discrete color.** The number of colors required by your application depends on the kinds of images that you want to display. If your application uses smooth shading, or displays images taken from the real world (such as from a scanner or video source), then you need the ability to display *continuous color*, and a 24-bit frame buffer is typically used (but see the discussion of quantization and dithering, in Section 3.3.5.9, for ways to do continuous color using an 8-bit frame buffer). In a continuous color system, every possible color is represented directly in the frame buffer.

Other applications do not need so many colors. For example, an application might use color to label the different wedges in a pie chart, or to differentiate streets from highways in a map. In a *discrete-color* system, the application uses a *color palette* containing the fixed number of possible colors (for example, up to 256 colors for an 8-bit frame buffer). The application's color palette is loaded into the hardware color map when the application runs. There are basically two ways for an application to define its color palette: *by color* or *by object.*

If a color palette is defined by color, then a fixed set of colors is loaded into the color map. For example, black might be the color at index 0, white might be at index 1, red at index 2, green at index 3, blue at index 4, and so on. If we want to color a certain object red, we assign that object color index 2; when we render that object, we set each pixel in the object to color 2. If we want to display a color that is not in the palette, and we have free slots in the color map, then we assign a new color index and give it the desired color.

If a color palette is defined by object, then each different kind of object is given its own color index. For example, a window system may assign the window-border color to be color index 15, and the window-background color to be color index 16. To set the window-background color to blue, we set color palette entry 16 equal to blue. The advantage of assigning palettes by object is that we can change the color of all objects of the same type by changing a single value in the color palette. We assign new slots in the color palette only when we create new kinds of objects.

It is also common to mix the two schemes. For example, a statistics application may reserve a fixed number of slots in the color palette for objects such as graph axes or annotation text (by object), and use the rest of the color palette to color in the wedges in pie charts or the bars in bar graphs (by color).

3.3.5.9      **Quantization and dithering.** It is also possible to display continuous-color images in a mapped-color frame buffer. Again, we can do so either by object, called *quantization*, or by color, called *dithering.*

To display a continuous-color image using quantization, we analyze the image to see how many different colors it contains. If the number of different colors is smaller than the size of the color map, we just assign each color a slot in the color map, and display the image with the colors translated into the correct color indices. More likely, however, the number of different colors in the image will be greater than the number of slots in the color map. In this case, we can find colors that are close to each other and treat them as the same color. We continue merging colors until we have fewer than the number of slots in the color map, and then we display as before.

Displaying a continuous-color image in a mapped frame buffer using quantization introduces color inaccuracies and, usually, a little color banding. More severe problems are that this technique is computationally expensive, and requires a different color palette for each image. If we are using a window system and have more than one image displayed on the screen at the same time, we can load only one image's color palette into the hardware color map at any one time, so all but one of the images will look completely wrong (you may have noticed this problem if you have ever used an 8-bit frame buffer to display more than one dig-itized photograph — because each image has its own color palette, only one im-age can be displayed correctly at a time).

Alternatively, we can display continuous-color images on mapped-color hard-ware using a color palette that is defined by color. To do so, we define a standard color palette containing colors that are spread out evenly across all possible con-tinuous colors. Each color in the image is then replaced by the closest color in the fixed color palette. This substitution obviously leads to numerous color errors, since we are typically using only 256 (or fewer) colors to represent millions of different colors. In smoothly shaded images, color banding will be clearly visi-ble. In images taken from the real world, colors will look blotchy (an effect called *posterization*) and inaccurate (for example, skin tones might look greenish).

We can reduce the color problems that we encounter when we display continuous-color images in a mapped-color frame buffer by using a technique called *dither-ing*. Dithering takes advantage of the fact that the human eye has less resolution for color information than for black and white. Thus, although a high-resolution system is needed to display lots of fine lines or text, lower resolution is sufficient for different shades of color. Using dithering, if we want to display orange, and we have only the colors red and yellow in our color palette, we can instead display alternating red and yellow pixels, and the eye will blend together the two colors and will see orange. To make a slightly redder orange, we use slightly more red pixels than yellow ones. Thus, we can use a small number of colors to give accept-able continuous-color images.

**3.3.5.10**     **Gamma correction.** The light emitted by a CRT is not linear with respect to the signal voltage applied to it, so the color of a pixel is not directly proportional to the color value in the frame buffer. If not corrected, this nonlinearity tends to make images appear too dark and can shift colors (for example, make flesh tones appear too red). Correcting for this nonlinearity is called doing *gamma correc-tion*. Gamma correction can be done either in hardware or in software, and is mainly applicable to CRTs.

## 3.4        User Input

So far, this chapter has discussed only the output side of graphics systems, but input is equally important to an interactive graphics application. Input can be characterized in two ways: by the type of hardware input device, and by the type of input value.

### 3.4.1        Hardware Input Devices

Practically every computer includes a *keyboard* for entering characters. There are two different ways that characters can be received from keyboards: as text strings or as raw button presses.

Most computers today also include a *pointing* device, such as a mouse, trackball, tablet, force-sensitive button, joystick, or touchscreen. A pointing device is typically used along with a cursor on the screen to provide screen positions. It is one of those small miracles of the human brain that we seamlessly connect the movement of a mouse by our hand with the movement of the cursor on the screen.

Less common are 3D pointing devices that provide 3D positions in space, or 6-degrees-of-freedom devices that give both a position and an orientation in space. The latter is commonly used by head-mounted displays in virtual-reality systems to determine the position of the user and the direction in which the user is looking.

Most of the examples in this book assume that you have a typical computer with a keyboard and a pointing device (probably a mouse).

### 3.4.2        Types of Input Values

The second way that input is characterized is by the type of input event. We distinguish different kinds of input event by the way that the application uses the input, rather than by the kind of device that generated the event.

### 3.4.2.1        **Text.** Text input treats input from a keyboard as connected strings of characters. Normally, the typed text string is not sent to the application until the user presses the "enter" or "return" key. The operating system gathers up the text and processes control actions, such as use of the "backspace" or "delete" key to correct input. Even the pointing device can be used in text input to move the text insertion point in the current input string.

**125**

**3.4.2.2**     **Buttons.** Another way to treat a keyboard is as a bank of buttons. Each button press is sent to the application immediately as it is entered on the keyboard. It is up to the application to interpret control keys such as the "backspace" and "enter" keys. This kind of input is sometimes called *raw* input (as opposed to text input, which is *cooked*).

Most pointing devices, such as mice and joysticks, also have one or more buttons that are treated similarly to keyboard buttons.

Depending on the keyboard and operating system, we might be able to process button presses at an even lower level. Some systems allow an application to access *device-level* keyboard input. At the device level, a keyboard produces input when a button is pressed, and produces a separate input event when the button is released. Even presses of modifier keys, such as "shift" or "control," are sent as separate input events — it is up to the application to figure out that the sequence "shift-down, a-down, a-up, shift-up" should produce an uppercase A. Some keyboards distinguish between the "shift" key on the left side of the keyboard and the one on the right side. There is typically no concept of keyboard repeat (where holding down a key sends the value of that key repeatedly). Because we are receiving input directly from the keyboard, device-level input is highly device dependent and will almost certainly not be portable from one system to another.

**3.4.2.3**     **Locations.** The simplest kind of input value from a pointing device is an $x, y$ location. A location input event is normally delivered to the application when a button is pressed or released, or if the location changes (for example, the mouse is moved). Most pointing devices report changes in position only; the operating system or window system translates these changes into an absolute position in either device coordinates for the display or window local coordinates.

**3.4.2.4**     **Selection.** Selection input, also called *picking*, uses the pointing device to determine at what the user is pointing. Put another way, selection converts a location into a graphics object. Picking is complicated by the fact that a location may correspond to more than one object. Consequently, selection input normally returns a set of objects, with the front object first. Some objects (such as lines) are difficult to pick, so selection input returns objects within a certain distance of the location; this distance is called the *selection proximity*.

 As mentioned in Section 3.1.7.2, one of the advantages of a retained-mode graphics system is that such a system can perform selection directly on the display list. Without a display list, the only way to perform a selection is to have the application resend the entire scene to the graphics system, and to see whether any object lies close enough to the cursor to be picked.

**3.4.2.5**     **Time.** Many applications need to be able to determine when a specified amount of time has passed — for example, to display frames of an animation at a constant rate, or to tell when an input request times out. To measure elapsed time, we treat the clock as an input device.

**3.4.2.6**     **Complex input.** Multiple input events often are combined into a single input event. Even after the event is delivered to the application, it might be further converted into a different kind of input event, or combined with other events to create a new event. For example, consider an application where the user can either click on a graphical button to select it, double-click an object, or press and hold the mouse button over an object and drag that object to a new location. All these actions start as two kinds of input events: location events from the mouse, and button events from the mouse button.

When the user performs a single-click on a graphical button, the location and mouse-button events are combined and converted into a selection event for the graphic representing the button. This selection event is then further converted into a new button event (for the graphical button). For a double-click action, the system uses time input to time the interval between the two clicks, to decide whether to convert the input events into a single double-click action or into two separate single-click actions. For a press-and-drag action, the system uses additional location events to determine the new location of the object.

# 4 The HOOPS Database

This chapter covers the structure and organization of the HOOPS graphics database. HOOPS consists of three main parts: a graphics database, one or more rendering pipelines, and an input subsystem. We have already described some of this structure in Chapter 3, but the interesting parts are the details.

## 4.1 Application Structure

To your application, HOOPS looks like a subroutine library. Your application invokes HOOPS subroutines to insert and delete objects from the graphics database, to initiate and control rendering, and to receive input events. The order in which these operations occur is called the *control flow* of the application; control flow was a major topic of Chapter 2.

The control flow of a typical graphics application cycles through the following six steps:

1. Your application code makes changes to the graphics database.

2. When it is finished making changes to the graphics database, your application tells HOOPS to update the display (either by explicitly calling HC_Update_Display or by waiting for input).

3. HOOPS walks the database and sends the primitives to be drawn to the renderer.

4. The renderer draws the scene and sends it to some output device.

**5.** The user sees the new picture, thinks for a while, and then generates input through the user interface.

**6.** Your application code receives this input and makes further changes to the HOOPS database.

This cycle repeats until the user terminates the application.

We can visualize the control flow as a repeating cycle (Figure 4.1). This cycle contains the three main parts of HOOPS — the database, renderer, and user-input subsystem — in addition to your application code, and (of course) the end user.

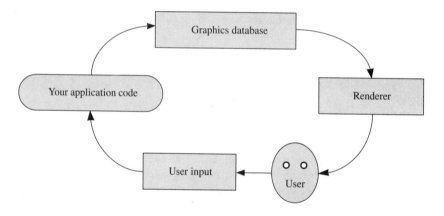

**Figure 4.1**     Control flow of a graphics application.

 Note that some libraries that are described as graphics systems contain only a renderer, and have no facilities for storing graphics information or for handling input events. When you are using such a graphics system, the application has to fill in for the missing parts. That requires more work on the part of the application writer and can make the resulting programs less portable.

## 4.2    Database Structure

To draw a picture of an analog clock, we store in the graphics database the
graphics primitives that make up the clock. Figure 4.2 is a picture of the clock.

**Figure 4.2**    A simple analog clock.

The clock consists of three main parts: the clock face and two hands. The face
itself is made up of two subparts: a circular rim and a central hub for the hands.

The HOOPS graphics database stores graphics scenes as a hierarchy (a tree),
normally depicted with the root at the top. Figure 4.3 shows a tree representing
one possible configuration of the HOOPS database for the clock.

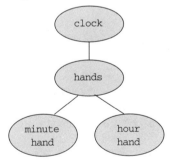

**Figure 4.3**    HOOPS graphics-database structure for the clock.

In this hierarchy, the clock face is stored in the top node of the hierarchy (called
"clock").

## 4.2.1     Segments

In HOOPS, each node in the tree is a *segment*. Program 4.1 creates the HOOPS segment hierarchy for the clock, shown in Figure 4.3. Note that, although Program 4.1 is a valid HOOPS program, it will not draw anything, because we have not put in the commands to create the geometry (we shall add those commands in Chapter 5).

```
1  HC_Open_Segment("clock");
2      // insert geometry for clock face: rim and hub
3      HC_Open_Segment("hands");
4          HC_Set_Color("red");
5          HC_Open_Segment("minute hand");
6              // insert geometry for minute hand
7          HC_Close_Segment();
8          HC_Open_Segment("hour hand");
9              // insert geometry for hour hand
10         HC_Close_Segment();
11     HC_Close_Segment();
12 HC_Close_Segment();
```

**Program 4.1**     Segment hierarchy for the clock.

Segments are the primary organizational principle in HOOPS. A segment can have subsegments (for example, the segment named "clock" has a subsegment named "hands", and the segment named "hands" has subsegments named "minute hand" and "hour hand"). In addition, segments can contain geometry (the segments named "clock", "minute hand", and "hour hand" all contain geometry) and attributes (the segment named "hands" contains the red color attribute set on it, on line 4 of Program 4.1). Note that there is no prohibition against a segment that has subsegments also having geometry or attributes; in fact, it is common for segments to have all three (see Figure 4.4). (We might say that *geometry*, *attributes*, and *subsegments* are the *gas* that makes segments go.)

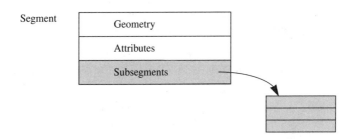

**Figure 4.4**    A segment that contains geometry, attributes, and subsegments.

In the database created by Program 4.1, the segment named "clock" has both geometry (the clock face) and a subsegment (the segment named "hands"). Note that we could have also created an additional subsegment of "clock" named "face" and placed the geometry for the clock face there, as shown in Figure 4.5.

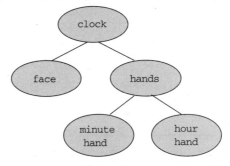

**Figure 4.5**    Alternative segment organization for clock.

In this alternative organization, all segments would contain either geometry or subsegments, but not both. Decisions such as how to organize the graphics database for an application are design issues that you will have to address; good database organization is covered in Section 10.1.1.

 In Program 4.1, we placed each clock hand in its own segment so that we could apply a different rotation factor to each hand as time passes. That is the reason why we left the clock face in the top node of the hierarchy, while placing the hands in their own nodes.

**4.2.1.1**    **Segments as objects.** A segment is an *object*, in the object-oriented programming sense. In particular,

- A segment encapsulates a public interface — the vast majority of HOOPS commands modify the state of a segment, or return information about a segment or its contents.

- A segment uses data hiding to protect the internal details of its representation from the programmer. Hiding unnecessary details makes life simpler for the programmer, and allows HOOPS to modify its internal representation on different platforms for portability, to take advantage of faster algorithms, or to incorporate improved rendering techniques.

- A segment has *attributes*, which act similarly to the member variables of an object.

- A segment can have one or more *subsegments*. The hierarchy formed by the segments in the database is like the class hierarchy in an object-oriented language (but is more dynamic).

- Just as member variables are inherited by a class's subclasses, attributes are inherited by a segment's subsegments. This form of inheritance is called *attribute inheritance*.

- A segment can be reused through the use of include segments (discussed in Section 4.2.2) and style segments (discussed in Section 4.2.4.5).

- A segment contains a single list; this list contains the geometry that belongs to that segment. This list is similar to the list member of a Smalltalk object. A segment can contain any number of pieces of geometry in its list, including zero.

In object-oriented languages, a member variable of an object can have only a single value at a time. Because a segment is an object, any one particular attribute of a segment can have only a single value at a time. For example, if a segment has its color attribute set to green and we then set the color attribute to red, the value green is replaced by the value red. The color attribute for the entire segment now has the value green and this new attribute applies to all geometry in the segment. If you want to draw two lines, one red and one green, *you must use two segments,* one with a color attribute of red and one with a color attribute of green.

Because each segment can have only a single value for an attribute, it is easy to find the value of an attribute. We simply ask the segment to return the value for that attribute. We can then change the value of the attribute and know exactly to what geometry the new attribute will apply — namely, all the geometry in that segment.

134

The fact that the value of an attribute applies to all geometry in a segment might seem obvious now that object-oriented programming is well accepted, but other graphics systems (including PHIGS, OpenGL, and Inventor) do not behave in this way. In these graphics systems, you can set the color to green and insert a line. If you then change the color to red and insert a second line, and you will get two lines, one of each color. Which attribute applies to which geometry depends on the order in which the graphics commands are executed, and on the order in which the graphics database is traversed.

4.2.1.2    **Declarative versus procedural graphics systems.** Even though HOOPS has many characteristics that qualify it to be called object oriented, historically the term *object oriented* has not been used to describe such graphics systems. Instead, graphics systems in which the value of an attribute applies to all geometry in a segment are called *declarative* graphics systems, to distinguish them from *procedural* graphics systems, where the procedural ordering of attributes is significant.

Procedural graphics systems are more difficult to use than are declarative graphics systems. Because a segment can contain more than one value for an attribute in a procedural graphics system, it is much harder to find the value of any particular attribute, and it is harder still to change the value of an attribute and to know to what geometry the attribute will apply. In addition, such systems cannot support attribute inheritance (in the object-oriented sense), which HOOPS does support.

4.2.2    **Include Segments**

HOOPS has two kinds of subsegments: regular segments and *include segments*. Include segments support a form of reuse. Include segments are similar to symbolic (soft) links in the UNIX file system, because they allow multiple links to the same object.

A segment to be included actually lives as a normal segment (with its own geometry, attributes, and subsegments) in another part of the graphics database. For convenience, HOOPS provides a place called "?Include Library" to store include segments, but segments to be included can exist anywhere in the HOOPS tree.

We create a link to such a segment, called an *instance* of the segment, using the HC_Include_Segment command. The instance behaves like a regular subsegment, except that the parent of an included segment is always that segment's real parent, rather than the segment that includes the included segment.

For example, if we are defining an automobile, we can define a segment tree representing a tire, and then include four instances of the tire, as in Program 4.2.

```
1  HC_Open_Segment("tire1");
2      HC_Include_Segment("?Include Library/tire");
3  HC_Close_Segment();

4  HC_Open_Segment("tire2");
5      HC_Include_Segment("?Include Library/tire");
6  HC_Close_Segment();

7  HC_Open_Segment("tire3");
8      HC_Include_Segment("?Include Library/tire");
9  HC_Close_Segment();

10 HC_Open_Segment("tire4");
11     HC_Include_Segment("?Include Library/tire");
12 HC_Close_Segment();
```

**Program 4.2**     Reuse of a segment with HC_Include_Segment.

The main advantages of include segments are that we can change the tire in one place and have the changes appear in all instances of the tire, and that there is a savings of space, because only one copy of the tire needs to be stored in the database.

### 4.2.3     Database Traversal

To render the graphics database, HOOPS walks the database tree, visiting each node that contains any primitives to be drawn. To draw a segment, HOOPS sends to the renderer any geometry that the segment contains, and then recursively draws any subsegments. Consequently, drawing a segment draws the entire branch of the tree with that segment as the root.

Because HOOPS is a declarative graphics system, the order in which HOOPS traverses the tree (or even whether it traverses the entire tree) is not important. Thus, HOOPS can choose how it walks the database. For example, if HOOPS can determine that a certain branch of the database tree does not contain any visible objects (for example, because its bounding box is off-screen, or because there is an attribute that turns off visibility), then HOOPS does not have to walk that part of the tree; HOOPS knows that nothing in that branch can affect the scene.

As we discussed in Chapter 3, what gets sent to the renderer to be drawn is a sequence of graphics primitives, where each primitive consists of some geometry and some attributes. If a segment contains geometry to be rendered, the HOOPS tree-walking routine constructs one or more primitives and sends them to the renderer. For each such primitive, each and every attribute that is applicable to that primitive must be known before the primitive can be drawn. For example, before we can draw a line, the renderer must know the line's color, its thickness, whether it is dashed, its modeling transformation, how it is lit, and so on. A primitive can have dozens — or even hundreds — of attributes; specifying them all would be substantial work.

## 4.2.4    Attribute Inheritance

Attribute inheritance in HOOPS works like inheritance in an object-oriented language. If an attribute value is not set locally on a segment, then it is inherited from a parent segment. The main difference between attribute inheritance and object-oriented inheritance is that the number of different kinds of attributes about which HOOPS knows is fixed (with the exception of user-defined attributes, described in Section 4.5.2.1).

Attribute values that are set explicitly on a segment are called *local attributes*. These attributes are set with any HOOPS Set command, such as HC_Set_Color or HC_Set_Line_Weight.

When HOOPS renders the database, it needs to know the attribute values for all the geometry in the database. For example, to draw a line, HOOPS needs to know the line color, thickness, and all other attributes that apply to a line. To determine the values of attributes, HOOPS first looks at local attributes set on the current segment. If any required attributes have not been set on the local segment, HOOPS looks in the parent of this segment to see whether a local attribute was set on the parent; HOOPS then looks at the parent's parent, and so on, until it finds a value for the attribute.

The effective value of an attribute — the value used to render the geometry in a segment — is called the *net value* of the attribute (or just the *net attribute*). As we shall see, HOOPS guarantees that every segment can determine the net value for every attribute (it must, because we need the net attribute values to render any geometry in a segment).

In Figure 4.6, containing the database diagram for the clock example, the color blue has been set on the clock segment, the color red has been set on the hands segment, and no color has been set on the "minute hand" or "hour hand" segments. What is the net attribute value for color for each segment?

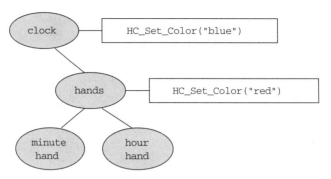

**Figure 4.6**        Clock database with attributes.

The segments "minute hand" and "hour hand" have no local color attribute set on them, so they inherit their color attribute. Since the "hands" segment has a local color attribute set on it, the "minute hand" and "hour hand" segments will use the color attribute from "hands" as their net color attribute. So the net color attributes used to draw this scene are blue for the "clock" segment, and red for the other three segments.

We can ask HOOPS for the net value of an attribute using one of the HOOPS routines that begin with "HC_Show_Net". In Program 4.3, the HC_Show_Net_Color command on line 8 returns the net color value for the segment named "minute hand".

```
1     HC_Open_Segment("clock");
2         HC_Set_Color("blue");

3         HC_Open_Segment("hands");
4             HC_Set_Color("red");

5             HC_Open_Segment("minute hand");
6                 char buffer[256];
7                 // get net value of attribute
8                 HC_Show_Net_Color(buffer);
9                 printf("net color of minute hand = %s\n",
10                    buffer);
11            HC_Close_Segment();

12        HC_Close_Segment();

13    HC_Close_Segment();
```

**Program 4.3**     Retrieval of the net color attribute of a segment.

If you think that Program 4.3 will print out "net color of minute hand = red", then you might want to try running it. Recall from Chapter 3 that the color of an object is not just a simple value, but rather consists of several components (diffuse, specular, and so on) and that you can specify separate colors for the edges and faces of polygons. You can use the HC_Set_Color command to set any component of the color attribute. The `HC_Set_Color("red")` command is an abbreviation that sets the diffuse component of all kinds of geometry (faces, edges, markers, lines, and text). When you print out the net value for the color attribute, you get the whole attribute — you get more than what you specified explicitly.

**4.2.4.1**   **Default attribute values.** When it starts up, HOOPS sets a local value for every attribute on the root segment of the database tree (HOOPS can do so because there is a fixed number of attributes). When it is looking for the value of an attribute, HOOPS will always eventually find its way up to the root of the tree, and will then use the value it finds there. Thus, the local attribute value set on the root segment of the database acts as a default value for the net attribute value. If you do not want to use the default value assigned by HOOPS, you can change it by changing the local attribute value on the root segment of the tree.

 Table 3.3 in the *HOOPS Reference Manual* contains a listing of the values for all the local attributes that are set on the root segment. These values are the default values for all the net attributes.

Another way to look at attribute inheritance is that, any time that you set a local attribute on a segment, you are establishing a default value for all segments below that one in the tree. Thus, in a scene with multiple complex graphical objects, each one represented by its own subtree, you can have different default values for each object by setting local attributes on the root segments of their subtrees.

**4.2.4.2**   **Renditions.** Of course, HOOPS does not actually search the database for net attribute values — that would be much too slow. Instead, for each segment, HOOPS constructs a structure called a *rendition* that caches the net value for every possible net attribute. HOOPS can build renditions because the number of attributes is fixed.

Since the root segment of the graphics database has a value set for every attribute, the rendition for the root segment is simply the value of all these local attributes taken together. A simplified version of the rendition for the root segment might look like Figure 4.7.

| Color | Line weight | Face pattern | Transform | Lighting | Visibility | Selectability |
|-------|-------------|--------------|-----------|----------|------------|---------------|

**Figure 4.7**     The rendition for the root segment.

Caching the net attributes in renditions is possible because HOOPS is a declarative graphics system. In a nondeclarative system, the net values for the attributes are dependent on the order in which the database tree is walked, so setting a local attribute in one part of the database tree can affect net attributes in completely unrelated parts of the tree, which would invalidate the renditions and force them to be recomputed completely whenever a change was made to the database.

 Note that the preceding description of renditions does not describe the way that HOOPS is implemented. Since renditions are not visible to the programmer (only the component net attributes are), HOOPS is free to use an even more efficient scheme to compute and cache net attributes.

**4.2.4.3**     **Nonstandard attribute inheritance.** Most attributes inherit in the way described previously (in the way the color attribute does), but a few attributes inherit in other ways. Consider a modeling transform: a translate, rotate, or scale. Modeling transformations are always performed with respect to the parent segment. When we rotate an object, for example, we want all its children to rotate too (even if they have their own local modeling transformations). In the clock, when a hand rotates, we want it to rotate in relation to the center of the clock, even when a transformation is used to move (or scale, or reorient) the entire clock.

As we discussed in Chapter 3, a segment's local modeling transformation is concatenated (using matrix multiplication) onto the net modeling transformation of that segment's parent — the local modeling transformation does not simply replace the parent's modeling transformation. If a segment has no local modeling transformations, the net transformation for the segment is the same as its parent's net modeling transformation.

In Figure 4.8, if the clock is rotated 20 degrees, and the hour hand is rotated an additional 90 degrees, then the net transformation for the hand is 110 degrees.

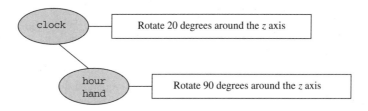

**Figure 4.8**     Nested rotations.

There are also a few attributes that inherit *up* the tree — for example, bounding volumes (see Section 3.1.7.1 for a description of bounding volumes, and Section 10.2.9 for tips on how to use bounding volumes in HOOPS). The bounding volume of a parent segment is the union of the bounding volumes of the children segments, plus the bounding volume of the parent segment's geometry.

A few attributes, such as normal vectors, do not inherit at all.

Unless stated explicitly otherwise, you can assume that an attribute inherits in the standard way. But, if you cannot remember how a specific attribute inherits, do not worry. Attributes always inherit in the way that makes the most sense.

**4.2.4.4**     **Attribute lock.** It is also possible to override local attributes temporarily, using *attribute lock*. When a specific attribute is locked in a segment, that attribute applies to all subsegments, even if they have a local attribute set on them for the same attribute. For example, you can use attribute lock to highlight a part of the database by changing the color of everything to red, temporarily ignoring any local color attributes. Program 4.4 will change the color to bright red of any geometry in the specified segment (and the specified segment's subsegments), regardless of the real colors.

```
1  void highlight (char * segment_to_highlight) {
2     HC_Open_Segment(segment_to_highlight);
3        HC_Set_Color("bright red");
4        HC_Set_Rendering_Options(
5              "attribute lock = color");
6     HC_Close_Segment();
7  }
```

**Program 4.4**     Use of attribute lock to highlight a segment tree.

**4.2.4.5**      **Style segments.** There is one more twist to the story of attribute inheritance. Let us say that, distributed across the hierarchy of our clock, there are numerous screws and nuts. These fasteners may be different lengths, and they may have hex heads, slotted heads, or some other topology, but they all have something in common — we want them all to be the same color. Initially, this color is a shiny steel gray, but we might want to be able to change the color to brass, or black, or some other color.

One way to have them all be the same color would be to set the color and lighting attributes (specular reflection, gloss, and so on) on each segment containing a fastener. That is not only inefficient, but also inconvenient, because changing the color of the fasteners will involve changing attributes on a large number of segments. Instead, HOOPS provides a convenient way to take a set of attributes and to make them apply to a large number of segments. We create a segment called a *style segment*. A style segment is just like any other segment, except that it (usually) does not contain any geometry; it contains only attributes.

We set up the style segment with the local attributes that we want, then we use this segment to *style* all the other segments. HOOPS provides a convenient place to put style segments, called "?Style Library". Style segments do not have to be located there, but putting a segment in "?Style Library" is a good way to document for what the segment is going to be used. Remember that a segment name that begins with a question mark (such as "?Style Library" or "?Picture") is an alias for the actual segment name (see the Section 4.2.5.3 for more information on aliases).

Lines 1 to 4 of Program 4.5 contain the code to create a style segment for the fasteners. This style segment is a segment named "fastener", which is a child of the segment named "?Style Library". To use this segment to style another segment, we use the HC_Style_Segment command (on lines 9 and 16).

```
1   HC_Open_Segment("?Style Library/fastener");
2       HC_Set_Color("diffuse=light gray, specular=white");
3       HC_Set_Color("gloss = 20.0");
4   HC_Close_Segment();

5   HC_Open_Segment("clock");

6       HC_Open_Segment("hands");

7           HC_Open_Segment("hour hand");
```

```
 8          HC_Open_Segment("screw 1");
 9            HC_Style_Segment("
10                    ?Style Library/fastener");
11            // geometry for screw 1
12          HC_Close_Segment();

13        HC_Close_Segment();

14        HC_Open_Segment("minute hand");

15          HC_Open_Segment("screw 2");
16            HC_Style_Segment(
17                    "?Style Library/fastener");
18            // geometry for screw 2
19          HC_Close_Segment();

20        HC_Close_Segment();

21     HC_Close_Segment();

22  HC_Close_Segment();
```

**Program 4.5**     Style segments.

Style segments themselves can have style segments; in particular, the "fastener" segment could contain an HC_Style_Segment command. Attributes that are "styled" act like local attributes for the purpose of further styling.

**4.2.4.6**     **Attribute inheritance summary.** Rendering the database consists of walking the database tree constructing primitives, and rendering these primitives.

From the viewpoint of the renderer, a segment consists of geometry and net attributes (Figure 4.9).

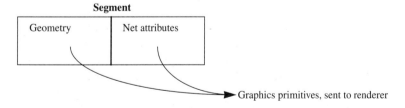

**Figure 4.9**     A segment from the viewpoint of the renderer.

The geometry and the net attribute values are what is drawn by the renderer.

From the viewpoint of the database tree walker (Figure 4.10), the net attributes of a segment come from three places: locally set attributes, style segments, and parent segments (this discussion applies to only those attributes that inherit normally).

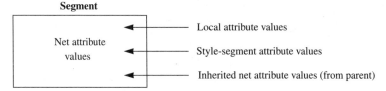

**Figure 4.10**     A segment from the viewpoint of the database tree walker.

In Figure 4.10, local attribute values are attributes that are explicitly set on a segment (via one of the HOOPS "Set" commands). Style-segment attribute values come from the local attributes of a segment that is used to "style" the current segment via the HC_Style_Segment command. Inherited net attribute values (typically) come from the net attributes of a parent segment of this segment.

Given any local attributes, style segments, and net attribute values for the parent segment, the net attribute values for the current segment are calculated as follows:

- If attribute lock is turned on for a specific attribute, the net attribute value from the parent (the inherited value) is used for the net attribute value.

- If attribute lock is off, and the attribute has a local value set on the current segment, that value is used as the net attribute value.

- Otherwise, if the current segment has any style segments, the attribute value from the style segment is used for the net attribute value (if a segment has more than one style segment and the same attribute has a local value in more than one of the style segments, the choice is arbitrary).

- Finally, if none of the preceding three methods work, the inherited net value from the current segment's parent segment is used (this method always provides a value, because all segments have a parent, and the parent has a net value for all attributes).

Note that an included segment inherits attributes from the segment that included it, rather than from its "real" parent. This rule allows different instances of an included segment to have different net attributes. Thus, each instance of an included segment has its own rendition (if an include segment is included in more than one place, it will have a set of net attribute values for each place that it is included). For example, if we use includes to include four instances of a tire for an automobile, each tire will have a different modeling transform attribute (to place each tire into the proper position), so the tire segment will have four renditions, one for each instance.

### 4.2.5    Segment Names and Keys

There are several different ways to reference a segment: implicit, explicit by name or alias, and explicit by key. If you always use a key to refer to a segment, then it is not necessary to name the segment.

**4.2.5.1**    **Implicit.** So far, we have always referred to segments implicitly, using the currently open segment. For example, the HC_Set_Color command sets a color attribute on the currently open segment.

**4.2.5.2**    **Explicit by name.** If you want to set an attribute on a segment other than the currently open segment, you can name the segment explicitly in the command. Commands that take an explicit segment name are prefixed with the letter Q (for Quick). For example,

```
HC_QSet_Color("clock", "green");
```

is completely equivalent to the following sequence of commands:

```
HC_Open_Segment("clock");
    HC_Set_Color("green");
HC_Close_Segment();
```

Most commands that operate on the currently open segment have a Q variant. Of course, if you are going to perform more than one operation on a segment, it is usually better (and faster) to open the segment first.

**4.2.5.3**    **Aliases.** Any command that takes a segment name, such as HC_Open_Segment or HC_QSet_Color, can also take an alias. You can define an alias using the HC_Define_Alias command. There are also several predefined aliases in HOOPS, such as "?Picture" and "?Style Library". An alias name always begins with a question mark.

In our clock example, we are going to be moving the hands to keep track of the time. It is bothersome to have to remember the segment hierarchy to get to the minute hand and the hour hand, so instead we can define two aliases:

```
HC_Define_Alias("?minute",
                "?Picture/clock/hands/minute hand");
HC_Define_Alias("?hour",
                "?Picture/clock/hands/hour hand");
```

Then, to advance the hour hand one hour, we can just say

```
HC_QRotate_Object("?hour", 0.0, 0.0, -30.0);
```

to rotate the hour hand 30 degrees clockwise around the *z* axis. If we ever want to reorganize the segment hierarchy of the database, then we need to change the alias in only one place, rather than in every place that the segment is named explicitly.

**4.2.5.4**
**Keys.** There is a second mechanism for referring to objects in HOOPS, called *keys*. You can write many HOOPS programs without the use of keys, but using keys often is more convenient and also is slightly faster than is using names (because keys do not require a name lookup). A key in HOOPS is a long integer. Routines that return a key are prefixed by the letter K. For example,

```
long key1 = HC_KOpen_Segment(
              "?Picture/clock/hands/hour hand");
```

Keys are used by HOOPS commands that end with the phrase "By_Key". For example, to open the hour hand segment by key, we use

```
HC_Open_Segment_By_Key(key1);
```

Keys are also useful because they can be used to refer to geometry inside of a segment. All the commands that insert geometry have K variants that return a key. For example,

```
long key2 = HC_KInsert_Circle(p1, p2, p3);
```

We can then use the key to edit or delete the new geometry.

Only segments can be named, so keys are the only way to refer to geometry. If you do not use a command that returns a key to insert geometry into a segment (by using Insert instead of KInsert), then it is difficult to get access to that piece of geometry to edit or delete it (other than by flushing all geometry from the segment, or doing a contents search on the segment). Commands that operate on geometry, such as HC_Edit_Polygon or HC_Move_Image, take a key argument but are not suffixed with the phrase "By_Key", because geometry is always referred to by key.

Keys should not be thought of as a replacement for names. In particular, there are no variants of commands such as HC_Set_Color that take a key as an argument — to set a color on a segment given a key, you have to open the segment using HC_Open_Segment_By_Key, and then do an HC_Set_Color on the open segment.

 There is a way to change a key into a segment name. It is useful for those few HOOPS commands that must take a segment name, when all you have is a key. To change a key to a segment name, format the key value as an ASCII hexadecimal string, and put an @ (at sign) on the front of it. The resulting string can be used as a segment name (just be sure that the key refers to a segment, rather than to geometry). For example, if a segment key has the decimal value 3917 (hex 0xf4c), then we can set a color on this segment with the command HC_QSet_Color("@f4c", "red"). One way to create the segment name is to use the %x format of sprintf.

In a typical application's database organization, segment names are used at the top levels of the database to refer to major components, but keys are used for individual objects in the database. For example, in a database representing a bicycle, we would not expect the application to create a name for every spoke on a wheel (let alone for every nut or bolt). Instead, the application would keep track of these objects using a C++ array of keys.

4.2.5.5     **No-name segments.** A segment does not need to be given a name. No-name segments are useful when the segment will be referred to exclusively by key. To omit naming a segment, use an empty string (not a null pointer) to create the segment — for example, HC_Open_Segment(" ").

## 4.2.6     Segment-Name Syntax

Segment names in HOOPS are made up from the normal alphanumeric characters A to Z, a to z, and 0 to 9, plus the characters "# + – $ _ ." and space. Segment names are not case sensitive — the name "CLOCK" is the same as "clock" (or "Clock", and so on). If a segment name contains space characters, more than one space character in a row is equivalent to a single space. In addition, leading and trailing spaces are not significant.

Any ASCII character can be used in a segment name if it is enclosed in matching quotation marks (you can use single quotation marks, double quotation marks, or even back quotation marks). For example, if you want a slash inside of a segment name, use the name "abc'/'def". Quoted alphabetic characters are case sensitive. The only time that quoted characters are useful is when a segment name is a string specified by the user, or is a file name. Putting such a string in quotation marks makes characters that have special meaning to HOOPS legal in the segment name (except for quotation marks, of course). Other than that, quoted characters are almost never used, and should be avoided.

A segment name that begins with a "?" (question mark) is an alias that refers to a segment.

The / (slash) character is used to combine segment names into a *path name* (like a UNIX file-system path name). The name "clock/hands" refers to the hands subsegment of the clock segment.

A path name that begins with a slash is an *absolute path name*, which names a segment with a path that starts at the root segment. Absolute path names uniquely identify a segment. In HOOPS, you will rarely write absolute path names. Instead, HOOPS provides aliases for you to use (such as "?Picture" and "?Include Library") whose values are absolute path names.

The root segment is simply named "/" (slash).

A path name (or single name) that does not begin with a slash is a *relative path name* that names a segment relative to the currently open segment.

The currently open segment can be referred to by the name "." (a single period). The name "./hands" (a period followed by a slash, followed by the name "hands") is the same as "hands". The only time the use of a period for a segment name is necessary is for commands that require a segment name — for example, HC_Flush_Contents(".") flushes the contents of the currently open segment.

You can refer to the parent of the currently open segment with either "^" (carat) or ".." (two periods).

**4.2.6.1**     **Wild cards.** Most commands that take a segment name as an argument can take a segment name containing *wild cards*. A wild card allows a single string to refer to more than one segment at the same time, and consequently allows many HOOPS commands to operate on more than one segment at a time. Wild cards are not used all that often, but they come in handy on a few occasions.

The simplest form of wild card is a set of names separated by commas and enclosed in parentheses. For example "clock/hands/(minute hand, hour hand)" refers to both hands of the clock. The wild card can be part of a name, so "clock/hands/(minute,hour) hand" has the same meaning.

The * (asterisk) character is used to replace zero or more characters in a segment name. For example, "clock/hands/* hand" may or may not refer to the same segments as "clock/hands/(minute hand, hour hand)", depending on whether we have defined any additional hands, such as one to sweep out the seconds.

The % (percent) character is used to replace a single character. For example, if you have defined sister subsegments named "seg#1", "seg#2", and "seg#–1", you can refer to the first two as "seg#%".

HOOPS also has an unusual (and particularly useful) wild card "..." (three periods) that you can use to refer to zero or more segment names in a path name. For example, "clock/.../*hand" refers to any segment name that ends with the word "hand", no matter where it lives in the subtree rooted under the segment named "clock". You can also use this wild card to refer to all segments in a sub-tree. For example, HC_Flush_Geometry("?Picture...") removes all geometry from the HOOPS database, starting with the "?Picture" segment. The command HC_Flush_Geometry("?Picture/...") does exactly the same action — the slash is optional. To flush geometry from all subsegments of "?Picture", but not from "?Picture" itself, use HC_Flush_Geometry("?Picture/*...").

Wild cards should not be used in commands that require a single segment name — for example, HC_Open_Segment (there can be only a single currently open segment).

## 4.3    Drivers

HOOPS uses aliases to shield you from worrying about the absolute structure of the database. When you insert new segments and geometry into "?Picture", they are placed somewhere in the database that causes them to be drawn, but, when you place segments or geometry into "?Include Library" or "?Style Library", they are placed somewhere else that causes them to not be drawn. How does HOOPS know which geometry to draw?

The values of "?Include Library" and "?Style Library" are simple: They are "/include library" and "/style library", respectively.

**149**

The "?Picture" alias is slightly more complicated — here is how that works. HOOPS defines a segment named "/driver". Underneath this segment are a dozen or more subsegments with names such as "x11", "msw", and "postscript" (because segment names are not case sensitive, the name X11 is the same as x11). There is one segment for each kind of device about which HOOPS knows — these subsegments of "/driver" are called *driver segments* (Figure 4.11).

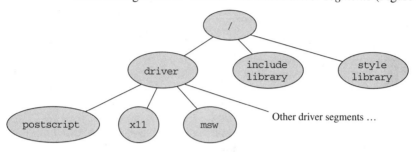

**Figure 4.11**    Driver segments.

You can use Program 4.6 to print out the names of all driver segments in HOOPS.

```
1  HC_Begin_Segment_Search("/driver/*");
2     char segname[128];
3     while (HC_Find_Segment(segname))
4        printf("%s\n", segname);
5  HC_End_Segment_Search();
```

**Program 4.6**    Driver segments.

If you execute Program 4.6 and look at the output, you will notice that, no matter on what platform you are running, your copy of HOOPS has a driver segment for every driver about which HOOPS knows on all platforms. For example, there is a driver segment for msw (Microsoft Windows) on UNIX platforms, and vice versa. In addition to the generic X11 driver, there are several drivers for UNIX platforms with special graphics hardware, with names such as "xgl" (for Sun XGL hardware), "gl" (for Silicon Graphics GL hardware) and "sbx" (for HP Starbase hardware). Only the drivers that make sense on a platform will actually work, but they are all there so that you can see what is available.

There are also other drivers, such as "cgm" (computer graphics metafile — a standard file format for transferring graphical information), "hpgl" (Hewlett-Packard graphics language — a printer and plotter format), "image" (the image driver — used to create images), "printf" (a driver that prints what it would draw, instead of drawing — for debugging), and "null" (a null driver that ignores everything sent to it). Drivers are documented in the *HOOPS Installation Guide* (which is included on the CD-ROM).

In HOOPS 4.1, there are 21 driver segments. One of these segments, named "3rdparty", does not correspond to a driver. Instead, it is a place where new drivers can be added by parties other than Autodesk. For example, graphics-display-board manufacturers have written drivers that take advantage of their graphics-accelerator technology. Or you can write a driver that implements a specialized renderer.

Driver segments have only one special characteristic: They each have the driver attribute set on them. The driver attribute is set with the HC_Set_Driver command (this command is normally never called by the user). The argument to HC_Set_Driver is a pointer to a function — this function is the actual device driver for that device. Like any attribute, the device-driver attribute is inherited by all subsegments of the driver segment. When HOOPS traverses the graphics database to render a scene, the graphics primitives are sent to their net device-driver function to be drawn.

When HOOPS starts up, it assigns a value to the "?Picture" alias that corresponds to the appropriate driver segment. It normally does so by reading the environment variable HOOPS_PICTURE, but it will choose a default value (and will issue a warning message) if HOOPS_PICTURE is not set. Note that HOOPS_PICTURE can be set externally in your computer's environment, or it can be set by your program before the first HOOPS command is executed.

You can show the value of the "?Picture" alias with the HC_Show_Alias command, as shown in Program 4.7.

```
1  char value[128];
2  HC_Show_Alias("?Picture", value);
3  printf("%s\n", value);
```

**Program 4.7**     The value of "?Picture".

Program 4.7 will print something like "?driver/msw/window0" or "?driver/x11/unix:0.0" (depending on what platform you are using). The value of the alias "?driver" is just "/driver" — so the value of "?Picture" refers to a segment that is a subsegment of a driver segment.

As the name "/driver/msw/window0" suggests, each subsegment of the msw driver segment corresponds to a window on the display device. The segment "window0" is created under the Microsoft Windows driver segment named "/driver/msw", and the creation of this segment causes HOOPS to create a new window on the screen. Any geometry placed under the "?Picture" alias (or in subsegments of "?Picture") is drawn into this window.

Some HOOPS device drivers use the name of the subsegment for information. For example, in X11, the value of the "?Picture" alias would be something like "?driver/x11/unix:0.0". The X11 driver uses the name "unix:0.0" to identify the display to which to send the picture. The name "unix:0.0" is X11 syntax for the main display on the local computer. For the PostScript driver, the subsegment name is used as the name of the file into which the PostScript output is written.

In summary, each subsegment of /driver is a driver segment for a different platform, and each subsegment of a particular driver segment is an *instance* of that driver (Figure 4.12). For a display driver on a window system such as X11 or Windows, each instance corresponds to a window on the display. For a hardcopy driver such as PostScript, each instance corresponds to a file to be printed.

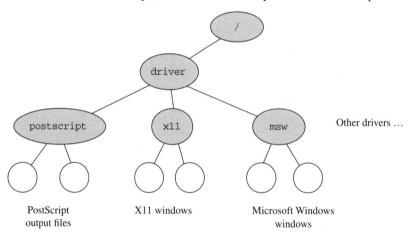

**Figure 4.12**          Driver-instance segments.

Any geometry and attributes placed into a segment under a driver instance will be drawn as part of that instance. In other words, any geometry placed into "/driver/msw/window0" will be drawn into window0, and any geometry placed into "/driver/postscript/file.eps" will be output as PostScript into the file named "file.eps".

You can create new windows for HOOPS to draw into simply by creating new subsegments of your driver segment. We shall discuss how to do that in Chapter 7; for now, Program 4.8 contains a simple example:

```
1  char newseg[128];
2  HC_Show_Alias("?Picture", newseg);
3  strcat(newseg, "+A");
4  HC_Open_Segment(newseg);
5      HC_Insert_Text(0.0, 0.0, 0.0, "second window");
6  HC_Close_Segment();
```

**Program 4.8**     Creation of a new window.

Program 4.8 creates two segments: the default one created by HOOPS (whose name is the value of "?Picture"), plus the new one (whose name Program 4.8 forms by concatenating "+A" onto the value of the "?Picture" alias, in line 3). Because each segment under a driver segment causes HOOPS to create a new output window for the driver, creating a new driver instance segment (in line 4) creates a second window on the screen. Note that, because we did not change the position or size of either of the windows, you might have to move the top window to see the one underneath.

If you want the same objects to appear in both windows, you can put the objects into a subsegment of "?Include Segment", and then use HC_Include_Segment to include the objects in both "?Picture" and "newseg".

Because X11 is a network window system, it can send display output to another computer over a network. For example, if there is a computer named "ralph" running X11 on your network, then you can send HOOPS output to ralph by creating a driver instance named "/driver/x11/ralph:0.0". The name "ralph:0.0" is X11 syntax for the main display on the machine named ralph.

## 4.4     Drawing the Database

As shown in Figure 4.13, when your application wants to draw a picture, the HOOPS database walker walks the database tree creating graphics primitives, which it sends to the appropriate renderer. The renderer sends its output to the device driver. The device driver is the interface between the renderer and your system's graphics hardware. Drawing of a picture in HOOPS is a cooperative effort among the database walker, a renderer, a device driver, and a device.

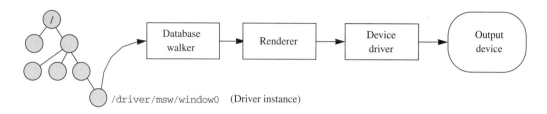

**Figure 4.13**     A driver instance and the rendering pipeline.

### 4.4.1     HOOPS Device Interface

To be portable to many different hardware platforms, HOOPS must be flexible. A few platforms, such as high-end graphics workstations, provide dedicated 3D rendering hardware. In this case, the goal of HOOPS is to feed the 3D graphics primitives from the database directly to the hardware, as fast as possible. Some platforms have 2D hardware that can draw simple lines and flat-shaded polygons. In this case, the device driver uses a HOOPS renderer to do all the 3D transformations and hidden-surface calculations, but uses the hardware to draw the 2D primitives. At the low end, some platforms just provide a simple frame buffer. In this case, the device driver has to do everything itself.

Ignoring differences across platforms, even on a single platform, HOOPS must be flexible. For example, an application might sometimes want fast rendering at the expense of realism, and at other times want perfect photorealistic images, no matter how much time they take. So HOOPS must be able to use different rendering algorithms (even in the same scene), some of which might be supported in hardware. HOOPS also supports hardcopy devices in addition to a normal, frame-buffer–based display.

In addition, even on platforms with 3D hardware, there are circumstances under which the HOOPS renderer will have to do all the work, because rendering hardware by its very nature has fixed limitations. For example, most 3D shading hardware allows only a fixed number of light sources in a scene (typically a small number, such as three or eight). If you want to draw a scene with more light sources than the hardware allows, then HOOPS has to abandon the shading hardware and to do the lighting calculations itself.

**154**

Many graphics systems simply ignore light sources beyond what the hardware will handle; this means that a scene that contains four light sources will be rendered incorrectly on hardware that supports only three light sources. Of course, performing lighting calculations in software is usually slower than is doing them in hardware, so your application might slow down when the user adds another light source, but at least the user will see the light.

You can find out how many lights are supported in hardware with the following command (note that the HC_Show_Device_Info command returns the result number as an alphanumeric string).

```
char result[32];
HC_Show_Device_Info("?Picture",
                "hardware lights", result);
```

HOOPS accomplishes its goal of flexibility by using a layered device interface called the *HOOPS Device Interface (HDI)*. HDI is the interface between the renderer and the device driver. If a platform provides graphics hardware (and it is faster than is HOOPS doing the same function in software), then HOOPS takes advantage of that hardware. If it does not, HOOPS fills in with software. Even on a system with graphics hardware, in some cases, the HOOPS software can be faster than the hardware.

## 4.4.2 Options

As we have seen, almost all information in HOOPS is stored as attributes (even device drivers). To draw a scene, the device driver and the renderer need to be supplied with information, such as what rendering algorithm or kind of lighting to use. Naturally, that information also is stored as attributes. Information used to control how a database is drawn is called an *option*. Options that are stored as attributes come in three flavors: driver options, rendering options, and heuristics.

### 4.4.2.1

**Driver options.** Driver options are commands to a particular device driver. For example, if your system can support double buffering, you can turn on that option with HC_Set_Driver_Options("double buffering"). You can also set the title of the HOOPS output window (for example, HC_Set_Driver_Options("title = graphics output")), or set the size of the output window (for example, HC_Set_Driver_Options("subscreen = (–0.5, 0.5, –0.5, 0.5)")).

Driver options affect only drivers, so it does not make sense to set them on a segment below a driver instance. The most common place to set driver options is on a driver instance (such as "?Picture"). Alternatively, you can set a driver option on a driver segment (such as "/driver/msw"), so that the option is inherited by all instances of that driver, or you can set a driver option on "/driver" (or equivalently, on "/"), so that it is inherited by all drivers (and their instances). Like those for all attributes, default values for all the driver options are set by HOOPS on the root segment.

In a typical HOOPS program, driver options are set on "?Picture". The only time that a HOOPS program would typically set a driver option anywhere else is when more than one driver instance is being used by the program. For example, you might set different driver options on a hardcopy driver and a display driver. Or, if you have multiple output windows, you can use the subscreen driver option to place each window in a different location on the screen.

**4.4.2.2**    **Rendering options.** Rendering options are used to control the rendering algorithm used by HOOPS. For example, unless your computer has special hardware, the default rendering algorithm is the painter's algorithm. On most platforms, the software Z-buffer algorithm is faster than the painter's algorithm (it is not the default for historical reasons, and because it uses more memory). Try adding the command

```
HC_Set_Rendering_Options(
        "hsr algorithm = software Z-buffer");
```

to the "?Picture" segment of a HOOPS program to see whether the program runs faster — if you have enough memory, it should run much faster (see Section 4.4.6 for a way to set options without recompiling your program). You can also use rendering options to control what kind of lighting to use, whether to use dithering, and so on. Rendering options affect how the graphics primitives in the database are rendered, so they can be set anywhere in the database tree. For example, Program 4.9 renders the same object twice — once using the painter's algorithm, and once using the software Z-buffer.

```
1   HC_Open_Segment("?Picture");
2      HC_Open_Segment("view 1");
3         HC_Translate_Object(0.5, 0.0, 0.0);
4         HC_Set_Rendering_Options(
5               "hsr algorithm = painters");
6         HC_Include_Segment("?Include Library/object");
7      HC_Close_Segment();
```

```
 8        HC_Open_Segment("view 2");
 9           HC_Translate_Object(-0.5, 0.0, 0.0);
10           HC_Set_Rendering_Options(
11                "hsr algorithm = software Z-buffer");
12           HC_Include_Segment("?Include Library/object");
13        HC_Close_Segment();

14  HC_Close_Segment();
```

**Program 4.9**     Two views with two different renderers.

The use of rendering options is yet another way in which HOOPS is declarative. A rendering option *declares* what renderer to use for a specific part of the database. In a procedural system, you would have to tell the system to use one renderer, then to render one part of your database, to switch renderers, and finally to render the other part of the database. HOOPS does this work for you.

**4.4.2.3**     **Heuristics.** Heuristics are hints that HOOPS can use to speed up rendering. Heuristics are similar to rendering options, but differ in that they are only suggestions. HOOPS is free to ignore them — they are *optional* options. For example,

```
HC_Set_Heuristics("backplane cull");
```

tells HOOPS to remove back-facing polygons *if doing so would speed up rendering.* If you are running on a system with rendering hardware, it might actually be slower to cull back-facing polygons, so setting this heuristic does not guarantee that back faces will not appear.

If your scene is only 2D (like the spreadsheet example in Chapter 2), or contains only lines, you can use

```
HC_Set_Heuristics("no hidden surfaces");
```

to turn off hidden-surface removal, which will significantly speed up rendering on most platforms.

Like rendering options, heuristics can be set anywhere in the database tree. For example, if one of the objects in your database will be drawn as a wireframe, you can turn off hidden surfaces for that object only.

A rendering option is information you give to change the way the HOOPS output appears. A heuristic is a hint that you give HOOPS to help it render your graphics more quickly. You should not depend on a heuristic to make any difference in the output image; a heuristic affects only how fast the image appears.

**4.4.2.4**    **Use of options.** You can set more than one option of the same type with the same command by separating the options with commas (spaces before or after commas are optional). For full information on all the possible options, see Section 4.4.3, or the entries in the *HOOPS Reference Manual* for HC_Set_Driver_Options, HC_Set_Rendering_Options, and HC_Set_Heuristics.

Options are a double-edged sword. You can dramatically speed up your graphics, but doing so might tune your application to a specific platform and so could make it less portable. It will always run on all platforms, but tuning for one platform may make it run slower on another (see Section 4.4.6 for a way to optimize a single executable to multiple platforms).

HOOPS programmers sometimes have trouble remembering whether a specific option is a driver option, a rendering option, or a heuristic. As we stated previously, the primary distinction between rendering options and heuristics is that heuristics are optional; they are only hints to HOOPS that it can use to speed up rendering.

Driver options are distinct because they apply to only a driver, whereas rendering options and heuristics apply to any segment in the database. If you are using two drivers (for example, a hardcopy driver and a display driver), or two instances of a driver (for example, for multiple windows), then you might set different driver options on the two driver segments. For example, you might change the window title on the display driver. The window title is a driver option because it does not make sense for a segment other than a driver segment to have a window title. On the other hand, turning off hidden surfaces is a heuristic, because one part of your database may contain hidden surfaces, yet another part may not.

The difference between driver options and rendering options is highlighted by the driver option "double-buffering" and the rendering option "technology = software frame buffer". Both of these options tell HOOPS to draw the output image into an off-screen buffer, and then to copy (blit) the buffer onto the display all at once. They can both be used to make animation smoother. On first look, they appear to serve the same purpose and thus might appear redundant. Let us examine why they are different, and why one is a driver option, whereas the other is a rendering option.

Double buffering is a driver option — it tells the HOOPS driver to allocate two frame buffers. The driver may do this allocation by dividing the hardware frame buffer in half; for example, if you have a 16-bit frame buffer, the driver could

**158**

treat it as two 8-bit frame buffers. In any case, HOOPS sends the scene to the driver one piece at a time, and the driver manages the two buffers.

The software frame buffer is a rendering option. In this case, the renderer — rather than the driver — allocates a separate frame buffer. This buffer is allocated in main memory, rather than in the graphics hardware, so it will never affect the number of colors displayed. In this case, the renderer draws the scene into the software frame buffer, and then sends this scene to the driver all at once.

On some systems, the software frame buffer is more efficient. For example, on Windows, the driver interface to the hardware (GDI) has a high overhead. Rendering the scene in a software frame buffer, then sending it through GDI as a single image to blit can make your graphics much faster. On other systems — particularly those with enough video memory to hold two frame buffers — using double buffering would be faster.

There are a few cases when using both double buffering and a software frame buffer would be a good idea. Consider a situation where HOOPS is running with X11, and the output is being sent over a local-area network to be displayed on a separate machine (an X server) from the one running HOOPS (the X client). In this case, specifying double buffering tells X11 to allocate a second frame buffer on the X server machine (where the image is being displayed), whereas specifying the software frame buffer allocates the frame buffer on the X client (the machine running HOOPS).

This use of the software frame buffer also affects how the scene is sent over the network. Normally, the scene is sent primitive by primitive to the X server, but when a software frame buffer is used, it is sent all at once as an image. Which way is faster depends on what the size of the output image is, on what the number of primitives to be rendered is, and on whether the X client or the X server is faster at rendering.

Finally, a driver option can be set on only a driver instance, so turning double buffering on and off affects everything drawn by that driver. On the other hand, the software frame buffer is a rendering option, so different parts of the HOOPS database can have different settings for this attribute.

In many HOOPS programs (those that use only a single driver and use the same rendering options and heuristics on the entire database), driver options, rendering options, and heuristics are all set on "?Picture", so they all affect the entire scene. In these programs, the distinctions between driver options and rendering options can be subtle. When you use multiple drivers, or use different rendering options on different parts of the database, the distinctions become more important.

**4.4.2.5**     **System options.** Alas, not every option in HOOPS can be treated as an attribute; options that affect the entire HOOPS system (rather than being set on an individual segment) are called *system options*. System options are set with the HC_Define_System_Options command and are returned with the command HC_Show_System_Options (note the use of the verb "Define" in the command, instead of "Set").

System options affect all of HOOPS. For example, you may have noticed that many of our examples use HOOPS commands that return information in an array of characters. Unfortunately, we had to guess how big to make the array, since HOOPS does not know the array's length and could easily overflow it, with potentially disastrous consequences. An alternative is to choose a fixed array size — say, 256 bytes — and to call HC_Define_System_Options("C string length = 256"). If the C string length is set and HOOPS tries to return information that is larger than the specified string length, it will fail and signal an error.

**4.4.3**     **Index of Options**

Table 4.1 contains a list of every HOOPS option and heuristic, with the names of the HOOPS commands that set them. You can show the value of an option by replacing the word Set or Define with Show in the command. For more information on each option, see the page for the appropriate command in the *HOOPS Reference Manual*.

| **Option or Heuristic** | **Command** |
| --- | --- |
| application | HC_Define_System_Options |
| atmospheric attenuation | HC_Set_Rendering_Options |
| attribute lock | HC_Set_Rendering_Options |
| backing store | HC_Set_Driver_Options |
| backplane cull | HC_Set_Heuristics |
| border | HC_Set_Driver_Options |
| bounding volumes | HC_Define_System_Options |
| C string length | HC_Define_System_Options |
| clipping | HC_Set_Heuristics |
| code generation | HC_Define_System_Options |
| color consolidation | HC_Set_Driver_Options |
| color index interpolation | HC_Set_Rendering_Options |
| color interpolation | HC_Set_Rendering_Options |
| concave polygons | HC_Set_Heuristics |
| continuous update | HC_Define_System_Options |
| control area | HC_Set_Driver_Options |
| debug | HC_Define_System_Options |

| | |
|---|---|
| debug | HC_Set_Driver_Options |
| debug | HC_Set_Rendering_Options |
| disable input | HC_Set_Driver_Options |
| double-buffering | HC_Set_Driver_Options |
| errors | HC_Define_System_Options |
| event checker | HC_Define_System_Options |
| face displacement | HC_Set_Rendering_Options |
| fatal errors | HC_Define_System_Options |
| first color | HC_Set_Driver_Options |
| fixed colors | HC_Set_Driver_Options |
| font directory | HC_Define_System_Options |
| force black-and-white | HC_Set_Driver_Options |
| gamma correction | HC_Set_Driver_Options |
| hidden surfaces | HC_Set_Heuristics |
| hsr algorithm | HC_Set_Rendering_Options |
| incremental updates | HC_Set_Heuristics |
| info | HC_Define_System_Options |
| intersecting polygons | HC_Set_Heuristics |
| landscape orientation | HC_Set_Driver_Options |
| license | HC_Define_System_Options |
| light scaling | HC_Set_Driver_Options |
| lighting interpolation | HC_Set_Rendering_Options |
| locater transform | HC_Set_Driver_Options |
| memory purge | HC_Set_Heuristics |
| message limit | HC_Define_System_Options |
| number of colors | HC_Set_Driver_Options |
| obsolete checking | HC_Define_System_Options |
| output format | HC_Set_Driver_Options |
| partial erase | HC_Set_Heuristics |
| pen speed | HC_Set_Driver_Options |
| perspective correction | HC_Set_Rendering_Options |
| physical size | HC_Set_Driver_Options |
| polygon handedness | HC_Set_Heuristics |
| quantization | HC_Set_Rendering_Options |
| quick moves | HC_Set_Heuristics |
| related selection limit | HC_Set_Heuristics |
| sanity checking | HC_Define_System_Options |
| selection proximity | HC_Set_Driver_Options |
| software frame buffer options | HC_Set_Rendering_Options |
| special events | HC_Set_Driver_Options |
| subscreen | HC_Set_Driver_Options |

| | |
|---|---|
| subscreen moving | HC_Set_Driver_Options |
| subscreen resizing | HC_Set_Driver_Options |
| subscreen stretching | HC_Set_Driver_Options |
| technology | HC_Set_Rendering_Options |
| texture interpolation | HC_Set_Rendering_Options |
| title | HC_Set_Driver_Options |
| transformations | HC_Set_Heuristics |
| update control | HC_Define_System_Options |
| update interrupts | HC_Set_Driver_Options |
| use colormap ID | HC_Set_Driver_Options |
| use window ID | HC_Set_Driver_Options |
| warnings | HC_Define_System_Options |
| write mask | HC_Set_Driver_Options |

**Table 4.1**    List of HOOPS options and heuristics.

### 4.4.4    Info

In addition to options, there is a separate kind of information that HOOPS calls *info*. The difference between an option and info is that an option can be changed, whereas info is fixed information about a specific device or feature that cannot be changed. There are three types of info in HOOPS: system info, device info, and font info.

**4.4.4.1**    **System info.** Returned with the HC_Show_System_Info command, system info is information about the specific HOOPS library you are using. For example, you can ask what the version number of HOOPS is, whether intermediate mode is available, which renderers are available, and whether this version of HOOPS supports the Kanji Japanese character set.

**4.4.4.2**    **Device info.** Returned with the HC_Show_Device_Info command, device info is information about a driver or a device. For example, you can find out whether your hardware is capable of double buffering by using the command HC_Show_Device_Info("?Picture", "double buffer", answer), where answer is a character array that returns the answer "copy", "swap", or "none" (see Section 3.1.4 or the *HOOPS Reference Manual* for information on what these values mean). You can also find out the resolution of the display, the number of colors, the depth of the Z-buffer, and more. The HC_Show_Device_Info command takes a driver instance as an argument, since device info will be different for different drivers.

**4.4.4.3**    **Font info.** Returned with the HC_Show_Font_Info command, font info is information about a specific text font on a specific device. For example, you can find out whether a specified font is proportionally spaced, and in what sizes it is available. Or you can find out whether a font is available on both the display and a hardcopy device.

**4.4.5**    ## Index of Info

Table 4.2 contains a list of all the (nonchangeable) information that HOOPS can return to your program, with the names of the HOOPS commands that return these items. For the possible values of the information and what they mean, see the page for the appropriate command in the *HOOPS Reference Manual*.

| Info | Command |
| --- | --- |
| a.i.r. present | HC_Show_System_Info |
| a.i.r. version | HC_Show_System_Info |
| alive | HC_Show_Device_Info |
| character widths | HC_Show_Font_Info |
| colors | HC_Show_Device_Info |
| current window ID | HC_Show_Device_Info |
| define | HC_Show_Font_Info |
| display | HC_Show_Device_Info |
| display type | HC_Show_Device_Info |
| double buffer | HC_Show_Device_Info |
| driver type | HC_Show_Device_Info |
| driver version | HC_Show_Device_Info |
| exists | HC_Show_Device_Info |
| exists | HC_Show_Font_Info |
| generic name | HC_Show_Font_Info |
| Gouraud shading | HC_Show_Device_Info |
| hardware cutting planes | HC_Show_Device_Info |
| hardware lights | HC_Show_Device_Info |
| hoops version | HC_Show_System_Info |
| i.m. present | HC_Show_System_Info |
| i.m. version | HC_Show_System_Info |
| kanji present | HC_Show_System_Info |
| keyboard | HC_Show_Device_Info |
| locater | HC_Show_Device_Info |
| locater buttons | HC_Show_Device_Info |
| locater type | HC_Show_Device_Info |
| max colors | HC_Show_Device_Info |

| | |
|---|---|
| max character | HC_Show_Font_Info |
| max pixels | HC_Show_Device_Info |
| max size | HC_Show_Device_Info |
| Phong lighting | HC_Show_Device_Info |
| pixel aspect ratio | HC_Show_Device_Info |
| pixels | HC_Show_Device_Info |
| planes | HC_Show_Device_Info |
| points to sru | HC_Show_Font_Info |
| proportional | HC_Show_Font_Info |
| resolution | HC_Show_Device_Info |
| rotatable | HC_Show_Font_Info |
| scalable | HC_Show_Font_Info |
| size | HC_Show_Device_Info |
| sizes | HC_Show_Font_Info |
| slantable | HC_Show_Font_Info |
| started | HC_Show_Device_Info |
| window aspect ratio | HC_Show_Device_Info |
| windowing system | HC_Show_Device_Info |
| Z buffer depth | HC_Show_Device_Info |

**Table 4.2**     List of HOOPS info.

## 4.4.6        Setting of Options at Run Time

Since options (including heuristics) are character strings, they can be interpreted at run time. A big advantage of this ability is that they can be changed at run time without requiring a recompilation of your program. HOOPS provides a simple way to change them. When a HOOPS application starts up, HOOPS checks several environment variables to see whether they are defined.

- HOOPS_DRIVER_OPTIONS. The value of this variable is passed to HC_Set_Driver_Options, applied to the root segment.

- HOOPS_RENDERING_OPTIONS. The value of this environment variable is passed to HC_Set_Rendering_Options, applied to the root segment.

- HOOPS_HEURISTICS. The value of this variable is passed to HC_Set_Heuristics, applied to the root segment.

- HOOPS_SYSTEM_OPTIONS. The value of this variable is passed to HC_Define_System_Options.

These environment variables make it easy to tune your application. You can try out different options without recompiling your program, to see what runs the best. In addition, these variables allow you to tune your graphics application for a specific platform without making the application less portable. Your application passes in the tuning parameters through environment variables, which can be set by an installation script or manually by an advanced user.

Passing in information through environment variables is so useful that HOOPS uses several other environment variables. One of these is HOOPS_PICTURE, which is used to set the value of the "?Picture" alias (see Section 4.4.7). Other useful environment variables are HOOPS_APPLICATION, HOOPS_COLORS, HOOPS_TEXT_FONT, HOOPS_FONT_DIRECTORY, HOOPS_VISIBILITY, HOOPS_PICTURE_OPTIONS, and HOOPS_LICENSE. For more information on these environment variables, see Chapter 3 in the *HOOPS Reference Manual*.

How you set environment variables depends on your platform. For example, on UNIX systems, environment variables are set with the set or setenv commands, depending on whether you are using csh (the C shell) or sh (the Bourne shell). On Windows systems (Windows 95 and NT), you can set environment variables using the System control panel or the Registry editor. See Chapter 11 of the *HOOPS Installation Guide* for information about setting environment variables on your platform.

### 4.4.7 HOOPS_PICTURE Environment Variable

HOOPS assigns the alias "?Picture" to the segment name of the driver instance used to display the HOOPS database. In most cases, however, you will want to override this value. You can do so from inside your program, by assigning a new value to the "?Picture" alias, or from the command line by setting the value of the HOOPS_PICTURE environment variable.

If HOOPS_PICTURE is set, then its value is appended onto the alias "?driver", and the result assigned to the alias "?Picture". For example, if HOOPS_PICTURE has the value "ps/file1", then the HOOPS output is sent to the file named "file1" in PostScript format, rather than to the screen.

The HOOPS_PICTURE alias is useful if the default value of "?Picture" does not take advantage of special graphics hardware or software that you have available on your computer. For example, on many UNIX systems, the default driver is "x11", but if you have special graphics hardware, you might be better off using the hardware manufacturer's native language for it (such as GL on a Silicon

Graphics system, Starbase on an HP system, or XGL on a Sun). See Section 4.3, or the chapter of the *HOOPS Installation Guide* for your system, for more information.

On a system running X11, HOOPS_PICTURE can be used to reroute the display output to a remote X display. For example, if HOOPS_PICTURE is set to "x11/ralph:0.0", then HOOPS output is sent to the display on the machine named "ralph" (the string "ralph:0.0" is X syntax; for more information, see your documentation for X11).

## 4.5    Mapping of Model and View

In Chapter 2, we saw the advantages of separating your application's model from its views. In this section, we discuss how to set up a correspondence between your application's data model and a view stored in the HOOPS database (Figure 4.14).

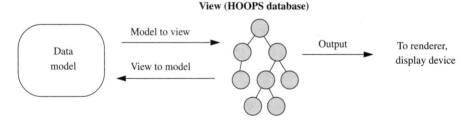

**Figure 4.14**    Mapping of model and view.

For simplicity, in this section, we shall assume that there is only a single active view, but multiple views of the same data model could be handled the same way.

To set up the correspondence between model and view, we have to solve two problems:

**1.** Given a data structure in your application's data model, how do you find the HOOPS segment that holds a view of that data structure?

**2.** Given a segment in the HOOPS graphics database that represents a view, how do you find its corresponding data structure in the data model?

For example, the spreadsheet program developed in Chapter 2 (Programs 2.5 through 2.8) consisted of multiple cells. To write that program, we needed a way to map between the data structure representing a cell (C++ class Cell) and a segment in the HOOPS database.

Note that the correspondence between data structures in your data model and segments in the HOOPS database might not be a one-to-one correspondence. In particular, a data structure in the data model can correspond to an object in the HOOPS database that is made up of more than one segment. In this case, we normally refer to the object in the HOOPS database using the segment at the root of the subtree that represents the object.

### 4.5.1     Mapping of Model to View

There are two ways to set up a mapping between your application's data model and the view stored in the HOOPS database: using segment names or using keys.

**4.5.1.1**     **Segment names.** In Chapter 2, the spreadsheet program (Programs 2.5 through 2.8) used segment names to map model to view. Each cell in the spreadsheet had a number, and the segment in the HOOPS database that corresponded to each cell had the name "cell $n$", where $n$ was the number of the cell. Therefore, to create a view of cell number 5, we used

```
HC_Open_Segment("cell 5");
```

and placed the appropriate geometry and attributes there.

In the spreadsheet example, all segments representing spreadsheet cells had the same parent segment, so we could use a single segment name to open the cell (assuming that the parent segment had already been opened). In a more complicated model, we might need to store a path name to the segment.

The main advantage of using segment names to map model to view is simplicity. The use of segment names is easy to program and simple to understand. It also makes your application easier to debug, since you can tell from the name of a segment what that segment does. However, there are a couple of disadvantages to using segment names. First, using a segment name requires that you either store the name as a character string in your data model, or reformat the name each time that you need it (as we did in the spreadsheet example). Second, opening a segment by giving a name (especially a path name) is slower than other methods, such as using keys (and can get slower as more segments are added).

**4.5.1.2**     **Keys.** A more common way to map model to view is through the use of keys; in fact, keys were added to HOOPS primarily to aid you in mapping model to view. The key for a segment is stored in the data model (as a 32-bit integer). Normally, the integer would be stored in the data model when you initially set up the view.

In the spreadsheet example, you could add a member variable to class Cell called d_segment_key, and could use this member to store the key of the segment corresponding to this cell. Then, to open the segment, you would use the command

```
HC_Open_Segment_By_Key(d_segment_key);
```

Using this command is about as simple as using segment names, but it does require an extra member variable in class Cell to hold the key (unless you renumber the keys — a trick that we shall discuss in Section 4.5.1.3).

An additional advantage of using keys is that, unlike names, keys can refer to geometry. This ability allows you to avoid using extra segments. For example, imagine that we are drawing a map of a computer network (such as the Internet). Each computer site is represented as a fixed point, and each connection is represented as a line drawn between two sites. Assuming that all these lines have the same attributes, we do not need to place each line into its own segment. Instead, we can use the key returned from HC_KInsert_Line, and can access each line directly.

**4.5.1.3**     **Renumbering of keys.** HOOPS has a facility that makes it even more convenient to use segment keys to map model to view. Normally, HOOPS assigns a key for each segment (or geometry), but you can change the key value with the HOOPS command HC_Renumber_Key.

For example, Program 4.10 creates a bar-graph view of a spreadsheet cell, for the spreadsheet example from Chapter 2. The HC_Renumber_Key command (on line 4) renumbers the key of each segment representing a cell to be the cell number.

```
1  void Cell::create_cell_view(long cell_num) {
2     HC_Open_Segment("?Picture/bar graph view");
3        long old_key = HC_KOpen_Segment("");
4           HC_Renumber_Key(old_key, cell_num, "global");

5           // code to set up attributes and
6           // geometry for the cell

7        HC_Close_Segment();
8     HC_Close_Segment();
9  }
```

**Program 4.10**     Renumbering of the key to be the cell number.

Renumbering the key to be the cell number makes accessing a cell convenient. Given the number of a cell, you can open the cell with the HOOPS command HC_Open_Segment_By_Key. For example, to open cell number 5, you simply use

```
HC_Open_Segment_By_Key(5);
```

Renumbering the key removes the need to store the key as a data member in the Cell class. Notice also that the segments used for each cell do not need to be named (the name is specified as an empty string, on line 3 in Program 4.10).

If your application has some sort of object identifier for each object in its data model (for example, the cell number), then it is convenient to use the command HC_Renumber_Key to set the HOOPS database key to be the object identifier. You can even renumber a key to be a C++ pointer to a data structure (see the example of how to do this renumbering in Section 4.5.2.2).

The key in Program 4.10 was specified as *global* (by the third argument to HC_Renumber_Key on line 4) — thus, each key in the database must be unique (or HOOPS will complain). You can also specify a key as *local*, in which case only keys for objects with the same parent segment have to be unique. A disadvantage of using local keys is that the parent segment must already be open before the child can be opened by key.

User-supplied keys must be nonnegative (positive or zero). The keys assigned by HOOPS are always negative.

Keys assigned by HOOPS are an encoding of the address of the HOOPS internal data structure used to store the segment or geometry.

Using renumbered keys is slightly slower than is using the original key, but is always faster than is using segment names. You can always restore the original key by calling HC_Renumber_Key and specifying the special value –1 (negative one) as the new key.

## 4.5.2    Mapping of View to Model

Mapping view to model is primarily necessary when you are handling input events, such as selection events. When the user selects some object on the screen, HOOPS returns to your application the segment and object that was selected. Your application needs a way to map that segment back to a data structure in your data model. For example, in our spreadsheet example, the user might select one of the bars in the bar graph, and we need a way to figure out to which cell that bar corresponds.

This problem can be summarized as follows: Given a segment in the HOOPS database, how do you find the data structure in your data model that corresponds to that segment? Basically, you must store a pointer to your model data structure in the HOOPS segment. HOOPS provides several ways to store such a pointer, each one appropriate to a different situation.

4.5.2.1          **User options.** The simplest way to store application-specific information in the HOOPS database is with *user options*. A user option is an attribute, and behaves just like a normal attribute, except that it is supplied and interpreted by the user. You can have any number of user options; each user option is identified by a name, and has a value. Both the option name and value are strings.

In the spreadsheet example, we can create a user option named "cell number" whose value is the (string representation) of the cell number. For example, in the segment corresponding to cell 5 in the data model, we would store the user option as follows:

```
HC_Set_User_Options("cell number=5");
```

You can retrieve all the user options set on a segment with the command HC_Show_User_Options (if a segment has multiple user options, they are all returned in a single string, separated by commas). It is usually more useful to show a single user option; for example, the following code returns the value of the "cell number" user option:

```
char option_value[128];
HC_Show_One_User_Option("cell number", option_value);
```

The returned string will contain "5" as a string value, which you can convert into a numeric value (for example, using the atoi function).

Since user options inherit just like any other attribute, it is less error prone to return the net value of a user option, rather than the local attribute value.

```
HC_Show_One_Net_User_Option("cell number",
   option_value);
```

There are two main advantages to showing the net value of a user option. First, a segment has a local attribute value only if the latter was explicitly set on it. If you use HC_Show_One_User_Option and there was no user option "cell number" set on the current segment, then HOOPS will issue a warning. A segment always has a net value for every attribute. The default value for any user option is the empty string (""). If the user option called "cell number" has no value, then the HC_Show_One_Net_User_Option will return the empty string, rather than issuing a warning.

The second advantage to using HC_Show_One_Net_User_Option is that you will net any inherited value, rather than just a locally set value. For example, if a cell in a spreadsheet is drawn using multiple segments, we need to set a user option on only the parent segment of the subtree representing this cell, and the other segments in the subtree will inherit the value. That way, if the system does a selection event, and the user picks some geometry down inside the segment hierarchy corresponding to a cell, your program will still get back the user option for the appropriate cell number.

In this section, we stored a simple integer value for a cell number (albeit as a string). You can also store a C++ pointer value, by converting it into a hexa-decimal string and storing it as a user option.

**4.5.2.2**       **Keys.** Using HC_Renumber_Key, we can use a single key to map model to view and view to model, all at the same time. We renumber the segment key to be a pointer to the data structure in the data model. Given a segment, we can use its key to access the data structure in the data model. Conversely, given the data structure, we can use its address to open the segment by key.

First, however, we need to use a little trick. The problem with using a pointer as a key is that a user-defined key must be positive, and, when a pointer is converted into a signed long integer, it might be either positive or negative. The trick is to recognize that the least-significant bit of a pointer is always zero, because data structures are always aligned on word boundaries and the smallest word bound-ary of any architecture on which HOOPS runs is 2 bytes (of course, there have been computers in the past that aligned structures on byte boundaries, and some-one could always build a computer that will do that again, but we doubt that someone will, since the trend today is toward aligning structures on 4-byte or even 8-byte boundaries). This (relatively obscure) fact allows us to store a pointer as a nonnegative signed integer by shifting it one place to the right. For example, Program 4.11 uses this trick to store a pointer to the Cell data structure in the key.

```
1   void Cell::create_cell_view() {
2       HC_Open_Segment("?Picture/bar graph view");
3           long old_key = HC_KOpen_Segment("");
```

```
4            unsigned long addr = (unsigned long) this;
5            assert((addr & 0x01) == 0);
6            addr >>= 1;
7            HC_Renumber_Key(old_key,
8                    (long) addr, "global");
9            // set up attributes and geometry
10        HC_Close_Segment();
11     HC_Close_Segment();
12  }
```

**Program 4.11**    Use of an address as a key.

---

**C++**    The C++ reserved word "this" on line 4 is a pointer to the current C++ object; because create_cell_view is a member of class Cell, "this" contains the address of the current cell. Casting "this" to an unsigned long integer makes sure that the sign bits are ignored during the shift operation. We then cast addr to a (signed) long integer before passing it to HC_Renumber_Key (line 8). The assert statement (line 5) is checked only during debugging, but it also serves as documentation to let a reader know what this code is supposed to do. On some systems, assert is spelled ASSERT (using uppercase letters).

---

Given a HOOPS segment key, the function in lines 13 through 16 of Program 4.11 will return a pointer to the cell in the data model it represents.

```
13  Cell * view_to_model(long key) {
14      if (key < 0) return (Cell *) 0; // error
15      else return (Cell *) (((unsigned long) key) << 1);
16  }
```

**Program 4.11 (continued)**  Mapping of view to model using keys.

One problem with using keys to map view back to model is that keys do not inherit (only attributes inherit). If a selectable object is made up of multiple HOOPS segments, we need to make sure that all segments in the object map back to the same selected data structure in our data model. When we used a user option to map view to model, this mapping happened automatically when we set the user option on the root of the segment subtree corresponding to the object, because all the other segments inherited the user option from the root segment. If we map view to model by renumbering the key of the root segment of the object, the other segments do not inherit the renumbered key. If the user selects a segment that has not had its key renumbered, the view_to_model function will return a null Cell pointer. We cannot solve this problem by renumbering the key of all segments corresponding to the object, since keys must be unique (even if we use local keys, segments that have the same parent must have unique keys).

One way to solve this problem is to modify the view_to_model function to check the parent of the current segment (and its parent, recursively) if the current segment's key was not renumbered (by testing to see whether the key is negative).

Another way to solve this problem is through careful use of the HC_Set_Selectability command to make sure that only segments that have had their key renumbered can be selected. For each object in the HOOPS database that has more than one segment, we renumber the key of the root segment, make the root segment selectable, and make all of its child segments not selectable. When the user selects the object, the selection event will return the lowest segment that is selectable, and that will be the segment whose key was renumbered. HC_Set_Selectability is discussed in Section 8.2.4.

---

On some segmented architectures (including old versions of DOS and Windows), a pointer to a function will not fit in a long integer, so you cannot use a key to store a pointer to a function. Instead, you must store the pointer to the function in a data structure, or else make the function be a member function of a data structure, and then store a pointer to the data structure in the key. User options do not have this problem, because they are not limited to a long integer value, but it is still a good idea to store only data pointers, rather than function pointers.

---

4.5.2.3     **Other (not-recommended) techniques.** There are two other techniques that can be used to store application-specific information in the HOOPS database: user values, and nonsense geometry.

Before user options were added to HOOPS, you could store a single long integer in a segment using the HC_Set_User_Value command. This command is now obsolete (you will still find it in the back of the *HOOPS Reference Manual*, along with warnings advising you to use user options or to renumber keys instead). There are two advantages to using a user value instead of a user option: (1) the user value is stored as a long integer, so it does not have to be converted into a string (unlike a user option); and (2) it can be negative (unlike a key).

If you need to store a large amount of application-specific information in the HOOPS database, a possible scheme is to convert this information into an array of points or an image, and to store it in the database as geometry. The only advantage of this technique is that the data will be written out into a HOOPS metafile (see Section 6.3 for information about metafiles), and can be read back in. Just make sure that you turn off visibility for that part of the database (unless you are one of those people who likes watching TV after the station has gone off the air).

## 4.6     The Tao of HOOPS

Like any good computer system, HOOPS embodies a language and a philosophy. Learning a few simple principles will make it easier for you to use HOOPS.

As its name specifies, HOOPS is a *hierarchical, object-oriented picture system*. HOOPS takes advantage of this hierarchy in ways significantly beyond those found in any other graphics system. The objects in this hierarchy are *segments*, and the majority of operations in HOOPS are performed on segments.

### 4.6.1     Language

The language of HOOPS has just a few dozen nouns and verbs, but, as you can in any language, you can make many sentences with just a few words. There are about 1000 commands in HOOPS — far too many for you to learn all of them — but if you know the vocabulary of HOOPS, you will almost always guess the right command for a particular task on the first try.

A HOOPS command consists of a verb followed by a noun; for example, in HC_Set_Color, the verb is Set and the noun is Color. There are also adverbs, prepositions, and a few other common parts of speech. Sections 4.6.1.1 through 4.6.1.6 contain the grammar rules for HOOPS.

#### 4.6.1.1     Nouns. The nouns in HOOPS are

- *Attributes*: for example, Color or Line_Weight

- *Geometry*: for example, Circle or Polygon

- *Events*: for example, Location_Event or Selection_Event

- Other objects: for example, Segment

**174**

**4.6.1.2**     **Verbs.** The most common HOOPS verbs are

- *Set*: Set assigns a value for an attribute. The Set verb is used with a noun that is an attribute — for example, HC_Set_Color or HC_Set_Line_Weight. A Set command sets the value of an attribute on the currently open segment. If this segment already has a value for the attribute being set, the old value is discarded.

- *UnSet*: UnSet is the opposite of Set. It removes a local attribute from a segment, so that the attribute can be inherited. On a newly created segment, all attributes are initially unset, so you typically need to unset an attribute only if you set it previously.

  For attributes that have values on and off, setting the attribute off is not the same as unsetting it. For example

  ```
  HC_Set_Visibility("off");
  ```

  makes the current segment invisible, whereas

  ```
  HC_UnSet_Visibility();
  ```

  says that the current segment inherits its visibility attribute from its parent segment (whose visibility may be on or off, or itself inherited).

- *UnSet_One*: Although many attributes have single values (such as visibility and line weight), a few attributes are *composite* — they are made up of multiple values. For example, the Color attribute is a composite attribute. We can use the HC_Set_Color command to set the color of lines, polygon faces, text, and lights, and we can also use it to set material attributes, such as the diffuse, specular, gloss, and transmissive colors. The HC_UnSet_Color command discards *all* color information in a segment. If you want to unset a single color attribute, use the HC_UnSet_One_Color command. For example, to unset the line color only, you can say

  ```
  HC_UnSet_One_Color("lines");
  ```

  and the line color will be inherited, and the other color attributes (face color, diffuse color, and so on) will be left alone.

- *Insert*: The Insert verb inserts a new piece of geometry into the currently open segment. The arguments depend on the kind of geometric entity being inserted. Examples are

  ```
  HC_Insert_Circle(point1, point2, point3);
  HC_Insert_Cutting_Plane(a, b, c, d);
  HC_Insert_Local_Light(0.0, 5.0, 10.0);
  HC_Insert_Text(0.0, 0.0, 0.0, "hello, world!");
  ```

- *Define*: In HOOPS, almost every possible setting on the graphics system is implemented as an attribute on a segment. This characteristic is one of the ways that HOOPS is object oriented and declarative. Even so, there are a few settings that are global — they affect all the HOOPS system, rather than only a segment. For example, the HC_Define_Alias command defines aliases such as "?Picture", the HC_Define_System_Options command defines options that apply to the entire system, and the HC_Define_Color_Name command lets you add new color names (such as "avocado" or "harvest gold") to the ones HOOPS knows. Commands that change global settings always use the verb Define.

- *Show*: Commands that use the verb Show always return information about HOOPS to the caller. This information may be an attribute that was set with the Set verb, the geometry of an object created by an Insert command, global information that was set with the Define verb, information about an input event, or system information. Here are examples:

```
// the color of the current segment
char color[256];
HC_Show_Color(color);

// the definition of a named color
char definition[256];
HC_Show_Color_Name("moose brown", definition);

// the elapsed time
float time;
HC_Show_Time(&time);
```

- *Show_One*: Like the UnSet_One verb, the Show_One verb is used to display one attribute of a compound attribute. For example, to show the diffuse color attribute of the current segment, we can use

```
char diffuse_color[80];
HC_Show_One_Color("diffuse", diffuse_color);
```

- *Show_Net, Show_One_Net*: The Show_Net verb is used to show the net value of an attribute (as opposed to a locally set value). The Show_One_Net verb is used to show the net value of one attribute in a compound attribute. If you want to see the value of an attribute that will be used by the renderer, you should show the net value of the attribute. It is a common programming mistake to use Show or Show_One to show an attribute value when you should use Show_Net or Show_One_Net (luckily, it is an easy mistake to track down).

- *Compute*: The Compute verb is used by utility commands. The utility commands are usually not strictly necessary to the operation of HOOPS; they are simply there to help you write your application. For example, the function HC_Compute_Dot_Product computes the vector dot product of two input vectors.

**4.6.1.3**     **Adverbs.** There are variations on HOOPS verbs that are indicated by the single letter prefixes Q and K, and by the suffix "By_Key". The 10 verbs in Section 4.6.1.2, coupled with these variants, make up approximately 90 percent of all HOOPS commands.

- *Q*: Q stands for the adverb *quickly*. Verbs that are prefixed with Q operate on explicitly named segments. For example, using HC_QSet_Color is equivalent to opening a segment, setting the color, and closing the segment. Note that "quickly" does not imply that the resulting program runs particularly fast — just that it is easy to write. Every command that operates on the currently open segment, using verbs such as Set, UnSet, UnSet_One, Insert, and Show, has an equivalent quick variant (called QSet, QUnSet, QUnSet_One, QInsert and QShow).

- *K*: The K prefix is used for commands that return a *key*. There are key-returning variants of the commands that insert geometry into a segment (for example, the verb KInclude), or create a subsegment, style segment, or an instance of an include segment (for example, HC_KOpen_Segment and HC_KStyle_Segment).

- *By_Key*: Commands that take a key as an argument (instead of operating implicitly on the currently open segment or taking an explicit segment name, as the Q commands do) are suffixed by the adverb "By_Key". An example is HC_Delete_By_Key. A few commands, such as HC_Edit_Polygon, whose noun is some kind of geometry, always take a key (since geometry is always referred to with a key), so they do not bother with the "By_Key" suffix.

- Combinations: Some of the adverbs can be used at the same time. The Q and K prefix are commonly combined. For example, HC_QKInsert is a quick insert that returns a key. The Q always comes before the K. Three commands — HC_KShow_Owner_By_Key, HC_KInclude_Segment_By_Key, and HC_KStyle_Segment_By_Key — combine the K prefix and the By_Key suffix, because they both take a key argument and return a new key. The Q and By_Key adverbs are mutually exclusive.

**4.6.1.4**     **Verbs That Apply to Specific Objects.** Several verbs are categorized most accurately by the object of the verb.

- *Verbs for segments:* Some commands — for example, the commands HC_Open_Segment, HC_Close_Segment, HC_Copy_Segment, HC_Create_Segment, HC_Delete_Segment, HC_Include_Segment, HC_Rename_Segment, and HC_Style_Segment — all have the same noun, "Segment". With the exception of Open, Close, and Delete, these verbs are used only with segments. The command HC_Flush_Contents, and its variants HC_Flush_Geometry and HC_Flush_Attributes, also operate on segments (see Section 4.6.1.6 on idioms).

- *Verbs for deleting entities by key:* If you have a key for an entity (a segment or some geometry), you can delete that entity with the HC_Delete_By_Key command. You can also delete the contents of an entity with the command HC_Flush_By_Key. These commands do not take a noun, because the key can refer to different kinds of entities (segments or geometry).

- *Verbs for transformations:* Even though transformations are attributes, they are different from other attributes in that performing a transformation on a segment does not replace the existing transformation. Instead, the new transformation is concatenated onto the old transformation. For example, a rotation of 5 degrees followed by a rotation of 10 degrees results in a total rotation of 15 degrees. Consequently, HOOPS has no HC_Set_Rotation command (since the Set verb would imply replacement of the existing attribute value); instead, this command is called HC_Rotate_Object. The HC_Scale_Object and HC_Translate_Object commands are similar.

  There is an HC_Set_Modelling_Matrix command that explicitly sets the modeling matrix (replacing any previous modeling matrix, and so deleting any previous Rotate, Scale, or Translate), and also a command HC_Append_Modelling_Matrix that appends a modeling matrix onto the existing transformation matrix. These two commands are used rarely. (Note that these two commands spell modeling as "modelling", with two letter ls.)

- *Verbs for editing geometry:* You can modify complex geometric entities — such as images, shells, meshes, polygons, polylines, and text — to change their geometry. The Edit verb takes one of these kinds of geometry as a noun (for example, HC_Edit_Polygon). In the case of a shell, you can edit the faces or the points separately with the commands HC_Edit_Shell_Faces and HC_Edit_Shell_Points.

- *Verbs for moving geometry:* You can change the position of images and text using the Move verb (for example, HC_Move_Image and HC_Move_Text). You can also move the position of a light (with HC_Move_Light_Position or HC_Move_Distant_Light), or the direction in which the light is shining (for example, HC_Move_Light_Target for a spot light).

  The one exceptional use of the Move verb is for the HC_Move_By_Key command, which is used to move an object (subsegment or geometry) from one segment to another (rather than to change the object's coordinates).

- *Verbs for opening and closing geometry:* Shells and meshes are complex enough that you can set attributes on their subparts. For example, you can set a color on each face of a shell or mesh. To do so, you open the entity (in the same way that you open a segment) using the HC_Open_Geometry command, then open the subpart (Edge, Face, or Vertex) on which you want to set an attribute, set the attribute, close the subpart, then close the entity.

  There is one special verb, MSet, used to set attributes on multiple shell or mesh vertices simultaneously, for speed.

- *Verbs for cameras:* The noun "Camera" has its own set of verbs using terminology from the film-making industry. The verbs that can be used with a camera are Dolly, Orbit, Pan, Roll, and Zoom (for example, the command HC_Zoom_Camera).

- *Verbs for events:* Another group of verbs is used for events. Some of these verbs are used with the noun "Event", such as HC_Await_Event, HC_Requeue_Event, and HC_Check_For_Events (note plural). Others are used with specific kinds of events. For example, the Enable, Disable, and Queue verbs can be used for Button_Events, Location_Events, Selection_Events, String_Events, or Wakeup_Events (for example, HC_Enable_Selection_Events). You can also define your own kind of event with HC_Queue_Special_Event, and can get rid of all current events with HC_Flush_All_Events.

- *Verbs for direct input:* The verb Get is used to get one piece of input. Get can be used with the nouns Button, Location, Selection, String, and Wakeup (note the similarity to verbs for events). The Get commands are convenience commands that enable a certain kind of event, wait for one event, and then return the value from the event. Although simple to use, they are limited to getting one kind of input. For example, if your application calls HC_Get_Selection, HOOPS dutifully waits for a selection and ignores all other input. If the user instead types on the keyboard, those events will be lost. We avoid using the Get commands in this book.

- *Verbs for metafiles:* The Read and Write verbs are used to read and write HOOPS metafiles (for example, HC_Write_Metafile).

- *Verbs for searching:* The Begin, Find, and End verbs are used for searching the database. The possible kinds of searches are Alias, Callback_Name, Color_Name, Contents, Font, Open_Segment, Segment, and Texture. For example, to print out all aliases about which HOOPS knows, you can use the following:

```
char alias_name[256], alias_value[256];
HC_Begin_Alias_Search();
while (HC_Find_Alias(alias_name) {
   HC_Show_Alias(alias_name, alias_value);
   printf("%s = %s\n", alias_name, alias_value);
}
HC_End_Alias_Search();
```

You can perform the same task with a color-name search to print out all the color names that HOOPS knows.

**4.6.1.5**     **Miscellaneous Commands.** For completeness, this section contains a complete list of the HOOPS commands that do not fall into one of the categories listed in the previous sections:

- HC_Abort_Program

- HC_Bring_To_Front

- HC_Control_Update

- HC_Exit_Program

- HC_Modify_Color_Map

- HC_Parse_String

- HC_Pause

- HC_Print_Version

- HC_Relinquish_Memory

- HC_Renumber_Key

- HC_Report_Error

- HC_Reset_System

- HC_Restart_Ink

- HC_Scroll_Text

- HC_Update_Display

Most of these commands are self-explanatory (you can look up those that are *not* in the *HOOPS Reference Manual*).

**4.6.1.6**    **Idioms.** Like any language with a history, HOOPS contains its share of idioms. Some of these exist for historical reasons; others are merely inexplicable.

For example, Q is a prefix, but By_Key is a suffix, even though the two perform similar functions. In addition, the Q prefix is much more common than the By_Key suffix. Almost every command that operates on the current segment has a quick variant, but only a few commands have a By_Key variant. The Q prefix and the By_Key suffix are never used together (because, if a segment is specified by key, then there is no need to specify it quickly by name).

Commands with the K prefix are identical to their non–K-prefixed brethren, except that they return a key. In C++ (and C), this prefix is superfluous, because the command could always return a key, and the programmer could ignore that key if desired. Unfortunately, FORTRAN requires subroutines and functions to have different names, so, to make it possible to call HOOPS commands from FORTRAN, there are two versions of all these commands.

Nobody seems to know why the commands to rotate, scale, and translate the geometry in a segment are HC_Rotate_Object, HC_Scale_Object, and HC_Translate_Object, instead of HC_Rotate_Segment, and so on. We imagine that this choice of noun indicates that a segment really is an object in HOOPS, that or HC_Rotate_Segment just sounded funny.

There are two different ways that you can delete objects in HOOPS, and correspondingly there are two verbs: Delete and Flush. You can use the command HC_Delete_By_Key, and you can use HC_Flush_By_Key. The Delete verb deletes the object indicated by the key, whereas the Flush verb deletes the object's contents, leaving the object itself intact. So far, so good. You can also use HC_Delete_Segment to delete a named segment, but you cannot use HC_Flush_Segment; instead, you can use the command HC_Flush_*Geometry*, HC_Flush_*Attributes*, or HC_Flush_*Contents*. These commands allow you fine control over what you flush out of a segment. (An earlier version of HOOPS had an HC_Flush_Segment command, but that command was made obsolete when the others were introduced.)

HOOPS distinguishes between attributes (set with the verb Set) and global settings (defined with the verb Define), but both of them use the same verb (Show) to show what was set or defined.

Even though the camera attribute is a compound attribute consisting of a camera position, camera target, up vector, field of view, and projection, it does not use the Show_One verb in the same way as other compound attributes do. For example, to show the camera position, you use the command HC_Show_Camera_Position, rather than HC_Show_One_Camera("position"). This syntax was necessary because the different components of the camera attribute return different values, so they need to have different commands with different arguments. In addition, there is no way to unset one camera attribute (because individual camera attributes do not inherit).

There are three commands that use the Set verb, but do not set an attribute on a segment: HC_Set_Normal, HC_Set_Priority, and HC_Set_Parameter. These commands set attributes on a subpart of a geometric entity (see "Verbs for opening and closing geometry" in Section 4.6.1.4). For example, the command HC_Set_Normal is used to set the normal vector of a face, edge, or vertex of a polygon mesh or shell. Because these commands cannot operate on a segment, they cannot take a Q prefix.

HOOPS is not consistent in its use of names for different coordinate spaces. Most of the time, the words *world* and *user* are used interchangeably to refer to world (user) coordinates, and the word *camera* to refer to camera coordinates. One command (HC_Compute_Coordinates), however, uses the word *camera* to refer to world coordinates (the claim is that this coordinate system is the one in which the position of the camera is set — ouch!), and calls camera coordinates *viewpoint* coordinates.

## 4.6.2     Philosophy

HOOPS has a definite philosophy. We have witnessed more than one discussion, when a new feature was being added to HOOPS, concerning the "HOOPS way" to implement the feature. Writing down that philosophy might entail filling an entire book. A few points that might affect you as a user of HOOPS are given in Sections 4.6.2.1 to 4.6.2.7.

**4.6.2.1**     **Lights, Cameras, Action.** In other graphics systems, the graphics database is used to store only primitives (geometry and attributes); other information needed to render a scene is kept separately. For example, we have already seen how HOOPS rendering options and driver options are stored as attributes in the database. Other information that is needed before a scene can be drawn includes the location and kind of lights, and the location and orientation of the camera. HOOPS takes the bold step of storing this information in the database too, right along with the graphics primitives.

For example, HOOPS treats lights as geometry. Thus, you use the Insert verb to insert a light (for example, HC_Insert_Spot_Light). On the other hand, a camera is an attribute, so you create a camera using the Set verb (e.g., HC_Set_Camera).

Because a light is geometry, it can be affected by attributes, so you can use HC_Set_Color to set the color of a light, or you can let the light inherit its color from a parent. Because a camera is an attribute, it can be inherited by the children of the segment on which it is set. Storage of information such as lights, cameras, and rendering options in the database reflects the declarative nature of HOOPS.

4.6.2.2 **Defaults.** Many graphics systems (including PEX, OpenGL, and PHIGS) require you to specify a substantial amount of information before you can draw anything. For example, you might have to specify a color and a line width before you can draw a line, or a font before you can draw a character. HOOPS has reasonable defaults for every possible attribute, so drawing a picture with HOOPS can be as simple as writing three lines of code. HOOPS uses inheritance to allow the programmer to accept or override these values as needed.

4.6.2.3 **Convenience.** HOOPS often provides multiple ways to accomplish the same goal, so you can choose the one that is most convenient for you. For example, colors can be specified by name (e.g., "dark reddish orange") or with an RGB (red, green, blue), HSV (hue, saturation, value), HLS (hue, lightness, saturation), or HIC (hue, intensity, chromaticity) triple, or as an index into a color map.

One problem with allowing attributes to be set in multiple ways is that, if you show such an attribute (for example, with HC_Show_Color), you may not get back the exact value that you specified (you will get back an equivalent value, but it may be represented differently). To solve this problem, you can use a command such as HC_Compute_Color to convert the returned value back to your preferred color system.

4.6.2.4 **Consistency across platforms.** HOOPS attempts to create the same image on all platforms, regardless of the underlying hardware. If you request a certain feature and the hardware does not provide it, HOOPS will fill in with software. For example, in many graphics systems, if you request Phong shading and the hardware provides only Gouraud shading, you get Gouraud shading. When you use HOOPS, you get Phong shading. The image may come up slower than it would were it computed with special hardware, but if speed is important, your application can always ask whether a specific kind of hardware is available with the HC_Show_Device_Info command.

Of course, if you request the color red and you have only a black-and-white display, there is nothing HOOPS can do short of writing you a check for a new system. Nevertheless, HOOPS goes significantly beyond any other commercial graphics system in delivering the same image across multiple platforms, regardless of hardware.

 Creating the same image regardless of hardware seems such an obvious goal, but most older graphics libraries were written by hardware vendors, rather than by software developers. It is to a hardware vendor's advantage to support only those features that are implemented directly by its hardware — that makes the hardware look better, and encourages you to buy the latest (fancy, expensive) hardware if you do not have a feature you need. Consequently, consistency across platforms is rare in graphics libraries.

**4.6.2.5**    **Heuristics.** HOOPS takes the view that it is good for the application writer to provide HOOPS with hints on the most effective ways to render a scene; these hints are called heuristics. Often, specifying a few heuristics can speed up your application dramatically.

**4.6.2.6**    **Strings.** Many attributes in HOOPS are specified as character strings. For example, colors can be specified with names such as "dark reddish orange" (there is also a way to specify a color by numeric value). One advantage of using strings is portability — HOOPS runs on platforms where an integer is as short as 16 bits and as long as 64 bits. Character strings are much more portable (even on newer systems that use 16-bit characters or Unicode). The use of strings also allows you to set attributes using environment variables, and to save them in ASCII meta-files. HOOPS contains a fast parser for character strings.

The use of strings also lets the programmer specify variable amounts of information clearly and succinctly. For example, you can use the HC_Set_Color command to set simple colors; to set different colors for the diffuse, specular, and ambient lighting; and to set separate colors for different kinds of geometry — and you can do so using your choice of color spaces (RGB, HLS, HSV, HIC). Likewise, you can use HC_Set_Rendering_Options, HC_Set_Driver_Options, and similar commands to set many different options, with different kinds of values. Without the use of strings, commands such as these would be complicated and would be much more difficult to use.

**184**

The only problem with the use of strings is that your compiler cannot check commands that change attributes to see whether they make sense. For example, if a program tries to pass a color to HC_Set_Driver_Options, the problem will be detected at run time, rather than at compile time.

**4.6.2.7**    **Segments.** As stated in Section 4.2.1, segments are the primary organizational principle in HOOPS. In HOOPS, however, segments primarily organize *attributes*, rather than geometry. In particular, attribute inheritance is controlled through the segment structure of the database. Consequently, the most effective way to use segments is to group together primitives with similar attributes. We shall discuss this idea in Section 10.1.1.

Although segments are meant to be plentiful and cheap, their overuse can swell the execution size of your program and can slow down rendering.

# 5 Geometry

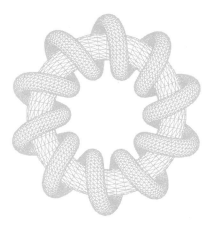

Chapter 4 dealt with two major aspects of the HOOPS graphics database: segments and attributes. This chapter covers the third major aspect: geometry. It also discusses the attributes that apply to each kind of geometry.

## 5.1 Coordinates

In HOOPS, as in most graphics systems, points in space are specified with Cartesian coordinates. Coordinates in 3D space are commonly called $x$, $y$, and $z$. HOOPS commands always take three coordinates; thus, all points in HOOPS are 3D. If we want to specify something in 2D, we simply use a $z$ coordinate of zero. HOOPS will notice the value and will automatically switch to using 2D routines as appropriate.

We specify coordinates in HOOPS using single-precision floating-point numbers, which on all current machines are 32 bits long. By default, however, C and C++ perform floating-point arithmetic using double-precision (64-bit) numbers. These double-precision numbers will be converted to single precision when they are passed to a HOOPS command.

| **C++** | On many C++ compilers, you can avoid this conversion cost by performing floating-point arithmetic in single precision. Make sure that all variables and constants in your floating-point expressions are single precision. Of course, you should ensure that single-precision numbers provide sufficient numerical accuracy for your computations. Note, however, that x86 processors do not have single-precision floating-point arithmetic, so they always perform floating-point computations using double precision. |
|---|---|

Some compilers (notably the Microsoft Visual C++ compiler) will complain when a double-precision value is converted to single precision, because of the possible loss of precision, even if it is obvious that no precision will be lost. For example, the following declaration will produce a warning message:

```
float foo = 1.0;
```

To avoid this annoying message, you can use the "f" suffix to designate a literal constant as single precision, as follows:

```
float foo = 1.0f;
```

For expressions, you can explicitly cast the value to single precision.

### 5.1.1      Points

HOOPS is inconsistent in the way that points are specified. A point is always three single-precision floating-point numbers, but points are passed to HOOPS in several different ways:

- Some HOOPS commands use three separate arguments to pass the three coordinates of a point. Each argument is a floating-point number. For example,

```
float x, y, z;
HC_Insert_Text(x, y, z, "hello, world!");
float x1, y1, z1, x2, y2, z2;
HC_Insert_Line(x1, y1, z1, x2, y2, z2);
```

- Some HOOPS commands take the points themselves as arguments. These routines always expect the *address* of the point. For example,

```
HC_Insert_Circle(&point1, &point2, &point3);
```

Physically, HOOPS requires you to pass it an address of three consecutive single-precision floating-point numbers, but there are several ways that you can create such a pointer. The two most common ways are as the address of an array of three floats, or as the address of a structure containing three floats. In the following code, the point p1 is an array of three floats, and p2 is a structure containing three floats.

```
float p1[3];  // array of three floats
struct Point { float x, y, z; };
Point p2;  // structure containing three floats
```

The actual declaration in HOOPS commands for a point argument (in hc.h) is a "void *". Because the memory organization of an array of three floats and that of a struct containing three floats are the same, either can be passed (as can any other data structure with the same memory organization). Unfortunately, this flexibility is purchased at the expense of type checking; later in this section, we shall describe a way to restore strong type checking to points.

If you use an array of three floats for a point, rather than a struct, then the "address of" (&) operator is optional when you pass a point to a HOOPS command, because arrays are passed as pointers in C++. The disadvantage of using an array is that the individual $x$, $y$, and $z$ components of a point are accessed via a subscript, rather than via a name (for example, the $x$ coordinate is p1[0], rather than p1.x), and assigning one point to another can be tricky because simply assigning one array to another does a pointer assignment.

- Some HOOPS commands take an array of points as an argument (usually preceded by a count of how many points are in the array):

```
HC_Insert_Polygon(5, array_of_5_points);
HC_Insert_Polyline(9, array_of_9_points);
```

In this case, you can use either a 2D array or an array of point structures (or some other data structure that has the same memory organization):

```
float array_of_5_points[3][5];
Point array_of_9_points[9];
```

In this book, we shall always use a structure to represent a point (and an array of structures for an array of points).

You can tell HOOPS which kind of point you will be using, so that it can do type checking. You just #define the preprocessor variable HC_POINT to be the C++ type name that you are using. An example is given in Program 5.1.

```
1    struct Point { float x, y, z; };
2    #define HC_POINT Point
3    #include <hc.h>
```

**Program 5.1**    Definition of type Point to be a struct of three floats.

Note that you must define HC_POINT *before* the file hc.h is included. Program 5.1 changes the declarations of all the HOOPS routines that take a point argument to expect a struct of three floats. If you define a point to be a struct of three floats in this way, then you cannot use an array of three floats for a point, of course.

You can define a point to be any other data structure with the same memory organization. For example, you can define a point to be an array of three floats by changing line 1 of Program 5.1 to

```
typedef float Point[3];
```

In this book, we shall always define a point to be a struct of three floats. Actually, the definition of struct Point that we shall be using also has a member function to allow the coordinates of a point to be set with a single function call (as shown in Program 5.2). Note that the *z* coordinate defaults to 0.0 (on line 4), so we can use the same function to set 2D points.

```
1  struct Point {
2     float x, y, z;
3     Point & set_point(float xx, float yy,
4                       float zz = 0.0) {
5        x = xx; y = yy; z = zz;
6        return *this;
7     }
8  };
```

**Program 5.2**     Definition of type Point.

For the examples in this book, you can assume that a point has the definition given in Program 5.2.

 **C++**     C++ allows a struct to have member functions, just like a class.

Any number of trailing arguments to a function can have default values. The function can then be called with fewer arguments, and the missing ones will use their default values.

The set_point function returns a reference to the point, so the resulting point can be used immediately in an expression (even in another call to set_point).

## 5.2     HOOPS Geometry

The kinds of geometry that HOOPS supports are markers, text, lines, circles, ellipses, polygons, meshes, shells, grids, images, lights, and cutting planes. Most of these kinds of geometry were introduced in Chapter 3; in this chapter we shall discuss mainly how to use them in HOOPS.

### 5.2.1      Information That Applies to All Kinds of Geometry

All HOOPS geometry obeys certain conventions.

**5.2.1.1**      **Boundary representation.** All geometric entities in HOOPS are represented by their boundaries — there are no solid objects in HOOPS. To create an object that appears to be solid, you define the infinitely thin surface of the object, called the object's *boundary representation*. For example, a sphere is represented by its surface, like the surface of a balloon, and a cube is represented by six square polygons. Such a surface looks solid, but if you insert a cutting plane (using HC_Insert_Cutting_Plane) to cut away part of this surface, you will see that the object is hollow. In addition, if you are not careful when you define an object, you might inadvertently leave holes in the surface, which would also expose the object as hollow.

**5.2.1.2**      **Tessellation.** The surfaces of objects are made up solely of flat polygons. For an object whose sides are all flat (such as a cube), flat sides are fine. But for objects with smoothly curved surfaces, such as cylinders and spheres, we must somehow represent the curved surfaces using only flat polygons. Creating a smoothly curved surface by breaking it up into polygons is called *tessellating* the surface. Unfortunately, such an object can look faceted, like a cut diamond. If we use enough facets and play a few tricks with our lighting calculations, however, we can get a surface that looks surprisingly smooth.

**5.2.1.3**      **Single versus multiple.** HOOPS geometry can be created in two forms, called *single* and *multiple*. The single form inserts a single object; the multiple form inserts multiple objects of the same type. For example, you can insert a single line using HC_Insert_Line, or you can insert multiple (connected) lines using HC_Insert_Polyline. Likewise, a polygon is a single object (despite its name), but you can insert multiple polygons using a mesh or shell (some graphics languages call a shell a polypolygon — but using *poly* polymorphously is too perverse for HOOPS!).

As we shall see, using a multiple form is not the same as using multiple instances of a single form. For example, a polyline with five line segments is not the same as the same five line segments drawn individually, and a shell or mesh is not the same as the identical set of separate polygons.

There are many attributes that apply to only multiple-form geometry. For example, in a shell or mesh, we can use smooth shading or texture mapping across multiple polygons, which is not possible with multiple individual polygons. In a polyline, the HC_Set_Line_Pattern command can specify how the individual line segments are connected (for example, using rounded, mitred, or beveled joints).

**5.2.1.4**      **Editing of geometry.** Some geometry can become large — especially geometry inserted via a multiple form. For example, a polyline can contain hundreds, or even thousands, of line segments, and a shell can contain equally large numbers of polygons. If an application wants to make a small change to a large piece of geometry, it can delete the old geometry and then reinsert the new one, but that approach is excessively slow. Instead, HOOPS provides a way to make changes to geometry in its database. For example, you can change a polyline using HC_Edit_Polyline. There are also commands to edit images, meshes, polygons, shells, and text.

**5.2.1.5**      **Attributes.** A few HOOPS attributes, such as transformations and cameras, can affect any kind of geometry, but other attributes were designed to affect only certain kinds of geometry. For example, line weight affects only lines. We shall discuss such attributes with each kind of geometry.

Some attributes — such as color, visibility, and selectability — can be specified on individual kinds of geometry. For example,

```
HC_Set_Color("text=blue, lines=red");
```

The syntax for specifying such attributes is flexible. Spaces before or after commas are optional, as are spaces before or after equal-to signs. The trailing "s" in words such as "lines" also is optional. You can use uppercase letters if you wish. Multiple specifications with the same color can be folded together — for example, "lines = faces = red".

You can also change the color of all geometry (of all kinds) — for example,

```
HC_Set_Color("geometry = green");
```

or just

```
HC_Set_Color("green");
```

Either of these last two commands changes the color of lines, text, markers, faces, and edges to green (but does not affect lights or windows). For more information, see the *HOOPS Reference Manual* entries for HC_Set_Color, HC_Set_Visibility, and HC_Set_Selectability; also see Chapter 9 in this book.

## 5.2.2     Markers

The simplest geometry in HOOPS is a marker, which marks a single location in space. The location is drawn with a symbol such as an ✕, a dot, or a circle. You can use markers to mark data points in a graph (such as the filled-in circles in the graph in Figure 5.1), or locations on a map (such as the ✕ in the map in Figure 5.1).

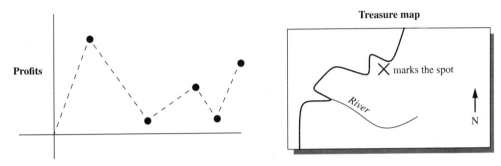

**Figure 5.1**     Markers.

Note that the two examples in Figure 5.1 are 2D, but markers are actually points in 3D space. For a larger example that contains the use of markers, see the clock-face program in Section 5.2.5.

HOOPS provides a large number of marker symbols, from which you can choose with the HC_Set_Marker_Symbol command. The default marker is a small open circle: ○.

Markers are considered to be annotation, rather than part of a scene. Thus, markers are always drawn in screen space, oriented to face the camera. That is, the marker's 3D position in the scene is transformed into a 2D position on the screen, and the marker is drawn there, upright and with a fixed size. Consequently, when a marker moves within a scene, only its position on the screen changes; its size and orientation remain fixed. As markers get farther away from the camera, they do not get smaller, and, if the scene rotates, the markers continue to face the camera (so that they are always readable).

You can change the color of the marker symbols in a segment using HC_Set_Color — for example,

```
HC_Set_Color("markers=blue");
```

You can change the size of the marker symbols in a segment using the
HC_Set_Marker_Size command.

There is no command to insert multiple markers. In the case of markers, there
is no difference between multiple markers and multiple instances of single
markers, so there is no need for a routine to insert multiple markers. If you
want one, you can define it as follows:

```
void HC_Insert_Polymarker(int size, Point array[]) {
    for (int i = 0; i < size; i++)
        HC_Insert_Marker(array[i].x, array[i].y,
            array[i].z);
}
```

The *HOOPS Reference Manual* mentions that you can insert multiple markers
using a mesh with face and edge visibility turned off. This technique is
slightly more efficient in terms of space, and produces identical results.

### 5.2.3     Text

You can choose whether text is treated as annotation or as a part of the scene.
Annotation text provides information about a scene, but is not part of the scene,
such as a label "origin" at coordinates (0, 0, 0). Numbers on the face of a clock,
or "flying logos", are examples of text that is part of a scene.

#### 5.2.3.1

**Annotation text.** By default, text is treated as annotation: It is drawn in screen
space, oriented to face the camera, horizontal, and upright. Text size and
orientation are not affected by any transformations in the scene; only the position
of the text is transformed. As you rotate and move a scene, annotation text will
continue to face you and will remain fixed in size.

The default size of text is 0.03 screen relative units (sru). Thus, the size of the text
is fixed relative to the size of the HOOPS output window, or, more precisely
(since text is measured by its height), the text size is fixed relative to the height of
the output window. The size 0.03 sru specifies the text to be 3 percent of the
height of the HOOPS output window on the screen. If the window is resized, the
text will change in size to match.

You can also specify the size of text in pixels— for example,

```
HC_Set_Text_Font("size = 5 pixels");
```

Text whose size is specified in pixels will not change in size when the output window is resized. You can specify size in pixels to keep small text readable, regardless of the resolution of the output display.

It is often desirable to specify the size of text in points — for example,

```
HC_Set_Text_Font("size = 12 points");
```

A *point* (not to be confused with a coordinate point) is a common text measurement approximately equal to 1/72 inch. When the text size is specified in points, the text will stay the same size, regardless of the size of the output window, and also regardless of the resolution of the display.

If your output display has a resolution of 72 pixels per inch, then a pixel is the same size as a point. If you have a 13-inch display, 72 pixels per inch corresponds roughly to a resolution of 640 by 480; on a 21-inch display, it corresponds roughly to a resolution of 1024 by 780.

So that text on the screen will be the right size when specified in points, HOOPS has to know the size and resolution of your screen monitor. HOOPS can find out the screen resolution, but there is no way for it to know how big your monitor is, so it guesses the monitor size assuming that a pixel is 1/72 inch (a point). If your monitor is a different size, or if your pixels are not square, you can use the "physical size" driver option to tell HOOPS the actual size of your monitor.

A text size is often specified in combination with a font name — for example,

```
HC_Set_Text_Font("Roman, size=12 points");
```

See the HC_Set_Text_Font and HC_Begin_Font_Search commands in the *HOOPS Reference Manual* for more information on fonts.

Finally, if your output window contains HOOPS subwindows (we shall discuss subwindows in Chapter 7), then it may be convenient to set the text size in window relative units (wru).

5.2.3.2    **Scene text.** You can also treat text as part of the scene (and make it fully transformable) with the command

```
HC_Set_Text_Font("transforms=on");
```

If your text is part of a scene (is transformable), you probably want to have the text size be in the same units of measure as the rest of your scene. In this case, you should use object relative units (oru). For example, the following command sets the text to be 0.1 units high:

```
HC_Set_Text_Font("transforms=on, size=0.1 oru");
```

How big 0.1 oru turns out to be on the screen depends on the camera and on any local transformations in the scene. With the default camera and transformations, the HOOPS output window goes from –1.0 to 1.0 in width and height, so text 0.1 oru high at the origin will be one-twentieth of the height of the output window, which is equal to 0.05 sru. Like text specified in sru but unlike text specified in points or pixels, text specified in oru will change size as the size of the output window changes. Transformable text specified in oru will also change size as it gets closer to or farther away from the camera (assuming a perspective projection).

5.2.3.3     **Other text attributes.** By default, text is aligned centered about its insertion point, so the command

```
HC_Insert_Text(0.0, 0.0, 0.0, "origin");
```

will place the word "origin" right in the middle of the output window. You can change the alignment of text with HC_Set_Text_Alignment. For example, to left justify text, you can use

```
HC_Set_Text_Alignment("<");
```

You can change the vertical alignment of text with the same HOOPS command. The default is to center the text vertically. To align text to the baseline of the text (the bottom of the capital letters), you can specify

```
HC_Set_Text_Alignment("v");
```

The "v" is supposed to look like a down-pointing arrow. You can specify a vertical and horizontal alignment in the same command. For more information and other options, see the *HOOPS Reference Manual* entry for HC_Set_Text_Alignment.

You can change the color of text with HC_Set_Color — for example,

```
HC_Set_Color("text=dark gray");
```

5.2.3.4     **Text as geometry.** You can convert text characters into other HOOPS geometry, such as shells. For more information, see the demo programs flylogo and fonteng in the demo/common/feature directory on the CD-ROM.

## 5.2.4      Lines

HOOPS has three ways to insert lines: single lines, polylines, and ink.

**5.2.4.1**      **Single lines.** A single line is a straight line segment. For example, to insert a line that goes from the origin to 1 unit in the $y$ direction, use

```
HC_Insert_Line(0.0, 0.0, 0.0, 0.0, 1.0, 0.0);
```

**5.2.4.2**      **Polylines.** A polyline is a sequence of connected line segments. To draw a unit square centered about the origin, use Program 5.3.

```
1  Point pts[5] = {
2      { -0.5, -0.5, 0.0 },      // lower left
3      { 0.5, -0.5, 0.0 },       // lower right
4      { 0.5, 0.5, 0.0 },        // upper right
5      { -0.5, 0.5, 0.0 },       // upper left
6      { -0.5, -0.5, 0.0 }       // lower left
7  };
8  HC_Insert_Polyline(5, pts);
```

**Program 5.3**      A unit square drawn with a polyline.

Notice that the first point had to be repeated at the end to close the figure, because polylines are not assumed to be closed.

**5.2.4.3**      **Ink.** An alternate way to insert a polyline is with the HC_Insert_Ink command. Ink works like the ink coming out of a pen on a pen plotter. The first call to HC_Insert_Ink moves the hypothetical pen to its starting position. Each subsequent call to HC_Insert_Ink moves the pen to a new position, inking a straight line segment as it goes. For example, to draw the same square as Program 5.3, given the same array, you can use

```
for (int i = 0; i < 5; i++)
    HC_Insert_Ink(pts[i].x, pts[i].y, pts[i].z);
```

The advantage of ink is that you do not need to construct an array of points. For example, you can read in coordinates from a file, and ink each one without having to wait until the entire file is read so that you can allocate an array for all the points. You do not even have to ink the entire polyline at the same time — you can close the segment being inked, and later can come back to it and resume inking where you left off.

You can terminate the line by calling HC_Restart_Ink. After that, the next call to HC_Insert_Ink will start a new polyline.

A polyline drawn via ink is considered to be multiple form, even though each line segment is drawn with its own HOOPS commands. That is, an inked polyline is equivalent to a regular polyline in all respects, but both are different from a sequence of calls to HC_Insert_Line.

**5.2.4.4**       **Line attributes.** You can change the width of a line using HC_Set_Line_Weight. The default weight is 1.0, which is usually a line one pixel wide (except on very-high-resolution devices — greater than 1000 pixels high — when it is one-thousandth of the screen height). You can force the line to be the minimum possible (a *hairline*) by specifying 0 as the line weight.

You can make a line dashed with HC_Set_Line_Pattern. The pattern is (usually) specified figuratively. For example, here are a few possible line patterns:

```
HC_Set_Line_Pattern("----");  // solid
HC_Set_Line_Pattern("- ");    // simple dashed line
HC_Set_Line_Pattern("-- --"); // long dashes
HC_Set_Line_Pattern(". . ."); // dotted line
HC_Set_Line_Pattern("-.-.");  // dashes and dots
HC_Set_Line_Pattern("center");// drafting centerline
```

There are other line patterns available; see the *HOOPS Reference Manual* entry for HC_Set_Line_Pattern for details.

Lines whose weight is greater than 1.0 are able to have *line treatments*. You can treat the ends of lines, and, for a polyline, you can treat how the individual segments join. The endcap of a line is specified as a prefix, and the line join is specified as a suffix, on the line pattern; you must specify a pattern to specify a treatment. For example, to round the ends of a solid line, and to mitre the joints where the line segments of a polyline meet, specify

```
HC_Set_Line_Pattern("(-->")
```

The leading parenthesis "(" specifies that the ends are to be rounded, the two dashes "−−" specify a solid line pattern, and the trailing angle bracket (greater-than sign) ">" specifies that the individual segments are to be joined with a mitre joint. The result looks something like Figure 5.2.

You can change the color of lines just the way you might expect — for example,

```
HC_Set_Color("lines=green");
```

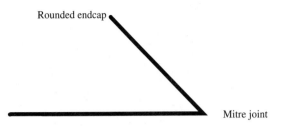

**Figure 5.2**     Polyline with line treatments.

### 5.2.5     Clock Example Using Lines and Markers

We now have enough geometry to draw the clock described in Chapter 4. Initially, we shall use lines for the clock hands, a polyline for the rim of the clock, text for the hour numerals, and a marker for the central hub.

This example (Program 5.4) begins with the definition of struct Point, and the inclusion of several standard header files. Remember that HC_POINT must be defined before hc.h is included.

```
1  struct Point {
2     float x, y, z;
3     Point & set_point(float xx, float yy,
4          float zz = 0.0) {
5        x = xx; y = yy; z = zz;
6        return *this;
7     }
8  };
9  #define HC_POINT Point
10 #include <hc.h>
11 #include <math.h>
12 #include <stdio.h>
```

**Program 5.4**     Clock example using lines and markers; initial definitions.

The next part of our example defines the main function. First, we open the segment "?Picture" and set options on it.

```
13   void main() {
14       HC_Open_Segment("?Picture");

15       HC_Set_Driver_Options(
16               "subscreen = (-0.5, 0.5, -0.5, 0.5)");
17       HC_Set_Heuristics("no hidden surfaces");
```

**Program 5.4 (continued)**   Driver options and heuristics.

The HC_Set_Driver_Options command sets the size and location of the output window. The display is assumed to go from –1 to +1 in each dimension, so this command creates a window that is one-half of the height and width of the display, positioned in the middle of the display.

The heuristic "no hidden surfaces" (line 17) tells HOOPS that the geometry that we will be using consists of lines and text, with no surfaces (no polygons or other filled objects). Thus, HOOPS does not need to perform hidden-surface calculations. We will get the same picture if we do not specify this heuristic, but it will usually be produced more slowly. It is always a good idea to specify this heuristic if your scene does not contain any hidden surfaces.

Another option that *probably* will be useful is

```
HC_Set_Rendering_Options(
        "technology=software frame buffer");
```

The rendering option "technology = software frame buffer" tells the renderer to draw everything into an off-screen buffer, and then to copy the buffer onto the display at once. This heuristic is useful for platforms that are slow at drawing primitives into the display (in particular, Microsoft Windows and Windows NT). Depending on what kind of graphics card you have, and assuming that you have enough RAM for the off-screen buffer, this option can dramatically speed up drawing. Some experimentation might be in order for your platform.

Now we get into the heart of this example. Remember that the "?Picture" segment is currently open (it was opened on line 14).

```
18           // clock geometry
19           HC_Open_Segment ("clock");
20             HC_Set_Color("dark blue");
21             HC_Set_Text_Font(
22                     "size = 0.1 oru, transforms");
```

**Program 5.4 (continued)**   Attributes on ?Picture.

The color of the clock is set to dark blue, and the size of the hour numerals is set to 0.1 oru. Thus, the size of the numbers is set relative to the other objects in the scene, rather than relative to the size of the output window (the default). We also turn on text transforms, because in this case the text is part of the scene (numbers on the face of the clock), and is not just annotation.

```
23              const float rimr = 0.98f;  // radius of rim
24              const float numr = 0.80f;  // radius of nums
```

**Program 5.4 (continued)**   Size of the clock elements.

The constants rimr and numr control the distance of the edge of the clock and the numerals from the center of the clock. Since the output window goes from −1 to +1 in both the *x* and *y* dimensions, the clock will nearly fill the output window.

Lines 26 to 39 contain a loop from 0 to 12 (making a total of 13 iterations). Inside this loop, we use HC_Insert_Ink to draw a polyline for the rim of the clock face, and HC_Insert_Text to place the numerals for the hours.

```
25              // for each hour
26              for (int hour = 0; hour <= 12; hour++) {
27                  double angle = hour * (3.14159/6.0);
28                  float x = (float) sin(angle);
29                  float y = (float) cos(angle);

30                  // rim of face
31                  HC_Insert_Ink(rimr * x, rimr * y, 0.0);

32                  // hour numerals
33                  if (hour > 0) {
34                      char buffer[32];
35                      sprintf(buffer, "%d", hour);
36                      HC_Insert_Text(numr * x, numr * y, 0.0,
37                          buffer);
38                  }
39              }
```

**Program 5.4 (continued)**   Clock rim and numerals.

The final part of the clock face is the central hub. For the hub we use a marker — a solid circle specified figuratively as "(*)" — whose color is set to reddish blue.

```
40          // central hub
41          HC_Open_Segment("hub");
42              // use solid dot for marker
43              HC_Set_Marker_Symbol("(*)");
44              HC_Set_Marker_Size(1.5);
45              HC_Set_Color("reddish blue");
46              HC_Insert_Marker(0.0, 0.0, 0.0);
47          HC_Close_Segment();  // hub
```

**Program 5.4 (continued)**    Central hub of clock.

Note that we have put the hub in its own segment, to keep its attributes separate from those of the rest of the clock. This separation is good programming style in HOOPS. In this example, however, the only attribute that conflicts is the color of the hub, so we could have left everything in the same segment and set the marker color with the command

HC_Set_Color("markers = reddish blue");

If we later change the hub from a marker to a polygon, it is easier to find and change the attributes that apply to it if the hub is in its own segment.

Next, we create the clock hands. Each hand has a different line-weight attribute, so each must be in a separate segment. But both hands are red, so we create a separate parent segment to hold the common color attribute.

```
48          HC_Open_Segment("hands");
49              HC_Set_Color("red");

50              HC_Open_Segment("minute hand");
51                  HC_Set_Line_Weight(2.0);
52                  HC_Insert_Line(0.0, -0.2, 0.0,
53                      0.0, 0.7, 0.0);
54              HC_Close_Segment();  // minute hand

55              HC_Open_Segment("hour hand");
56                  HC_Set_Line_Pattern("(--");
57                  HC_Set_Line_Weight(4.0);
58                  HC_Insert_Line(0.0, -0.1, 0.0,
59                      0.0, 0.5, 0.0);
60              HC_Close_Segment();  // hour hand

61          HC_Close_Segment();  // hands

62      HC_Close_Segment();  // clock
```

```
63      HC_Close_Segment();  // ?Picture

64      HC_Pause();
65   }
```

**Program 5.4 (continued)**   Clock hands.

The finished clock is shown in Figure 5.3.

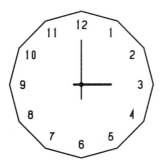

**Figure 5.3**      Clock drawn with lines, markers, and text.

Just for fun, we can make the hands of our clock move like those of a real clock. The lines in Program 5.5 replace the HC_Pause command on line 64 of Program 5.4.

```
1       // Define aliases for the hour and minute hands
2       HC_Define_Alias("?hour", "?Picture/.../hour hand");
3       HC_Define_Alias("?minute",
4            "?Picture/.../minute hand");

5       while (1) {     // forever
6          HC_Get_Wakeup(60.0);     // wait 60 seconds
7          HC_QRotate_Object("?minute", 0.0, 0.0, -6.0);
8          HC_QRotate_Object("?hour", 0.0, 0.0, -0.5);
9          HC_Update_Display();
10      }
```

**Program 5.5**      Moving clock hands.

The clock will run forever (until you kill it). Once each minute, the minute hand rotates 6 degrees (360 degrees in a circle, divided by 60 minutes in an hour) and the hour hand rotates 0.5 degree (the hour hand moves 360 degrees, divided by 60

**203**

minutes in an hour, divided by 12 hours, or one-twelfth the speed of the minute hand). Also try commenting out line 6 of Program 5.5 (the HC_Get_Wakeup command that causes the clock to wait 1 minute between updates) to see how fast your system can update the clock. My, how time flies!

 This clock does not keep accurate time, because it does not account for the time taken up by drawing. The HC_Get_Wakeup command waits 60 seconds, but HOOPS also takes a small but finite amount of time to recalculate and redraw the clock, so the clock will fall behind. We can fix this problem by using HC_Enable_Wakeup_Events and HC_Await_Event to get a series of wake-up events spaced 1 minute apart. We introduced events in Chapter 3; we shall discuss them in detail in Chapter 8. In addition, to make our clock useful, we would need a way to set the time, so that the clock did not always start at midnight.

### 5.2.6     Polygons

A polygon defines a flat surface in space. The polygon has an edge and a face. To draw a unit square centered about the origin, use Program 5.6.

```
1  Point pts[4] = {
2      { -0.5, -0.5, 0.0 },    // lower left
3      { 0.5, -0.5, 0.0 },     // lower right
4      { 0.5, 0.5, 0.0 },      // upper right
5      { -0.5, 0.5, 0.0 },     // upper left
6  };

7  HC_Insert_Polygon(4, pts);
```

**Program 5.6**     Unit square drawn with a polygon.

The square drawn by Program 5.6 is similar to the unit square that we drew using a polyline (in Program 5.3), except that now we need to specify only four points, because HOOPS will close the polygon automatically (it is not an error to specify the closing point, but HOOPS will ignore the redundant point). In addition, a polygon defines a surface, so this unit square will be colored in. Finally, unlike a polyline, a polygon must be flat. The points specified must all lie on a plane (if they do not, HOOPS will not complain, but hidden-surface elimination and lighting may not work properly). One way to ensure that polygons sent to HOOPS are planar is to break up your polygons into triangles, since triangles are always planar.

**5.2.6.1**     **Polygon attributes.** A polygon consists of two separate parts: the edge and the face. You can set attributes on these two parts independently. You can also choose to display either or both of them using the HC_Set_Visibility command. By default, both edges and faces are visible. To see just the outline of the polygon (so that it looks like a closed polyline), use

```
HC_Set_Visibility("faces = off");
```

To turn back on visibility for faces, you could use the same command with "faces=on", but it is usually better to unset visibility (so that it will inherit), rather than to turn it on explicitly. For example, to turn back on face visibility in a segment where it was turned off, you would say

```
HC_UnSet_One_Visibility("faces");
```

That way, if you want to turn off all faces in a drawing (for example, to get a wireframe view), you can just set to *off* the visibility of faces on "?Picture", and all faces in the drawing will vanish. If you had explicitly set to *on* the visibility of faces somewhere down in the database, then those faces would remain on.

To set the line weight of the polygon edge, use HC_Set_Edge_Weight; to set the line pattern of the edge, use HC_Set_Edge_Pattern. These commands work analogously to HC_Set_Line_Weight and HC_Set_Line_Pattern. Because polygon edges are always closed with no ends, the endcap line treatment of the edge pattern is ignored. The line-join treatment does work — it defines how the line segments in the edge of a polygon are joined (but, as is true for polylines, only if the edge weight is greater than 1). For example, to define a polygon with rounded corners, use

```
HC_Set_Edge_Weight(4.0);
HC_Set_Edge_Pattern("--)");
```

You can apply a pattern to the face of a polygon using HC_Set_Face_Pattern. A face pattern is similar to — but not the same as — a texture (in any case, a texture can be applied to only a shell, mesh, or window). As are line and edge patterns, a face pattern is specified figuratively. Here are some common face patterns (see HC_Set_Face_Pattern in the *HOOPS Reference Manual* for more patterns):

```
HC_Set_Face_Pattern("##");     // crosshatch
HC_Set_Face_Pattern("::");     // dotted
HC_Set_Face_Pattern("<><>");   // diamonds
HC_Set_Face_Pattern("||");     // vertical lines
HC_Set_Face_Pattern("==");     // horizontal lines
```

**205**

The pattern is drawn using the face-contrast color, whose default is white. To change the face-contrast color, use

```
HC_Set_Color("face contrast = gray");
```

Similarly, you can set the edge and face colors of a polygon:

```
HC_Set_Color("faces=orange, edges=purple");
```

By default, the edges and faces of a polygon are the same color. As an optimization, the edge of a polygon is drawn only if it is a color different from that of the face of the polygon, or if the edge weight is not 1.

**5.2.6.2**     **Clock example using a polygon.** Program 5.4 drew the rim of the clock using a polyline. If we want to color in the face of the clock, we must use a polygon instead. There is no "ink" equivalent for polygons, so we must create an array to hold the points in the polygon. Lines 1 to 18 of Program 5.7 replace the loop beginning on line 26 in Program 5.4.

```
1          Point poly_points[12];  // point array

2          // for each hour (starting from 1)
3          for (int hour = 1; hour <= 12; hour++) {
4              double angle = hour * (3.14159/6.0);
5              float x = (float) sin(angle);
6              float y = (float) cos(angle);

7              // rim and interior of clock face
8              poly_points[hour-1].set_point(
9                      rimr*x, rimr*y, 0.0);

10             // hour numerals
11             char buffer[8];
12             sprintf(buffer, "%d", hour);
13             HC_Insert_Text(numr * x, numr * y, 0.0,
14                     buffer);
15         }

16         HC_Set_Color("faces=light silver");
17         HC_Set_Edge_Weight(3.0);
18         HC_Insert_Polygon(12, poly_points);
```

**Program 5.7**     Clock example using a polygon.

The loop now goes from 1 to 12 (12 iterations, instead of 13), because we do not need to close the polygon. The poly_points array, however, is subscripted from 0 to 11, so we have to subtract 1 from the subscript in line 8.

Note that, for now, we shall continue to specify the heuristic "no hidden surfaces", even though our scene now contains a surface. We shall discuss this issue in Section 5.2.8.

The clock now looks like the picture in Figure 5.4.

**Figure 5.4**     Clock example using polygons.

Note that we changed the face color to light silver on line 16 of Program 5.7. If we had not done so, then the face color would be dark blue, just like the rest of the geometry in the face, and the hands would not be visible. You can also change the text color (for the hour numerals) and the edge color (for the rim of the clock) independently. You can change the face pattern using HC_Set_Face_Pattern. For a "retro" look, try changing the edge of the clock face to a dotted line, and the face pattern to dotted.

### 5.2.7     Circles and Ellipses

A circle is defined by three points on the edge of the circle. These points cannot be colinear (if they are, HOOPS will complain).

Why does HOOPS not define a circle with a center point and a radius? Because HOOPS circles are 3D, and a center point and radius define a circle only in 2D. It turns out that, in 3D, the easiest way to specify a circle is with three points. In the clock example, everything is in the 2D plane, where the $z$ coordinate is 0, so Program 5.8 is a simple routine to draw a circle in the $z = 0$ plane, given a center point and a radius.

```
1  void insert_2D_Circle(float x, float y, float r) {
2      Point cp1, cp2, cp3;
3      cp1.set_point(x, y+r, 0.0);   // 12 o'clock
4      cp2.set_point(x+r, y, 0.0);   // 3 o'clock
5      cp3.set_point(x, y-r, 0.0);   // 6 o'clock
6      HC_Insert_Circle(&cp1, &cp2, &cp3);
7  }
```

**Program 5.8**     Routine to draw a 2D circle.

Program 5.8 uses the points at the top, right, and bottom of a circle to define that circle. Any three distinct points on the circle would have worked as well.

In addition to commands to insert circles, HOOPS also has commands to insert circular arcs, circular chords, circular wedges, ellipses, and elliptical arcs. For more information, see the respective entries in the *HOOPS Reference Manual,* or look at the example in Section 5.4, which creates a scene containing one primitive of each possible type.

**5.2.7.1**     **Circle attributes.** Like a polygon, a circle has an edge and a face. All attributes that apply to polygons also apply to circles (including edge pattern, but not including the "line join" part of the edge pattern, since the edges of circles do not contain separate segments with line joins).

**5.2.7.2**     **Clock example using circles.** In the next version of the clock, we use two circles: one to replace the face of the clock, and one to replace the central hub. We use the insert_2D_circle routine defined in lines 1 through 7 of Program 5.8.

The segment containing the hands is the same, so we shall look at only the rest of the clock, which draws the clock face and the hour numerals. The next part of Program 5.8 is the same as Program 5.4, except that the loop that draws the hour numerals no longer contains the commands to draw the clock face.

```
8      HC_Open_Segment ("clock");
9          HC_Set_Color("dark blue");
10         HC_Set_Text_Font(
11             "transforms, size = 0.1 oru");
12         const float rimr = 0.98; // radius of rim
13         const float numr = 0.80; // radius of numbers
```

```
14          // for each hour
15          for (int hour = 1; hour <= 12; hour++) {
16              double angle = hour * (3.14159/6.0);
17              float x = (float) sin(angle);
18              float y = (float) cos(angle);

19              // hour numerals
20              char buffer[8];
21              sprintf(buffer, "%d", hour);
22              HC_Insert_Text(numr * x, numr * y, 0.0,
23                      buffer);
24          }
```

**Program 5.8 (continued)**  Clock example using a circle — the hour numerals.

We draw the clock face using the insert_2D_Circle routine.

```
25          // rim and interior of clock face
26          HC_Set_Color("faces=light silver");
27          HC_Set_Edge_Weight(3.0);
28          insert_2D_Circle(0.0, 0.0, rimr);
```

**Program 5.8 (continued)**  The clock face drawn using a circle.

Finally, the hub is also drawn as a (filled-in) circle. Note that the radius of this circle is 0.03. By default, markers are approximately 3 percent of the screen height, so a radius of 0.03 makes our circle the same size as the marker that was used for the central hub in Program 5.4.

```
29          // central hub
30          HC_Open_Segment("hub");
31              HC_Set_Color("reddish blue");
32              const float markr = 0.03;
33              insert_2D_Circle(0.0, 0.0, markr);
34          HC_Close_Segment();   // hub
```

**Program 5.8 (continued)**  The clock hub drawn using a circle.

The rest of this program is the same as Program 5.4.

```
35              HC_Open_Segment("hands");
36                  // define hands here...
37              HC_Close_Segment();  // hands
38          HC_Close_Segment();  // clock
```

**Program 5.8 (continued)**   The remainder of the clock.

The clock now looks like the image in Figure 5.5.

**Figure 5.5**     Clock drawn with circles.

## 5.2.8     Drawing Order

The clock example is essentially 2D, because all objects lie in a single plane (where the $z$ coordinate is 0). At the same time, some of the objects are in front of other objects. For example, the hub is in front of the hands, the hands are in front of the clock face, and the hour numerals are in front of the face. Such a scene — where the objects lie in a single 2D plane, but some of the objects lie in front of other objects — is called a $2\frac{1}{2}$-dimensional ($2\frac{1}{2}$D) scene.

At this point, you may be wondering how, in the previous clock programs, did the hour numerals end up in front of the clock face, did the hub end up in front of the clock hands, and did the hands end up in front of the face? How did HOOPS know to draw the circle representing the hub in front of the circle representing the face? The answer is partly luck, and partly the rules HOOPS uses to constrain drawing order.

The primary rule that HOOPS uses to constrain drawing order (when hidden surfaces are off) is that the geometry in any subsegments is drawn after the geometry in the current segment. Thus, subsegments always appear in front of their parent segments. In the clock example, this fact guaranteed that the hub and the hands (which are both in subsegments) were drawn in front of the clock face. But we still do not know why the hub ended up in front of the hands, or why the hour numerals text ended up in front of the clock face. As a declarative graphics system, HOOPS is free to change the drawing order to suit its needs, and a future release of HOOPS (perhaps because of a new, faster rendering algorithm) may well change the order and cause the previous examples in this chapter to draw incorrectly. We need a way to guarantee which objects will be drawn in front.

We shall discuss three ways to guarantee that one object is drawn in front of another. One way is to turn back on the hidden-surface algorithm by removing the "no hidden surfaces" heuristic from the "?Picture" segment, and then to modify the $z$ coordinates of all objects slightly to put some in front of others. For example, we could give the hub a $z$ coordinate of 0.00, the hands a $z$ coordinate of 0.01, the hour numerals each a $z$ coordinate of 0.02, and the face a $z$ coordinate of 0.03. Larger $z$ coordinates are farther away from the camera, so objects with smaller $z$ coordinates (such as the hub) will be drawn in front.

---

Note that we kept the $z$ coordinates close together. By default, HOOPS uses a perspective camera projection, so objects that are farther away will be drawn smaller. Making the $z$ coordinates close together minimized this distortion. An alternate solution is to use the command

```
HC_Set_Camera_Projection("orthographic");
```

on the "?Picture" segment to turn off perspective distortion.

---

The second way is similar to the first, except that, instead of using the $z$ coordinate to define which objects are in front, we use a separate value called the *priority*. Each piece of geometry in the HOOPS database is given a priority value based on the order in which it is inserted into the database. The priority is a long integer that starts at 0, with each successive piece of geometry assigned successively increasing integers. If the "hidden surface removal algorithm" rendering option has been set to "priority", then HOOPS uses the priority value to determine the drawing order. Objects with a higher priority (inserted later) will be drawn later, and so will appear in front. You can find out what this priority value is for a particular piece of geometry with HC_Show_Priority; you can change it to a new priority with HC_Set_Priority.

The third way to guarantee that one object is in front of another is to use the HC_Bring_To_Front command. This command works on only those segments where the "no hidden surfaces" heuristic has been specified (or inherited). When hidden surfaces are off, geometry in subsegments is always in front of geometry in the current segment, but you can use HC_Bring_To_Front to put geometry from one child segment in front of geometry in another child segment.

Program 5.9 contains the clock example (with all extraneous attributes and code removed for clarity) with the ordering guaranteed by use of HC_Bring_To_Front. The main changes are on lines 28 and 29.

```
1   HC_Open_Segment ("?Picture");
2      HC_Set_Heuristics("no hidden surfaces");

3      // clock geometry
4      HC_Open_Segment ("clock");

5         HC_Open_Segment("numerals");
6            // for each hour
7            for (int hour = 1; hour <= 12; hour++) {
8               HC_Insert_Text(numr * x, numr * y, 0.0,
9                     buffer);
10           }
11        HC_Close_Segment();  // numerals

12        // rim and interior of clock face
13        insert_2D_Circle(0.0, 0.0, rimr);

14        // central hub
15        HC_Open_Segment("hub");
16            insert_2D_Circle(0.0, 0.0, markr);
17        HC_Close_Segment();  // hub

18        HC_Open_Segment("hands");
19           HC_Open_Segment("minute hand");
20              HC_Insert_Line(0.0, -0.2,
21                    0.0, 0.0, 0.6, 0.0);
22           HC_Close_Segment();     // minute hand

23           HC_Open_Segment("hour hand");
24              HC_Insert_Line(0.0, -0.1,
25                    0.0, 0.0, 0.4, 0.0);
26           HC_Close_Segment ();     // hour hand
27        HC_Close_Segment ();     // hands

28        HC_Bring_To_Front("hands");
29        HC_Bring_To_Front("hub");
```

**212**

```
30          HC_Close_Segment ();     // clock
31      HC_Close_Segment ();     // ?Picture
```

**Program 5.9**    Clock example with drawing order guaranteed.

We put the hour numerals in their own subsegment, so now all geometry except the clock face is in child segments of the "clock" segment. Thus, the clock face will be drawn in back of all other geometry. The HC_Bring_To_Front command on line 28 brings the hands to the front, and the same command on line 29 brings the hub in front of everything (including the hands). Because the hour numerals are now in a segment of their own, they do not need to be brought in front of the clock face.

It is also possible to reorder geometry within a single segment, without adding any subsegments. To do so, you can insert the geometry "by key", and use the command HC_Bring_To_Front_By_Key. You can also use HC_Bring_To_Front_By_Key to reorder segments by key. But remember that geometry in child segments will always be drawn in front of geometry in parent segments.

It is usually best to avoid the use of HC_Bring_To_Front to order geometry. After all, HOOPS is really a 3D graphics package, and we could argue that a clock should not be a $2\frac{1}{2}$D object anyway. Real clocks have depth and volume. If we want the hub to be in front of the hands, then we should place it in front of the hands by giving it a smaller $z$ coordinate. In Section 5.2.10, we shall define a clock with depth and volume.

The main situation in which the HC_Bring_To_Front command is useful is when HOOPS is used as a window system, when you can use the HC_Bring_To_Front command to bring one window in front of another. Windows will be discussed in Chapter 7.

## 5.2.9    Shells

A *shell* is a collection of polygons that forms a 3D object. If the shell is *closed*, with no holes in it, then the shell divides 3D space into two parts called the *inside* and the *outside* of the shell. A shell consists of one or more polygonal *faces*. Shells are typically used to represent common geometric objects, such as cubes and spheres. The advantages of using a shell, rather than using multiple independent polygons, are that the shell takes up less memory in the database, is faster to render, and can be smoothly shaded.

**5.2.9.1**     **Shell geometry.** You specify a shell using two arrays, an array of points called the *point list,* and an array of indices into the point array, called the *face list.* A separate array of points is used so that faces of the shell can share points with one another. For example, when you define a cube, each vertex is shared by four different faces, so you need only eight vertices to define six faces. If you defined the same cube using separate polygons (each with its own vertices), then each polygon would require storage for four points, for a total of 24 points stored in the database.

The face list is an array of integers. The first integer is the number of vertices in the first face, followed by an integer for each vertex, which are indices into the point array. For example, if the face list contains (3 0 1 2), then a triangle is formed from the first three points in the point array. The next entry in the face list starts another face, and so on.

Each face must be planar; in other words, all its vertices must lie in the same plane. In addition, the edges of a face must not intersect one another. Finally, all faces in a shell must have the same handedness; that is, the points must all be defined in the same direction (clockwise or counterclockwise), viewed from outside the shell. Other than that, the definition of shells is flexible. The faces do not even have to be connected, edges can share more than one face, and faces can contain holes.

Program 5.10 defines a simple rectangular box using a shell. The arguments to the routine are the location of the center of the box, and the box's dimensions. The returned value is the key of the new shell.

```
1   long insert_box (
2           Point & center,
3           float length_x,
4           float length_y,
5           float length_z) {
```

```
 6      // Initialize the point list
 7      Point points[8];  // array for shell point list
 8      points[0].set_point(center.x - length_x/2.0,
 9                          center.y - length_y/2.0,
10                          center.z - length_z/2.0);
11      points[1].set_point(center.x + length_x/2.0,
12                          center.y - length_y/2.0,
13                          center.z - length_z/2.0);
14      points[2].set_point(center.x + length_x/2.0,
15                          center.y + length_y/2.0,
16                          center.z - length_z/2.0);
17      points[3].set_point(center.x - length_x/2.0,
18                          center.y + length_y/2.0,
19                          center.z - length_z/2.0);
20      points[4].set_point(center.x - length_x/2.0,
21                          center.y - length_y/2.0,
22                          center.z + length_z/2.0);
23      points[5].set_point(center.x + length_x/2.0,
24                          center.y - length_y/2.0,
25                          center.z + length_z/2.0);
26      points[6].set_point(center.x + length_x/2.0,
27                          center.y + length_y/2.0,
28                          center.z + length_z/2.0);
29      points[7].set_point(center.x - length_x/2.0,
30                          center.y + length_y/2.0,
31                          center.z + length_z/2.0);

32      // Initialize the face list
33      static int face_list[30] = {
34              4, 0, 1, 2, 3,
35              4, 4, 5, 1, 0,
36              4, 2, 1, 5, 6,
37              4, 7, 4, 0, 3,
38              4, 7, 6, 5, 4,
39              4, 3, 2, 6, 7 };

40      return HC_KInsert_Shell(8, points, 30, face_list);
41  }
```

**Program 5.10**   Routine to create a rectangular box.

The points array contains eight points: one for each vertex of the box. The face_list array contains 30 integers and defines six faces.

Using this routine, you can insert a unit cube, centered at the origin, with the commands on lines 42 to 44 of Program 5.10.

```
42  Point origin;
43  origin.set_point(0.0, 0.0, 0.0);
44  insert_box(origin, 1.0, 1.0, 1.0);
```

**Program 5.10 (continued)** Insertion of a rectangular box.

5.2.9.2     **Shell attributes.** Since shells are collections of polygons, they have the same attributes as polygons do. For example, you can change the face and edge colors of a shell, the face and edge pattern, the face and edge visibility, the edge weight, and so on. Shells also have four features that go beyond the capabilities of polygons:

1. Vertex markers

2. Silhouette and perimeter edges

3. Attributes on subparts

4. Smooth shading

5.2.9.3     **Vertex markers.** Like a polygon, a shell has faces and edges; in addition, the vertices of a shell can have markers. You can change the marker symbol and the size for these markers, and you can turn off the markers with the command HC_Set_Visibility("markers=off"). For most uses of shells, it is common to turn off the visibility of markers.

5.2.9.4     **Silhouette and perimeter edges.** The individual faces of a shell all have edges, and you can set the visibility of these edges on and off as usual. For a shell that is not a closed surface, you might want to see only the *perimeter* edges of the shell — those edges that are attached to only one face in the shell — and not to see the interior edges between two faces in the shell (see Figure 5.6). You can turn on the visibility of perimeter edges with a special option of the HC_Set_Visibility command:

```
HC_Set_Visibility("edges=(off, perimeters=on)");
```

This command turns off the visibility of edges, and then turns back on the visibility of perimeter edges, so that only they are visible.

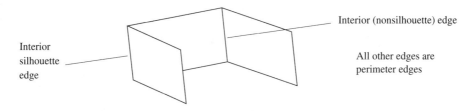

Interior silhouette edge

Interior (nonsilhouette) edge

All other edges are perimeter edges

**Figure 5.6**        Silhouette edges.

Another alternative is that you might want visible what are called *interior silhouette* edges. An interior silhouette edge is an interior edge (rather than a perimeter edge) that is visible in silhouette. An edge is visible in silhouette if one of its two attached faces is facing toward the viewpoint, and the other is facing away. In Figure 5.6, there are two interior edges, and one is a silhouette edge. All other edges are perimeter edges (they have only one attached face).

To make visible interior silhouette edges (as well as perimeter edges), you can use

```
HC_Set_Visibility("edges=(off, perimeters=on,"
                  "interior silhouettes=on)" );
```

There are other possible combinations. For more information, refer to the entry for HC_Set_Visibility in the *HOOPS Reference Manual*.

**5.2.9.5**        **Attributes on subparts.** Unlike for the other kinds geometry that we have seen so far, for a shell, you can set attributes on individual faces, edges, and vertices. This ability allows individual faces (and edges and vertices) in a single shell to have attributes completely different from one another. To change the color of a face, you first open the shell. Opening a shell is just like opening a segment, except that you must use a key (since shells are not named). Geometry is opened with the HC_Open_Geometry command. Open geometry is closed with the HC_Close_Geometry command.

Within matching open and close geometry commands, you can open an individual face, edge, or vertex, and can change its attributes. For example, you can open a face with the HC_Open_Face command. The argument to this command is the index of the face in the face list. For example, Program 5.11 sets attributes on the faces of a shell created using the routine defined in Program 5.10.

```
1  long key = insert_box(origin, 1.0, 1.0, 1.0);
2  HC_Open_Geometry(key);

3     HC_Open_Face(0);        // open the first face
4        HC_Set_Color("red");
5     HC_Close_Face();

6     HC_Open_Face(1);        // open the second face
7        HC_Set_Color("green");
8     HC_Close_Face();

9  HC_Close_Geometry();
```

**Program 5.11**    Setting of attributes on individual faces in a shell.

Program 5.11 opens the first face (index zero in the face list) in the cube, and sets that face's color to red. It then opens the second face (index 1 in the face list), and sets the color to green. The other faces in the cube are not changed. If a face has not had a particular attribute set on it explicitly, that attribute is inherited from the regular segment attributes.

You can set any attribute on a face of a shell that you can set on the face of a single polygon, including the face color, face pattern, and visibility. You can also unset these attributes (for example, using HC_UnSet_Color), and can show them (for example, using HC_Show_Color), just as you would unset or show an attribute on a segment.

You can also open an edge using the HC_Open_Edge command. The arguments to HC_Open_Edge are two numbers, which are indices into the points array of the currently open shell. There must be an edge between these two points. For example, Program 5.12 opens the edge that is shared by the first and second faces of the cube (which happens to be the edge between points 0 and 1 in the points array).

```
1  long key = insert_box(origin, 1.0, 1.0, 1.0);
2  HC_Open_Geometry(key);
3     HC_Open_Edge(0, 1);
4        HC_Set_Color("reddish green");
5     HC_Close_Edge();
6  HC_Close_Geometry();
```

**Program 5.12**    Opening of an edge in a shell.

You can set (or unset, or show) any attribute on an edge of a shell that you can set on the edge of a single polygon, including the edge color, edge weight, edge pattern, and visibility.

Finally, you can open a vertex using the HC_Open_Vertex command. The argument to HC_Open_Vertex is an index into the points array. For example, Program 5.13 marks each vertex of a cube with a different marker symbol.

```
1    HC_Open_Segment("?Picture");

2        Point origin;
3        origin.set_point(0.0, 0.0, 0.0);
4        long key = insert_box(origin, 1.0, 1.0, 1.0);

5    HC_Open_Geometry(key);
6        char * symbols[8] = {
7            "()", "(*)", "(x)", "(())",
8            "(+)", "[]", "[*]", "[x]" };

9        for (int i = 0; i < 8; i++) {
10            HC_Open_Vertex(i);
11                HC_Set_Marker_Symbol(symbols[i]);
12            HC_Close_Vertex();
13        }

14    HC_Close_Geometry();
15  HC_Close_Segment();  // ?Picture
```

**Program 5.13**  Opening of a vertex in a shell.

You can set any attribute on a vertex that you can set on a marker, including the marker symbol, marker size, marker color, and visibility.

**5.2.9.6**  **Shells and smooth shading.** One of the most significant capabilities that shells have (that goes beyond the capabilities of multiple separate polygons) is the ability to be smoothly shaded via lighting interpolation. Smooth shading is described in Section 3.3.4.5. There are two forms of smooth shading: Gouraud shading and Phong shading. Either can be applied to a shell.

The default is Gouraud shading. You can specify Phong shading using the HC_Set_Rendering_Options command. You can also specify whether to shade either faces or edges. To turn off smooth shading, use the following command:

```
HC_Set_Rendering_Options("no lighting interpolation");
```

Of course, if you want perform lighting interpolation, your scene should contain one or more lights.

HOOPS must be able to obtain a normal vector for each vertex in the shell. If you do not provide these normals, HOOPS will generate them by averaging the normal vectors for each face that shares that vertex. Even for simple shapes, such as spheres and cylinders, this average may not be realistic, and can produce lighting anomalies. To avoid this problem, you can set normal vectors explicitly using HC_Set_Normal. The HC_Set_Normal command is unusual in that it is valid only inside of an open face, edge, or vertex; it cannot be applied to a segment.

For the purposes of smooth shading, it is best to set normal vectors on the vertices, but you can also set normal vectors on the faces or edges of a shell, and HOOPS will average these normals to obtain the vertex normals for smooth shading. Alternatively, you can set the edge color or face color on an open vertex, and HOOPS will use these color values directly for color interpolation.

You can also unset a normal (so that it will go back to being calculated by HOOPS), and can show the value of the normal. The HC_Show_Net_Normal command returns the value you have set, or, if you have not set a value, returns the calculated value that HOOPS will use for that normal (there is no "inherited" value for a normal). The value returned by either HC_Show_Normal or HC_Show_Net_Normal may not agree exactly with a value that you set because of normalization (normalizing a vector keeps it pointing in the same direction, but sets its length to 1.0).

5.2.9.7        **Pseudo-coloring.** In addition to performing lighting interpolation (smooth shading), you can interpolate colors across a shell. You can use interpolation to visualize data using pseudo-coloring. For example, you can use color to indicate temperature across a surface. To interpolate colors, you need to set a color on each vertex using HC_Open_Vertex and HC_Set_Color (or some other color-setting command). You can turn off color interpolation with the "no color interpolation" option of HC_Set_Rendering_Options.

There are several variations on color interpolation; which one you use will depend on the kind of data that you want to visualize. For example, you can interpolate color values so that the color changes smoothly across a face, or you can interpolate color indices so that you get contour bands. The former might be useful for displaying temperatures when you want the color to change smoothly as temperature increases; the latter might be useful for displaying altitude on a map when you want all altitudes between (for example) 500 and 1000 feet to be the same color. See the *HOOPS Reference Manual* descriptions of the "color interpolation" and "color index interpolation" options in the command HC_Set_Rendering_Options, and the command HC_Set_Color_By_FIndex, for more information.

**5.2.9.8**     **The MSet verb.** Setting attributes on individual vertices can be tedious and slow, so HOOPS provides a special verb to set individual attributes on multiple vertices at the same time. For example, you can set all the normal vectors in a shell from an array of vectors with HC_MSet_Vertex_Normals. You can also set the vertex colors (using either the HC_MSet_Vertex_Colors_By_FIndex command or HC_MSet_Vertex_Colors_By_Value) and texture-map vertex coordinates (using HC_MSet_Vertex_Parameters). See the *HOOPS Reference Manual* for more information on these commands.

**5.2.9.9**     **Editing of a shell.** A shell can be large, containing hundreds or even thousands of polygons. If an application is making incremental changes to a shell, it will be far too expensive to require the entire shell to be deleted and then reinserted into the HOOPS database after each change. Instead, you can make changes to a shell while it is in the HOOPS database, using the commands HC_Edit_Shell_Faces and HC_Edit_Shell_Points.

A common use of these commands is to allow interactive editing of single points in a shell — to allow a user to grab a point on a shell and to move that point into a new position. Program 5.14 contains a routine to change the position of a single point in a shell. The arguments are the key of the (already-inserted) shell, the point to modify (the first point is point 0), and the new value of the point. If the value of the second argument ("which") is –1, then the final point in the shell is modified.

```
1   void change_shell_point(long key, int which,
2         Point &newpoint) {
3     HC_Edit_Shell_Points(key, which, 1, 1, &newpoint);
4   }
```

**Program 5.14**     Routine to change a single point in a shell.

The third argument to HC_Edit_Shell_Points is a count of the number of points to delete from the shell; the fourth argument is the number of points to insert. If these two arguments are equal, then the shell is updated in place, making this command particularly efficient. You can also use the HC_Edit_Shell_Points command for more complicated editing operations, such as adding new points to an existing shell.

To edit a shell, you might need to find out the current contents of the shell. You can get this information with the HC_Show_Shell and HC_Show_Shell_Size commands. You use the HC_Show_Shell_Size command to find out the sizes of the point list and face list, so arrays can be allocated for them. For example, use

```
1  int point_list_size, face_list_size;
2  HC_Show_Shell_Size(key, &point_list_size,
3                    &face_list_size);
4  Point * point_list = new Point[point_list_size];
5  int * face_list = new int[face_list_size];
6  HC_Show_Shell(key, &point_list_size, point_list,
7                    &face_list_size, face_list);
```

You can also use HC_Show_Partial_Shell and HC_Show_Partial_Shell_Size to retrieve part of a shell. For example, you can find out the value of a single point in the shell with the following command:

```
1  Point the_point;
2  HC_Show_Partial_Shell(key, which, 1, &the_point,
3                    0, 0, 0, 0);
```

The first argument is the key of the (previously inserted) shell. The second argument is the index of the point to be returned. The third argument is the number of points to return in the fourth argument (in this case, just one). The final four arguments return faces from the face list; in this case, they are not used.

**5.2.9.10**      **Optimization of a shell.** You can use the HC_Compute_Minimized_Shell command to remove redundant vertices and degenerate faces from a shell. This operation makes the shell more compact and faster to draw. This command takes the point and face-list arrays for a shell, and returns a new point and face list for the optimized shell. For more information, see the entry in the *HOOPS Reference Manual* for HC_Compute_Minimized_Shell. As an example of the use of this command, in Section 6.7, there is a program that constructs a shell from an arbitrary collection of polygons, and then optimizes it with HC_Compute_Minimized_Shell.

**5.2.10**      **Clock Example Using Shells**

This section creates a clock, once again, but this time built entirely using shells. The hub is a sphere, and the rim is a torus. The minute hand is a cylinder with a cone on the end for a pointer, and the hour hand is a cylinder with a cube on the end. The hour numerals have been left off. Figure 5.7 is what the clock will look like.

**Figure 5.7**    Clock example drawn using shells.

**5.2.10.1**    **Cylinder.** We have already seen the definition of the insert_box routine (Program 5.10), used to create a cube in Programs 5.11 through 5.13. In Program 5.15, we define a routine called insert_cylinder that creates a cylinder. A cylinder has a curved surface, so this routine tessellates that surface into a number of flat faces. The number of faces is controlled by the "resolution" argument. Program 5.15 leaves the two ends of the cylinder open; a different version might include two additional faces to close off the ends.

Each face in the shell is a thin rectangle. We must be careful that the handedness of all faces is the same (otherwise, HOOPS will issue a warning).

```
1  // tessellate a cylinder and insert as a
2  // HOOPS shell primitive
3  // the final argument is the number of
4  // faces in the tessellation
5  void insert_cylinder (
6      Point &center,
7      float radius,
8      float height,
9      int   resolution) {
```

```
10      // compute cylinder points and pack into an array
11      int   count_points = 2 * resolution;
12      Point * points = new Point[count_points];
13      float angle = TWO_PI / resolution;

14      // create two circles in xz plane
15      for (int loop = 0; loop < resolution; loop++) {
16         // circle at top of cylinder
17         points[loop].set_point(
18               center.x + radius * cos(loop * angle),
19               center.y + height/2.0,
20               center.z + radius * sin(loop * angle) );
21         // circle at bottom of cylinder
22         points[resolution + loop].set_point(
23               center.x + radius * cos(loop * angle),
24               center.y - height/2.0,
25               center.z + radius * sin(loop * angle) );
26      }

27      // compute the shell face-list array
28      int   face_list_length = 5 * resolution;
29      int * face_list = new int[face_list_length];
30      int * fp = face_list;

31      // compute all but final face
32      for (loop = 0; loop < resolution - 1; loop++) {
33         *fp++ = 4;       // number of vertices in the face
34         *fp++ = loop;
35         *fp++ = loop + 1;
36         *fp++ = loop + resolution + 1;
37         *fp++ = loop + resolution;
38      }

39      // compute final face; done separately to make
40      // sure the final face connects to the first face
41      *fp++ = 4;       // number of vertices in the face
42      *fp++ = resolution - 1;
43      *fp++ = 0;
44      *fp++ = resolution;
45      *fp = (2 * resolution) - 1;
```

**224**

```
46    // insert the Shell
47    HC_Insert_Shell(count_points, points,
48                    face_list_length, face_list);
49    // clean up memory
50    delete [] points;
51    delete [] face_list;
52  }
```

**Program 5.15**   Clock example — routine to create a cylinder.

**5.2.10.2**   **Cone.** The pointer for the minute hand is a cone. The definition of a cone is similar to that of a cylinder, except that one end is a point. Unlike in Program 5.15 (for defining a cylinder), in Program 5.16, the bottom of the cone is closed with an additional face (you could use the same approach to close both ends of the cylinder).

```
1   // tessellate a cone and insert as a HOOPS shell
2   void insert_cone (
3       Point & center,
4       float radius,
5       float height,
6       int   resolution) {
7       // create array of Points
8       int count_points = resolution + 1;
9       Point * points = new Point[count_points];
10      float angle = TWO_PI / resolution;
11      // base of cone is circle in the xz plane
12      for (int loop = 0; loop < resolution; loop++) {
13          points[loop].set_point(
14              center.x + radius * cos (loop * angle),
15              center.y - height/2.0,
16              center.z + radius * sin (loop * angle) );
17      }
18      // store point for tip of cone
19      points[resolution].set_point (center.x,
20              center.y + height/2.0, center.z);
```

```
21      // create the shell face list
22      int   face_list_length =
23         // triangular faces from base to tip
24         resolution * 4 +
25         // plus one circular base face
26         resolution + 1;
27      int * face_list = new int[face_list_length];
28      int * fp = face_list;

29      // compute all but final face in side
30      for (loop = 0; loop < resolution - 1; loop++) {
31         *fp++ = 3;// number of vertices in the face
32         *fp++ = loop;
33         *fp++ = loop + 1;
34         // tip of cone is at points[resolution]
35         *fp++ = resolution;
36      }

37      // compute last face in side; done separately to
38      // make sure that face connects to the first face
39      *fp++ = 3;       // number of vertices in the face
40      *fp++ = resolution - 1;
41      *fp++ = 0;
42      *fp++ = resolution;

43      // compute the base face
44      *fp++ = resolution;
45      loop = resolution;
46      while (loop--) *fp++ = loop;

47      // insert the shell
48      HC_Insert_Shell(count_points, points,
49                      face_list_length, face_list);

50      delete [] points;
51      delete [] face_list;
52   }
```

**Program 5.16**    Clock example — routine to create a cone.

**5.2.10.3**    **Sphere.** A sphere is a geometric object simpler than a cylinder or cone, but it is more complicated to define as a shell. The insert_sphere routine, in Program

**226**

5.17, breaks up the sphere into bands of latitude (with circles parallel to the equator dividing the bands). Each band is then tessellated into quadrilaterals, except the two polar endcaps, which are tessellated into triangles (one point of each triangle is the pole). Of course, there are many other ways to tessellate a sphere.

```
1   // tessellate a sphere and insert as a HOOPS shell
2   void insert_sphere (
3       Point & center,
4       float radius,
5       int    resolution) {

6       // create the array of Points
7       int    rows = resolution;
8       int    columns = 2 * resolution;
9       int    count_points = columns * (rows - 1) + 2;
10      Point * points = new Point[count_points];
11      Point * pp = points;
12      float angle = PI / resolution;

13      // create the points for the sphere
14      for (int vv = 1; vv < rows; vv++) {
15          // start at vv=1 to leave holes at poles,
16          // these holes will be capped with single points
17          // and triangles, instead of with quads

18          // create a circle of latitude in the xy plane
19          float latitude = radius * sin (vv * angle);
20          for (int uu = 0; uu < columns; uu++) {

21              // sweep a circle in yz plane that goes
22              // through point(vv) on semicircle
23              (pp++)->set_point(
24                  center.x + radius * cos(vv * angle),
25                  center.y + latitude * sin(uu * angle),
26                  center.z + latitude * cos(uu * angle) );
27          }
28      }

29      // now have a grid of points in (uu, vv) space of
30      // dimension (rows - 1 by columns)
```

```
31      // add points for endcaps
32      (pp++)->set_point(center.x + radius
33            center.y, center.z);
34      (pp++)->set_point(center.x - radius,
35            center.y, center.z);
36      // compute the face list
37      int face_list_length =
38            // number of quad faces
39            5 * columns * (rows - 2) +
40            // plus number of triangles
41            4 * 2 * columns;
42      int * face_list = new int[face_list_length];
43      int *fp = face_list;
44      int count_faces = 0;

45      // vv walks across rows
46      for (vv = 0; vv < rows - 2; vv++) {

47          // uu walks across columns
48          for (int uu = 0; uu < columns - 1; uu++) {
49              // quad faces connect row(vv) to row(vv + 1)
50              *fp++ = 4;// number of vertices in face
51              *fp++ = vv * columns + uu;
52              *fp++ = vv * columns + uu + 1;
53              *fp++ = (vv + 1) * columns + uu + 1;
54              *fp++ = (vv + 1) * columns + uu;
55          }

56          // tie the start and end together
57          *fp++ = 4;
58          *fp++ = (vv + 1) * columns + uu;
59          *fp++ = vv * columns + uu;
60          *fp++ = vv * columns;
61          *fp++ = (vv + 1) * columns;
62      }
```

```
63      // compute endcaps (use triangles)
64      for (int uu = 0; uu < columns - 1; uu++) {
65          *fp++ = 3;      // 3 points in face
66          *fp++ = count_points - 2;
67          *fp++ = (uu + 1);
68          *fp++ = uu;
69          *fp++ = 3;
70          *fp++ = count_points - 1;
71          *fp++ = (rows - 2) * columns + uu;
72          *fp++ = (rows - 2) * columns + uu + 1;
73      }

74      // tie the start and end together
75      *fp++ = 3;      // 3 points in face
76      *fp++ = count_points - 2;
77      *fp++ = 0;
78      *fp++ = columns - 1;
79      *fp++ = 3;
80      *fp++ = count_points - 1;
81      *fp++ = (rows - 1) * columns - 1;
82      *fp++ = (rows - 2) * columns;

83      HC_Insert_Shell(count_points, points,
84                      face_list_length, face_list);

85      // clean up memory
86      delete [] points;
87      delete [] face_list;
88  }
```

**Program 5.17**   Clock example — routine to create a sphere.

**5.2.10.4**   **Torus.** The rim of the clock is a torus (doughnut shape). We divide the torus into ringlike circular bands; then we tessellate the bands using quadrilaterals. We must be careful when we connect the two "ends" of the torus, to make sure that polygon handedness is kept consistent.

```
1   // tessellate a torus and insert as a HOOPS shell
2   void insert_torus (
3       Point & center,
4       float radius_inner,
5       float radius_outer,
6       int   resolution) {

7       // create the array of Points
8       int   count_points = resolution * resolution;
9       Point *points = new Point[count_points];
10      Point *pp = points;
11      float angle = TWO_PI / resolution;

12      // radius of toroid's cross-sectional circle
13      float radius_circle = radius_outer - radius_inner;

14      // radius from center of cross-section
15      // to center of torus
16      float radius_torus =
17              (radius_outer + radius_inner) / 2.0;
18      for (int vv = 0; vv < resolution; vv++) {
19          // compute circle in xz plane with
20          // radius = radius_outer - radius_inner
21          // circle is centered at center + radius_torus
22          float position_x = radius_torus + radius_circle
23                  * cos(vv * angle);
24          float position_z = radius_circle
25                  * sin(vv * angle);

26          for (int uu = 0; uu < resolution; uu++) {
27              // revolve each point in the circle around
28              // the line through center and parallel
29              // to the z axis
30              (pp++)->set_point(
31                      center.x + position_x * cos(uu*angle),
32                      center.y + position_x * sin(uu*angle),
33                      center.z + position_z );
34          }
35      }
```

```
36      // create the face list
37      int   count_faces = resolution * resolution;
38      int   face_list_length = 5 * count_faces;
39      int * face_list = new int[face_list_length];
40      int * fp = face_list;

41      for (vv = 0; vv < resolution - 1; vv++) {
42          for (int uu = 0; uu < resolution - 1; uu++) {
43              *fp++ = 4;// number of vertices in face
44              *fp++ = vv * resolution + uu;
45              *fp++ = vv * resolution + uu + 1;
46              *fp++ = (vv + 1) * resolution + uu + 1;
47              *fp++ = (vv + 1) * resolution + uu;
48          }

49          // tie the ends together
50          *fp++ = 4;
51          *fp++ = vv * resolution + resolution - 1;
52          *fp++ = vv * resolution;
53          *fp++ = (vv + 1) * resolution;
54          *fp++ = (vv + 1) * resolution + resolution - 1;
55          *fp++ = 4;
56          *fp++ = vv + 1;
57          *fp++ = vv;
58          *fp++ = (resolution - 1) * resolution + vv;
59          *fp++ = (resolution - 1) * resolution + vv + 1;
60      }

61      // finally, connect the corners
62      *fp++ = 4;
63      *fp++ = (resolution * resolution) - resolution;
64      *fp++ = 0;
65      *fp++ = resolution - 1;
66      *fp++ = resolution * resolution - 1;

67      HC_Insert_Shell(count_points, points,
68                  face_list_length, face_list);

69      delete[] points;
70      delete[] face_list;
71  }
```

**Program 5.18**    Clock example — routine to create a torus.

**5.2.10.5**      **Clock.** Once we have defined all the primitives that we need (box, cylinder, sphere, and torus), defining the actual clock is similar to defining previous clocks. Note that, on line 14 of Program 5.19, we turn off the visibility of markers and edges, so that the markers and edges will not be displayed in the shells (only faces will be displayed).

Also note that the pointer for the hour hand, which is a box, is placed into its own segment (appropriately named "box") on line 32. We put it there so that we can turn off the "lighting interpolation" rendering option for it. Unlike what we want for a sphere or a torus, we want the faces of the box to be flat — they are not an approximation to a curved surface, so we do not want the edges of the box to be smoothed over. The other objects in the clock use smooth shading to make them appear curved.

If the objects are to look solid and 3D, they must be lit. We light them with a single light, on line 11 (try deleting the light to see what the clock looks like). Lights will be discussed in Section 5.2.14.

```
1  void main() {
2      Point center;

3      HC_Open_Segment ("?Picture");

4          // these options may not be necessary
5          // depending on your platform
6          HC_Set_Rendering_Options(
7                  "hsr algorithm = software z-buffer");
8          HC_Set_Rendering_Options(
9                  "technology = software frame buffer");

10         // light the clock
11         HC_Insert_Distant_Light(5.0, 5.0, -5.0);

12         // clock geometry
13         HC_Open_Segment("clock");
14             HC_Set_Visibility("no markers, no edges");
15             HC_Set_Color("darker blue");

16             center.set_point(0.0, 0.0, 0.0);
17             insert_torus(center, 0.9, 0.95, 30);

18             center.set_point(0.0, 0.0, 0.0);
19             insert_sphere(center, 0.1, 20);

20             HC_Open_Segment("hands");
21                 HC_Set_Color("red");
```

```
22              HC_Open_Segment("minute hand");
23                  center.set_point(0.0, 0.375, 0.0);
24                  insert_cylinder(center,
25                      0.05, 0.75, 20);

26                  center.set_point(0.0, 0.75, 0.0);
27                  insert_cone(center, 0.15, 0.2, 20);
28              HC_Close_Segment();

29              HC_Open_Segment("hour hand");
30                  center.set_point(0.0, 0.2, 0.0);
31                  insert_cylinder(center, 0.05, 0.4, 20);

32                  HC_Open_Segment("box");
33                      center.set_point(0.0, 0.4, 0.0);
34                      insert_box(center, 0.2, 0.2, 0.2);
35                      HC_Set_Rendering_Options(
36                          "no lighting interpolation");
37                  HC_Close_Segment();

38              HC_Close_Segment();      // hour hand
39            HC_Close_Segment();      // hands
40          HC_Close_Segment();      // clock

41          // aliases
42          HC_Define_Alias("?clock", "?Picture/clock");
43          HC_Define_Alias("?hour hand",
44                          "?clock/hands/hour hand");
45          HC_Define_Alias("?minute hand",
46                          "?clock/hands/minute hand");

47      HC_Close_Segment();      // ?Picture

48      // animate the hands
49      for (int i = 0; i < 12; i++) {
50        HC_Update_Display();
51        HC_QRotate_Object("?minute hand",
52            0.0, 0.0, -30.0);
53        HC_QRotate_Object("?hour hand",
54            0.0, 0.0, -2.5);
55      }

56      HC_Pause ();
57  }
```

**Program 5.19**   Clock example constructed using shells.

### 5.2.11      Meshes

A mesh is similar to a shell in that it is a collection of faces, but a mesh is simpler than a shell, and that simplicity allows it to be stored and displayed more efficiently. A mesh is like a rectangular wirescreen mesh — it can be bent into an arbitrary curved surface, but it is still topologically a quadrilateral (it has four edges).

A mesh is defined by a 2D array of points. Figure 5.8 shows a 3 by 5 mesh (3 rows by 5 columns, for a total of 15 points).

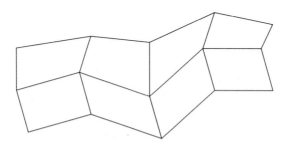

**Figure 5.8**      A 3 by 5 mesh containing eight faces.

This mesh would be defined as follows:

```
HC_Insert_Mesh(3, 5, point_array);
```

where point_array is an array of 15 points, specified row by row. Because the way in which the quadrilaterals are connected is fixed, there is no need for a face list (as there is in a shell).

The points in the mesh are connected into quadrilaterals. The quadrilaterals in a mesh are often not planar (as required by the renderer), so they are further subdivided in half into triangles. The resulting bands of triangles are called *triangle strips*, or just *tri-strips*. Figure 5.9 shows the 3 by 5 mesh divided into 16 triangles (as it would be rendered).

It is common for high-end 3D graphics hardware to be optimized to display tri-strips, so using meshes is an especially fast way to display 3D surfaces.

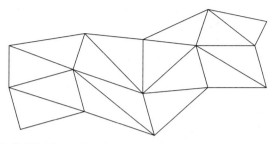

**Figure 5.9**     Mesh divided into tri-strips.

**5.2.11.1**     **Mesh attributes.** The attributes that apply to meshes are almost identical to those that apply to shells. For more information, refer to Sections 5.2.9.2 through 5.2.9.8 on shell attributes.

One difference between shells and meshes is that meshes have one additional option for the visibility of edges — it is possible to turn on and off the visibility of the *mesh-quad* edges separately. The mesh-quad edges are all the edges in the mesh *except the diagonal ones*. Normally, when edges are visible, all edges are drawn, including the diagonal edges. To turn off the visibility of diagonal edges, we turn off the visibility of edges, and then turn back on the visibility of mesh quads.

```
HC_Set_Visibility("edges=(off, mesh quads=on)");
```

This operation is so common that there is an abbreviation:

```
HC_Set_Visibility("edges=mesh quads only");
```

With the visibility set this way, our mesh looks like Figure 5.10.

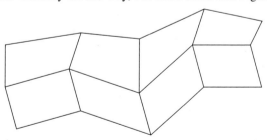

**Figure 5.10**     Mesh with only mesh quads visible.

You can also set, unset, and show attributes on individual parts (vertices, edges, and faces) of a mesh, just as you can those of a shell. The vertices are numbered as they are arranged in the point list. For the vertex at row R and column C, the vertex number is (R × K + C), where K is the number of columns. Figure 5.11 shows the vertices as they would be numbered for HC_Open_Vertex (and as they are arranged in the point list).

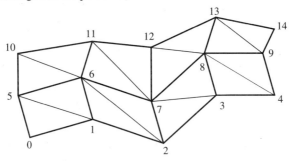

**Figure 5.11**  The vertices in a mesh.

Because a mesh has no face list, however, we need a scheme to number the faces. Here is how we do it. Vertex 0 has one triangle adjacent to it (the triangle between vertices 0, 1, and 5); it is called face 0. Likewise, face 1 is the triangle between vertices 1, 2, and 6, and so on, up to face 8 (vertices 8, 9, and 13). Note that there is no face 4. That method covers one-half of the triangles. For the others, we use negative face numbers. Consider face 6, which is the face between points 6, 7, and 11. The face on the opposite side of vertex 6 (the face between vertices 6, 5, and 1) is called face –6. A good way to remember this is that the quadrilateral between vertices 0 and 6 consists of two faces called face 0 and face –6. The final face in the mesh is face –14. Figure 5.12 shows our mesh with the faces numbered.

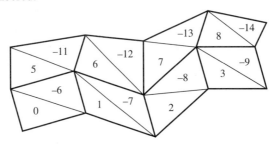

**Figure 5.12**  The faces in a mesh.

**5.2.11.2** **Mesh example.** Program 5.20 contains a routine that takes an arbitrary function of two variables and generates a surface graph of the function, using a mesh. The arguments are a pointer to the function to graph, and — for both *x* and *y* — the start and end values for the interval in which the function is to be evaluated, and the number of points at which to evaluate the function. The number of points defines the size of the mesh. We use the result of the function to define the height of the mesh (the *y* value of each vertex).

```
1   long graph_function(
2       float (*funct)(float x, float y),
3       float xstart,
4       float xend,
5       int xpoints,
6       float ystart,
7       float yend,
8       int   ypoints) {
9       Point * point_list = new Point[xpoints * ypoints];
10      Point * pl = point_list;
11      float xinc = (xend - xstart) / (xpoints - 1);
12      float yinc = (yend - ystart) / (ypoints - 1);
13      float xendr = xend + xinc/2.0;
14      float yendr = yend + yinc/2.0;
15      for (float y = ystart; y < yendr; y += yinc) {
16          for (float x = xstart; x < xendr; x += xinc) {
17              pl->x = x;
18              // evaluate function
19              pl->y = (*funct) (x, y);
20              pl->z = y;
21              pl++;
22          }
23      }
24      long key = HC_KInsert_Mesh(xpoints, ypoints,
25                          point_list);
26      delete [] point_list;
27      return key;
28  }
```

**Program 5.20** Routine to graph a 2D function.

Lines 29 through 48 of Program 5.20 constitute a test program that defines and displays a function with the graph_function routine.

```
29  float sin_cos(float x, float y) {
30      float xfreq = 4.0;
31      float yfreq = 2.0;
32      return ((0.25 + 0.5 * sin(x * 1.5 + 1.0))
33              * sin (xfreq*x) * cos (yfreq*y));
34  }

35  void main() {
36      HC_Open_Segment("?Picture");
37          HC_Set_Rendering_Options(
38                  "hsr algorithm = software z-buffer");
39          HC_Insert_Distant_Light(5.0, 5.0, -5.0);

40          graph_function(&sin_cos,
41                  -1.0, 1.0, 20, -1.0, 1.0, 20);
42          HC_Rotate_Object(-20.0, 10.0, 0.0);
43          HC_Set_Visibility(
44                  "no markers, edges=mesh quads only");
45          HC_Set_Color("faces=dark green");
46      HC_Close_Segment();

47      HC_Pause();
48  }
```

**Program 5.20  (continued)**  Define and display a function.

Figure 5.13 shows the output.

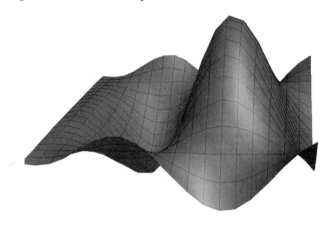

**Figure 5.13**      The graph of a function using a mesh.

If you want to see the mesh appear one triangle at a time, delete the HC_Set_Rendering_Options command on line 37.

### 5.2.12    Grids

A grid is like a sheet of graph paper. Grids are useful as a base on which to place other objects. The individual grid blocks do not have to be square — they can be arbitrary parallelograms. In addition, you can define a radial grid (like a radar screen). See the *HOOPS Reference Manual* entry for HC_Insert_Grid for more information.

One advantage of grids is that they can be infinite in extent, so, if you are using a grid as a background, you do not have to worry about how big to make the grid. HOOPS figures out what parts of the grid are visible, and draws only those parts. And, when viewed in perspective, infinite grids are drawn all the way to infinity, smoothly vanishing toward the horizon (see Program 5.21 and Figure 5.14).

#### 5.2.12.1

**Grid attributes.** Grids are similar to shells and meshes, and have the same attributes. The main difference is that you cannot set attributes on subparts of a grid.

#### 5.2.12.2

**Grid example.** Program 5.21 defines a regular (quadrilateral, not radial) grid that is infinite in extent.

```
1        Point origin, ref1, ref2;
2        origin.set_point(0.0, 0.0, 0.0);
3        ref1.set_point(0.2, 0.0, 0.0);
4        ref2.set_point(0.0, 0.2, 0.0);
5        HC_Insert_Grid("quadrilateral",
6                    &origin, &ref1, &ref2, 0, 0);
7        HC_Rotate_Object(75.0, 0.0, 0.0);
8        HC_Set_Visibility("no markers, no faces");
```

**Program 5.21**    Infinite grid.

The arguments to HC_Insert_Grid specify that this quadrilateral grid starts at the origin. The point ref1 gives the direction to move to the next grid point in one dimension, and ref2 gives the direction for the other dimension. The final two arguments give the number of grid points in each dimension; the value 0 specifies that the grid is infinite.

Line 7 rotates the grid so that it is seen in perspective. Notice in Figure 5.14 how HOOPS stops drawing the grid lines as they become too close together to be clearly visible.

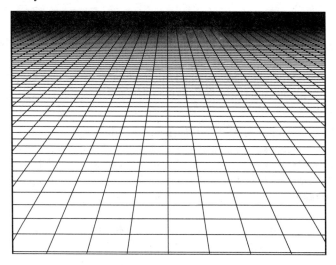

**Figure 5.14**     An infinite grid.

## 5.2.13     Images

An *image* is a 2D array of pixels. Images are like markers and annotation text in that they are always drawn in screen space — one pixel of the image per pixel on the display.

 You can get an image to display in object space by treating the image as a texture map and painting it onto the surface of a polygon. Then, the image will be transformed as the polygon is transformed. See Chapter 9 for more information on texture maps.

Program 5.22 creates and displays a simple image: a set of eight color bars.

```
1  #include <hc.h>

2  struct Color {
3      unsigned char r, g, b;
4  };

5  const unsigned char on = 0xff;
6  const unsigned char off = 0x00;
```

```
 7  Color colors[8] = {
 8     {  on, off, off },    // red
 9     { off,  on, off},     // green
10     { off, off,  on },    // blue
11     { off,  on,  on },    // cyan
12     {  on, off,  on },    // magenta
13     {  on,  on, off },    // yellow
14     {  on,  on,  on },    // white
15     { off, off, off }     // black
16  };

17  void main() {
18     const int width = 25;    // width of each color bar
19     const int height = 200; // height of each color bar

20     unsigned char image[3 * 8 * width * height];
21     unsigned char *p = image;

22     // create the image
23     for (int h=0; h<height; h++) {
24        for (int bar=0; bar<8; bar++) {
25           for (int w=0; w<width; w++) {
26              *p++ = colors[bar].r;
27              *p++ = colors[bar].g;
28              *p++ = colors[bar].b;
29           }
30        }
31     }

32     // insert the image
33     HC_Open_Segment("?Picture");
34        HC_Insert_Image(0.0, 0.0, 0.0, "RGB",
35              width * 8, height, image);
36     HC_Close_Segment();

37     HC_Pause();
38  }
```

**Program 5.22**   Color bars created with an RGB image.

In Program 5.22, each pixel was defined as an RGB value, with 3 bytes taken up in the image array for each pixel. An alternative way to define an image is to use color indices into a color map. In Program 5.23, each pixel only needs 1 byte in the image array. Each byte in the image array is an index into the local color map. The local color map is set on line 8. Note that a color map is an attribute in HOOPS, so different segments can have different color maps. HOOPS color maps are discussed further in Section 9.1.2.3.

```
1   #include <hc.h>
2   void main() {
3       const int width = 25; // width of each color bar
4       const int height = 200; // height of each color bar

5       unsigned char image[8 * width * height];
6       unsigned char *p = image;

7       // create the color map
8       HC_Set_Color_Map("red, green, blue, cyan, "
9           "magenta, yellow, white, black");

10      // create the image
11      for (int h=0; h<height; h++) {
12          for (int bar=0; bar<8; bar++) {
13              for (int w=0; w<width; w++) {
14                  *p++ = bar;
15              }
16          }
17      }

18      // insert the image
19      HC_Open_Segment("?Picture");
20          HC_Insert_Image(0.0, 0.0, 0.0, "mapped",
21                  width * 8, height, image);
22      HC_Close_Segment();

23      HC_Pause();
24  }
```

**Program 5.23**    Color bars created with a mapped image.

Of course, color bars are not a particularly interesting image. In fact, it probably would be better for us to define color bars using a mesh, or at least as eight polygons. The problem with using an image is that the appearance of an image is platform dependent, because images are defined in screen space (one image pixel per screen pixel). An image will appear larger or smaller depending on the resolution of the display. On a device with a very high resolution, such as a printer, an image will appear very small.

A more common use of HOOPS images is to display externally generated images. HOOPS can display images that either are in raw bitmap form, or use indices into a color map. Most externally generated images, however, use some sort of compression to reduce storage requirements. For example, images are often stored in GIF or JPEG format. In the demo/common/gifrdr directory on the CD-ROM is an example program that reads in an image in GIF format and displays it as a HOOPS image. Program 5.24 uses this routine to display a GIF image from disk. The demo/common/txtruniv directory contains several example GIF images.

```
1   #include <hc.h>
2   extern "C" long gif_to_hoops(
3         char *, char *, char *, char *);
4   void main() {
5      char fname[] =
6         "/hoops/demo/common/txtruniv/stop2.gif";
7      HC_Open_Segment("?Picture");
8         HC_Set_Color("window = black");
9         long image_key = gif_to_hoops(
10               fname, ".", "rgb", "stop_sign");
11      HC_Close_Segment ();
12      HC_Pause();
13   }
```

**Program 5.24**   Program to read and display GIF format images.

Note that you probably will have to change the file name on line 6, depending on where you installed HOOPS from the CD-ROM. You will also need to link with the file gif2hps.c in the demo/common/gifrdr directory.

You can retrieve the data from an image using the HC_Show_Image command. You can also determine the size, format, and location of an image using the HC_Show_Image_Size command. You can edit the individual pixels in an image using the HC_Edit_Image command. See the *HOOPS Reference Manual* for more information.

**5.2.13.1**     **Image attributes.** The primary HOOPS attribute that applies to an image is a color map for a mapped image. We used a HOOPS color map in Program 5.23. See Section 9.1.2.3 for a discussion of color maps. Note that a HOOPS color map is not the same as a hardware color map.

**5.2.13.2**     **Images as attributes.** An image is normally considered to be geometry, but an image can be also used as an attribute. In particular, an image can be used like a color, to color a face of a polygon, mesh, or shell. An image can also be used as a texture map. See Section 9.2 for more information on how to use an image as a color or as a texture map.

**5.2.13.3**     **Generation of images.** The output from HOOPS is an image, normally displayed on the screen, but HOOPS can also be used to store images in files. The use of HOOPS to generate images is discussed in Section 6.2.3.

**5.2.14**     **Lights**

HOOPS treats scenes with lights in them differently from the way it treats scenes without lights.

**5.2.14.1**     **Unlit scenes.** If you do not insert any lights at all into a scene, then the scene is *unlit* (this is also called *flat lighting*). In this case, the color of each object is just the color of that object's net color attribute (which is the diffuse color attribute). For example, if you set the color attribute of an object to green, then that object will be green. Objects are not shaded, so a green object is uniformly green — it will not be lighter on one side or on top where the light hits it (because there are no lights).

Unlit scenes look flat. This effect might be just what you want, such as for a scene that only contains lines, or for charts and graphs. If you want any degree of realism, however, you will want to light your scene. For example, Figure 5.15 shows the clock made up of shells, without any lights.

Figure 5.16 shows the same scene, this time with a single light.

**Figure 5.15**    The clock example with no lights.

**Figure 5.16**    The clock example with a single light.

5.2.14.2     **Lit scenes.** If a scene contains any lights, then HOOPS performs lighting calculations for all the objects in the scene. The color of each object will then depend not only on that object's color, but also on the amount and color of the light falling on it. Thus, inserting the first light into a scene can sometimes make the scene look darker, because the sides of objects facing away from the light source will be darker than before.

The lighting calculation for a scene includes an ambient-light term, which you set using HC_Set_Color. The default ambient light value is

```
HC_Set_Color("ambient = dark gray");
```

For more information on lighting calculations, see Section 3.3.4. For more information on setting and using colors, see Section 9.1.

As we discussed in Chapter 3, there are three main kinds of light sources in graphics scenes: distant lights, local lights, and spotlights.

If all you want to do is provide diffuse light to a scene, so that HOOPS draws objects brighter on one side than on the other to convey a sense of depth, then you probably want a distant light. To insert a distant light, you can use

```
HC_Insert_Distant_Light(x, y, z);
```

In the case of a distant light, the arguments *x*, *y*, and *z* are not a location in space; they are a direction from the origin toward the light source. The light source acts as though it were infinitely far away: the light rays are all parallel to one another, and the light intensity does not drop off with distance.

Less frequently used are local lights and spotlights. Spotlights have a useful feature in that their location can be specified in camera relative units (lights are normally in object relative units, like other geometry). For example, you can "mount" a spotlight on your camera.

 If your system performs lighting in hardware, there is usually a limit on how many lights you can insert into a scene before HOOPS has to switch to software. You can determine this limit by asking HC_Show_Device_Info for the number of "hardware lights".

5.2.14.3     **Lights as geometry.** HOOPS treats lights as geometry, whereas it treats cameras as attributes. What would happen if lights were treated as attributes? If a light were an attribute, then it would inherit like any other attribute. A light would be inherited by — and so would illuminate only — geometry contained in segments below it in the database hierarchy. To light the entire scene, we would have to insert all our lights into the driver-instance segment (typically, "?Picture"). That, in turn, would make it difficult to use a color attribute to change the color of one light in a scene, because objects in the same segment must all have the same attributes. If we placed two lights in separate segments, so that we could change one light's color, then each light would be at the root of a separate subtree, and thus would not illuminate the same scene.

Instead, it makes more sense to treat lights as geometry. Then, a light is part of the entire scene, rather than just a part of the segments underneath it in the tree. A light illuminates all other geometry in the same scene (that is, all geometry under the same driver-instance segment), whether it is placed in the root segment of the scene or is buried somewhere down in the depths of the scene tree. Thus, we can have multiple lights in the same scene, each with different attributes.

**5.2.14.4**    **Light attributes.** The main attributes affecting lights are color and visibility. A light inherits its color just like any geometry. The "lightness" of the color controls the brightness of the light. For example, to set the color of a light to red, you can use

```
1   HC_Open_Segment("");
2       HC_Insert_Distant_Light(5.0, 5.0, -5.0);
3       HC_Set_Color("lights=red");
4   HC_Close_Segment();
```

If you want to create a scene with multiple lights of different colors, you must put the lights into separate segments, each with a different light color. Setting the light color affects only lights in the current segment or in its children (since the light color is inherited).

You can turn lights on and off by setting the visibility of lights on and off. In addition, turning off the visibility of lights prevents lights elsewhere in the same scene from shining on any geometry in this part of the tree. For example, consider the segment tree in Figure 5.17.

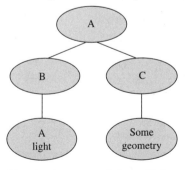

**Figure 5.17**    A graphics database containing a light.

If you issue the following command on segment B,

```
HC_Set_Visibility("lights=off");
```

then you effectively turn off the light in B. But if you issue the same command on segment C, then you prevent the light in segment B from shining on the geometry in segment C.

If you issue the following command on segment B,

```
HC_Set_Color("lights=red");
```

you change the color of the light in B, and so affect the color of the light illuminating the geometry in segment C. But if you issue the same command on segment C, it has no effect on anything (unless there is a light in segment C).

## 5.2.15    Cutting Planes

A *cutting plane* allows you to cut away part of a scene. For example, if you have a scene representing a house, you can cut away everything above the ceiling line (to remove the roof), so that you can see the layout of the rooms. A cutting plane is considered geometry, and it affects (cuts) all geometry in the same scene (under the same driver-instance segment). A scene can contain more than one cutting plane — geometry is removed if it is cut away by any cutting plane.

The following command inserts a cutting plane:

```
HC_Insert_Cutting_Plane(a, b, c, d);
```

where the arguments are (floating-point) coefficients for the plane equation for the cutting plane. The plane equation is

$$ax + by + cz + d = 0$$

The plane itself is all points $(x, y, z)$ in space that satisfy this equation. The part of the scene that is cut away is all points $(x, y, z)$ that satisfy the following inequality:

$$ax + by + cz + d > 0$$

You can visualize how the plane equation defines a plane as follows: for some arbitrary cutting plane in space, imagine the line that passes through the origin and is perpendicular to the cutting plane (see Figure 5.18). The (a, b, c) part of the plane equation is a point on this line, and d is the distance from the plane to the origin, in units of the vector from (a, b, c) to the origin. This formulation works even if the plane contains the origin. Note that, for any plane, there is an infinite number of values for (a, b, c, d) that define it (since we can multiply both sides of the plane equation by any positive constant).

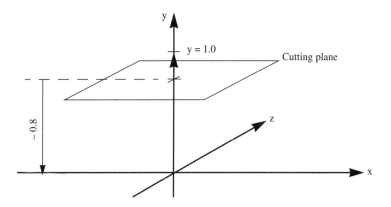

**Figure 5.18**     Cutting plane.

Continuing our house example, let us say that we want to cut away everything whose *y* coordinate is greater than 0.8, so the cutting plane is perpendicular to the *y* axis. The vector (0, 1, 0) is in the direction of the *y* axis, and is conveniently chosen to be of length 1.0. The distance from the cutting plane to the origin in units of this vector is –0.8.

The equation of the cutting plane in Figure 5.18 is $0x + 1y + 0z + -0.8 = 0$, which gives us

```
HC_Insert_Cutting_Plane(0.0, 1.0, 0.0, -0.8);
```

Everything above this plane — in the direction of the vector (0, 1, 0) — will be cut away. To cut away everything below this plane, we negate each of the arguments, as follows:

```
HC_Insert_Cutting_Plane(0.0, -1.0, 0.0, 0.8);
```

If cutting planes are done in hardware on your system, there may be a limit on how many planes you can insert before HOOPS has to switch to using software. You can determine this limit by asking HC_Show_Device_Info for the number of "hardware cutting planes".

Cutting planes do not affect lights. Depending on your system, a cutting plane may or may not cut away part of a single text character or marker. Wide lines may be clipped by a cutting plane differently on different systems.

A common use of a cutting plane is to remove everything from a scene that is closer than a certain distance from the front of the camera (viewpoint). Doing so keeps a single polygon right in front of the camera from blocking the entire view. Such a cutting plane is called a *hither* plane. Hither planes were discussed in Section 3.3.2.

For example, if our camera is at (0, 0, –5), which is 5 units from the origin on the negative *z* axis, we can clip everything that is more than 4 units from the origin on the negative *z* axis with the command

```
HC_Insert_Cutting_Plane(0.0, 0.0, -1.0, -4.0);
```

The fourth argument (–4.0) gives the *z* coordinate of the clipping plane. Note that this command removes everything from behind the camera as well.

Likewise, you can use a cutting plane to remove everything more than a certain distance from the camera. Such a cutting plane is called a *yon* plane. Yon planes were discussed in Section 3.3.2.

For example, to clip anything more than 100 units on the positive *z* axis, we change the fourth argument to 100.0, and then multiply all the arguments by –1 (so we clip everything that has a *z* coordinate greater than that of the cutting plane), resulting in the command

```
HC_Insert_Cutting_Plane(0.0, 0.0, 1.0, -100.0);
```

In this case, the fourth argument is the negative of the *z* coordinate of the clipping plane (because we multiplied through by –1).

**5.2.15.1**      **Cutting-plane attributes.** Like all geometry, the cutting plane is affected by the net transformation matrix of the segment where it is located. The transformation matrix allows you to rotate and translate a cutting plane in space.

Other than that, the main attribute that affects cutting planes is visibility. The command

```
HC_Set_Visibility("cutting planes = off");
```

will effectively turn off a cutting plane, and will keep a cutting plane in another part of the database tree from affecting local geometry. For example, consider the segment tree in Figure 5.19.

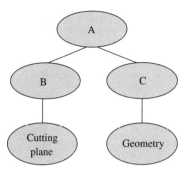

**Figure 5.19**     A graphics database containing a cutting plane.

Normally, the cutting plane in segment B will cut all geometry in the same window, including the geometry in segment C. If you turn off cutting-plane visibility in segment B, then the cutting plane is effectively turned off (it has no effect on any geometry in the scene). If you turn off cutting-plane visibility in segment C, then the geometry in segment C is not affected by the cutting plane in segment B (but geometry in other segments will still be affected).

We can use the ability to turn off cutting-plane visibility selectively, to do partial cutaways. For example, imagine a scene containing a sphere and a cube, with the cube entirely inside the sphere. We want to cut away one-half of the sphere, so that we can see the cube inside, but we do not want to cut the cube. We put the cube and sphere into separate segments, and turn off cutting-plane visibility for the cube.

## 5.2.16     User-Defined Geometry

What do you do if HOOPS does not provide a kind of geometry that your application needs? You define the geometry yourself using HOOPS Intermediate Mode (I.M.).

For example, you might want to define a piece of geometry that looks like a train track — two parallel lines with evenly spaced cross ties (Figure 5.20). Of course, you can store the train track by tessellating it into individual lines (two polylines for the tracks, and numerous lines for the cross ties) and storing those lines in the HOOPS graphics database. With HOOPS I.M., however, you can store a simple polyline to indicate the path of the track, and then use HOOPS I.M. to convert the polyline into a train track when the scene is rendered.

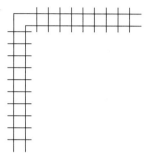

**Figure 5.20**      A train track drawn with HOOPS Intermediate Mode.

HOOPS I.M. uses callback routines to pass back control to the application during the traversal of the HOOPS graphics database. Callback routines can be associated with individual segments or with particular kinds of geometry inside a segment.

Unfortunately, a complete explanation of the use of HOOPS I.M. is beyond the scope of this book. The individual routines are documented in the *HOOPS Reference Manual*, and there are numerous example programs in the demo/ common/im directory on the CD-ROM (in particular, the train-track example is in the file tracks.c). The demo routines for HOOPS I.M. are cataloged in Section 10.5.6.

## 5.3      Geometry Tips

This section contains two techniques that can make your HOOPS application more efficient or easier to write.

### 5.3.1      Insertion of Geometry by Reference

Normally, when you insert geometry into the HOOPS database, HOOPS makes a copy of the data that you supply. For some kinds of geometry, these data can be voluminous, and making a copy wastes space and makes your application bigger and slower than it needs to be. To avoid this problem, HOOPS allows you to insert meshes, shells, and images *by reference*. If you insert geometry by reference, you are telling HOOPS that it does not need to make a copy of the data. For a mesh, the data are the points in the point list. For a shell, the data are the point list and the face list. For an image, the data are the pixels.

Once you insert geometry by reference, you must not make any changes to that geometry's data. In particular, it may be tempting to change the object in the database by changing its data. That will not work. For example, if you create a mesh by reference, you cannot move one of its vertices by changing the value of one of the points in the point list.

 On some platforms, HOOPS may need to make a copy of the data anyway, so any changes you make will not be reflected in the output. Even if HOOPS does not copy the data, HOOPS often calculates intermediate information, such as bounding boxes, and caches it, so making a change to the data can cause major internal distress to HOOPS.

The proper way to edit a shell, mesh, or image inserted by reference is with one of the edit routines, such as HC_Edit_Mesh. However, these changes might not be reflected back into your data.

For example, in Program 5.20, we evaluated a function of two variables to create a mesh. After we had finished creating the mesh, we inserted it into the HOOPS database, so HOOPS made a copy of the point list, and then we deleted our copy of the point list. A more efficient implementation would allocate the point list, and then create the mesh by reference.

```
1   Point * point_list = new Point[xpoints * ypoints];
2   long key = HC_KInsert_Mesh_By_Ref(xpoints, ypoints,
3                                       point_list);
```

At this point, we can neither make any changes to the contents of point_list, nor delete point_list. If point_list has been allocated on the heap, as in the preceding example, you should save its address so that you can delete the allocated memory when you have finished displaying the mesh.

We are allowed to make changes to the mesh using HC_Edit_Mesh. For example, to set the point at a specific row and column, we can use

```
1   void set_point(long key, int row, int col,
2        Point * value) {
3     HC_Edit_Mesh(key, row, col, 1, 1, value);
4   }
```

This change may or may not be reflected back into point_list.

### 5.3.2     Retrieval of Geometry

Most changes to geometry require you to supply a key for the geometry, but you might not want to go to the bother of remembering all the keys for all the geometry in your application. A trick that you can use to get a key for any piece of geometry in the HOOPS database is a *contents search*.

For example, if the current segment contains a mesh, Program 5.25 will retrieve a key for it.

```
1  HC_Begin_Contents_Search(".", "mesh");
2  long key;
3  char type[32];
4  int found = HC_Find_Contents(type, &key);
5  HC_End_Contents_Search();
```

**Program 5.25**     A search for a mesh.

The arguments to HC_Begin_Contents_Search are the segments to search (wild-cards are legal, so you can use "..." as the first argument to search the entire tree beginning with the current segment), and the type of object for which to look (in this case, a mesh). HC_Find_Contents returns three values. The function itself returns true if an object was found. The first argument returns the type of the found object (in this case, the only type that can be found is a mesh), and the second argument returns the key for the found object.

Contents searches often come in handy. You can use them to find out what kinds of geometry are in a segment, to search for a piece of geometry in the database, or to compute statistics about the geometry in a HOOPS database tree. There is more information about searching in Section 6.5.

## 5.4     Geometry Example

This section defines a program that displays every kind of HOOPS geometry, except lights and cutting planes. Program 5.26 starts with the standard declaration for type Point, and includes two files:

```
 1   #include <math.h>
 2   struct Point {
 3      float x, y, z;
 4      Point & set_point (
 5         float xx,
 6         float yy,
 7         float zz) {
 8         x = xx;
 9         y = yy;
10         z = zz;
11         return *this;
12      }
13   };

14   #define HC_POINT Point
15   #include "hc.h"
```

We define a class Object_Positioner to position the objects in the scene relative to one another. To use class Object_Positioner, you create an instance of it, tell it how many rows and columns there are, and (optionally) change the spacing of the rows and columns. After that, each call to the member function set_position invokes a HOOPS transformation, so that each object can be created at its own origin.

```
16   class Object_Positioner {

17     private:
18       int _rows;
19       int _columns;
20       float _row_spacing;
21       float _column_spacing;

22     public:
23       Object_Positioner(int rows = 4, int columns = 4):
24               _rows (rows), _columns (columns) {
25          _row_spacing = 3.0; _column_spacing = 4.0;
26       }

27       void set_position(int grid_spot);
28       void set_position(int row, int column);
```

```
29    void set_row_spacing(float row_spacing) {
30        _row_spacing = row_spacing;
31    }
32    void set_column_spacing(float column_spacing) {
33        _column_spacing = column_spacing;
34    }

35    float get_column_spacing() {
36        return _column_spacing;
37    }
38    float get_row_spacing() {
39        return _row_spacing;
40    }
41 };

42 void Object_Positioner::set_position(int grid_spot) {
43    // compute the row and column position in the grid
44    // and call other set_position member function
45    set_position(grid_spot/_columns, grid_spot%_rows);
46 }

47 void Object_Positioner::set_position(
48        int row, int column) {
49    // given an (r,c), compute the translation needed
50    // to take the object's origin to this grid spot
51    HC_Translate_Object(_column_spacing * column,
52                        - _row_spacing * row, 0.0);
53 }
```

The compute_mesh routine is similar to the graph_function routine that we defined in Program 5.20.

```
54 void compute_mesh(
55    float xstart,
56    float xend,
57    int xnodes,
58    float ystart,
59    float yend,
60    int ynodes,
61    float (*funct)(float x, float y),
62    Point * ipl) {
```

```
63        Point * pl = ipl;
64        float x, y;
65        float xinc, yinc;
66        xinc = (xend - xstart) / (xnodes - 1);
67        float yinc = (yend - ystart) / (ynodes - 1);
68        xendr = xend + xinc/2.0;
69        float yendr = yend + yinc/2.0;
70        pl += xnodes * ynodes;
71        for (x = xstart; x < xendr; x += xinc) {
72            for (y = ystart; y < yendr; y += yinc) {
73                --pl;
74                pl->x = x;
75                pl->y = (*funct) (x, y);
76                pl->z = y;
77            }
78        }
79    }
```

The sin_cos routine is used as in the graph_function to generate the mesh.

```
80    float sin_cos(
81        float x,
82        float y) {
83        float xfreq = 4.0f;
84        float yfreq = 2.0f;
85        return ((0.25 + 0.5 * sin(x * 1.5 + 1.0))
86                    * sin(xfreq*x) * cos(yfreq*y));
87    }
```

Lines 88 through 350 (the remainder of Program 5.26) contain the main routine. It creates and initializes each kind of HOOPS geometry one at a time, putting each into position with an Object_Positioner.

```
88    void main() {
89        Point    point1, point2, point3;
90        Point    center, major_axis, minor_axis;
91        float    text_offset = -0.8;

92        // create a grid of the HOOPS primitives --
93        // cutting planes and lights are omitted
94        // each primitive should be bounded by (-1.0, 1.0)
95        // in each of the x, y, and z dimensions,
96        // including a text label
```

```
97     // create an Object_Positioner
98     Object_Positioner op(4, 4);
99     op.set_row_spacing(3.0);
100    op.set_column_spacing(4.0);

101    // create the primitives
102    HC_Open_Segment("?Picture/HOOPS Primitives");
103       HC_Set_Visibility("edges = on, faces = off");
104       HC_Set_Heuristics("no hidden surfaces");

105       HC_Open_Segment("Title");
106          HC_Insert_Text(1.5 * op.get_column_spacing(),
107                   3.0, 0.0, "HOOPS 4.1 Primitives");
108          HC_Set_Text_Alignment("**");
109       HC_Close_Segment();

110       HC_Open_Segment("Text");
111          HC_Insert_Text(0.0, 0.9, 0.0, "3D");
112          // will only work if you have Kanji enabled
113          HC_Insert_Text_With_Encoding(0.0, 0.0, 0.0,
114                         "JEC", "Kanji  \x8F\xA1");
115          HC_Insert_Text(0.0, text_offset, 0.0,
116             "Text");
117          op.set_position(15);
118       HC_Close_Segment();

119       HC_Open_Segment("Ellipse");
120          center.set_point(0.0, 0.4, 0.0);
121          major_axis.set_point(0.6, 0.4, 0.0);
122          minor_axis.set_point(0.0, 0.7, 0.0);
123          HC_Insert_Ellipse(&center,
124             &major_axis, &minor_axis);
125          HC_Insert_Text(0.0, text_offset, 0.0,
126             "Ellipse");
127          op.set_position(14);
128       HC_Close_Segment();
```

```
129        HC_Open_Segment("Elliptical Arc");
130            center.set_point(0.0, 0.4, 0.0);
131            major_axis.set_point(0.6, 0.4, 0.0);
132            minor_axis.set_point(0.0, 0.7, 0.0);
133            HC_Insert_Elliptical_Arc(&center,
134                    &major_axis, &minor_axis, 0.0, 0.5);
135            HC_Insert_Text(0.0, text_offset, 0.0,
136                    "Elliptical Arc");
137            op.set_position(13);
138        HC_Close_Segment();

139        HC_Open_Segment("Line");
140            HC_Insert_Line(-0.6, 0.4,
141                    0.0, 0.6, 0.4, 0.0);
142            HC_Insert_Text(0.0, text_offset, 0.0,
143                    "Line");
144            op.set_position(12);
145        HC_Close_Segment();

146        HC_Open_Segment("Quad Grids");
147            Point origin;
148            Point ref1, ref2;
149            origin.set_point(-0.6, -0.2, 0.0);
150            ref1.set_point(-0.6, 0.4, 0.0);
151            ref2.set_point(0.0, -0.2, 0.0);
152            HC_Insert_Grid("quadrilateral",
153                        &origin, &ref1, &ref2, 2, 2)
154            HC_Insert_Text(0.0, text_offset, 0.0,
155                    "Quad Grid");
156            HC_Set_Visibility("no markers");
157            op.set_position(11);
158        HC_Close_Segment();
```

```
159     HC_Open_Segment("Radial Grids");
160         origin.set_point(0.0, -0.2, 0.0);
161         ref1.set_point(0.5, -0.2, 0.0);
162         ref2.set_point(0.3535, 0.1535, 0.0);
163         HC_Insert_Grid("radial", &origin,
164             &ref1, &ref2, 2, 4);
165         HC_Insert_Text(0.0, text_offset, 0.0,
166             "Radial Grid");
167         HC_Set_Visibility("no markers");
168         op.set_position(10);
169     HC_Close_Segment();

170     HC_Open_Segment("Image");
171         int    rows = 30;
172         int    columns = 30;
173         int    data_array_size = rows * columns * 3;
174         unsigned char * data =
175             new unsigned char[data_array_size];
176         // could come up with a better image...
177         for (int i = 0; i < data_array_size; ++i) {
178             data[i] = i % 256;
179         }
180         HC_Insert_Image(0.0, 0.4, 0.0, "RGB",
181                         rows, columns, data);
182         HC_Insert_Text(0.0, text_offset, 0.0,
183             "Image");
184         op.set_position(9);
185         delete [] data;
186     HC_Close_Segment();
```

```
187        HC_Open_Segment("Marker");
188          HC_Set_Visibility("markers = on");
189          HC_Open_Segment("Marker 1");
190            HC_Insert_Marker(0.0, 0.9, 0.0);
191            HC_Set_Marker_Symbol("*");
192          HC_Close_Segment();
193          HC_Open_Segment("Marker 2");
194            HC_Insert_Marker(0.0, 0.4, 0.0);
195            HC_Set_Marker_Symbol("<>");
196          HC_Close_Segment();
197          HC_Open_Segment("Marker 3");
198            HC_Insert_Marker(0.0, -0.1, 0.0);
199            HC_Set_Marker_Symbol("(x)");
200          HC_Close_Segment();
201          HC_Insert_Text(0.0, text_offset, 0.0,
202              "Markers");
203          op.set_position(8);
204        HC_Close_Segment();

205        HC_Open_Segment("Mesh");
206          int   xcount = 20;
207          int   ycount = 20;
208          Point * points = new Point[xcount * ycount];
209          compute_mesh(-1.0, 1.0, xcount,
210              -1.0, 1.0, ycount, sin_cos, points);
211          HC_Open_Segment("Mesh Geometry");
212            HC_Insert_Mesh(xcount, ycount, points);
213            HC_Rotate_Object(15.0, 15.0, 0.0);
214            HC_Set_Visibility(
215              "no markers, edges=mesh quads only");
216          HC_Close_Segment();
217          HC_Insert_Text(0.0, text_offset, 0.0,
218              "Mesh");
219          op.set_position(7);
220          delete [] points;
221        HC_Close_Segment();
```

```
222        HC_Open_Segment("Polygon"); {
223            Point points[6];
224            points[0].set_point(-0.6,  -0.2,  0.0);
225            points[1].set_point( 0.6,  -0.2,  0.0);
226            points[2].set_point( 0.2,   0.4,  0.0);
227            points[3].set_point( 0.6,   1.0,  0.0);
228            points[4].set_point(-0.6,   1.0,  0.0);
229            points[5].set_point(-0.2,   0.4,  0.0);

230            HC_Insert_Polygon(6, points);
231            HC_Insert_Text(0.0, text_offset, 0.0,
232                    "Polygon");
233            HC_Set_Visibility("edges = on, faces = on");
234            HC_Set_Color("edges = blue, faces = pink");
235            HC_Set_Heuristics("concave polygons");
236            op.set_position(6);
237        } HC_Close_Segment();

238        HC_Open_Segment ("Polyline"); {
239            Point points[6];
240            points[0].set_point(-0.6,  -0.2,  0.0);
241            points[1].set_point( 0.6,  -0.2,  0.0);
242            points[2].set_point( 0.2,   0.4,  0.0);
243            points[3].set_point( 0.6,   1.0,  0.0);
244            points[4].set_point(-0.6,   1.0,  0.0);
245            points[5].set_point(-0.2,   0.4,  0.0);

246            HC_Insert_Polyline(6, points);
247            HC_Insert_Text(0.0, text_offset, 0.0,
248                    "Polyline");
249            op.set_position(5);
250        } HC_Close_Segment();

251        HC_Open_Segment("Shell"); {
252            int point_count = 8;
253            Point points[point_count];
254            int face_list_length = 30;
```

```
255            points[0].set_point(-0.6,  -0.2,  -0.6);
256            points[1].set_point(-0.6,  -0.2,   0.6);
257            points[2].set_point(-0.6,   1.0,   0.6);
258            points[3].set_point(-0.6,   1.0,  -0.6);
259            points[4].set_point( 0.6,   1.0,  -0.6);
260            points[5].set_point( 0.6,  -0.2,  -0.6);
261            points[6].set_point( 0.6,  -0.2,   0.6);
262            points[7].set_point( 0.6,   1.0,   0.6);

263            // array for face list
264            static int face_list[] = {
265                       4, 0, 1, 2, 3,
266                       4, 0, 3, 4, 5,
267                       4, 3, 4, 7, 2,
268                       4, 1, 2, 7, 6,
269                       4, 2, 3, 4, 7,
270                       4, 7, 4, 5, 6 };

271            HC_Set_Line_Pattern("- -");
272            HC_Set_Line_Weight(0.5);
273            HC_Insert_Text(0.0, text_offset, 0.0,
274                "Shell");
275            HC_Set_Visibility(
276                "edges=on, markers=off, faces=off");

277            HC_Open_Segment("Shell Geometry");
278               HC_Insert_Shell(point_count, points,
279                        face_list_length, face_list);
280               HC_Rotate_Object(15.0, 0.0, 0.0);
281            HC_Close_Segment();
282            op.set_position(4);
283         } HC_Close_Segment();

284      HC_Open_Segment("Circular Arc"); {
285         point1.set_point( 0.8, 0.0, 0.0);
286         point2.set_point( 0.0, 0.8, 0.0);
287         point3.set_point(-0.8, 0.0, 0.0);
288         HC_Insert_Circular_Arc(&point1, &point2,
289             &point3);
290         HC_Insert_Text(0.0, text_offset, 0.0,
291             "Circular Arc");
292         op.set_position(3);
293      } HC_Close_Segment();
```

```
294        HC_Open_Segment("Circular Chord"); {
295            point1.set_point( 1.0, 0.0, 0.0);
296            point2.set_point( 0.0, 1.0, 0.0);
297            point3.set_point(-0.8,
298                        1.0 - sqrt(0.36), 0.0);
299            HC_Insert_Circular_Chord(&point1,
300                   &point2, &point3);
301            HC_Insert_Text(0.0, text_offset, 0.0,
302                   "Chord");
303            op.set_position(2);
304        } HC_Close_Segment();

305        HC_Open_Segment("Circular Wedge"); {
306            point1.set_point(-1.0,
307                        -0.2 + sqrt(0.44), 0.0);
308            point2.set_point(0.0, 1.0, 0.0);
309            point3.set_point(1.0,
310                        -0.2 + sqrt(0.44), 0.0);
311            HC_Insert_Circular_Wedge(&point1,
312                   &point2, &point3);
313            HC_Insert_Text(0.0, text_offset, 0.0,
314                   "Wedge");
315            op.set_position(1);
316        } HC_Close_Segment();

317        HC_Open_Segment("Circle"); {
318            point1.set_point( 0.6, 0.4, 0.0);
319            point2.set_point( 0.0, 1.0, 0.0);
320            point3.set_point(-0.6, 0.4, 0.0);
321            HC_Insert_Circle(&point1, &point2, &point3);
322            HC_Insert_Text(0.0, text_offset, 0.0,
323                   "Circle");
324            HC_Set_Color("polygons = red");
325            op.set_position(0);
326        } HC_Close_Segment();
```

Lines 327 through 347 translate and scale the scene so that it will fill the output window and be centered. In Section 6.1.7.2, we shall see how to manipulate the HOOPS camera so that we can fit the camera to the scene, rather than fitting the scene to the camera, as in this program.

```
327        // scale and translate the scene so that it will
328        // fit into the default camera's field of view
329        // (2, 2) at z=0.0
330        float x_length = op.get_columns() *
331                            op.get_column_spacing();
332        float y_length = op.get_rows () *
333                            op.get_row_spacing();

334        // compute the centroid of the scene and
335        // translate it to the origin
336        Point centroid;
337        centroid.set_point((-3.0 + x_length) / 2.0,
338            (4.0 - y_length) / 2.0, 0.0);
339        HC_Translate_Object(-centroid.x, -centroid.y,
340                            -centroid.z);

341        // scale each dimension by the inverse of the
342        // maximum length;
343        // this step preserves the aspect ratio of the
344        // world space (isotropic scaling)
345        float max = 0.0;
346        if (x_length > y_length) max = x_length;
347        else max = y_length;
348        HC_Scale_Object(2.0 / max, 2.0 / max, 2.0/max);

349   HC_Close_Segment();      // ?Picture/HOOPS
```

Finally, we pause to see the results.

```
350   HC_Pause();
351 }
```

**Program 5.26**    Geometry example.

Figure 5.21 shows the output from Program 5.26.

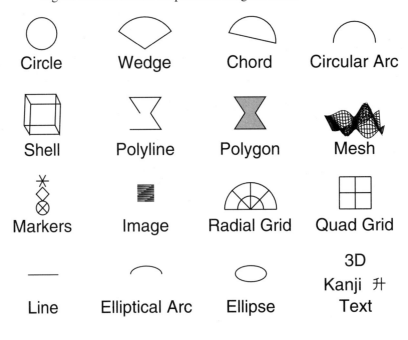

**Figure 5.21**        Every kind of HOOPS geometry.

# 6     Viewing and Searching

Previous chapters have discussed how to create a scene using HOOPS geometry, attributes, and segments. Once you have generated a scene, you typically want to do something with it. This chapter covers several of the possibilities. In particular, you can view the scene (from different angles and in different ways), you can print or plot it, you can create an image of it, you can save the image to a file, you can save the scene database to a file, and you can collect statistics about the scene.

## 6.1     Cameras

In computer graphics, a *camera,* or *viewpoint,* is what allows us to view a scene. The camera is our surrogate, allowing us to "see" what the mathematical description of a scene in the graphics database actually looks like. It converts the objective world of a scene into the subjective world of an image (and, in computer graphics, as the saying goes, "image is everything").

In HOOPS, a camera is an attribute. As is true of any attribute, if you set the camera attribute on a segment, then that camera is inherited by the children of the segment, unless they explicitly override it with their own locally set camera. Each segment has a net value for the camera attribute — either a locally set camera or an inherited camera — and this net value is the camera used to view the geometry in that segment.

Like any attribute, the camera attribute can be set multiple places in the database. What does it mean for a scene to have more than one camera? Do you get more than one view of the same scene? No. Since each segment has only one net value for the camera attribute (as it does for any attribute), each piece of geometry in a scene will be viewed by only a single camera — the camera defined by its net camera attribute. Thus, different segments in a scene can be viewed by different cameras, but each segment will be viewed only once (unless that segment is included more than once in the scene via HC_Include_Segment).

If you have trouble thinking of a camera as an attribute, remember that a camera is just a viewing transformation, which is used by the HOOPS driver to transform a scene from world coordinates into screen coordinates. The net value of the viewing transformation (the camera) for a particular segment is used to transform the geometry in that segment. Different segments can have different values for their net viewing transformation.

---

Alternatively, HOOPS could have treated a camera as a piece of geometry, so a camera in a scene would view all the other geometry in the same scene, and multiple cameras would create multiple views of the entire scene. After all, HOOPS treats lights as geometry — each light illuminates all other objects in the scene.

As we shall see in Chapter 7, HOOPS treats windows as attributes, and, because cameras are usually associated with windows, treating a camera as an attribute makes associating cameras with windows a little easier (and a little more consistent).

The only problem with treating a camera as an attribute is that it is hard to think of a camera in the same way that you think of a color or a line style. Perhaps it would have been clearer to call the camera attribute the viewing-transform attribute, since it is easier to think of a viewing transform as an attribute (as you do the modeling-transform attribute). But HC_Zoom_Viewing_Transform just does not have the same ring to it as HC_Zoom_Camera.

---

### 6.1.1    Camera Components

A camera attribute consists of several components. The components of a camera are shown in Figure 6.1.

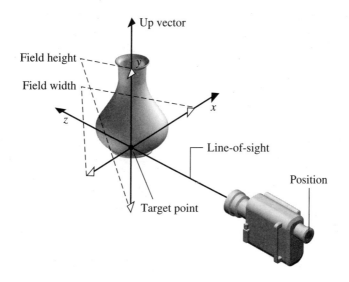

**Figure 6.1**     The components of a camera.

**6.1.1.1**     **Position.** The *position* of the camera is a point that represents the position of the viewpoint (in world coordinates). Normally, the camera position is placed slightly away from the objects that you wish to view.

**6.1.1.2**     **Target.** The *target* is a point (specified in world coordinates) toward which the camera is looking. The camera target is usually in the middle of the objects that you wish to view. The camera target must not be at the same position as the camera. The vector between the camera position and the camera target is called the *line of sight*.

**6.1.1.3**     **Up vector.** The *up vector* is a vector that defines "which way is up." If you specified only the camera's position and target, the camera could still rotate around the line of sight, so the up vector fixes the orientation of the camera. The up vector must not be all zeros, and cannot be parallel to the line of sight.

Logically, the up vector should be perpendicular to the line of sight. If it is not, the up vector is projected onto a plane perpendicular to the line of sight. The resulting projected vector is used to define the direction of the positive $y$ axis on the screen.

**6.1.1.4**     **Field.** The *field* of the camera comprises two numbers — a width and a height — that define the minimum area around the target that will be visible in the output window. The camera field, along with the distance between the camera position and the camera target, determine (in photographic terms) what kind of lens the camera is using. If the field is larger than the distance from the camera position to the target, then we have the equivalent of a wide-angle lens. If the distance between the camera position and target is much larger than the camera field, then we have the equivalent of a telephoto lens. Changing the size of the field (if the camera position and target remain fixed) is the same as zooming the lens.

The ratio of the width to the height of the field is called the *aspect ratio*.

**6.1.1.5**     **Projection.** The *projection* determines how HOOPS represents the 3D coordinates of a scene using only the 2D coordinates on the screen. A *perspective projection* scales the $x$ and $y$ coordinates depending on the $z$ coordinate (depth), such that objects that are farther away appear smaller on the screen. Other projections are *orthographic, stretched, oblique perspective,* and *oblique orthographic*. Projections are discussed in Section 3.3.1.1 (see also Section 6.1.9, on oblique projections, and Section 6.1.10, on stretched projections).

**6.1.2**     **Camera Inheritance**

The components of a camera taken together inherit as a single attribute, unlike most other composite attributes, where each component inherits individually as though it were a separate attribute. For example, color and visibility are composite attributes that consist of components (such as face color and edge color); these components can be set individually and inherit separately.

When you set a new camera, it does not inherit any components from any camera attribute higher up in the database tree. Instead, the new camera completely overrides the inherited camera. If you later unset a camera attribute that was explicitly set on a segment, the segment goes back to inheriting the entire camera. You cannot unset an individual component of a camera.

## 6.1.3     The Default Camera

Of course, we have already been using a camera to view our graphics scenes, without explicitly creating one. Since a camera is an attribute, HOOPS supplies a default value for it. Unless you explicitly set a camera attribute on a segment, the default camera is inherited by all segments in the database, and so is used to view all the segments in the database.

The default camera is positioned at (0.0, 0.0, –5.0), which is 5 units in the negative $z$ direction. Recall that, in the left-handed coordinate system normally used in computer graphics, the positive $z$ axis points away from the viewer. The camera's target is the origin, and the up vector is (0.0, 1.0, 0.0) — the positive $y$ axis. The field of the camera is 2.0 units wide and 2.0 high, and the projection is perspective. The default camera is shown in Figure 6.2.

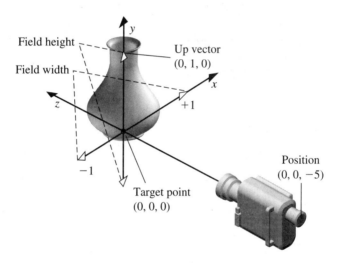

**Figure 6.2**     The default camera.

This default camera looks squarely at the $x, y$ plane from 5 units away on the negative $z$ axis, with "up" in the positive $y$ direction; it sees a field that is a square 2 units per side, centered at the origin (between –1.0 and +1.0 on the $x$ and $y$ axes). Thus, if we define our objects such that they are centered at the origin, and are close to but no bigger than 1.0 unit in both their positive and negative $x$ and $y$ dimensions, then they will be viewed well by the default camera. And, in fact, that is exactly how we defined the geometry in the clock example in Chapter 5 (not to mention in most of the other examples that we have seen so far). In the clock example, the face of the clock (a torus) was defined to be centered at the origin, to lie in the *x, y* plane, and to have a radius of 0.95 units. We could have defined the geometry of the clock with a different position, orientation, or size, but then we would have needed a different camera to view the clock properly.

## 6.1.4      Screen Coordinates

A camera is primarily a transformation that changes the world-coordinate system of a graphics scene into a 2D screen-coordinate system. This change of coordinate systems is called the *viewing transformation.* Viewing transformations were discussed in Section 3.3.1.1.

### 6.1.4.1      Mapping of the camera field to screen coordinates.
The screen-coordinate system is a rectangle with its origin at the center and with width and height equal to the field width and height. For example, the default camera defines the screen-coordinate system as a square whose width and height are both 2 units. Figure 6.3 shows the default screen-coordinate system as it would appear mapped onto a window on the screen.

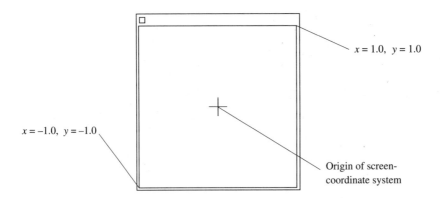

x = 1.0,  y = 1.0

x = –1.0,  y = –1.0

Origin of screen-coordinate system

**Figure 6.3**      Screen coordinates.

If the camera field is changed, then the screen-coordinate system will change. For example, we might have a scene that contains objects that range from +5 to –5 in both *x* and *y* (in world coordinates). Using the default camera, we would see only those objects that are within 1 unit of the origin. We can change the camera field such that its width and height are both 10 units (between +5 and –5). Figure 6.4 shows the new screen-coordinate system.

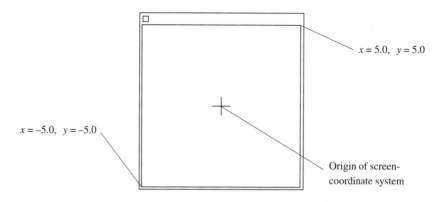

$x = 5.0, \quad y = 5.0$

$x = -5.0, \quad y = -5.0$

Origin of screen-
coordinate system

**Figure 6.4**      Screen coordinates for a camera field larger than that in Figure 6.3.

The origin of the screen-coordinate system is *always* in the center of the output window, and corresponds to the target position in world coordinates.

Of course, the magnitude of the screen-coordinate system (like that of the world-coordinate system) is completely arbitrary. For example, a molecular-modeling application might use coordinates with magnitudes such as 550 nanometers, and would thus set the camera field to a size appropriately small; an astronomy application might set the camera field to be 100 trillion kilometers wide, so that it could view an area 10 light-years across.

 It is usually a good idea to scale your application's units such that your coordinates are neither extremely small nor immensely large. For example, it would probably be a bad idea to choose your units to be meters for an astronomy application (so you would have coordinates that were very large) or a molecular-modeling application (so you would have coordinates that were very small). Even though coordinates are floating-point numbers in HOOPS, most of the HOOPS defaults work best with coordinates that range close to +1.0 and −1.0. You can also run into numerical-accuracy problems when you mix numbers with different scales in the same computation, especially since HOOPS uses single-precision floating-point numbers to store coordinates.

**6.1.4.2**      **Aspect ratio.** The ratio of the width to the height of a coordinate system is called the *aspect ratio*. For example, the default screen-coordinate system has an aspect ratio of 1 to 1 (defined by the width and height of the camera field). A window on the screen also has an aspect ratio. If the aspect ratio of the screen window exactly matches the aspect ratio of the camera field, then the camera field fits perfectly into the window, as was shown in Figures 6.3 and 6.4 (the window border does not count).

When the user resizes the HOOPS output window on the screen, the aspect ratio of the screen window can change. In addition, your program can change the aspect ratio of the camera field (using the commands HC_Set_Camera_Field, HC_Set_Camera_By_Volume, or HC_Set_Camera). What happens when the aspect ratio of the window does not match the aspect ratio of the camera field? By default, HOOPS centers the camera field in the screen window, so that all the camera field is visible. Thus, the camera field defines the *minimum* area around the target in the scene that is guaranteed to be visible in the output window. HOOPS pads either the width or the height of the camera field as necessary to make the camera field fit the screen window.

For example, if the output window is resized such that it is 50 percent wider than it is tall (the aspect ratio becomes 1.5 to 1), then the $y$ coordinates will range from $-1.0$ to $1.0$ (as before), but the $x$ coordinate will range from $-1.5$ to $1.5$. HOOPS does not clip the scene to the camera field, so objects that are slightly outside of the camera field may become visible, as shown in Figure 6.5.

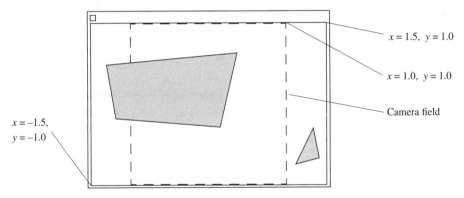

**Figure 6.5**     Fitting of the camera field into a nonsquare window.

In Figure 6.5, the camera field is indicated by dashed lines. These dashed lines do not actually appear in the HOOPS output window.

It is possible to tell HOOPS to keep the aspect ratio of the output window constant, using the "no subscreen stretching" option of the command HC_Set_Driver_Options. In fact, this value is the default for this option. When this option is in effect, the user can change the size of the output window, but the ratio of the window's width to height will remain fixed.

The "no subscreen stretching" driver option is useful in combination with the "subscreen" option of HC_Set_Driver_Options, which allows the application to set the initial size of the output window. By default, the HOOPS output window takes up the entire screen. We can set the output window to be square (assuming a screen with an aspect ratio of 4 to 3) with the command

```
HC_Set_Driver_Options(
    "subscreen=(-0.75, 0.75, -1.0, 1.0)");
```

If we set the output window to be square and leave on "no subscreen stretching", then the user can change the size of the output window, but cannot change the window's shape from being square. Thus, the user can change the output window's size without inadvertently adding any extra space at the sides or the top and bottom.

You can prohibit the user from resizing the window with the "no subscreen resizing" option. You can even prohibit the user from moving the window around the screen with the "no subscreen moving" option.

As you resize the output window of a HOOPS application, such as the clock example from Chapter 5, the output scene scales such that it gets larger and smaller as the window gets larger and smaller, but the relationship of $x$ to $y$ coordinates does not change. Thus, a circle continues to look circular, rather than getting fatter or skinnier (becoming an ellipse), as the output window gets wider or taller. (See Section 6.1.10, on stretched projections, for an example of how to make objects scale nonuniformly to match the window).

## 6.1.5     Modification of the Camera

You can modify the camera settings by changing the value of the camera attribute that applies to your scene. You can change the value by setting a camera attribute on the segment at the top of your scene, which is normally "?Picture". That way, your new camera is inherited by all segments that are subsegments of "?Picture", which includes all the visible objects in the scene.

### 6.1.5.1     The HC_Set_Camera command.
HOOPS provides many different commands for working with cameras. Underpinning all these commands is the command HC_Set_Camera, which modifies all five components of a camera at the same time.

For example, say that we want to change the aspect ratio of the camera field to be the same as that of a standard monitor. A standard monitor has an aspect ratio of 4 to 3 (if it has a resolution such as 640 by 480, 800 by 600, or 1024 by 768).

Program 6.1 sets a camera attribute on "?Picture" that is the same as the default camera, except that the aspect ratio of the camera field is changed. Note that the field width and height can be any multiple of the aspect ratio. For the default camera with an aspect ratio of 1 to 1, the field width and height are both 2.0. To change the aspect ratio to 4 to 3, we leave the field height at 2.0 and change the field width to 2.667 (2 times 4 divided by 3).

```
1   Point position, target, up;
2   position.set_point(0.0, 0.0, -5.0);
3   target.set_point(0.0, 0.0, 0.0);
4   up.set_point(0.0, 1.0, 0.0);
5   float field_width = 8.0 / 3.0;    // 4/3 * 2
6   float field_height = 2.0;
7   HC_QSet_Camera("?Picture", &position, &target, &up,
8           field_width, field_height, "perspective");
```

**Program 6.1**     Changing of the camera field using HC_QSet_Camera.

In this example, we use HC_QSet_Camera to set the camera attribute on "?Picture". It is a good idea to use QSet (which names the segment on which to set the attribute), rather than Set (which sets the attribute on the currently open segment), to set the camera attribute, so that a camera is not accidentally set on a segment other than "?Picture" (that might cause some of the segments in your scene to continue to inherit the old camera).

If you want to modify a single component of the camera attribute but you do not know its current settings, you can show them with the HC_Show_Net_Camera command. For example, Program 6.2 changes the field width and height of the camera, but leaves the other components alone.

```
 1   Point position, target, up;
 2   float field_width, field_height;
 3   char projection[64];
 4   HC_Open_Segment("?Picture");
 5       HC_Show_Net_Camera(&position, &target, &up,
 6             &field_width, &field_height, projection);
 7       field_width = 8.0 / 3.0;
 8       field_height = 2.0;
 9       HC_Set_Camera(&position, &target, &up,
10             field_width, field_height, projection);
11   HC_Close_Segment();
```

**Program 6.2**     Changing of part of a camera using HC_Set_Camera.

---

**C++**     Note that points are always passed by address in HOOPS, but, for the
HC_Show_Net_Camera command (on line 5), the two float arguments for the
field also must be passed by address so that their values can be returned. Since
the final argument is a string, and a string is always passed via a pointer, there
is no need to take its address in either the Set or Show command.

Of course, HOOPS could have used C++ reference arguments to return
values, but that would have made HOOPS incompatible with C.

---

**6.1.5.2**     **Setting of a single component.** HOOPS provides a number of routines for
setting individual camera components. For example, the single command in
Program 6.3 performs same task as Program 6.2 — it sets the camera field to
have an aspect ratio of 4/3.

```
HC_QSet_Camera_Field("?Picture", 8.0 / 3.0, 2.0);
```

**Program 6.3**     Changing of the camera field with HC_QSet_Camera_Field.

This command behaves slightly differently, depending on whether a camera
attribute has been set previously on "?Picture". If "?Picture" already has a local
camera attribute, this command will change only the camera field of that camera,
and will leave the other components of the camera alone. But if "?Picture" does
not have a local camera attribute, this command will create a new camera with all
default values, change the camera field, and set this new attribute on "?Picture".

Thus, Program 6.3 is not equivalent to Program 6.2. Program 6.2 used the net
values for all the components of the new camera (except for the camera field),
whereas Program 6.3 uses the default values for all the components (other than
the field). Most of the time, however, the values inherited by "?Picture" for the

camera components are the same as the default values, so these two programs would produce the same results.

In addition to the HC_Set_Camera_Field command, the other components of a camera can be set with the HC_Set_Camera_Position, HC_Set_Camera_Target, HC_Set_Camera_Up_Vector, and HC_Set_Camera_Projection commands. Each of these commands creates a default camera if the segment does not already have a camera attribute set on it.

Each of the commands to set a component of the camera has a corresponding command to show the value of that component. For example, you can determine the camera field using HC_Show_Camera_Field. Or you can determine the net value of the camera field with HC_Show_Net_Camera_Field. This command will work only if the current segment has a local camera attribute set on it.

As you should with the HC_Set_Camera command, if you want to use one of these commands to change the camera for your entire scene, you should make sure that you set the camera attribute on "?Picture".

### 6.1.6     Camera Movement

Once you have a camera set up, you might want to move it around the scene. You can move it using HC_Set_Camera, but that would be clumsy, so HOOPS provides a number of routines to make it easier. These routines borrow their names from film-making jargon.

### 6.1.6.1

**Zoom.** The HC_Zoom_Camera command lets you act as though you have a zoom lens on your camera. This command takes a single floating-point argument — for example,

```
HC_Zoom_Camera(2.0);
```

A zoom by a factor of 2.0 makes everything look twice as big as before, but it also means that the camera sees less of the scene. The same command with an argument of 0.5 will zoom out by the same factor, which makes objects smaller but views more of the scene.

The HC_Zoom_Camera command actually modifies the camera field — a zoom by a factor of 2.0 makes the camera field one-half as big, in both dimensions.

If you are using a perspective projection (the default), then zooming in and out can change how objects look in perspective. Very wide camera angles (which act like a wide-angle lens) accentuate perspective and make objects look strange; very small camera angles (equivalent to a telephoto lens) reduce perspective. If you use a small enough camera angle, perspective will virtually disappear (indeed, an orthographic projection can be thought of as a camera infinitely far away with an infinitely large zoom factor).

**6.1.6.2**      **Dolly.** The HC_Dolly_Camera command moves both the position of the camera and the camera target. Dollying the camera produces the same change in the view as would occur if you translated the scene in the opposite direction (Figure 6.6).

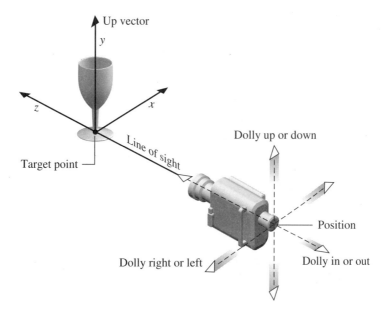

**Figure 6.6**      Dollying of the camera.

The HC_Dolly_Camera command takes three floating-point arguments. The first argument is the amount to dolly to the right (or, if negative, left), the second argument is the amount to dolly up (or, if negative, down), and the third argument is the amount to dolly in toward the target (or, if negative, away from the target).

Dollying the camera leaves unchanged the width and height of the camera field and the up vector (although they are now relative to the new camera target).

**6.1.6.3**      **Dolly versus zoom.** Dollying the camera forward and back and zooming the camera in and out might seem to have a similar effect on a view, but the effects are actually quite different. If you are using an orthographic projection, then dollying the camera will not make the objects in the scene get larger or smaller, because, in an orthographic view, the size of an object does not depend on that object's distance from the camera. To make objects larger or smaller in an orthographic projection, you need to zoom the camera (zooming changes the camera field).

In a perspective projection, zooming the camera in and out will make the objects larger or smaller, but it will also change the perspective in the scene. Dollying the camera forward and back will make objects in the scene larger or smaller without changing perspective, but if there is an object close in front of the viewpoint, then dollying the camera forward might put that object behind the camera (or, even more disconcerting, put the camera inside of the object). Likewise, dollying the camera back might put an object that used to be behind the camera in front of it, blocking the view.

**6.1.6.4**      **Orbit.** Another useful command is HC_Orbit_Camera. This command lets you view your scene from various angles. The name *orbit* indicates that this command acts as though the camera were a moon orbiting around the object that you wish to view (actually, around the camera target point). Orbiting the camera produces the same change in the view as would occur if you rotated the scene the opposite direction about the target point, as shown in Figure 6.7.

The two arguments to HC_Orbit_Camera are floating-point numbers. The first number is the amount to orbit around to the right (or, if negative, to the left). The second number is the amount to orbit up (or, if negative, down). If both arguments are nonzero, the left–right orbit is performed first.

For example, if we start with the default camera, then the command

```
HC_Orbit_Camera(90.0, 0.0);
```

orbits the camera such that the camera is looking at the scene from the positive *x* axis.

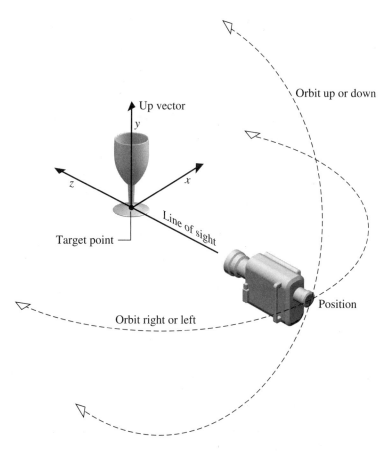

Up vector

$y$

$z$

$x$

Line of sight

Target point

Orbit up or down

Position

Orbit right or left

**Figure 6.7**      Orbiting of the camera.

If you orbit the camera up or down, the up vector is rotated by the same amount, so it remains perpendicular to the new line of sight. If you orbit the camera up 180 degrees (up and over the top), the scene will be upside down (with the up vector pointing in the negative *y* direction), but if you orbit the camera right 180 degrees, the scene will be right-side up (with no change to the up vector).

Each call to HC_Orbit_Camera (like calls to all the camera-movement commands) works relative to the current camera position, so successive calls are cumulative. Two calls, each of which orbits the camera 10 degrees to the right, will orbit the camera a total of 20 degrees.

**6.1.6.5**    **Pan.** Imagine the camera positioned on a tripod. Without changing the position of the tripod, you can swivel the head of the tripod right and left, or up and down. This movement is called *panning*. Panning the camera changes the camera target, but leaves the camera position unchanged. In addition, if you pan up or down, the camera up vector is rotated an equivalent amount, so it remains perpendicular to the new line of sight.

The two arguments to HC_Pan_Camera are the amount (in degrees) to pan to the right (or, if negative, to the left), and the amount to pan up (or, if negative, down). For example, if someone says "look, up in the sky, it's a...", you probably want the following command:

```
HC_Pan_Camera(0.0, 90.0);
```

If both an up–down pan and a right–left pan are specified, then the right–left pan is performed first.

Note that pan and orbit both rotate the camera, but HC_Orbit_Camera rotates the camera about the target point and changes the camera position, whereas the command HC_Pan_Camera rotates the camera about the camera position and changes the camera target.

**6.1.6.6**    **Roll.** The HC_Roll_Camera command rotates the camera about the line of sight, leaving both the camera position and target unchanged. It is equivalent to rotating the up vector. A positive roll rotates the camera counterclockwise, which makes the scene appear to rotate clockwise. Rolling the camera produces the same change to the view as would occur if you rotated the scene the opposite direction about the line of sight. Rolling the camera continuously is a good way to get horribly dizzy.

The following command causes the camera to stand on its head, turning the scene upside-down.

```
HC_Roll_Camera(180.0);
```

### 6.1.7    Filling of the Screen with Your Scene

The default HOOPS camera assumes that your scene lies between −1.0 and +1.0 on the *x* and *y* axes. In reality, of course, most scenes are not that cooperative. A scene might be much larger or smaller, or it might not even lie at the origin. This section presents simple programs that will make it easy for you to set up a camera in your application.

For example, say that your scene contains objects that lie between −100 and +100. You could change the camera field, but then your camera field would be much larger (200 units) than the distance between the camera position and the camera target (which, by default, is 5 units). This situation will give you the equivalent of a very wide lens and consequently a very distorted perspective view (objects closer to the camera position will appear overly large).

To make this image look normal, you also need to move the camera position back (just like a photographer might move back when photographing a large scene). How far should you move the HOOPS camera? In the default camera, the camera field is 2 units wide and the camera position is 5 units from the target, so, if our new camera field is 200 units wide, then it stands to reason that our new camera position should be 500 units back. To view this scene, we would use the following commands:

```
1  HC_Open_Segment("?Picture");
2     HC_Set_Camera_Position(0.0, 0.0, -500.0);
3     HC_Set_Camera_Field(200.0, 200.0);
4  HC_Close_Segment();
```

These commands work if our scene is centered about the origin, but what if it is not? For example, what if our scene lies between 0 and 200 on the *x* axis? We could translate the scene until it is centered, but that would be cheating. Instead, we set a new camera target (in addition to a new camera position and camera field), as follows:

```
1  HC_Open_Segment("?Picture");
2     HC_Set_Camera_Target(100.0, 0.0, 0.0);
3     HC_Set_Camera_Position(100.0, 0.0, -500.0);
4     HC_Set_Camera_Field(200.0, 200.0);
5  HC_Close_Segment();
```

Both the camera position (line 3) and the camera target (line 2) have been moved 100 units in the positive *x* direction; the camera no longer lies on the *z* axis, and it is not looking at the origin. Because both the camera position and target have been moved by the same amount, the new line of sight is parallel to the old line of sight (the *z* axis), but is translated 100 units in the positive *x* direction. Similarly, if the object were not centered on the *y* axis, we could change the *y* value of the camera position and target by changing the second argument to these two commands (on lines 2 and 3).

Because it is common to change the camera position, target, and field at the same time, HOOPS provides a single command to change all three. Instead of calculating and setting a new camera position, target, and field, we can use the HC_Set_Camera_By_Volume command. Given the *x* and *y* range of a scene, this command sets up a reasonable view for you. For example, to view the scene just described, which lies between 0 and 200 on the *x* axis and −100 and +100 on the *y* axis, you would use the following command:

```
HC_QSet_Camera_By_Volume("?Picture", "perspective",
    0.0, 200.0, -100.0, 100.0);
```

The HC_Set_Camera_By_Volume command also lets you set the projection.

HC_Set_Camera_By_Volume always sets the line of sight parallel to the *z* axis, with the camera displaced in the negative *z* direction from the target, looking toward the *x, y* plane, and with the up vector pointing in the positive *y* direction. If you do not want these defaults, you can first call HC_Set_Camera_By_Volume, and then orbit or roll the camera to the desired position.

As you should with the other camera-oriented commands, if you want the camera created by HC_Set_Camera_By_Volume to apply to your entire scene, you should be careful to use this command on a segment such as "?Picture".

### 6.1.7.1

**Setting the camera to a bounding volume.** You can use the command HC_Set_Camera_By_Volume even if you do not know the extent of a scene. Program 6.4 determines the extent of the geometry in the database tree under the "?Picture" segment using the HC_Compute_Circumcuboid command, and sets an appropriate camera on "?Picture" to view it:

```
1  HC_Open_Segment("?Picture");
2     Point min, max;
```

```
 3      // find the bounding box of the object
 4      int success = HC_Compute_Circumcuboid(".",
 5              &min, &max);
 6      if (!success) printf("no geometry in ?Picture");

 7      // convert to world coordinates
 8      HC_Compute_Coordinates(".",
 9              "object", &min, "world", &min);
10      HC_Compute_Coordinates(".",
11              "object", &max, "world", &max);

12      // the conversion of object -> world coordinates
13      // may have flipped the min and max points
14      if (min.x > max.x) {
15          float tmp = min.x; min.x = max.x; max.x = tmp;
16      }
17      if (min.y > max.y) {
18          float tmp = min.y; min.y = max.y; max.y = tmp;
19      }

20      HC_Set_Camera_By_Volume("perspective",
21                  min.x, max.x, min.y, max.y);

22  HC_Close_Segment();
```

**Program 6.4**     Setting of the camera to a bounding volume.

Line 1 of Program 6.4 opens "?Picture" as the current segment. Line 2 defines two points, called min and max, that will be used to hold the min and max points of the bounding volume of the scene. The bounding volume is retrieved in line 4 with the HC_Compute_Circumcuboid command. This command always takes a segment name as an argument, so we use "." to indicate that we want to know the bounding volume for the current segment ("?Picture").

The bounding volume is always returned without regard to any transformations on the current segment, so, in order to take into account any transformations on "?Picture", we need to transform the min and max points into world coordinates (note that, if we are absolutely sure that "?Picture" does not have any modeling transformations set on it, we can leave out lines 7 through 19). Lines 8 and 10 transform the min and max points from the object-coordinate system of the current segment into the world-coordinate system. Lines 12 through 19 make sure that min is still less than max after the transformation. Finally, line 20 sets up the camera to view the bounding volume of the scene.

**6.1.7.2**        **Keeping parts of the camera constant.** Program 6.4 ignored the current camera when it set up its camera. So regardless of what direction the old camera was facing, the new camera always viewed the scene from the negative $z$ direction (facing toward positive $z$). Sometimes, that is not what you want. Sometimes, you want to keep some parts of the old camera, but want to modify the camera (slightly) to fit the scene into the output window.

For example, you might want to keep viewing the scene from the same angle. Your graphics application may let the user orbit and dolly the camera around to view the scene from any desired angle or position, but you also want to provide a command to fit the scene into the output window. Users would be disconcerted if they were viewing the scene from (for example) the positive $y$ axis (from above), but when they pushed the button to fit the view to the scene, the view shifted abruptly such that they were viewing from the negative $z$ axis. Instead, you would like to keep viewing from the positive $y$ axis, but change other components of the camera to fit the view to the scene.

Alternatively, you might want to keep the same camera position, and to change the direction that the camera is facing. An example is an application that flies the camera around a scene during an animation, to look at the scene from all sides, but at the same time keeps the scene centered in the view.

We shall present two routines, one to solve each of these two problems. Both routines start with the current camera. The first routine (Program 6.5) dollies the camera (which keeps the line of sight parallel to the line of sight of the original camera) until the camera is looking at the center of the scene, and then dollies the camera (again) forward or back until the scene just fills the view. The second routine (Program 6.6) keeps the camera position the same, and pans until the camera is looking at the center of the scene, then dollies the camera forward or back until the scene fills the view.

Program 6.6 is slightly more intuitive, since, as humans, we look at a new object by turning our head to face it, rather than by keeping our head facing the same direction and translating our body until we can see the object. Program 6.5 has the advantage that it keeps the view angle the same, so it is more reasonable if all we are trying to do is to center the scene in the view. Dollying the camera (as in Program 6.5) is equivalent to translating the object by the opposite amount, whereas a pan (used in Program 6.6) also appears to rotate the object.

The first routine works as follows:

1. Find the centroid of the scene to be viewed.

2. Preserving the angle of the current line-of-sight vector, dolly the camera such that the line of sight passes through the centroid of the scene. Do so by dollying the camera until it is positioned exactly at the center of the scene.

3. Back off the position of the camera so that the distance to the target is 2.5 times the field width. In addition, constrain the position to lie along the line of sight. Do so by dollying the camera in the negative $z$ direction (the dolly works in viewpoint space, and viewpoint $z$ is the line of sight).

4. Set the camera field width and height to be twice the length of the radius of the object's bounding sphere.

The two arguments to the dolly_camera_to_object function are the name of the segment containing the camera (typically "?Picture"), and the name of the segment containing the scene (can also be "?Picture").

```
1   void dolly_camera_to_object(
2       char * camera_path,
3       char * object_path) {

4       // find the centroid of the scene
5       Point center;
6       float radius;
7       HC_Compute_Circumsphere(object_path,
8           &center, &radius);

9       // find the current settings for the camera
10      HC_Open_Segment(camera_path);
11          Point position, target;
12          HC_Show_Net_Camera_Position(&position.x,
13              &position.y, &position.z);
14          HC_Show_Net_Camera_Target(&target.x,
15              &target.y, &target.z);

16          // dolly the camera to view the scene center
17          HC_Dolly_Camera(center.x - target.x,
18              center.y - target.y, center.z - target.z);
```

```
19          // back off
20          Point view_axis;
21          view_axis.set_point(center.x - position.x,
22                  center.y - position.y,
23                  center.z - position.z);
24          float distance =
25                  HC_Compute_Vector_Length(&view_axis);
26          // compute distance to back out the camera
27          float back_up = 2.5 * (2.0 * radius) - distance;
28          // the dolly moves the target as well
29          HC_Dolly_Camera(0.0, 0.0, - back_up);
30          // set the target back to the object centroid
31          HC_Set_Camera_Target(center.x,
32                  center.y, center.z);

33          // set the camera field width and height
34          if (radius == 0.0) radius = 1.0;
35          HC_Set_Camera_Field(2 * radius, 2 * radius);

36      HC_Close_Segment ();
37  }
```

**Program 6.5**     Dollying the camera to fit the scene in its view.

Program 6.6 is simpler than Program 6.5.

1. Find the centroid of the scene to be viewed.

2. Set the camera target to the scene's centroid; this action logically is a pan.

3. Set the camera field width and height to be twice the length of the radius of the object's bounding sphere.

4. Adjust the position of the camera such that the distance to the target is 2.5 times the field width, by dollying the camera in the negative $z$ direction.

```
1  void pan_camera_to_object(
2     char *camera_path,
3     char *object_path) {
```

```
 4      // find the centroid of the scene
 5      Point center;
 6      float radius;
 7      HC_Compute_Circumsphere(object_path,
 8              &center, &radius);

 9      HC_Open_Segment(camera_path);
10          // find the current settings for the camera
11          Point position;
12          HC_Show_Net_Camera_Position(&position.x,
13                  &position.y, &position.z);

14          // set the camera target to the scene's centroid
15          HC_Set_Camera_Target(center.x,
16                  center.y, center.z);

17          // set the camera field width and height
18          if (radius == 0.0) radius = 1.0;
19          HC_Set_Camera_Field(2 * radius, 2 * radius);

20          // back off
21          Point   view_axis;
22          view_axis.set_point(center.x - position.x,
23                  center.y - position.y,
24                  center.z - position.z);
25          float distance =
26                  HC_Compute_Vector_Length(&view_axis);
27          // compute distance to back out the camera
28          float back_up = 2.5 * (2.0 * radius) - distance;

29          // the dolly moves the target as well
30          HC_Dolly_Camera(0.0, 0.0, - back_up);
31          // put it back at the center
32          HC_Set_Camera_Target(center.x,
33                  center.y, center.z);

34      HC_Close_Segment();
35  }
```

**Program 6.6**   Panning the camera to fit a scene in its view.

**6.1.8**          **Creation of a New Camera**

As mentioned in Section 6.1.5, if you set a camera attribute on a segment that does not already have a camera attribute set on it, HOOPS will create a new camera for you, and will set it on that segment. Most of the time, when you are just modifying your scene's camera, you will be executing camera-oriented commands on "?Picture". There are a few times, however, when you might want to have more than one camera in a scene. You already know how to do that — simply call any camera-oriented command on a segment that does not already have the camera attribute set on it, and HOOPS will create a new camera — but what does it mean to have more than one camera in a scene?

The main reason to have more than one camera in a scene is if you want different parts of a scene to be viewed with different cameras. For example, you might want to be able to orbit the main camera to view an object from different directions, while using a separate camera to view a background pattern for your scene from a fixed position. Or you might create a scene that contains two objects, and you want one object to be viewed in perspective and the other object to be viewed orthographically.

As we discussed in Section 6.1, cameras are inherited just like any attribute. In Figure 6.8, a camera has been set on segment B. Everything in the scene will be viewed by the default camera except for those objects underneath (or in) segment B.

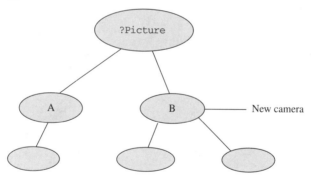

**Figure 6.8**          A scene with more than one camera.

You can find out the value of the camera that will be used to view the geometry in a segment by using the command HC_Show_Net_Camera (or you can show the net value of any of the camera's components, for example, by using the command HC_Show_Net_Camera_Field).

Note that simply inserting a camera does not cause anything to be sent to the display screen; that is the function of a driver. Any cameras that you create must still be under some driver segment (such as "?Picture") to be displayed. The camera attribute simply defines the viewing transformation that will be used by the driver to view the geometry. A good way to think of the difference between a camera and a driver is that a camera maps a scene into a window, whereas a driver instance maps a top-level window onto a display device.

You can also use multiple cameras to create multiple views of the same object. You normally use multiple views only when you have multiple windows, each with its own camera. Viewing the same object multiple times logically requires including the object more than once in the scene (for example, by using the HC_Include_Segment command). There is an example of the use of multiple views, with multiple cameras, in Section 6.1.9.3.

## 6.1.9    Oblique Projections

So far, we have talked about only orthographic and perspective projections. HOOPS also provides two oblique projections: *oblique perspective* and *oblique orthographic*. Oblique projections involving *skewing*.

**6.1.9.1**    **Oblique orthographic.** An orthographic projection is typically used in drafting applications so that objects do not get smaller as they get farther away, and so that parallel lines remain parallel. Unfortunately, a regular orthographic projection can cause some lines to be hidden. For example, in Figure 6.9, viewing a cube straight on in an orthographic view causes it to look like a square.

Orthographic                          Oblique orthographic

**Figure 6.9**    Orthographic and oblique orthographic views of a cube.

In an oblique orthographic view, the $x$ and $y$ coordinates are skewed depending on the $z$ coordinate. For example, a typical oblique orthographic view moves objects up and to the right (but does not make them smaller) as they get farther away. We can thus see the sides of the cube, even though we are still viewing it straight on. See the documentation in the *HOOPS Reference Manual* for the HC_Set_Camera_Projection command for more information.

An oblique orthographic view of a wireframe cube produces a well-known optical illusion called a Nekker Cube (the cube on the right in Figure 6.9). Our human preference is to interpret this cube as though it were viewed from above, but it could equally well be a cube viewed from below. Try mentally switching the front and the back face.

**6.1.9.2**     **Oblique perspective.** An oblique-perspective projection is useful when the target plane of a perspective projection is not perpendicular to the line of sight. There are a few (albeit specialized) situations where this kind of projection can be useful.

For example, consider a graphics system with three display monitors arranged side by side to display a panoramic view of a single scene. Logically, the three monitors are displaying a single view, but physically we need to create three separate views, one for each monitor. For the two side monitors, the screen is not perpendicular to the line of sight, so we must use a target plane (which is always parallel to the screen) that is not perpendicular to the line of sight. Figure 6.10 shows the situation viewed from above (looking down the $y$ axis).

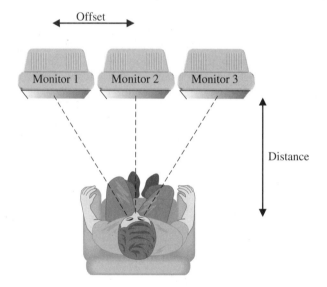

**Figure 6.10**     Use of oblique perspective with multiple monitors.

To make this setup work, we rotate the target plane about the *y* axis for the side views, using an oblique-perspective projection.

To determine the proper angle to rotate the target plane for each monitor, we take the offset from the camera target to the center of the monitor, divided by the distance from the viewpoint to the (entire) target plane, and take the arc tangent of the result. For example, if we are using a default camera for monitor 2, then monitor 1 is offset 2.0 units, and the distance from the viewpoint to the target plane is (the default) 5.0 units, which gives us arctan(2.0 / 5.0) = 21.8 degrees. For the camera corresponding to monitor 1, we issue the following command:

```
HC_Set_Camera_Projection(
        "oblique perspective = 21.8");
```

The camera for monitor 3 will have its target plane rotated –21.8 degrees.

The same trick may be useful even if you are not using multiple monitors. For example, consider a flight simulator used for training airplane pilots. Such simulators display the view that the pilot would see out of a window in a monitor positioned where the window would be. Often, these windows are not perpendicular to the pilot's line of sight, so an oblique-perspective view is required.

Another use for oblique-perspective views is for creating stereo images. To create a stereo image, we need to create two views of an object: one from the perspective of each eye. We already know how to create two views of the same object using two cameras. We offset each camera slightly left or right to approximate the position of each eye; however, then the line of sight for each eye is no longer perpendicular to the target. Figure 6.11 shows the situation viewed from above.

We rotate the target plane slightly for each eye with an oblique-perspective projection.

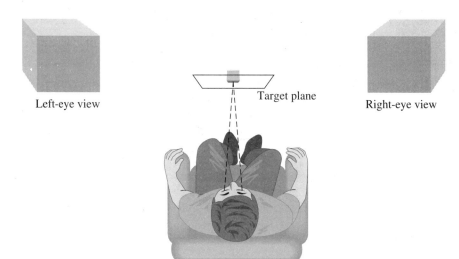

**Figure 6.11**     Use of oblique perspective for a stereo view.

**6.1.9.3**     **Multiple-projection example.** Program 6.7 creates four views of a cube. Each view uses a different kind of projection: perspective, orthographic, oblique perspective, and oblique orthographic.

```
1   void main() {
2       // create a cube centered at the origin
3       HC_Open_Segment("?Include library/cube");
4           static Point point_list[8] = {
5               {-0.3, -0.3, -0.3},
6               {0.3, -0.3, -0.3},
7               {0.3, 0.3, -0.3},
8               {-0.3, 0.3, -0.3},
9               {-0.3, -0.3, 0.3},
10              {0.3, -0.3, 0.3},
11              {0.3, 0.3, 0.3},
12              {-0.3, 0.3, 0.3} };
```

```
13          static int face_list[30] = {
14                4, 0, 1, 2, 3,
15                4, 4, 5, 1, 0,
16                4, 2, 1, 5, 6,
17                4, 7, 4, 0, 3,
18                4, 7, 6, 5, 4,
19                4, 3, 2, 6, 7 };
20          HC_Insert_Shell(8, point_list, 30, face_list);
21     HC_Close_Segment();
```

**Program 6.7**     Four views of a cube — definition of the cube.

The first part of Program 6.7 (lines 1 through 21) creates a cube in the include library (so that the cube can be included in the scene four times). This cube is centered at the origin and is 0.6 units in each dimension.

The remainder of the program creates four views of the cube. First, we open "?Picture" and turn off the visibility of faces and markers, so that only the edges of each cube will be visible (since we do not have any surfaces visible, we should also turn off hidden surfaces with HC_Set_Heuristics, but we do not bother for such a simple example). For each view, we translate the object into one quadrant of the window (so that the cubes do not all appear at the same place), set the appropriate projection, and include the cube.

```
22     // create four views
23     HC_Open_Segment("?Picture");
24        HC_Set_Visibility("faces=off, markers=off");

25        HC_Open_Segment("view 1");
26           // move to upper right
27           HC_Translate_Object(0.5, 0.5, 0.0);
28           HC_Set_Camera_Projection("perspective");
29           HC_Include_Segment("?Include library/cube");
30        HC_Close_Segment();

31        HC_Open_Segment("view 2");
32           // move to upper left
33           HC_Translate_Object(-0.5, 0.5, 0.0);
34           HC_Set_Camera_Projection("orthographic");
35           HC_Include_Segment("?Include library/cube");
36        HC_Close_Segment();
```

```
37          HC_Open_Segment("view 3");
38              // move to lower right
39              HC_Translate_Object(0.5, -0.5, 0.0);
40              HC_Set_Camera_Projection(
41                      "oblique perspective = (15, 15)");
42              HC_Include_Segment("?Include library/cube");
43          HC_Close_Segment();

44          HC_Open_Segment("view 4");
45              // move to lower left
46              HC_Translate_Object(-0.5, -0.5, 0.0);
47              HC_Set_Camera_Projection(
48                      "oblique orthographic = (15, 15)");
49              HC_Include_Segment("?Include library/cube");
50          HC_Close_Segment();

51      HC_Close_Segment();       // ?Picture
52      HC_Pause();
53  }
```

**Program 6.7 (continued)**   Four views of a cube.

Note that, because we set a camera projection inside each view, this scene actually has *five* different cameras: the default camera (which is not used to view any geometry), and a camera in each view.

Recall that individual camera components do not inherit separately, so, even if we changed a component in the default camera, that change would not affect any of the view cameras. For example, we cannot change the overall camera position by changing the camera position of the default camera and letting the position inherit. To change the camera position, we have to change it in all four view cameras.

Note that the orthographic view (upper left in Figure 6.12) looks like a square, since we are viewing the cube head on and there is no perspective to make the far face of the cube smaller. The perspective view (upper right in Figure 6.12) might look a little strange at first, because we are viewing the cube from slightly below

Figure 6.12 shows what the output looks like .

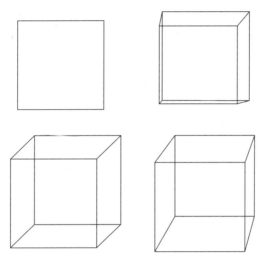

**Figure 6.12**     Four views of a cube, with different projections.

and to the left — the larger face is in front. The oblique-orthographic view (lower left in Figure 6.12) is like a standard engineering drawing of a cube — the faces do not get smaller as they get farther away, but they are offset up and to the right. Note the HC_Set_Camera_Projection command on lines 47 and 48, which sets both the $x$ offset and $y$ offset. Finally, the oblique-perspective view uses the same $x$ and $y$ offsets as does the oblique-orthographic view, but adds perspective.

### 6.1.10     Stretched Projections and 2D Scenes

In Section 6.1.4.2, we saw how HOOPS keeps the aspect ratio of a scene constant, even when we change the aspect ratio of the window. HOOPS keeps the aspect ratio constant by adding extra space to the camera field either on the sides or on the top and bottom. In some cases, however, we might want the camera field to fill the output window exactly, even if that means changing the aspect ratio of the scene. In HOOPS, we can fill the output window exactly with a *stretched projection.* A stretched projection stretches the scene to fit into the output window.

Program 6.8 draws a circle in the middle of the screen, and demonstrates stretched projections.

```
 1  HC_Open_Segment("?Picture");
 2      HC_Set_Driver_Options("subscreen stretching");
 3      Point p1 = {0.0, 0.5, 0.0};
 4      Point p2 = {0.5, 0.0, 0.0};
 5      Point p3 = {0.0, -0.5, 0.0};
 6      HC_Insert_Circle(&p1, &p2, &p3);
 7      HC_Pause();
 8      HC_Set_Camera_Projection("stretched");
 9      HC_Pause();
10  HC_Close_Segment();
```

**Program 6.8**    Circle drawn with two projections.

Initially, Program 6.8 draws the circle using the default (perspective) projection, and then pauses (on line 7). At this point, you should resize the output window, changing its aspect ratio. The command on line 2 allows you to change the aspect ratio by enabling subscreen stretching. As you resize the output window (and change its aspect ratio), the circle remains circular, as shown in Figure 6.13.

  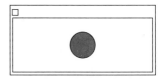

**Figure 6.13**    Regular projection — circle stays circular.

After you click the mouse inside the HOOPS output window, Program 6.8 changes the projection to "stretched" and pauses again (on line 9). If you now resize the output window, then the aspect ratio of the scene will change as you change the aspect ratio of the window. Thus, the circle will not remain circular, as shown in Figure 6.14.

  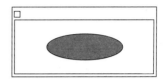

**Figure 6.14**　　Stretched projection — circle stretches to match window.

With a stretched projection, the scene stretches to fit the output window. Why would we want that to happen? Do we not want our circles to remain circular and our squares to remain square?

One case where we would use a stretched projection is to draw a border around the inside of a window. Program 6.9 draws a thick black border by drawing a black edge around the inside of the window.

```
1   HC_Open_Segment("?Picture");
2       HC_Set_Driver_Options("subscreen stretching");

3       HC_Open_Segment("border");
4           HC_Set_Camera_Projection("stretched");
5           Point border[4] = {
6                   {-1.0, -1.0, 0.0},
7                   { 1.0, -1.0, 0.0},
8                   { 1.0,  1.0, 0.0},
9                   {-1.0,  1.0, 0.0}
10          };
11          HC_Insert_Polygon(4, border);

12          HC_Set_Visibility("faces=off, edges=on");
13          HC_Set_Edge_Weight(50.0);

14      HC_Close_Segment();  // border

15  HC_Close_Segment();  // ?Picture

16  HC_Pause();
```

**Program 6.9**　　A window border using a stretched projection.

The segment named "border" (opened on line 3) contains a polygon (lines 5 through 11) that is exactly the same size as the camera frame. Since this segment has a stretched projection (set on line 4), this polygon will fit exactly inside the output window. Only the edges of the polygon are drawn (line 12), with an edge weight of 50 (line 13), to give a thick border.

Because edge weights are specified in screen relative coordinates, the border drawn in Program 6.9 does not scale (change in thickness) when you resize the output window. To draw a border that does scale with the window, you could draw a border with four skinny polygons, one along each edge of the window. Or you could draw a shell with a hole in it.

Note that line 4 — which sets the camera projection to "stretched" — creates a new camera in the segment named "border" (not in "?Picture"). Thus, only the geometry inside "border" will be drawn with a stretched projection; any objects in the "?Picture" segment, but not in "border", will be drawn with a nonstretched projection. For example, we can insert the circle from Program 6.8 under "?Picture", and it will not be affected by the camera in "border" (it will use the default camera). When the user resizes the window for this scene, the border will change aspect ratio to match the window, but the circle will keep a one-to-one aspect ratio and will remain circular, as shown in Figure 6.15.

**Figure 6.15**　　The border stretches, but the circle does not.

There are other cases where we might want to use a stretched projection, but they are mainly for 2D graphics. For example, in Chapter 2, Program 2.7, which draws a bar graph, uses a stretched projection. In the case of a bar graph — or almost any statistical graph — the aspect ratio of the scene is not important, so we prefer to have the graph fill the output window. (The exception is pie charts, which we want to remain circular.)

Another case where stretched projections are useful is when we want to place an object in a specific position of the output window, even if the output window is resized. For example, to place an object (such as a user-interface gadget) in the upper-right corner of the window, we can position it at $x = 1$, $y = 1$, but then it will appear in the upper-right corner only if the output window is square. By using a stretched projection, we can place objects accurately regardless of the aspect ratio of the output window. Another such use would be to place a toolbar along one of the sides of the window. The toolbar itself could then use a non-stretched projection, so that the tools (buttons and sliders) would not stretch.

The word *oblique* can be used as a modifier for any of the three kinds of projections. We have already seen the *oblique-orthographic* and the *oblique-perspective* projections; HOOPS also supports an *oblique-stretched* projection. The terms *orthographic, perspective*, and *stretched* are mutually exclusive, however, so you cannot specify a *stretched-perspective* projection. Stretched projections are always orthographic. Since stretched projections are used almost exclusively for 2D scenes, this limitation is not a problem.

## 6.2    Printer and Image Output

When the HOOPS database is rendered, the output is sent, by default, to the local computer's screen. It is also possible to send the output to a printer, or to an output file. In this section, we discuss the different places to which you can send the rendered output image, and the various ways that you can send it.

As we discussed in Section 4.3, the driver segment determines where the HOOPS output is sent. For example, if you place geometry under the segment named "/driver/msw/window0", then the msw (Microsoft Windows) driver will be used to draw the geometry in a window named window0.

In addition to the drivers for various displays, such as msw or x11, HOOPS has several other drivers. For example, the driver named "postscript" creates a file of PostScript commands, instead of drawing the output on a display screen. Thus, you can place some geometry under a segment named "/driver/postscript/file.ps", and, when HC_Update_Display is called, this geometry will be translated into PostScript commands and placed into a file named "file.ps". Likewise, the driver named "hpgl" generates Hewlett-Packard Graphics Language (HPGL) files to drive printers and plotters, and the "pict" driver generates Macintosh PICT files. The HOOPS drivers are documented in the *HOOPS Installation Guide* (which is included on the CD-ROM).

There is also a driver named "image" that does not produce any output. The image driver takes the result of rendering the HOOPS graphics database and places that result into a HOOPS image, where it can then be used like any HOOPS image (for example, as a texture map or a window background). The image driver is described in Section 6.2.2, and is documented in the *HOOPS Installation Guide*.

## 6.2.1    Sending of Output to Another Driver

There are several ways that a HOOPS program can send output to another driver, such as a printer driver: by redefining "?Picture" using the HOOPS_PICTURE environment variable, by defining the HOOPS_HARDCOPY environment variable, or by opening a new driver instance explicitly.

### 6.2.1.1    **Redefining "?Picture" using HOOPS_PICTURE.** For a simple HOOPS program that just displays a single image (such as many of the example programs in this book), the easiest way to get hardcopy output is simply to change the definition of the "?Picture" alias to refer to a hardcopy driver. You can do that inside the program with HC_Define_Alias, but there is an even easier way.

As we discussed in Sections 4.3 and 4.4.7, you can set the alias "?Picture" using the HOOPS_PICTURE environment variable. For example, if that variable HOOPS_PICTURE has the value "msw/window0", then the "?Picture" alias is set to "?driver/msw/window0", and any geometry placed under the "?Picture" segment will be drawn by the msw driver into window0. If HOOPS_PICTURE has not been set, then a reasonable default driver is chosen (depending on the current platform), and a warning message is issued.

To cause the output instead to be rendered by the PostScript driver into a file named "output.ps", you can just set HOOPS_PICTURE to "postscript/output.ps" and run the program. No output will be produced on the computer's screen; instead, the output will be placed into the file "output.ps". You can then print this file to any PostScript printer, include it in a document (that is how many of the illustrations in this book were produced), or even send it to another user.

You can use the same technique to produce HPGL, CGM, and PICT output. You can also use this technique to set the driver to be the printf driver; this option does not draw anything at all, but rather produces a file containing a printout of what HOOPS thought it was going to draw. The printf driver is useful when your program is not drawing what you think it should be drawing, perhaps because of a hardware problem, and you want to see what HOOPS thinks it is drawing.

The advantage of using HOOPS_PICTURE to change the driver is that your program does not need to be recompiled. The disadvantage is that this technique will work for only simple programs that produce a single output image. If your program accepts any user input, this technique will not work, because hardcopy drivers naturally do not handle user input.

In addition, there are several driver options that are not applicable to hardcopy drivers, such as those dealing with windows (for example, the use-window-id driver option), or options such as gamma correction. In addition, certain hardcopy drivers require you to set special driver options. For example, the CGM and HPGL drivers require you to set the "physical size" driver option to tell them how big the output image should be drawn (what the size of the plotter paper is). HOOPS allows you to set options such as this one (without recompiling your program) using the HOOPS_PICTURE_OPTIONS environment variable.

See the chapter for each driver in the *HOOPS Installation Guide* for a list of driver options that do not apply to that driver, and of special options that must be set. Also, see Section 4.4.6 for more information on environment variables used by HOOPS.

6.2.1.2     **Defining HOOPS_HARDCOPY.** There is a slightly more robust way to produce hardcopy output, but it requires slightly more work on the part of the programmer. Unlike using HOOPS_PICTURE to select a hardcopy driver, this technique allows a program to display output on the screen and to produce hardcopy output.

Similar to the "?Picture" alias, there is a "?Hardcopy" alias that is set by the HOOPS_HARDCOPY environment variable. Using this alias, your application can easily produce a hardcopy snapshot of the current HOOPS database, as shown in Program 6.10.

```
1   HC_Open_Segment("?Hardcopy");
2       HC_Include_Segment("?Picture");
3       HC_Update_Display();
4   HC_Close_Segment();
5   HC_Delete_Segment("?Hardcopy");
```

**Program 6.10**    Printing.

If the environment variable HOOPS_HARDCOPY is set to "postscript/out.ps", then line 1 creates a segment named "/driver/postscript/out.ps" (which is an instance of the PostScript driver). Line 2 includes everything in the "?Picture" segment, so that everything that currently appears on the screen will be printed.

Line 3 actually writes the output to the file "out.ps". Finally, we close the segment named "out.ps" and delete it. This action deletes the driver instance, which closes the output file.

If the HOOPS_HARDCOPY environment variable does not exist, then the "?Hardcopy" alias is not set, and, when line 1 is executed, HOOPS will issue an error message, saying that the alias is not defined. It is therefore a good idea for your program to check whether the HOOPS_HARDCOPY environment variable was set (using the HC_Show_Environment command). If the environment variable was not set, your application can assign a default value to the "?Hardcopy" alias, or can simply disable printing.

To print output that has more than one page, you can take advantage of the fact that HOOPS will output something only if that something is visible. In this case, we create the driver instance as before, but we set its visibility to off, as shown in lines 2 through 5 of Program 6.11.

Then, each time we want to print a page, we execute lines 7 through 9. Finally, when we are done printing and want to close the output file, we execute line 11.

```
1   // setup for hardcopy
2   HC_Open_Segment("?Hardcopy");
3       HC_Include_Segment("?Picture");
4       HC_Set_Visibility("off");
5   HC_Close_Segment();

6   // print a page
7   HC_QSet_Visibility("?Hardcopy", "on");
8   HC_Update_Display();
9   HC_QSet_Visibility("?Hardcopy", "off");

10  // close outfile
11  HC_Delete_Segment("?Hardcopy");
```

**Program 6.11**    Printing of multiple pages.

Some hardcopy drivers require you to set driver options, such as the size of the printer output. You can set them either inside your program (using HC_Set_Driver_Options on the appropriate driver instance segment), or using environment variables. You use the HOOPS_HARDCOPY_OPTIONS environment variable to set driver options on the "?Hardcopy" driver segment.

**6.2.1.3**    **Opening a driver explicitly.** Of course, your application does not need to use any environment variables if it does not wish; it can open any driver that it chooses and send output to that driver. For example, if your application has a "print" command, this command could display a dialog that allows the user to chose whether to produce the output in PostScript, HPGL, CGM, or PICT format. The user will also specify a file name. Your program will then concatenate the file name onto the appropriate driver name, and open a segment.

For example, if the user chooses to print a PICT file, and specifies the file name "myoutput", then the application will open a segment named "?driver/pict/myoutput". The application will proceed, starting with line 2 in Program 6.10 (or line 3 in Program 6.11).

## 6.2.2 Case Sensitivity and Special Characters

Note that HOOPS generally is not case sensitive; "?Picture" is the same as "?picture" or even "?pICTURE", and "?Hardcopy" is the same as "?hardcopy". Segment names are not case sensitive, and that can cause problems if you need to use a specific case for the output file name created by a hardcopy driver.

To create a segment name that is case sensitive, you need to enclose the name inside quotation marks (either single or double). For example, you can create a driver instance with the name "?driver/pict/'MyOutput'".

Quoted segment names are also useful if you need to place special characters in the name. For example, to use an absolute path name to specify the output file name, you could specify the name as "?driver/pict/'/user/wm/output'". The single quotation marks keep the slash marks in the file name from being interpreted by HOOPS as segment-name separators. They do so whether the segment name is specified inside your application, or via an environment variable. For example, the following command sets the HOOPS_HARDCOPY environment variable using csh (the C shell) on UNIX.

```
setenv HOOPS_HARDCOPY "pict/'/usr/wm/output'"
```

## 6.2.3 The Image Driver

The image driver is like any driver except that it does not produce any output (on the screen or into a file). Instead, the image driver places the rendered output image into a HOOPS image. You can then use the image in several ways: use it in the scene like any other image, write it out to a file, use it as a face pattern or window background, or use it as a texture map. Face patterns and texture maps are covered in Chapter 9. In this section, we deal with how to use the image driver to generate images.

To use the image driver, you need first to connect it to the HOOPS image into which it is to draw. After that, you can send objects to be rendered to the image driver, just as you would send them to any other driver. See Section 6.2.1 for information on how to use alternate drivers.

To connect the image driver to a HOOPS image, you use the "use window id" driver option on the image driver; instead of passing a window id, however, you pass the key of the image. The image itself can be anywhere in the HOOPS database. If you want the image itself to be visible, it should be in a segment under some display driver. If you want the image to be off-screen, then you can insert it anywhere in the HOOPS database that is not under a driver (or you can just turn off the visibility of the image).

Program 6.12 draws into an image, with the original scene and the resulting image both visible.

```
1   struct Point { float x, y, z; };
2   static Point point_list[8] = {
3          { -0.5F, -0.5F, -0.5F },
4          {  0.5F, -0.5F, -0.5F },
5          {  0.5F,  0.5F, -0.5F },
6          { -0.5F,  0.5F, -0.5F },
7          { -0.5F, -0.5F,  0.5F },
8          {  0.5F, -0.5F,  0.5F },
9          {  0.5F,  0.5F,  0.5F },
10         { -0.5F,  0.5F,  0.5F } };
11  static int face_list[30] = {
12         4, 0, 1, 2, 3,
13         4, 4, 5, 1, 0,
14         4, 2, 1, 5, 6,
15         4, 7, 4, 0, 3,
16         4, 7, 6, 5, 4,
17         4, 3, 2, 6, 7 };
```

```
18   void main() {
19     HC_Open_Segment("/Include Library/cube");
20         HC_Insert_Shell(8, point_list, 30, face_list);
21         HC_Set_Color("faces = blue");
22         HC_Set_Visibility("markers=off");
23         HC_Rotate_Object(30.0F, 30.0F, 0.0F);
24     HC_Close_Segment();
```

**Program 6.12**   The image driver — creating the scene.

Lines 1 through 17 define the point and face lists for a shell. Inside the main function (line 18), we create the scene in the include library (lines 19 through 24), so that we can include it both in the visible scene and in the scene to be rendered by the image driver.

```
25         HC_Open_Segment ("?Picture");

26         HC_Open_Segment("scene");
27             HC_Set_Window( -1.0, 0.0, -1.0, 1.0);
28             HC_Include_Segment("/Include Library/cube");
29             HC_Insert_Text(0.0, -0.9, 0.0, "Scene");
30         HC_Close_Segment();
```

**Program 6.12 (continued)**  The image driver — segment containing the scene.

Line 25 opens the "?Picture" segment. Underneath "?Picture", we create two segments, both of which are subwindows. The first, called "scene" (line 26), includes the cube from the include library (line 28) and inserts a text label (line 29).

```
31         HC_Open_Segment("image");
32             HC_Set_Window(0.0, 1.0, -1.0, 1.0);
33             HC_Insert_Text(0.0, -0.9, 0.0, "Image");

34             // create image under image driver
35             int width = 200;
36             int height = 150;
37             unsigned char * image_data =
38                     new unsigned char[3 * width * height];
```

```
39              long image_key = HC_KInsert_Image_By_Ref(
40                  0.0F, 0.0F, 0.0F, "RGB, name=cube",
41                  width, height, image_data);
42          HC_Close_Segment();
43       HC_Close_Segment();
```

**Program 6.12 (continued)** The image driver — segment containing the image.

The second subwindow, in a segment named "image" (line 31), contains a text label (line 33) and a single image. We specified the image to be 200 pixels wide and 150 pixels high, but it could have been any size. Line 37 allocates the memory for the image, but we do not need to initialize it, because the image will be created by the image driver. Line 39 inserts the image into the segment. Note that the image is inserted "By_Ref" (by reference). Inserting the image by reference is an optimization so that HOOPS does not make a copy of the image data (see Section 5.3.1). The key of the inserted image is saved in the variable "image_key".

```
44       // create an instance of the image driver
45       HC_Open_Segment("?driver/image/temp");
46          char buffer[64];
47          sprintf(buffer, "use window id = %ld",
48              image_key);
49          HC_Set_Driver_Options(buffer);
50          HC_Set_Rendering_Options("hsra = szb");
51          // include the segment tree from the file
52          HC_Include_Segment("/Include Library/cube");
53       HC_Close_Segment();
54       // initiate update cycle
55       HC_Pause ();
56       HC_Delete_Segment("?driver/image/temp");
57       delete [] image_data;
58    }
```

**Program 6.12 (continued)** The image driver itself.

Finally, on line 45, we create an instance of the image driver, by creating a subsegment (called "temp") under "?driver/image". Lines 46 through 49 set the "use window id" driver option of the image driver to the key of the inserted image. Line 50 sets the hsra (hidden-surface–rendering algorithm) rendering

**308**

option to be szb (software Z-buffer). Note that this option is not a driver option; it is a rendering option. Line 52 includes the cube from the include library.

 Use of the software Z-buffer algorithm is an optimization; when we are using the image driver, however, it is often a good choice. The main drawback of the software Z-buffer algorithm is that it has to allocate a Z-buffer the size of the output image; in this case, however, the output image is the size of the image into which we are rendering, which is small.

Line 55 calls HC_Pause, which initiates an update of the display. This command updates both whatever driver is attached to "?Picture" and the image driver. Since the output image from the image driver is part of the visible scene, we can see both the cube and the image of the cube on the screen (shown in Figure 6.16).

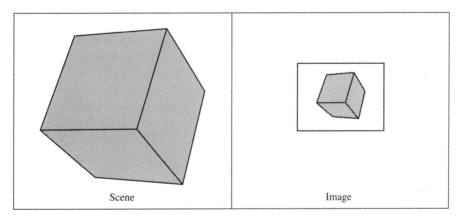

Scene                    Image

**Figure 6.16**    The scene and its image.

As well as simply viewing the image output by the image driver, as we did in Program 6.12, there are other ways you can use the output image. You can write out the image into a HOOPS metafile (see Section 6.3 for information about metafiles). If you want to write out the image in some other format, such as GIF or JPEG, you can retrieve the image data using the HC_Show_Image command, convert the RGB data into any format you wish, and write out the formatted data.

The image driver is also useful when used in conjunction with one of the hardcopy drivers (such as the PostScript, HPGL, CGM, and PICT drivers), to save the output as an image, instead of as a series of drawing commands. For example, if you want to save a scene as a PostScript image, you first render the scene using the image driver into an image, and then output the image using the PostScript driver into a file.

You can use this technique to help solve a problem that you are likely to encounter when you are trying to print scenes containing color-interpolated objects. A common example of this problem occurs when you create a PostScript file containing Gouraud-shaded objects. PostScript can use only flat shading on faces, so, to display a smooth-shaded image, the HOOPS PostScript driver will output an image at full resolution. Because a full-size PostScript image can be huge (on the order of 50 megabytes), such a file can be extremely slow to produce, and will overload many PostScript printers. By using the image driver, you can control the resolution of the output image to reduce the file size to something more manageable. This problem is discussed in Section 10.1.6.

See Chapter 16 of the *HOOPS Installation Guide* for more information on the image driver.

## 6.3        Metafiles

HOOPS provides a way to write out to a disk file part or all of the graphics database; this file is called a graphics *metafile*. A metafile can be read back into a HOOPS program. You can think of a metafile as a segment tree stored on disk. A metafile is a human-readable text file; it can be edited with a text editor, or read into or generated by other (non-HOOPS) programs.

Metafiles are useful for transferring graphic information between programs or users without sending an entire program. Metafiles are portable, so a metafile can be written on one system and read on another.

Metafiles can also be used as a sort of virtual memory. If your application has a large HOOPS database, it might not be desirable to keep the entire database in memory at the same time. Consider a game program that renders a series of rooms. There might be hundreds of rooms in the graphics database, but from any one viewpoint in the scene, you can see the interior of only one (or a few) of them. Keeping all the rooms in the graphics database uses up a lot of memory, and can slow down rendering. Instead, we can keep each room in a metafile, and read in the metafiles for only those rooms that are currently visible.

**6.3.1**    **Writing out a Metafile**

You can write out a metafile using the HC_Write_Metafile command. For example, Program 6.13 is the clock example from Chapter 5 (Program 5.8), modified so that it writes out the segment tree to a metafile. The only change to this program is the added HC_Write_Metafile command on line 57. We present the entire program because we shall refer back to it.

```
1   void insert_2D_Circle(float x, float y, float r) {
2       Point cp1, cp2, cp3;
3       cp1.set_point(x, y+r, 0.0);        // 12 o'clock
4       cp2.set_point(x+r, y, 0.0);        // 3 o'clock
5       cp3.set_point(x, y-r, 0.0);        // 6 o'clock
6       HC_Insert_Circle(&cp1, &cp2, &cp3);
7   }
8   void main() {
9       HC_Open_Segment("?Picture");
10          HC_Set_Heuristics("no hidden surfaces");
11          HC_Set_Rendering_Options(
12              "technology = software frame buffer");

13          // clock geometry
14          HC_Open_Segment("clock");
15              HC_Set_Color("dark blue");
16              HC_Set_Text_Font(
17                  "transforms, size = 0.1 oru");
18              const float rimr = 0.98; // radius of rim
19              const float numr = 0.80; // radius of numbers

20              // for each hour
21              for (int hour = 1; hour <= 12; hour++) {
22                  double angle = hour * (3.14159/6.0);
23                  float x = (float) sin(angle);
24                  float y = (float) cos(angle);
25                  // hour numerals
26                  char buffer[8];
27                  sprintf(buffer, "%d", hour);
28                  HC_Insert_Text(numr * x, numr * y, 0.0,
29                          buffer);
30              }
```

```
31              // rim and interior of clock face
32              HC_Set_Color("faces=light silver");
33              HC_Set_Edge_Weight(3.0);
34              insert_2D_Circle(0.0, 0.0, rimr);

35              // central hub
36              HC_Open_Segment("hub");
37                  HC_Set_Color("reddish blue");
38                  const float markr = 0.03;
39                  insert_2D_Circle(0.0, 0.0, markr);
40              HC_Close_Segment();

41              HC_Open_Segment("hands");
42                  HC_Set_Color("red");

43                  HC_Open_Segment("minute hand");
44                      HC_Set_Line_Weight(3.0);
45                      HC_Insert_Line(0.0, -0.2,
46                          0.0, 0.0, 0.6, 0.0);
47                  HC_Close_Segment(); // minute hand

48                  HC_Open_Segment("hour hand");
49                      HC_Set_Line_Pattern("(--");
50                      HC_Set_Line_Weight(10.0);
51                      HC_Insert_Line(0.0, -0.1,
52                          0.0, 0.0, 0.4, 0.0);
53                  HC_Close_Segment ();

54              HC_Close_Segment ();     // hands
55          HC_Close_Segment ();     // clock
56      HC_Close_Segment ();     // ?Picture

57      HC_Write_Metafile("?Picture", "clock.hmf", "");

58      HC_Pause ();
59  }
```

**Program 6.13**    Write a metafile for a clock.

The HC_Write_Metafile command (line 57) takes the segment tree starting at "?Picture" and writes it to the file "clock.hmf" (in the current directory). The third argument is used to specify options.

One useful option is "follow cross-references", which tells HOOPS to write out style and include segments. Normally, when writing out include or style segments, HOOPS writes out a reference to the name of the include or style segment, rather than writing out the segment and its contents (including any children). If you do not follow cross references, however, you should remember to write out the referenced objects to the metafile explicitly.

One problem with cross references (to include and style segments) in metafiles is that they are written out using absolute path names. When a metafile containing a cross reference is read back in, the cross reference contains the same absolute path name. This absolute path name can cause two problems. If the metafile originally written out did not follow cross references, then you need to ensure that the cross reference points to a valid segment.

Even more problematic, if the metafile originally written out did use the "follow cross-references" option, then the include (or style) segment itself was written out using an absolute path name. When such a metafile is read back in, any included or styled segments will be read back into an absolute location in the segment tree. Thus, reading in a metafile can cause objects to be placed into your segment tree in unexpected places. In general, you should be careful when writing out metafiles for segment trees containing include and style segments.

There are other options for setting the directory to write the file. See the *HOOPS Reference Manual* entry for HC_Write_Metafile for other options.

HOOPS metafiles are stored as readable text. Program 6.14 is a listing of the metafile written out by Program 6.13. Compare it to the structure of the program that produced it.

```
1   ;; HMF V1.24 TEXT
2   (Rendering_Options "technology=software frame buffer")
3   (Heuristics "no hidden surfaces")
```

```
 4  (Segment "clock" (
 5   (Color_By_Value "Line,Marker,Text,Edge" "RGB" 0 0
       0.65)
 6   (Color_By_Value "Face" "RGB" 0.818 0.818 0.818)
 7   (Edge_Weight 3)
 8   (Text_Font "size=0.1 oru,transforms")
 9   (Circle (0 0.98 0) (0.98 0 0) (0 -0.98 0))
10   (Text -4.24574e-6 0.8 0 "12")
11   (Text -0.400003 0.692818 0 "11")
12   (Text -0.692822 0.399997 0 "10")
13   (Text -0.8 -3.18431e-6 0 "9")
14   (Text -0.692819 -0.400002 0 "8")
15   (Text -0.399998 -0.692822 0 "7")
16   (Text 2.12287e-6 -0.8 0 "6")
17   (Text 0.400001 -0.692819 0 "5")
18   (Text 0.692821 -0.399999 0 "4")
19   (Text 0.8 1.06144e-6 0 "3")
20   (Text 0.69282 0.400001 0 "2")
21   (Text 0.4 0.69282 0 "1")

22   (Segment "hands" (
23     (Color_By_Value "Geometry" "RGB" 1 0 0)

24     (Segment "hour hand" (
25       (Line_Pattern  "(---)")
26       (Line_Weight 10)
27       (Line 0 -0.1 0 0 0.4 0)))

28     (Segment "minute hand" (
29       (Line_Weight 3)
30       (Line 0 -0.2 0 0 0.6 0)))))

31   (Segment "hub" (
32     (Color_By_Value "Geometry" "RGB" 0.34549 0 1)
33     (Circle (0 0.03 0) (0.03 0 0) (0 -0.03 0))))))))
```

**Program 6.14**    Metafile generated by Program 6.13.

HOOPS metafiles use parentheses to set off the tree structure of the database. Each attribute or piece of geometry is placed in a separate parenthesized list.

Notice that colors are written out as RGB values (on lines 5, 6, 23, and 32). The "use color names" option of the HC_Write_Metafile command tells HOOPS that it is okay to write out color names if the colors were specified by name. If you write out color names, then lines 5 and 6 in the metafile will be replaced by the following single line:

```
(Color "Line=Marker=Text=Edge=dark blue, Face=light
silver")
```

Because HOOPS is declarative, the color attribute on a segment is the total effect of all the individual commands that modify the color on that segment. In particular, the color descriptor for the segment named "clock" in the metafile is the total effect of the HOOPS commands that modify any colors for the "clock" segment (lines 15 and 32 in Program 6.13).

 You can use the HC_Set_Metafile command to set a metafile as an attribute on a segment. When you set a metafile attribute on a segment, HOOPS will write out the segment tree into the metafile, and also will keep the metafile synchronized with any changes to the database. For example, if you change an attribute in the segment tree, HOOPS will update the metafile. Although the HC_Set_Metafile command is more declarative than is HC_Write_Metafile, it is rarely used.

The viewer application, contained on the CD-ROM, is useful for examining HOOPS metafiles (see Sections 10.5.8 and 10.5.10).

## 6.3.2 Reading in a Metafile

To read a metafile into the HOOPS database, you use the HC_Read_Metafile command. For example, Program 6.15 reads in the metafile generated by Program 6.12 (stored in the file named clock.hmf) and displays it.

```
1  void main() {
2      HC_Read_Metafile("clock.hmf", "?Picture", "");
3      HC_Pause();
4  }
```

**Program 6.15**   Read and display a metafile.

HOOPS comes with several dozen interesting metafiles, which you can read in just like the clock. These metafiles can be found in the HOOPS installation directory under demo/common/hmf.

Once you have read a metafile into a segment tree, it is just like any other segment tree in the database, so you can manipulate it as usual. For example, Program 6.16 does a little animation with the clock.

```
 1   void main() {
 2      HC_Read_Metafile("clock.hmf", "?Picture", "");
 3      HC_Define_Alias("?hour", "?Picture/.../hour hand");
 4      HC_Define_Alias("?minute",
 5            "?Picture/.../minute hand");
 6      for (int i=0; i<60; i++) {
 7         HC_QRotate_Object("?minute", 0.0, 0.0, -6.0);
 8         HC_QRotate_Object("?hour", 0.0, 0.0, -0.5);
 9         HC_Update_Display();
10      }
11      HC_Pause();
12   }
```

**Program 6.16**     Read and modify a metafile.

### 6.3.3     Metafile Directory

The file-name argument to the HC_Read_Metafile and HC_Write_Metafile commands is the name of the metafile to be read or written. If this name is not a full path name, then HOOPS uses the current directory to read or write the metafile. You can change the directories that HOOPS uses for metafiles with the HC_Define_System_Options command. For example, on Microsoft Windows, our program might contain the following command:

```
HC_Define_System_Options(
      "metafile directory=c:\\hoops\\hmf");
```

Note that backslashes in the file name must be doubled, because C++ uses the backslash to introduce special characters (such as \n). To help you to avoid this problem, and to make path names more portable, HOOPS also accepts forward slashes (even on Windows and Macintosh platforms) — for example,

```
HC_Define_System_Options(
      "metafile directory=c:/hoops/hmf");
```

You can also set the metafile directory to a list of directories (separated by commas and enclosed in parentheses). In this case, HOOPS searches the directories in order when reading a metafile, and writes metafiles into the first directory in the list.

Because file names are normally not portable between different computers, HOOPS allows you to set the metafile directory using the environment variable HOOPS_METAFILE_DIRECTORY. For example, on Windows, you would say

```
set HOOPS_METAFILE_DIRECTORY=c:\hoops\hmf
```

As we mentioned in Section 6.3.2, HOOPS comes with several dozen interesting metafiles. It is a good idea to set the HOOPS_METAFILE_DIRECTORY environment variable to this directory (normally demo/common/hmf under the HOOPS installation directory), so that HOOPS programs can read them without knowing in what directory they reside. For example, on Windows, if HOOPS is installed in c:\hoops, you could say

```
set HOOPS_METAFILE_DIRECTORY=c:\hoops\demo\common\hmf
```

## 6.4    Inquiries

Thus far in this chapter, we have discussed how to view a HOOPS database and how to write out a database as a metafile. Both of these actions treat the relationship between your application and HOOPS as a one-way street — your application sends data to HOOPS, and HOOPS consumes the data. It is also possible for your application to retrieve data from the HOOPS database. We have already seen two ways to do data retrieval:

1.  You can use Show and Show_Net commands to return the values of local and net attributes in the database. For example, the HC_Show_Color command will return any local color attribute on a segment.

2.  You can use Show commands to return geometries stored in the database. For example, the HC_Show_Line command will return the endpoints of a line stored in the database.

Both of these techniques require you to know something about the database. For example, HC_Show_Color returns an error if the color attribute has not been set on the specified segment, and HC_Show_Line requires a key as an argument.

How can you see what is in a database if you know nothing about it? If someone hands you a metafile, for example, how can you tell how big it is, or whether it contains any shells?

If you know the name (or key) of a segment, you can determine what that segment contains by using the HC_Show_Existence command. This command is particularly useful for determining whether a certain attribute has been set on a segment. For example, Program 6.17 looks for a local color attribute.

```
1  HC_Open_Segment("?Picture");
2      int count = HC_Show_Existence("color");
3      if (count > 0) {
4          char buffer[256];
5          HC_Show_Color(buffer);
6      }
7  HC_Close_Segment();
```

**Program 6.17**     Determine whether a color attribute has been set on "?Picture".

An attribute (such as color) has only a single value, so the HC_Show_Existence command on line 2 will return only 0 or 1 depending on whether "?Picture" has a color attribute set on it.

If you called the HC_Show_Color command on "?Picture" (line 5) and it did not have a locally set color attribute, then HOOPS would signal an error. The HC_Show_Existence command allows you to check to make sure that a local color attribute has been set on a segment before you show its value.

 You can always call an HC_Show_Net command (such as HC_Show_Net_Color) on any segment, because all segments have a net value for all attributes.

You can also use the HC_Show_Existence command to check for the existence of geometry, of specific kinds of geometry, of attributes (to see whether any attributes have been set on a segment), of child segments, of include segments, of style segments, and of everything (to see if a segment contains anything). See the *HOOPS Reference Manual* page for HC_Show_Existence for more information.

## 6.5     Searching

The HC_Show_Existence command discussed in Section 6.4 requires us to know the name of a segment. We still need a way to see what is in a database about which we know nothing.

Of course, one way to approach this problem is to print out a metafile. We can then look at the metafile (either manually, or with a program), to see exactly what is in the database. There is a better way: using HOOPS searching commands.

There are eight kinds of searches in HOOPS. They can be divided into two categories:

1. Searches on nonattribute options

2. Searches that return information about the HOOPS database

Each kind of search begins with a command that uses the "Begin" verb, and ends with a command that uses the "End" verb. In between the begin and end, you can use commands with the "Find" verb to return matching objects, and you can show the number of matching objects.

Searches can be nested, so one search can start even if another search of the same type is already in progress. However, only one search of each type can be active (returning values) at a time. The active search is the most recent one started with a "Begin" command. When the active search is finished (via an "End" command) and there are nested searches (of the same type), then the one most recently interrupted becomes the active search.

## 6.5.1    Nonattribute Option Searches

You use nonattribute option searches to find out the value of information that is not stored as an attribute in the HOOPS database. Nonattribute options either are built in to HOOPS (or a specific display device), or are defined by the user with a command that starts with the "Define" verb (see Chapter 4 for more information about nonattribute options). There are five kinds of nonattribute option searches:

1. An *alias search* is used for searching through all the aliases that HOOPS knows ("?Picture" is an alias). In addition to the HOOPS built-in aliases, new aliases can be set by the user with the HC_Define_Alias command.

2. A *callback name search* is used for searching through all the callback names defined to HOOPS with the HC_Define_Callback_Name command. It is mainly useful with HOOPS intermediate mode.

3. A *color name search* is used for searching through all the color names that HOOPS knows (for example, "red" or "greenish"). Besides the many color names that HOOPS recognizes, new color names can be defined with the HC_Define_Color_Name command.

4. A *font search* is used for searching through all the fonts available on a particular display or defined by the user with HC_Define_Font.

5. A *texture search* is used for searching through all textures that have been defined with the HC_Define_Texture command.

For example, Program 6.18 prints out all the system-specific fonts that are available on the current output device ("?Picture").

```
1   HC_Begin_Font_Search("?Picture", "specific");
2   int count;
3   HC_Show_Font_Count(&count);
4   printf("This device has %d fonts\n", count);
5   printf("Here they are:\n");

6   int flag = (count > 0);
7   while (flag) {
8      char fname[256];
9      flag = HC_Find_Font(fname);
10     if (flag) printf("%s\n", fname);
11  }
12  HC_End_Font_Search();
```

**Program 6.18**     Print out all available system-specific fonts.

The HC_Find_Font command on line 9 returns true each time that a font is found.

If you need more information about a font than just its name, you can call the HC_Show_Font_Info command for each font name found by the font search. See the *HOOPS Reference Manual* pages for HC_Begin_Font_Search and HC_Show_Font_Info for more information.

## 6.5.2     Database Searches

There are three kinds of searches that return information from the HOOPS segment hierarchy:

1. An *open-segment search* searches through all the currently open segments (segments that have been opened by HC_Open_Segment, but have not yet been closed by HC_Close_Segment).

**2.** A *contents search* returns the contents of a segment (or a set of segments).

**3.** A *segment search* searches through all segments in a set (it is a restricted form of a contents search).

Contents and segment searches are the most useful for retrieving information from the HOOPS database.

**6.5.2.1**    **Open-segment search.** Program 6.19 closes all open segments and returns the number of segments that were closed.

```
1   int close_segments() {
2      HC_Begin_Open_Segment_Search();
3      int count;
4      HC_Show_Open_Segment_Count(&count);
5      for (int i = 0; i<count; i++) {
6         HC_Close_Segment();
7      }
8      HC_End_Open_Segment_Search();
9      return count;
10  }
```

**Program 6.19**    Close all open segments.

Program 6.19 is useful after a metafile has been read in. If the metafile was truncated accidentally, then it might not close all its segments properly when read in. This program will make sure that any open segments are closed.

**6.5.2.2**    **Segment searches.** The HC_Begin_Segment_Search command takes a segment name as an argument, and the HC_Find_Segment command returns any segment matched by that segment name, if one exists. Thus, you can use a segment search to discover whether a segment exists. Typically, however, the segment name passed to HC_Begin_Segment_Search will contain wild cards, and so will match a set of segments. These segments will be returned, one at a time, by the command HC_Find_Segment. Wild cards were defined in Section 4.2.6.1.

For example, Program 6.20 traverses the entire database recursively, starting with the currently open segment.

```
 1  void traverse() {
 2      HC_Begin_Segment_Search("*");
 3      char child[256];
 4      while (HC_Find_Segment(child)) {
 5          // do something with child
 6          HC_Open_Segment(child);
 7          traverse();
 8          HC_Close_Segment();
 9      }
10      HC_End_Segment_Search();
11  }
```

**Program 6.20**    Traverse database recursively.

The wild card "*" matches any child of the currently open segment. For each child segment, the segment is opened, and then this routine calls itself (on line 7) to search that child's children.

Program 6.20 shows how searches can be nested — in this case recursively, to an arbitrary depth. To search the database, however, you do not usually need to use nested searches and recursion. Another way to visit all the segments in the database is with a single (nonrecursive) search using the "..." wild card, shown in Program 6.21.

```
 1  void traverse() {
 2      HC_Begin_Segment_Search("*...");
 3      char child[256];
 4      while (HC_Find_Segment(child)) {
 5          // do something with child
 6      }
 7      HC_End_Segment_Search();
 8  }
```

**Program 6.21**    Traverse database nonrecursively.

The "*..." segment name (on line 2) contains two wild cards: "*" and "...". This segment name matches all children of the current segment, and their children. If we had used the "..." wild card by itself, then Program 6.21 would have returned the current segment as well as that segment's children.

Note that Programs 6.20 and 6.21 might return segments in slightly different order.

**6.5.2.3**   **Looking for specific kinds of objects.** Program 6.22 walks the database (using commands similar to those in Programs 6.21), but also checks (using HC_Show_Existence, on line 4) whether any of the returned segments have a color attribute set on them.

```
1   HC_Begin_Segment_Search("...");
2   char child[256];
3   while (HC_Find_Segment(child)) {
4      if (HC_QShow_Existence(child, "color")) {
5          char color[256];
6          HC_QShow_Color(child, color);
7          printf("segment %s\n", child);
8          printf("has color '%s'\n", color);
9      }
10  }
11  HC_End_Segment_Search();
```

**Program 6.22**   Find all color attributes.

If we run Program 6.22 on the database produced by Program 6.12 (the clock example), then we get the following output (of course, on a platform other than Microsoft Windows, the name "msw" will be different):

```
segment /driver/msw/window0/clock/hands
has color 'geometry=red'
segment /driver/msw/window0/clock/hub
has color 'geometry=reddish blue'
segment /driver/msw/window0/clock
has color 'line=marker=text=edge=dark blue,face=light
silver'
```

We can use a similar program to look for other attributes, geometry, or anything else for which HC_Show_Existence can look. Program 6.23 prints out all segments that contain text strings in the database.

```
 1  HC_Begin_Segment_Search("...");
 2  char child[256];
 3  while (HC_Find_Segment(child)) {
 4     int count = HC_QShow_Existence(child, "text")
 5     if (count > 0) {
 6        printf("segment %s contains %d text strings\n",
 7              child, count);
 8     }
 9  }
10  HC_End_Segment_Search();
```

**Program 6.23**     Find all text strings.

Program 6.23 tells us only which segments contain text. We would like a way to get access to the text strings themselves — for example, to print them out. We can do that with a contents search.

**6.5.2.4**     **Contents searches.** We can use a contents search to get access to objects in the database. It is especially useful for getting access to geometry. Program 6.24 is similar to Program 6.23 but is modified to print out all text strings in each segment. The HC_Show_Existence command has been replaced by a contents search.

```
 1  HC_Begin_Segment_Search("...");
 2  char child[256];
 3  while (HC_Find_Segment(child)) {
 4     HC_Begin_Contents_Search(child, "text");
 5     int count;
 6     HC_Show_Contents_Count(&count);

 7     if (count > 0) {
 8        printf("segment %s contains %d text strings\n",
 9              child, count);
10        char type[80];
11        long key;
```

```
12          while (HC_Find_Contents(type, &key)) {
13              float x, y, z;
14              int length;
15              HC_Show_Text_Length(key, &length);
16              char * text = new char[length + 1];
17              HC_Show_Text(key, &x, &y, &z, text);
18              printf("(%g, %g, %g) %s\n", x, y, z, text);
19              delete [] text;
20          }
21      }
22      HC_End_Contents_Search();
23  }
24  HC_End_Segment_Search();
```

**Program 6.24**    Print out all text strings by segment.

For each segment that contains one or more text strings, Program 6.24 prints out the name of the segment (on line 8), followed by each text string — including the string's *x, y, z* position (on line 18). We use the HC_Show_Text_Length command to get the length of the text string (on line 15), and allocate a buffer that is 1 character larger to hold the string and its terminating null character (on line 16). The type returned by HC_Find_Contents (on line 12) will always be "text", since that is all we are seeking.

Program 6.24 uses two kinds of searches: a segment search to visit each segment in the database, and a contents search to access all text in each segment. The two arguments to HC_Begin_Contents_Search (on line 4) are the segment to search and a string that indicates for what kind of object to look (the second argument takes the same values as the argument to HC_Show_Existence).

In Program 6.24, we used two nested searches. Alternatively, we can use a single contents search to find everything in the database. To do that, we use a wild card for the first argument to HC_Begin_Contents_Search. Program 6.25 uses this technique to return all text strings in the HOOPS database.

```
 1  HC_Begin_Contents_Search("...", "text");
 2  char type[80];
 3  long key;
 4  while (HC_Find_Contents(type, &key)) {
 5     float x, y, z;
 6     int length;
 7     HC_Show_Text_Length(key, &length);
 8     char * text = new char[length + 1];
 9     HC_Show_Text(key, &x, &y, &z, text);
10     printf("(%g, %g, %g) %s\n", x, y, z, text);
11     delete [] text;
12  }
13  HC_End_Contents_Search();
```

**Program 6.25**    Print out all text strings.

Program 6.25 prints out all text strings without organizing the strings by segment (unlike Program 6.24). In general, we would use a contents search inside of a segment search when we want to process the database one segment at a time, and a single contents search on all segments when we just want to process the contents of the database without regard to which segments contain which contents.

In addition, a contents search searches only in segments that match the segment name pattern. Because include segments (and style segments) are not actually part of the segment hierarchy, no wild card will match an include segment. If you need to walk the entire segment tree for a scene, including all include segments, you can use a segment search, and at each segment perform a contents search. If there are any include segments returned by the contents search, then you can do a segment search recursively on the included segment. Program 6.26 does just that.

```
 1  void searchall() {
 2     HC_Begin_Segment_Search("...");
 3     char child[256];

 4     while (HC_Find_Segment(child)) {
 5        HC_Begin_Contents_Search(child, "everything");
 6           char type[80];
 7           long key;
```

```
 8            while (HC_Find_Contents(type, &key)) {
 9                if (strcmp(type, "include") == 0) {
10                    long ikey =
11                          HC_KShow_Include_Segment(key);
12                    HC_Open_Segment_By_Key(ikey);
13                        searchall();
14                    HC_Close_Segment();
15                }
16            }
17        }
18        HC_End_Contents_Search();
19    }
20    HC_End_Segment_Search();
21 }
```

**Program 6.26**   Search entire database, including include segments.

If the key returned by HC_Find_Contents (line 8) is the key of an include (line 9), then we use the HC_KShow_Include_Segment command to get the key of the included segment (line 10), open the included segment (line 12), and then call the searchall function recursively (line 13).

The second argument to the HC_Begin_Contents_Search command (on line 5) controls what kind of objects are returned by HC_Find_Contents. The word "everything" does just what it says — returns everything, including geometry, attributes, child segments, style segments, and include segments. If we wanted to return only geometry and include segments, we would specify "geometry, include" (we do not need to return child segments; the segment search finds all of those).

**6.5.2.5**   **Determination of net attributes for geometry.** We can use a contents search to return all the geometry in a database. Once we have a piece of geometry, we can use the HC_Show_Owner_By_Key command to find the net attributes that apply to it. For example, given a key for a line, we use HC_Show_Owner_By_Key to get the segment that contains the line, and then use HC_Show_Net_Color to determine what color will be used to draw the line.

As an example, Program 6.27 prints out the type and color of all geometry in the database.

```
1   HC_Begin_Contents_Search("?Picture...", "geometry");
2   char type[80];
3   long key;
4   while (HC_Find_Contents(type, &key)) {
5       long owner = HC_KShow_Owner_By_Key(key);
6       HC_Open_Segment_By_Key(owner);
7           char color[80];
8           HC_Show_Net_Color(color);
9           printf("A %s %s\n", color, type);
10      HC_Close_Segment();
11  }
12  HC_End_Contents_Search();
```

**Program 6.27**    Contents search for geometry.

In a program such as Program 6.27, we often want to print out different information based on the type of the object. For example, if the object is a line, we might want to print out its net line weight. We can determine the type of an object by testing the first argument returned by HC_Find_Contents (on line 4) to see whether it is equal to "line" (or "circle", or whatever) and taking the appropriate action. Program 6.28 in the next section does just that.

# 6.6        Computation of Model Information

Program 6.28 uses searching to compute information about the contents of the HOOPS database. The heart of this program is the class Model_Info (in file model_info.hxx), which contains four public methods. The constructor for Model_Info takes the name of a segment in the HOOPS database from which to start computing statistics. The compute method computes the statistics for the model, and the print method prints them out. The display method is like the print method, but it displays the statistics using HOOPS output, rather than printf (we shall not show the display method in this book, but you can examine it in the program on the CD-ROM). The remainder of Model_Info is a set of counters, used to accumulate information about the database, and a few private methods.

```
1   class Model_Info {

2     public:
3       Model_Info(const char * segment_path);
```

```
4      void  compute();
5      void  print();     // print to console
6      void  display();   // display in HOOPS window
7    private:
8      char *_segment_path;
9      // geometry totals
10     int     _total_circle;
11     int     _total_circular_arc;
12     int     _total_circular_chord;
13     int     _total_circular_wedge;
14     int     _total_ellipse;
15     int     _total_elliptical_arc;
16     int     _total_grid;
17     int     _total_image;
18     int     _total_line;
19     int     _total_marker;
20     int     _total_mesh;
21     int     _total_polygon;
22     int     _total_polyline;
23     int     _total_shell;
24     int     _total_string_cursor;
25     int     _total_text;

26     // light totals
27     int     _total_spot_light;
28     int     _total_distant_light;
29     int     _total_local_light;

30     // cutting plane total
31     int     _total_cutting_plane;

32     // derived totals
33     // all faces in meshes & shells plus polygon total
34     int     _total_faces;
35     // all vertices in meshes and each shell face
36     // and all polygons
37     int     _total_vertices;
38     // (vert/face - 2) * _total_faces
39     int     _total_triangles;
```

```
40      // private methods
41      void _increment_count(char * type, long key);
42      void _count_shell(long key,
43          int * faces, int * vertices, int * triangles);
44      void _display_primitive_count(char * primitive,
45          int count, float y_position);
46      void _compute_tree(char * segment);
47  };
48
```

**Program 6.28**    Class Model_Info.

Before we define the member functions of class Model_Info, we shall define a few utility functions and classes. These functions and classes are all contained in the file common.hxx.

```
49  #include <string.h>

50  // 3D point structure
51  struct Common_Point {
52      float x, y, z;
53      Common_Point & set_point (
54          float xx,
55          float yy,
56          float zz) {
57          x = xx;
58          y = yy;
59          z = zz;
60          return *this;
61      }
62  };

63  // Boolean data type
64  typedef void * Common_Boolean;

65  inline Common_Boolean streq(const char * s0,
66          const char * s1) {
67      return (Common_Boolean) (strcmp (s0, s1) == 0);
68  }
```

**Program 6.28  (continued)**  Utility classes and functions in common.hxx.

Lines 51 through 62 define our standard point class, called Common_Point. We also define an inline function streq (lines 65 through 68) that returns true if two strings are equal.

---

**C++**

For a Boolean (true-or-false) value, we use a typedef of type void * (on line 64). A void pointer can be used as a truth value in an "if" statement, but cannot be used in arithmetic (as an integer could be, if it were used as the Boolean type). Note that later versions of C++ include a Boolean type.

---

The member functions for class Model_Info are all defined in the file model_info.cxx. The constructor makes a copy of the segment name, and zeros all the counters.

```
69   Model_Info::Model_Info(const char * segment_path) :
70        _segment_path(strcpy(
71            new char[strlen(segment_path) + 1],
72            segment_path)) {

73   // zero geometry totals
74   _total_circle = 0;
75   _total_circular_arc = 0;
76   _total_circular_chord = 0;
77   _total_circular_wedge = 0;
78   _total_ellipse = 0;
79   _total_elliptical_arc = 0;
80   _total_grid = 0;
81   _total_image = 0;
82   _total_line = 0;
83   _total_marker = 0;
84   _total_mesh = 0;
85   _total_polygon = 0;
86   _total_polyline = 0;
87   _total_shell = 0;
88   _total_string_cursor = 0;
89   _total_text = 0;

90   // zero light totals
91   _total_distant_light = 0;
92   _total_local_light = 0;
93   _total_spot_light = 0;
```

**331**

```
 94      // zero derived totals
 95      _total_faces = 0;
 96      _total_triangles = 0;
 97      _total_vertices = 0;

 98      // zero cutting-plane totals
 99      _total_cutting_plane = 0;
100  }
```

**Program 6.28 (continued)** Model_Info constructor.

The compute function calls the private member function _compute_tree on the saved segment name. The _compute_tree function does a contents search on the tree (on line 110). The object returned by the HC_Find_Contents command (line 112) is tested to see whether it is an include segment (line 113). If it is, the _compute_tree function is called recursively on the include segment. Normally, a contents search does not search inside included segments. If the object is not an include segment, the _increment_count function is called.

```
101  void Model_Info::compute() {
102      _compute_tree(_segment_path);
103  }

104  void Model_Info::_compute_tree(char * segment) {
105      long     key;
106      char     type[32];
107      // perform a contents search on segment and its
108      // subsegments, following includes

109      HC_Open_Segment(segment);
110        HC_Begin_Contents_Search("...",
111              "geometry, includes");
112        while (HC_Find_Contents(type, &key)) {

113            if (streq(type, "include")) {
114                char iseg[2048];
115                HC_Show_Include_Segment(key, iseg);
116                  _compute_tree(iseg);
117            }
118            else {
119                _increment_count(type, key);
120            }
```

```
121          }
122          HC_End_Contents_Search();
123      HC_Close_Segment();
124  }
```

**Program 6.28 (continued)** The compute and _compute_tree member functions.

The _increment_count private member function tests to see what kind of object was returned by the contents search. Most of the time, it just increments the appropriate counter. In a few cases, further investigation is warranted. If the object is a mesh, polygon, or shell, the number of faces, vertices, and triangles is determined. In the case of shells, this computation is complicated enough that a separate function, _count_shell, is called.

```
125  void Model_Info::_increment_count(
126      char *    type,
127      long      key) {

128      if (streq(type, "circle")) {
129          _total_circle++;
130      }

131      else if (streq(type, "circular arc")) {
132          _total_circular_arc++;
133      }

134      else if (streq(type, "circular chord")) {
135          _total_circular_chord++;
136      }

137      else if (streq(type, "circular wedge")) {
138          _total_circular_wedge++;
139      }

140      else if (streq(type, "cutting plane")) {
141          _total_cutting_plane++;
142      }

143      else if (streq(type, "distant light")) {
144          _total_distant_light++;
145      }

146      else if (streq(type, "ellipse")) {
147          _total_ellipse++;
148      }
```

```
149      else if (streq(type, "elliptical arc")) {
150          _total_elliptical_arc++;
151      }
152      else if (streq(type, "grid")) {
153          _total_grid++;
154      }
155      else if (streq(type, "image")) {
156          _total_image++;
157      }
158      else if (streq(type, "line")) {
159          _total_line++;
160      }
161      else if (streq(type, "local light")) {
162          _total_local_light++;
163      }
164      else if (streq(type, "marker")) {
165          _total_marker++;
166      }
167      else if (streq(type, "mesh")) {
168          int rows, columns;
169          HC_Show_Mesh_Size(key, &rows, &columns);
170          _total_faces += (rows - 1) * (columns -1);
171          _total_mesh++;
172          _total_vertices += rows * columns;
173          _total_triangles += 2 * _total_faces;
174      }
175      else if (streq(type, "polygon")) {
176          int count;
177          _total_polygon++;
178          _total_faces++;
179          HC_Show_Polygon_Count(key, &count);
180          _total_vertices += count;
181          _total_triangles += count - 2;
182      }
183      else if (streq(type, "polyline")) {
184          _total_polyline++;
185      }
```

```
186    else if (streq(type, "shell")) {
187        _total_shell++;
188        // obtain totals for shell components
189        int face_count = 0;
190        int vertex_count = 0;
191        int triangle_count = 0;
192        _count_shell(key, &face_count,
193              &vertex_count, &triangle_count);
194        _total_faces      += face_count;
195        _total_vertices   += vertex_count;
196        _total_triangles  += triangle_count;
197    }

198    else if (streq(type, "spot light")) {
199        _total_spot_light++;
200    }

201    else if (streq(type, "string cursor")) {
202        _total_string_cursor++;
203    }

204    else if (streq(type, "text")) {
205        _total_text++;
206    }
207 }

208 void Model_Info::_count_shell(
209    long      shell_key,
210    int *     faces,
211    int *     vertices,
212    int *     triangles) {

213    // find size of current shell and allocate memory
214    int   p_count = 0;
215    int   fl_length = 0;
216    HC_Show_Shell_Size(shell_key,
217          &p_count, &fl_length);
218    Common_Point * points =
219          new Common_Point[p_count];
220    int * flist = new int[fl_length];

221    HC_Show_Shell(shell_key, &p_count, points,
222          &fl_length, flist);
```

**335**

```
223    // step through the face list and
224    // count the number of faces and triangles
225    int      face_count = 0;
226    int      current_face = 0;
227    int      triangle_count = 0;
228    while (current_face != fl_length) {
229       // step over holes
230       if (flist[current_face] < 0) { // a hole
231          current_face += - flist[current_face] + 1;
232       }
233       // count facets
234       else { // a facet
235          // count the triangles in the face -
236          // ignores holes
237          triangle_count += flist[current_face] - 2;
238          current_face += flist[current_face] + 1;
239          face_count++;
240       }
241    }

242    // release memory
243    delete [] points;
244    delete [] flist;
245    *faces = face_count;
246    *vertices = fl_length - face_count;
247    *triangles = triangle_count;
248 }
```

**Program 6.28 (continued)** The _increment_count and _count_shell member functions.

Finally, the print member function prints out all the counters.

```
249 void Model_Info::print() {
250    printf("Geometry Found in and below:\n\n");
251    char path_name[2048];
252    HC_Show_Pathname_Expansion(_segment_path,
253          path_name);
254    printf("\t\t[%s]\n\n", path_name);

255    // geometry
256    printf("\n");
257    printf("\tGeometry\n");
```

```
258    printf("\t\tcircles        == %d\n",
259         _total_circle);

260    printf("\t\tcircular arcs  == %d\n",
261         _total_circular_arc);

262    printf("\t\tcircular chords== %d\n",
263         _total_circular_chord);

264    printf("\t\tcircular wedges== %d\n",
265         _total_circular_wedge);

266    printf("\t\tellipses       == %d\n",
267         _total_ellipse);

268    printf("\t\telliptical arcs== %d\n",
269         _total_elliptical_arc);

270    printf("\t\tgrids          == %d\n",
271         _total_grid);

272    printf("\t\timages         == %d\n",
273         _total_image);

274    printf("\t\tlines          == %d\n",
275         _total_line);

276    printf("\t\tmarkers        == %d\n",
277         _total_marker);

278    printf("\t\tmeshes         == %d\n",
279         _total_mesh);

280    printf("\t\tpolygons       == %d\n",
281         _total_polygon);

282    printf("\t\tpolylines      == %d\n",
283         _total_polyline);

284    printf("\t\tshells         == %d\n",
285         _total_shell);

286    printf("\t\tstring cursors == %d\n",
287         _total_string_cursor);

288    printf("\t\ttext strings   == %d\n",
289         _total_text);
```

```
290    // lights
291    printf("\n");
292    printf("\tLights\n");
293    printf("\t\tdistant lights == %d\n",
294        _total_distant_light);
295    printf("\t\tlocal lights   == %d\n",
296        _total_line);
297    printf("\t\tspot lights    == %d\n",
298        _total_spot_light);

299    // cutting planes
300    printf("\n");
301    printf("\tCutting Planes\n");
302    printf("\t\tcutting planes == %d\n",
303        _total_cutting_plane);

304    // derived totals
305    printf("\n");
306    printf("\tDerived Totals\n");
307    printf("\t\tTotal Faces        == %d\n",
308        (int) _total_faces);
309    printf("\t\tTotal Vertices     == %d\n",
310        (int) _total_vertices);
311    printf("\t\tAverage Vertices/Face == %2.3f\n",
312        (float)(_total_vertices) /
313        (float)(_total_faces));
314    printf("\t\tTotal Triangles    == %d\n",
315        _total_triangles);
316 }
```

**Program 6.28 (continued)** The print member function.

## 6.7     Conversion of Polygons into a Shell

Program 6.29 looks in a segment for any polygons, converts them into a single shell, and then optimizes the shell. This routine uses two contents searches and the HC_Compute_Minimized_Shell command. The argument is the name of the segment to be optimized. To optimize the entire database, you could use a search to find all segments containing polygons, then call this routine on each such segment.

```
1   void convert_to_shell(char * segment) {
2       HC_Open_Segment(segment);
3       char type[32]; // will always be "polygon"
4       long key;
```

**Program 6.29**   Convert polygons to an optimized shell.

This routine does two contents searches. The first one finds all the polygons in this segment and adds up the total number of points. The command HC_Show_Contents_Count returns the total number of polygons in the segment. Note that this routine changes the polygons into a shell even if there is only one polygon in the segment. We could change this behavior by changing the test on line 12. Each call of HC_Find_Contents (on line 13) finds one of the polygons and returns its key. The HC_Show_Polygon_Count command (on line 15) returns the number of points in each polygon. These counts are accumulated into polygon_points.

```
5           HC_Begin_Contents_Search(".", "polygons");
6               // points in all polygons
7               int polygon_points = 0;
8               // number of polygons
9               int polygon_count;
10              HC_Show_Contents_Count(&polygon_count);
11              // leave if there are no polygons
12              if (polygon_count == 0) return;
13              while (HC_Find_Contents(type, &key)) {
14                  int count;
15                  HC_Show_Polygon_Count(key, &count);
16                  polygon_points += count;
17              }
18          HC_End_Contents_Search();
```

**Program 6.29 (continued)**   Find polygons.

Next, we allocate two arrays for storing a point list and a face list. See Section 5.2.8 for more information on how shells are created.

```
19              // array for storing shell points
20              Point * points = new Point[polygon_points];
21              Point * current_point = points;
```

```
22          // array for storing shell face list
23          int face_list_length =
24                  polygon_points + polygon_count;
25          int * face_list = new int[face_list_length];
26          int * current_face_list_entry = face_list;

27          // offset in face list of current face
28          int face_offset = 0;
```

**Program 6.29 (continued)** Allocate arrays for a shell.

The second contents search stores all the data from each polygon in the newly allocated arrays. The HC_Find_Contents command (on line 31) finds each polygon and returns the polygon's key.

```
29          // fill the shell arrays just created
30          HC_Begin_Contents_Search(".", "polygons");
31              while (HC_Find_Contents(type, &key)) {
```

We use the HC_Show_Polygon_Count command again (on line 34) to return the number of points in this polygon. The HC_Show_Polygon command (line 35) returns the points in the polygon. We insert them directly into the points array using a pointer into the array called current_point.

```
32              int count;
33              // load the polygon points
34              HC_Show_Polygon_Count(key, &count);
35              HC_Show_Polygon(key,
36                      &count, current_point);
37              current_point += count;
```

Next, we create the face-list entries corresponding to this polygon. The face list consists of a series of face entries. Each face entry consists of a count of the number of vertices in the face, followed by the indices of the vertices in the points list.

```
38              // load the face list for the current
39              // polygon
40              // the first item in a face entry in
41              // the face list is the number of vertices
42              *current_face_list_entry++ = count;
```

```
43                    // the next 'count' items in a face entry
44                    // are the indices of the points;
45                    // indices go from
46                    // face_offset to face_offset + count - 1
47                    for (int i = 0; i < count; i++) {
48                        *current_face_list_entry++ =
49                                face_offset + i;
50                    }
51                    face_offset += count;
52                }
53            HC_End_Contents_Search();
```

**Program 6.29 (continued)** Initialize the shell.

Now that we have retrieved all the data from the polygons, we can delete them from the segment. An alternative way to delete them would have been to delete each polygon by key during the second contents search.

```
54          // get rid of all the old polygons
55          HC_Flush_Contents(".", "polygons");
```

The shell, as it is, will probably contain redundant points. For example, if a segment contains six polygons arranged in a cube, each polygon will share each vertex with two other faces in the shell. We can eliminate these redundant points using the HC_Compute_Minimized_Shell command. First, we allocate arrays for the new point list and face list. We allocate arrays that are the same size as the old (unoptimized) arrays, because we do not know yet how many data we can eliminate, but we do know that the optimized shell can be no larger than the unoptimized one.

The HC_Compute_Minimized_Shell command takes 11 arguments. The first four are for the old (unoptimized) shell arrays. The next argument is a string containing options, such as what tolerance is used for merging points and whether to delete unused points. In this case, we take all the default values for the options. The next four arguments are for the new (optimized) shell arrays. The final two are the (returned) mapping lists showing how the points and faces in the old shell map to the new shell. We are not interested in these mapping arrays, so we pass null pointers for the arguments. Once we have calculated the optimized shell (on line 61), we insert it into the segment (on line 69).

```
56          // allocate arrays for the optimized shell
57          Point * new_points = new Point[polygon_points];
58          int * new_face_list = new int[face_list_length];
59          int new_pcount;
60          int new_flist_length;

61          HC_Compute_Minimized_Shell(
62                  polygon_points, points,
63                  face_list_length, face_list,
64                  "",        // no options
65                  &new_pcount, new_points,
66                  &new_flist_length, new_face_list,
67                  (int *) 0, (int *) 0);

68          // insert the optimized shell
69          HC_Insert_Shell(new_pcount, new_points,
70                  new_flist_length, new_face_list);
```

**Program 6.29 (continued)**  Optimize and insert the shell.

Next, we free the memory that was allocated for the arrays.

```
71          delete [] points;
72          delete [] face_list;
73          delete [] new_points;
74          delete [] new_face_list;
```

Finally, we print out statistics to show how much space we have saved. The savings in points is a true savings, since we have eliminated redundant points. The reduction in the number of faces is somewhat artificial, since the original polygons did not use face lists at all (each polygon is only a single face).

```
75          // statistics (optional)
76          printf("reduced points from %d to %d\n",
77                  polygon_points, new_pcount);
78          printf("reduced face list from %d to %d\n",
79                  face_list_length - new_flist_length);

80      HC_Close_Segment();
81  }
```

**Program 6.29 (continued)**  Print a few statistics.

Note that, even if we do not eliminate any points (because all the polygons are completely separate and do not share any points — a rare situation), this routine is still worth running because most platforms draw shells more efficiently than they do individual polygons.

Note that, if smooth shading is enabled (which it is by default) and your scene contains at least one light, then the drawing might change when polygons are merged into shells, since polygons cannot be smoothly shaded, but shells can be. Your program will need to be careful with the use of Program 6.29, and to make sure that the proper color attributes are set to enable or disable smooth shading, as desired. You can disable smooth shading with the following command:

```
HC_Set_Rendering_Options("no lighting interpolation");
```

# 7 Windows

Most modern computer applications incorporate a 2D graphical user interface using windows, buttons, sliders, lists, and other components. When you are writing an application, you have a choice of tools to use to help you write your user interface. Most modern computers come with a native window system — for example, Microsoft Windows on a PC, X-Windows on a UNIX machine, or the toolbox routines on a Macintosh. If you are writing a nongraphical application, you typically use the native window system to write your user interface.

If you are writing a 3D graphics application, you can write your user interface using HOOPS. Even though HOOPS is a 3D graphics system, it is general enough that you can write a user interface completely using only HOOPS commands, without any calls to the native window system. Using HOOPS has the benefit of making your user interface portable, since a HOOPS application can run without change on practically any window system, whereas an application written for a specific window system typically will not run on another. The main disadvantage of writing your user interface using HOOPS calls is that doing so puts an extra layer between your program and the native window system.

Alternatively, you can write the user interface for your 3D graphics application using calls to your computer's native window system. The main advantage of using the native window system is that it gives your application more control over the user interface, since your application does not need to go through an extra HOOPS layer. The disadvantage, of course, is a lack of portability. For most commercial applications, however, the extra control is important enough to make it worthwhile to spend the time to write the user interface using the native window system.

If you write your application's user interface using the native window system, you will still need to use HOOPS to write the 3D parts of your user interface. For example, selection (picking) of 3D objects will require cooperation between the window system and the 3D graphics system.

There are some parts of your application's user interface that you could write using the native window system, but it is better to write them with the help of the 3D graphics system. For example, if you want the ability to rotate graphical objects in space, you could use three sliders (one each for rotation in $x$, $y$, and $z$), but it is more intuitive to use a *virtual trackball*, which allows the user to grab an object with the cursor and to rotate that object in 3D space.

If an application uses both native window-system calls and HOOPS commands, the 3D graphics-system calls will be portable to different operating systems and computers, but the window-system calls will not be. Porting a 3D graphics application will require rewriting the 2D graphical user interface, but so would porting any application that uses a native window system as its graphical user interface.

## 7.1        Use of HOOPS to Write a User Interface

As we mentioned previously, HOOPS is sufficiently powerful that you can use it to write a user interface, without making calls to a window system. There are two ways to do so: with or without an underlying window system.

When HOOPS was first developed, window systems were not common — neither X-Windows nor Microsoft Windows existed yet. In those days (for example, on DOS or UNIX), when a 3D graphics application was started, it normally took control of the entire display screen. If a user wanted multiple windows, it was up to HOOPS to create them, as there was no window system to provide them. Partly as a legacy from those days, HOOPS still has the ability to create multiple windows (both overlapping and tiled).

Note that the term *window* has two meanings. Most people think of a window as a regular application window on the screen (such as the "overall HOOPS window"). Such a window normally has user-interface controls (such as the close box drawn in the upper-left corner of the window in Figure 7.1). These windows also can be moved around the screen, and usually can be minimized (converted to an icon). Under this definition, Figure 7.1 contains only one window.

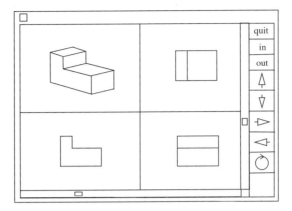

**Figure 7.1**    Windows and subwindows.

In a window system, however, the term *window* is used to refer to any (usually rectangular) subarea of the screen that contains a view or a user-interface gadget. For example, in most window systems, each button or slider has its own "window" — that area of the screen real estate that the slider occupies. In Figure 7.1, this kind of window includes the overall window, the close-box control window, the four subwindows that hold each view of the part, the two slider windows, and the eight buttons on the right side of the overall window.

Depending on how the user interface of an application is set up, there may be even more windows. For example, in Figure 7.1, the area containing the buttons may itself be a window (called the toolbar window). This window is the parent window of the button windows, and is itself a child of the overall window. Windows are often arranged in such a parent–child hierarchy (diagrammed in Figure 7.2).

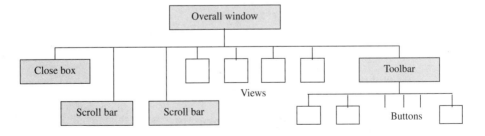

**Figure 7.2**    A hierarchy of windows.

**347**

In this book, we shall differentiate the two kinds of windows by calling the application window an *overall window,* and the windows inside of the application window *subwindows.* When we discuss a window that could either be an application window or a subwindow, we shall refer to it as simply a *window.*

Even when your user interface is written with the native window system, HOOPS windows are useful for creating subwindows. For example, in a 3D drafting application, you might want to provide multiple views of an object by dividing the overall HOOPS window into four subwindows for the top, side, front, and perspective view, as shown in Figure 7.1. HOOPS subwindows are also useful for creating user-interface gadgets, such as the buttons and sliders in Figure 7.1. So, even if you are writing your user interface using a window system, it is useful to know about HOOPS windows, so that you can use them for subwindows.

## 7.1.1    HOOPS Windows

In HOOPS, a window (as you might guess) is an attribute. In Chapter 2, we displayed the ledger view of a spreadsheet (Program 2.5) by using the window attribute to divide the overall window into separate subwindows, one for each cell in the spreadsheet. In Program 2.5, the windows did not overlap (they were *tiled*).

### 7.1.1.1

**The window attribute.** The window attribute is set on a segment with the HC_Set_Window command. This command takes four arguments, which define the left, right, bottom, and top coordinates of the window, specified with respect to the parent window. Setting the window attribute on a segment causes all geometry in that segment to be drawn inside the specified window area. The window attribute inherits like any regular attribute, so any geometry in this segment's subsegments also is drawn inside this window (unless a child segment has a window attribute set on it explicitly).

As we discussed in Section 6.1, a camera maps a 3D scene into a 2D window. In particular, the camera field defines the coordinates of the output window. By default, the camera field sets the coordinates of the output window to range between –1.0 and 1.0 in both $x$ and $y$. With a stretched camera projection, the camera output field is mapped exactly onto the output window. With a nonstretched projection, either the width or height of the camera field is padded to preserve the aspect ratio of the camera field.

The net window attribute defines the window on the display into which the camera field is mapped. Thus, when the window attribute is set on a segment, it causes any geometry that inherits the window attribute to be mapped into that window.

Program 7.1 divides the output window into four equal-sized subwindows. As we discussed in Section 4.3, the segment "?Picture" corresponds to the HOOPS output window (or to the whole screen, if there is no window system).

```
1   HC_Open_Segment("?Picture");

2       HC_Open_Segment("upper left window");
3           HC_Set_Window(-1.0, 0.0, 0.0, 1.0);
4       HC_Close_Segment();

5       HC_Open_Segment("upper right window");
6           HC_Set_Window(0.0, 1.0, 0.0, 1.0);
7       HC_Close_Segment();

8       HC_Open_Segment("lower left window");
9           HC_Set_Window(-1.0, 0.0, -1.0, 0.0);
10      HC_Close_Segment();

11      HC_Open_Segment("lower right window");
12          HC_Set_Window(0.0, 1.0, -1.0, 0.0);
13      HC_Close_Segment();

14  HC_Close_Segment();
```

**Program 7.1**    Four subwindows in HOOPS.

Program 7.1 creates a new segment for each window, and sets the window attribute on that segment with the coordinates of each quadrant. For example, the segment "upper left window" defines a window that goes from –1.0 to 0.0 in *x* and 0.0 to 1.0 in *y*. When we add geometry to the scene, the window in which it appears depends on into which of the four subsegments the geometry is placed. For example, if we want to draw an object that will appear in only the upper-left window, we place it in the segment named "upper left window". If we want the same object to appear in all four windows (for example, with four different cameras, as shown in Figure 7.1), then we use the HC_Include_Segment command to include the same object in all four subsegments, and set the appropriate camera on each one.

When we divide a window into subwindows, each new window is given its own coordinate system. The camera field is mapped into this coordinate system, as though the subwindow were a top-level window. So each subwindow has *x* and *y* coordinates that range from –1.0 to 1.0 (unless its camera field has been changed). The center of each subwindow corresponds to the net camera target for that segment, and the dimensions of the subwindow correspond to the net camera field for the segment.

**349**

Note that the segment "?Picture" is implicitly a window — the overall window corresponding to the HOOPS output window (or the entire screen, in the rare case that you are running HOOPS without a window system). You cannot set the window attribute (using HC_Set_Window) on "?Picture", because "?Picture" is already a window, and you cannot unset the window attribute (using the command HC_UnSet_Window). In general, you cannot modify the window attribute on any driver instance (including the values of the aliases "?Picture" or "?Hardcopy"). See Section 4.3 for more information about driver-instance segments.

If you want to change the coordinates of the overall window with respect to the screen, instead of calling HC_Set_Window on "?Picture", you can use the "subscreen" option of the HC_Set_Driver_Options command.

There is one additional limitation on HOOPS windows. When you set the window attribute (with HC_Set_Window), it must be on a segment whose parent also is a window (or a driver instance, such as "?Picture"). For example, if you want to define subwindows of "?Picture", you must set the window attribute on the immediate-children segments of "?Picture".

It is legal for the arguments passed to HC_Set_Window to be larger than the coordinates of the parent window's camera field. For example, if the camera field is the default −1.0 to 1.0, a subwindow can be set with coordinates from −2.0 to 2.0. Only that part of the subwindow that actually fits in the parent window will be visible, however; the rest will be clipped. You can use this ability to scroll a scene inside of a window.

**7.1.1.2**    **Subwindows of subwindows.** HOOPS subwindows can themselves have subwindows, and so on, recursively. Each subwindow is defined with respect to its parent window. For example, if you use Program 7.1 to divide the screen into four subwindows, then Program 7.2 will divide the upper-right window into two additional subwindows.

```
1   HC_Open_Segment("?Picture/upper right window");
2      HC_Open_Segment("left subwindow");
3         HC_Set_Window(-1.0, 0.0, -1.0, 1.0);
4      HC_Close_Segment();
```

```
5        HC_Open_Segment("right subwindow");
6            HC_Set_Window(0.0, 1.0, -1.0, 1.0);
7        HC_Close_Segment();
8    HC_Close_Segment();
```

**Program 7.2**    Subwindows of subwindows in HOOPS.

Each subwindow's coordinates are defined in terms of the coordinates of that subwindow's immediate parent, so the coordinates of the subwindow "left subwindow" are defined in terms of "upper right window" — the $x$ coordinate of "left subwindow" ranges from –1.0 to 0.0, which is one-half of "upper right window", rather than from 0.0 to 0.5, which would be one-eighth of "?Picture".

The root of the subwindow hierarchy must be the segment "?Picture" (or another driver instance). In addition, as we mentioned at the end of Section 7.1.1.1, a segment can have a window attribute set on it only if its immediate parent has a window attribute set (or its parent is "?Picture" or some other driver instance). Thus, if your application defines any subwindows (using the HOOPS command HC_Set_Window), these windows must all be defined contiguously, immediately under a driver instance at the top of the segment hierarchy.

Note, however, that it is legal to set the window attribute on an include segment, as long as the segment that includes the include segment has the window attribute set itself. You can use windowed include segments to include one window inside of multiple other windows — for example, to include a button in multiple places.

To guarantee that all windows are visible, HOOPS always displays children subwindows in front of their parent subwindows on the screen. In Program 7.2, for example, the two subwindows "left subwindow" and "right subwindow" will never be obscured by their parent "upper right window".

**7.1.1.3**    **Toolbars.** A common use of subwindows inside of subwindows is to define a toolbar: a row of buttons or other user-interface objects along one side of the output window (Figure 7.3).

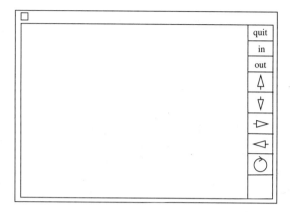

**Figure 7.3**        Toolbar window with button subwindows.

To create a toolbar window, you can divide the overall window into two subwindows: a tall narrow window at the right for the toolbar, and a large subwindow for the main output image. The toolbar subwindow is then further divided into separate subwindows, one for each button or other object in the toolbar (Program 7.3).

```
1   HC_Open_Segment("?Picture");
2      HC_Set_Camera_Projection("stretched");
3      HC_Open_Segment("main output");
4         HC_Set_Window(-1.0, 0.9, -1.0, 1.0);
5         HC_Set_Camera_Projection("perspective");
6         // main output goes here
7      HC_Close_Segment();
8      HC_Open_Segment("toolbar");
9         HC_Set_Window(0.9, 1.0, -1.0, 1.0);
10        HC_Open_Segment("quit button");
11           HC_Set_Window(-1.0, 1.0, 0.9, 1.0);
12           HC_Insert_Text(0.0, 0.0, 0.0, "quit");
13        HC_Close_Segment();
```

```
14        HC_Open_Segment("in button");
15            HC_Set_Window(-1.0, 1.0, 0.8, 0.9);
16            HC_Insert_Text(0.0, 0.0, 0.0, "in");
17        HC_Close_Segment();

18        // do other buttons

19      HC_Close_Segment();

20  HC_Close_Segment();
```

**Program 7.3**     Toolbar with buttons.

By making the buttons be themselves subwindows of the toolbar window, rather than subwindows directly of "?Picture", you can move the toolbar around without changing the definitions of the buttons. For example, you can move the toolbar to the left side of the output window simply by moving the toolbar window, rather than by moving each button individually.

**7.1.1.4**     **Overlapping windows.** You can use the HC_Set_Window command to create overlapping windows simply by creating windows whose coordinates overlap (Figure 7.4).

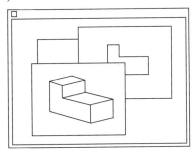

**Figure 7.4**     Overlapping windows in HOOPS.

As we discussed at the end of Section 7.1.1.2, children subwindows always appear in front of their parents, but when overlapping windows are siblings of one another (have the same parent segment), one window will partially obscure other windows (as shown in Figure 7.4). In HOOPS, each window is created in front of any existing sibling windows, so the most recently created window will appear in front of all its siblings. For multiple overlapping windows, the ordering (from back to front) is the same as the order in which the windows were created.

**353**

You can change the ordering of sibling windows using the HC_Bring_To_Front command. HC_Bring_To_Front makes its argument subwindow act as though that subwindow's segment were created most recently. If you want to specify the ordering of a set of sibling subwindows, you should call HC_Bring_To_Front on each one in order, from back to front.

You can use HC_Bring_To_Front on nonwindowed segments and HC_Bring_To_Front_By_Key on any piece of geometry, to order geometry and segments with respect to one another and to windows. Note, however, that HC_Bring_To_Front and HC_Bring_To_Front_By_Key work on geometry and nonwindowed segments only if hidden surfaces are off for the current segment (see HC_Set_Heuristics). HC_Bring_To_Front works on subwindows whether or not hidden surfaces are on. You can also use priority to control what appears in front. See Section 5.2.7 for more information.

**7.1.1.5**      **Other window attributes.** By default, windows are opaque — they obscure any window behind them. However, you can make a window transparent by setting the window pattern to be "clear":

```
HC_Set_Window_Pattern("clear");
```

In addition, you can use HC_Set_Window_Pattern to define a background pattern for a window. Except for the "clear" pattern, the possible window patterns are the same as polygon-face patterns — for example, "##" for a crosshatch, "::" for dotted, "[][]" for checkerboard, and "<><>" for diamonds. See the command HC_Set_Window_Pattern for more information.

Two options of the HC_Set_Color command apply to windows. For example,

```
HC_Set_Color("windows=light gray");
```

sets the window background color to light gray. When a window has a pattern (other than "solid" or "clear") applied to it, then the pattern is drawn with the window contrast color. For example,

```
HC_Set_Window_Pattern("::");
HC_Set_Color(
        "windows=purple, window constrast=yellow");
```

draws a window background consisting of yellow dots on a purple background (this example should not be taken as an endorsement of this particular color scheme).

You can also use an image as a window backdrop. See Section 9.2.2 for more information.

Finally, when HOOPS creates a window, it draws a one-pixel–wide border line around the edge of the window as a window frame. The image inside the window is shrunk slightly to take the frame into account. You can control whether HOOPS draws this window frame with the HC_Set_Window_Frame command. By default, window frames are on. To turn them off, use

```
HC_Set_Window_Frame("off");
```

The window frame is drawn using the window contrast color.

When HOOPS is used with a window system, normally the overall window (the window that corresponds to "?Picture") will have a border drawn around it by the window system, so HOOPS does not draw an additional frame around that window. The border drawn by the window system normally also contains a control area containing a close box, controls for resizing the window, scroll bars, and so on. You can control the frame of the overall window with the "border" and "control area" options of HC_Set_Driver_Options. For example, the following command instructs HOOPS to tell the window system not to draw a border or a control area around the overall window:

```
HC_Set_Driver_Options("no border, no control area");
```

If the "subscreen" driver option is left at its default value (the whole screen), setting these driver options will cause the HOOPS main output window to take over the entire screen. When the window system does not draw a border around the output window, you can tell HOOPS whether or not to draw its own frame around the output window by calling HC_Set_Window_Frame on "?Picture".

Note that the exact behavior of these driver options is somewhat dependent on the window system. On some window systems, they may not work at all. Another (usually better) way to control the appearance of the overall window is to create the overall window using the window system, and then to connect it to HOOPS (rather than letting HOOPS create the overall window). This topic is discussed in Section 7.3.

**7.1.1.6**     **Text size in windows.** In Section 5.2.2, we discussed how text size can be specified in sru (screen relative units), oru (object relative units), or points. If your scene contains HOOPS subwindows, then, in some cases, it is convenient to specify text size in wru (window relative units). When you use wru, the text size is set in relation to the smallest enclosing window, rather than in relation to the outermost window (as it is in sru). Setting text size in wru is useful for text inside a button or other user-interface gadget that is normally enclosed inside its own HOOPS window, so that the text will size automatically to the size of the button.

 The term *screen relative units* is a misnomer; it dates from the days when HOOPS was used without a window system, and the outermost window was the screen.

### 7.1.2     Multiple-Subwindow Example

Program 7.4 displays a cube in four HOOPS subwindows. Program 7.4 first creates the cube in a subsegment of the include library (lines 3 through 23). We place the cube in the include library so that we can include it into multiple HOOPS subwindows.

```
1   #include "hc.h"
2   void main() {
3       // create a cube centered at the origin
4       HC_Open_Segment("?Include library/cube");
5           static Point point_list[8] = {
6               {-0.4, -0.4, -0.4},
7               {0.4, -0.4, -0.4},
8               {0.4, 0.4, -0.4},
9               {-0.4, 0.4, -0.4},
10              {-0.4, -0.4, 0.4},
11              {0.4, -0.4, 0.4},
12              {0.4, 0.4, 0.4},
13              {-0.4, 0.4, 0.4} };
14          static int face_list[30] = {
15                  4, 0, 1, 2, 3,
16                  4, 4, 5, 1, 0,
17                  4, 2, 1, 5, 6,
18                  4, 7, 4, 0, 3,
19                  4, 7, 6, 5, 4,
20                  4, 3, 2, 6, 7 };
21          HC_Insert_Shell(8, point_list, 30, face_list);
22          HC_Set_Visibility("no markers, no faces");
23      HC_Close_Segment();
```

```
24    HC_Open_Segment("?Style Library/text overlay");
25       HC_Set_Camera_Projection("stretched");
26       HC_Set_Text_Alignment(">v");
27       HC_Set_Text_Font("size=0.04 wru");
28    HC_Close_Segment();

29    HC_Open_Segment("?Picture");

30       HC_Open_Segment("front");
31          HC_Include_Segment("?Include Library/cube");
32          HC_Set_Window(-1.0, 0.0, 0.0, 1.0);
33          HC_Open_Segment("title");
34             HC_Insert_Text(0.95, -0.95, 0.0,
35                   "Front");
36             HC_Style_Segment(
37                   "?Style Library/text overlay");
38          HC_Close_Segment();
39       HC_Close_Segment();

40       HC_Open_Segment("above");
41          HC_Include_Segment("?Include Library/cube");
42          HC_Set_Window(0.0, 1.0, 0.0, 1.0);
43          HC_Orbit_Camera(0.0, 30.0);
44          HC_Open_Segment("title");
45             HC_Insert_Text(0.95, -0.95, 0.0,
46                   "Above");
47             HC_Style_Segment(
48                   "?Style Library/text overlay");
49          HC_Close_Segment();
50       HC_Close_Segment();

51       HC_Open_Segment("side");
52          HC_Include_Segment("?Include Library/cube");
53          HC_Set_Window(-1.0, 0.0, -1.0, 0.0);
54          HC_Orbit_Camera(30.0, 0.0);
55          HC_Open_Segment("title");
56             HC_Insert_Text(0.95, -0.95, 0.0,
57                   "Side");
58             HC_Style_Segment(
59                   "?Style Library/text overlay");
60          HC_Close_Segment();
61       HC_Close_Segment();
```

```
62          HC_Open_Segment("Both");
63              HC_Include_Segment("?Include Library/cube");
64              HC_Set_Window(0.0, 1.0, -1.0, 0.0);
65              HC_Orbit_Camera(30.0, 30.0);
66              HC_Open_Segment("title");
67                  HC_Insert_Text(0.95, -0.95, 0.0,
68                      "both");
69                  HC_Style_Segment(
70                      "?Style Library/text overlay");
71              HC_Close_Segment();
72          HC_Close_Segment();

73      HC_Close_Segment();
74      HC_Pause();
75  }
```

**Program 7.4**     Multiple views in HOOPS subwindows.

On lines 24 through 28, we create a style segment in the style library. We use the attributes in the style segment to style text captions that will be placed in each subwindow.

In the remainder of Program 7.4, we create four subwindows under the segment "?Picture", called front, above, side, and both. For each window, we include the cube from the include library, set the window attribute, and place a title. For all except the first window, we also orbit the camera into the proper position for the view. For each view, we use only a single command (on lines 32, 42, 53, and 64) to create a window. Even with a title in each view (lines 33 through 38, 44 through 49, 55 through 60, and 66 through 72), Program 7.4 is short and simple.

Note how the title segment in each subwindow uses a stretched projection (defined in the style segment, on line 25), whereas the clock uses a nonstretched perspective projection in the same window. The stretched projection allows the text to be right justified at the far right side of the window. Because text is normally not transformed, the text itself in each title is not stretched out (as it would be, if we used HC_Set_Text_Font to turn on text transforms).

The output from Program 7.4 is shown in Figure 7.5.

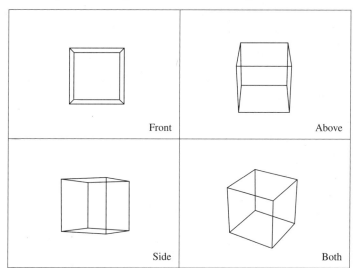

**Figure 7.5**    Multiple views in HOOPS subwindows.

## 7.1.3    Window-System Windows with HOOPS

In Section 7.1.1, we discussed how to create subwindows of the overall application window using HOOPS. In this section, we shall discuss how to create new window-system (overall application) windows from inside HOOPS.

As we discussed in Section 4.3, a driver-instance segment (a segment such as "?Picture" that is a child of a driver segment) corresponds to a window-system window, so you can create a new window on the screen simply by creating a new driver instance. This window is not a HOOPS subwindow; it is a full application window created by the window system, with a border, control area, and the user-interface gadgets that any normal application window has.

For example, Program 7.5 opens up a driver instance that is a sibling window of "?Picture".

```
1  char newseg[128];
2  HC_Show_Alias("?Picture", newseg);
3  strcat(newseg, "+A");
4  HC_Open_Segment(newseg);
5     HC_Insert_Text(0.0, 0.0, 0.0, "second window");
6  HC_Close_Segment();
```

**Program 7.5**     Opening of a new driver instance.

If you run Program 7.5 on an X11 system, then the "?Picture" alias will have the value "/driver/x11/unix:0.0", so this program will create a new segment with the name "/driver/x11/unix:0.0+A". So this program results in two segments that are children of the driver segment "/driver/x11". Each such segment is used by the driver to create a window on the screen.

The second window will be created with the same size and position as "?Picture", so we may have to move one window to see the other, but we can modify the window's position using the "subscreen" driver option. Note that, because we now have two driver instances, we can set separate driver options (such as "subscreen") on each one.

Why did we use the suffix "+A" to create the new window in Program 7.5? In HOOPS, the name of the driver instance can be used by the driver. For example, for the PostScript driver, the name of the driver instance is the file name used to write the PostScript output. For the X11 driver, the name of the driver instance is the X11 name of the display to which to send the output.

It turns out that the X11 driver is the only current HOOPS display driver that actually cares about the format of the driver-instance name. The syntax "0.0+A" tells X11 to create a new window. For more information, see the X11 documentation for your system.

What happens if we run Program 7.5 on a non-X11 system? On Microsoft Windows, the value of "?Picture" is "?driver/msw/window0", so Program 7.5 will create a new driver instance named "?driver/msw/window0+A". The msw (Microsoft Windows) driver uses the name "window0+A" to create the new window, but it does not care about the syntax of the name, so no harm is done. Thus, the "+A" makes X11 happy, and does not bother the other HOOPS drivers. For more information about what each driver does with the driver instance names, see the *HOOPS Installation Guide*.

**7.1.4**       **Multiple Window Example**

Program 7.6 is similar to Program 7.4, which displays a cube in four HOOPS subwindows, but is rewritten to use four window-system windows. Note that, even though HOOPS is using the window system to create the windows, this program does not contain any calls to the window system, so it is portable to any system that runs HOOPS.

The differences between Program 7.6 and 7.4 are minimal. Instead of opening up four subsegments of "?Picture", we open up four subsegments of the parent of "?Picture" (the driver segment). We also change the HC_Set_Window command into a HC_Set_Driver_Options command to set the subscreen driver option. The only other change is the code to create the proper names for the new driver instances.

```
1   #include "hc.h"
2   #include <string.h>
3   void main() {
4       // create a cube centered at the origin
5       HC_Open_Segment("?Include library/cube");
6           static Point point_list[8] = {
7               {-0.4, -0.4, -0.4},
8               {0.4, -0.4, -0.4},
9               {0.4, 0.4, -0.4},
10              {-0.4, 0.4, -0.4},
11              {-0.4, -0.4, 0.4},
12              {0.4, -0.4, 0.4},
13              {0.4, 0.4, 0.4},
14              {-0.4, 0.4, 0.4} };
15          static int face_list[30] = {
16              4, 0, 1, 2, 3,
17              4, 4, 5, 1, 0,
18              4, 2, 1, 5, 6,
19              4, 7, 4, 0, 3,
20              4, 7, 6, 5, 4,
21              4, 3, 2, 6, 7 };
22          HC_Insert_Shell(8, point_list, 30, face_list);
23          HC_Set_Visibility("no markers, no faces");
24      HC_Close_Segment();
```

```
25    HC_Open_Segment("?Style Library/text overlay");
26       HC_Set_Camera_Projection("stretched");
27       HC_Set_Text_Alignment(">v");
28       HC_Set_Text_Font("size=0.04 wru");
29    HC_Close_Segment();

30    HC_Open_Segment("?Picture");
31       HC_Include_Segment("?Include Library/cube");
32       HC_Set_Driver_Options(
33            "subscreen=(-1.0, 0.0, 0.0, 1.0)");
34       HC_Open_Segment("title");
35          HC_Insert_Text(0.95, -0.95, 0.0,
36                "Front");
37          HC_Style_Segment(
38                "?Style Library/text overlay");
39       HC_Close_Segment();
40    HC_Close_Segment();

41    char segname[128];
42    HC_Show_Alias("?Picture", segname);
43    strcat(segname, "+A");
44    // position of the letter A in segname
45    int charpos = strlen(segname) - 1;

46    // use suffix +A for the top view
47    HC_Open_Segment(segname);
48       HC_Include_Segment("?Include Library/cube");
49       HC_Set_Driver_Options(
50            "subscreen=(0.0, 1.0, 0.0, 1.0)");
51       HC_Orbit_Camera(0.0, 30.0);
52       HC_Open_Segment("title");
53          HC_Insert_Text(0.95, -0.95, 0.0,
54                "Above");
55          HC_Style_Segment(
56                "?Style Library/text overlay");
57       HC_Close_Segment();
58    HC_Close_Segment();
```

```
59        // use suffix +B for the side view
60        segname[charpos] = 'B';
61        HC_Open_Segment(segname);
62           HC_Include_Segment("?Include Library/cube");
63           HC_Set_Driver_Options(
64                 "subscreen=(-1.0, 0.0, -1.0, 0.0)");
65           HC_Orbit_Camera(30.0, 0.0);
66           HC_Open_Segment("title");
67              HC_Insert_Text(0.95, -0.95, 0.0,
68                    "Side");
69              HC_Style_Segment(
70                    "?Style Library/text overlay");
71           HC_Close_Segment();
72        HC_Close_Segment();

73        // use suffix +C for the oblique view
74        segname[charpos] = 'C';
75        HC_Open_Segment(segname);
76           HC_Include_Segment("?Include Library/cube");
77           HC_Set_Driver_Options(
78                 "subscreen=(0.0, 1.0, -1.0, 0.0)");
79           HC_Orbit_Camera(30.0, 30.0);
80           HC_Open_Segment("title");
81              HC_Insert_Text(0.95, -0.95, 0.0,
82                    "Both");
83              HC_Style_Segment(
84                    "?Style Library/text overlay");
85           HC_Close_Segment();
86        HC_Close_Segment();

87        HC_Pause();
88     }
```

**Program 7.6**   Multiple views in window-system windows in HOOPS.

Lines 1 through 29 of Program 7.6 are the same as those in Program 7.4. We create the cube, and set up a style segment for the text captions.

Next, instead of opening up four subsegments of "?Picture", we open up "?Picture" itself (line 30) and three additional siblings (lines 46, 61, and 75). We use "?Picture for the front view. The HC_Set_Driver_Options command (on line 32) sets the subscreen of "?Picture" to be the upper-left quadrant of the screen.

The way that we use this command is nearly identical to the way that we used the HC_Set_Window command in Program 7.4, except that the coordinates of the window are passed inside a string, rather than as four floats.

To open up siblings of "Picture", we save the value of the "?Picture" alias in the string "segname", and concatenate "+A" onto it (lines 41 to 43). We also save the position of the letter "A", so that we can change it later for the other two segments (line 45). We use segname for the other two views, changing the suffix to +B and +C (lines 60 and 74).

The output looks similar to that of Program 7.4, except that, instead of one window-system window divided into four subwindows, we now have four separate window-system windows, as shown in Figure 7.6.

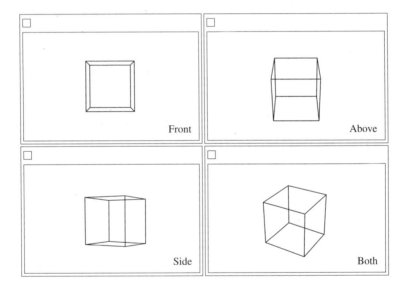

**Figure 7.6**    Multiple views in window-system windows.

In both Programs 7.6 and 7.4, we specified the size of the text font in wru (window relative units), so we set the size of the font in relation to the smallest enclosing window. If we had not specified the font size, then it would have defaulted to 0.03 sru (screen relative units), so we would have set the size of the font in relation to the outermost window. When we switched from one (window-system) window to four, the size of the font would have changed. By specifying the font in wru, we ensure that the font stays the same size in both programs.

### 7.1.5      The Problem with HC_Pause

If you ran Program 7.6, you might have noticed a problem. The HC_Pause command on line 87 is supposed to wait for user input, and then to terminate the program. But if you clicked in any window other than the upper-left one, nothing happened. Alternatively, if you pressed a key on the keyboard, the program terminated only if the window-system input focus was on the upper-left window. What was going on?

As we discussed in Section 8.2.9, the HC_Pause command is only a convenience command; it enables input events, and then waits for input. When it enables input events, it has to specify a driver instance, so it uses "?Picture"; therefore, HC_Pause waits for an input event on only "?Picture". Because we used "?Picture" for the upper-left window, we must supply an input event to the upper-left window before our program will terminate.

---

Note that Program 7.6 did not need to use "?Picture" as one of the four windows. Instead, it could have deleted the segment "?Picture" and created four new driver instances. If we had done that, however, we could not have used HC_Pause at all, since it would have tried to enable events on a nonexistent driver instance.

---

A real application will normally do something with user input, so the HC_Pause command is rarely used. In fact, HC_Pause is typically used for only simple output-only example programs, like the ones we have seen (up until now) in this book. We shall discuss real graphical input in Chapter 8; for now, we shall give you a simple routine that will perform the same function as HC_Pause, but will work with multiple windows (multiple driver instances).

Program 7.7 works by finding all driver instances using a segment search, and enabling mouse and keyboard events on them. The HC_Enable_Location_Events and HC_Enable_Button_Events commands will be covered in Chapter 8.

```
1  void common_pause() {
2      // enable Location and Button events on
3      // each driver instance
4      char seg[128];
```

```
 5      HC_Begin_Segment_Search("/driver/*/*");
 6         while (HC_Find_Segment(seg)) {
 7             HC_Enable_Location_Events(seg, seg, "v");
 8             HC_Enable_Button_Events(seg, "anything");
 9         }
10      HC_End_Segment_Search();

11      // wait for an event
12      char event_type[32];
13      HC_Await_Event(event_type);
14      HC_Requeue_Event();

15      // disable Location and Button events
16      HC_Begin_Segment_Search("/driver/*/*");
17         while (HC_Find_Segment(seg)) {
18             HC_Disable_Location_Events(seg, seg, "v");
19             HC_Disable_Button_Events(seg, "anything");
20         }
21      HC_End_Segment_Search();
22  }
```

**Program 7.7**     Replacement of HC_Pause with common_pause.

After enabling input events, we wait for an event using the HC_Await_Event command (line 13), which pauses the program. When we receive an event, we requeue it (this action will allow another HC_Await_Event command to look at the event). Finally, we disable input events on all driver instances (using another search) and return.

Now, if we replace the call to HC_Pause (line 87 in Program 7.6) with a call to common_pause, then we can click in any output window and our program will terminate.

Note that Program 7.7 will find all driver instances, rather than just the siblings of "?Picture". For example, if you are doing PostScript output to a segment named "/driver/postscript/filename", input events will be enabled on this segment (enabling output events on a hardcopy driver does not make much sense, but it does not do any harm). In some convoluted and rare programs, this routine might cause a problem, but, as we said earlier, most programs will use real input routines, rather than a routine like this one.

## 7.2  Native Window Systems

For a typical graphics application, you will write the 2D parts of the user interface using direct calls to the native window system, and the 3D parts using calls to HOOPS. In addition, HOOPS itself makes calls to the window system. For example, if you draw a 3D line using a HOOPS command, HOOPS will transform the line into 2D screen space, remove any parts of the line that are hidden by objects in front of the line, and then draw one or more 2D line segments using native window-system calls. Thus, both HOOPS and your application will be making calls to the native window system to draw objects into the same area of the screen. Consequently, HOOPS and the native window system need to coordinate their actions, such as deciding when to clear the screen, what order to draw objects, what to do when a window is minimized or destroyed, and so on. Luckily, this coordination is remarkably easy to do with HOOPS.

Connecting HOOPS to a window system involves two tasks: connecting the window system's user input loop to HOOPS so that HOOPS can handle selection events, and connecting HOOPS to a window-system window so that HOOPS knows where to draw its output.

### 7.2.1  User Input

We discussed the general principles of handling user input in Section 3.4; we shall cover how to handle user input in HOOPS in Chapter 8. When you write your user interface using a window system, however, all low-level user input (such as mouse and keyboard events) will be handled by the window system.

The only help with user input that you need from HOOPS is help handling selection events. To select a 3D object, the user clicks the mouse in a window containing HOOPS output. The window system handles the mouse event and passes it to your application. Your application's event handler then uses the mouse position from this event, and calculates what 3D object has been selected using the HOOPS command HC_Compute_Selection. Selection events will be covered in Section 8.5.

### 7.2.2  Connection to a Window-System Window

Normally, HOOPS creates its own output window for each driver instance (such as "?Picture"). When you write your user interface using a window system, the window system will be in charge of creating the output window. All you need to do is to tell HOOPS where this output window is, with the "use window id" driver option, so that HOOPS can draw into it.

To connect HOOPS to a window-system window, your application needs to perform the following six steps:

1. Delete the driver-instance segment associated with "?Picture", so that HOOPS will not create an output window or try to send output to it.

2. Create a window. You create the window using the native window system — HOOPS is not involved.

3. Create a new HOOPS driver-instance segment for the window.

4. Set the "use window id" driver option on the new driver-instance segment; this option connects the driver instance to the window-system window.

5. Disable HOOPS input, because user input will be handled by the window system. Use the "disable input" or "disable input = all" driver options.

6. When the window system destroys the window, delete the driver-instance segment.

Note that it is possible to change the relative order of some of the steps. For example, we could create the window-system window (step 2) before we delete the "?Picture" driver instance (step 1).

Different window systems use different techniques to create windows, and because this book is not about how to use window systems, we shall not go into detail on the subject (we shall simply present several examples). For more information about creating window-system windows, see the documentation for your window system. Regardless of which window system you use, it will return an id or handle that identifies the window to your application. This id is the one that is passed to the "use window id" driver option.

The driver option "disable input" in step 5 tells HOOPS not to process any input events, such as mouse clicks or key presses. It is up to your application to receive these events from the window system, and to process them appropriately. Even with the "disable input" driver option set, however, HOOPS will process certain (noninput) events from the window system, such as "expose" events that are generated when the HOOPS window is brought out from behind another window. If you want HOOPS to disable event processing completely, you should specify "disable input = all" as the driver option. In this case, you will need to tell HOOPS explicitly to redraw the scene (using HC_Update_Display) when your application receives an expose event or other similar event. See Section 8.5 for more information.

The CD-ROM included with this book contains several programs that create windows using a window system, and connect them to HOOPS. In the remainder of this chapter, we shall go over four of them. These demo programs are all located in the demo subdirectory of the HOOPS distribution:

- The file demo/common/cookbook/x11winid.c contains an X11 example.

- The directory demo/motif/simple contains a Motif example that uses the Motif uscr interface on top of X11.

- The directory demo/win32/win32wid contains a Microsoft Windows example.

- The directory demo/mfc/simple contains an MFC (Microsoft Foundation Classes) example for Microsoft Windows.

## 7.2.3    X11

Program 7.8 uses direct X11 (X-windows) calls to open a window on the screen. This example is useful to read, even if you do not plan to use X11, because it is the simplest example program, and shows each of the six steps from Section 7.2.2 clearly.

The first part of the code creates a window (step 2). The values that HOOPS needs are stored in the variables DisplayPtr (on line 5) and window (on line 16). The window variable is of type Window, which is actually an unsigned long integer.

```
1  #include "hc.h"
2  #include <X11/Xlib.h>
3  #include <X11/Xutil.h>

4  void main() {

5     Display * DisplayPtr = XOpenDisplay("");
6     if (DisplayPtr == (Display *) 0)
7        HC_Abort_Program("Cannot connect to X server");

8     int screen= DefaultScreen(DisplayPtr);
9     int border= 5;
```

**369**

```
10    XSizeHints normhint;
11    normhint.width = 200;
12    normhint.height= 200;
13    normhint.x= 400;
14    normhint.y= 600;
15    normhint.flags= PSize|PPosition;

16    Window window = XCreateSimpleWindow(
17        DisplayPtr, RootWindow(DisplayPtr,screen),
18        normhint.x, normhint.y, normhint.scrwidth,
19        normhint.scrheight, border,
20        BlackPixel(DisplayPtr,screen),
21        WhitePixel(DisplayPtr,screen));

22    Atom wm_delete_window = XInternAtom(DisplayPtr,
23        "WM_DELETE_WINDOW", False);
24    XSetWMProtocols(DisplayPtr, window,
25        &wm_delete_window, 1);
26    XSetNormalHints(DisplayPtr, window, &normhint);
27    XSelectInput(DisplayPtr, window,
28        KeyPress|ButtonPressMask|ExposureMask);
29    XMapWindow(DisplayPtr, window);
30    XFlush(DisplayPtr);
```

**Program 7.8**     Creation of a window in X11.

Next, we perform step 1, and delete the "?Picture" segment (line 31). Just to be paranoid, we also delete the alias (line 32). Deleting the alias is optional, but it keeps our program from opening the alias by mistake. Recall that the relative order of steps 1 and 2 is unimportant.

In lines 33 through 37, we perform step 3, and create a new driver instance for our new window. This segment is a subsegment of "?driver/x11" formed from the display name and the window number. Line 36 opens the new driver instance. Opening the driver instance is equivalent to opening "?Picture" in a HOOPS program that does not use window-system windows. We save the key for this window for later use.

Next, in lines 38 through 40, we set the "use window id" driver option (step 4). We disable HOOPS input (step 5) in the same command.

The rest of your application follows line 42.

When the user closes the window, or the application is finished, we delete the driver instance (line 43) and (optionally) call HC_Exit_Program to terminate HOOPS and the application (step 6). Alternatively, we could shut down HOOPS without terminating the application, using HC_Reset_System.

```
31  HC_Delete_Segment("?Picture");
32  HC_UnDefine_Alias("?Picture");

33  char str[100];
34  sprintf(str, "?driver/x11/%s+%d",
35          DisplayString(DisplayPtr), window);

36  long key = HC_KOpen_Segment(str);
37      if (window <= 0) HC_Exit_Program();

38      sprintf(str,
39          "disable input, use window ID= %u", window);
40      HC_Set_Driver_Options(str);
41  HC_Close_Segment();

42      // your application goes here

43      HC_Delete_By_Key(key);
44      HC_Exit_Program();
45 }
```

**Program 7.8 (continued)**   Use of HOOPS with X11.

A cute trick that is often done in X11/HOOPS applications is to renumber the key of the driver-instance segment. For example, we could insert the following line after line 37 in Program 7.8.

```
HC_Renumber_Key(key, window, "global");
```

Renumbering the key of the driver instance segment is useful in an application that will use multiple windows. When the application receives an input event from X, the window id is stored in the event. For example, for a ButtonPress event (such as a mouse button), the window id is stored in event.xbutton.window. By renumbering the key to be the window id, we can open the segment corresponding to the window using the following one line:

```
HC_Open_Segment_By_Key(event.xbutton.window);
```

Look in the demo program demo/common/cookbook/x11winid.c for more information.

### 7.2.4     Motif

When you are using Motif with X11, you can obtain the window id (of X11 type "Window") from the widget handle for the window (of Motif type "Widget") using the XtWindow function. This value is the one that is passed to set the "use window id" driver option of HOOPS. For example, Program 7.9 sets the "use window id" driver option from a newly created Motif window is whose handle is stored in a Motif widget named "canvas".

```
1  sprintf(str,
2      "disable input, use window ID= %u",
3      XtWindow(canvas));
4  HC_Set_Driver_Options(str);
```

**Program 7.9**     The window handle from a Motif widget.

The directory demo/motif/simple contains several simple demo programs (analyze.c, hoopsw_test.c, lookat.c, lookat_widget_hierarchy.c motiftst.c and twowin.c) that use Motif with HOOPS.

An even easier way to use HOOPS with Motif is to use the HOOPS Motif widget. The HOOPS Motif widget is a Motif widget that creates an output window and hooks up that window to HOOPS. The HOOPS Motif widget is used in the example program in demo/motif/viewer.

### 7.2.5     Microsoft Windows

In Microsoft Windows, the six steps for connecting HOOPS to the window system are spread out in several different places. Step 1, which deletes "?Picture", is normally done in the beginning of WinMain, in the initialization code for your application (before the event loop). In Program 7.10, we also delete the "?Picture" alias (line 2), to ensure that we do not accidentally try to open it in the program.

We also need to register a window class for the HOOPS output window. This step occurs in WinMain, as shown in lines 3 through 14 of Program 7.10. The function name HoopsWndProc (on line 5) is the name of your message-handler function for the HOOPS output window.

```
1  HC_Delete_Segment("?Picture");
2  HC_UnDefine_Alias("?Picture");
```

```
 3   WNDCLASS wc;
 4   wc.style = CS_HREDRAW | CS_VREDRAW | CS_OWNDC;
 5   wc.lpfnWndProc = HoopsWndProc;
 6   wc.cbClsExtra = 0;
 7   wc.cbWndExtra = sizeof(HLOCAL);
 8   wc.hInstance = hInstance;
 9   wc.hIcon = LoadIcon(NULL, IDI_APPLICATION);
10   wc.hCursor = LoadCursor(NULL, IDC_ARROW);
11   wc.hbrBackground = GetStockObject(WHITE_BRUSH);
12   wc.lpszMenuName = NULL;
13   wc.lpszClassName = "MdiHoopsChild";
14   RegisterClass(&wc);
```

**Program 7.10**   HOOPS with Microsoft Windows, fragments from WinMain.

The HoopsWndProc function receives messages sent by Windows in response to events. The first argument passed to this function is the handle for the window (of type HWND, which is usually a void *). Lines 15 through 55 contain the definition for HoopsWndProc (it can be in the same file as WinMain, or it can be in a separate file).

This function will handle various messages, but the one about which we are most concerned here is the WM_CREATE message, which is sent when a new HOOPS output window is created by the window system (step 2). Your HoopsWndProc function will normally contain a switch statement to handle the different messages that can be sent to it.

When we receive the WM_CREATE message (line 18), we create the driver segment for the window (step 3). Because we can have more than one active HOOPS window at a time, we number the windows sequentially using the static variable num_window. The driver instance is created under the msw driver segment. We use num_window to create the segment name, so multiple windows will have distinct segment names.

Next, on lines 24 to 27, we set the "use window id" driver option on the driver instance, using the window handle passed to this function as the window id.

As in the X11 example, we also need to store the key of the driver-instance segment (the variable "driver_key" that was defined in line 23), so that we can retrieve it later. One way to store it is in extra allocated window memory, as shown in lines 28 to 40.

The remaining cases of the switch statement follow line 41. These cases will handle events and commands generated for your window. For example, if you have created a menu with a "zoom" command, then, when the user chooses this command, you can do an HC_Zoom_Camera on the driver-instance segment.

Finally, when the window is closed, you simply delete the driver instance by retrieving its key from window storage, as shown on lines 42 to 50.

On lines 51 to 56, we clean up the allocated window memory when the window is destroyed.

```
15   long FAR PASCAL HoopsWndProc(HWND hWnd, UINT message,
16        UINT wParam, LONG lParam) {

17     switch (message) {
18       case WM_CREATE: {

19         char szSegment[80];
20         static int num_window = 0;
21         sprintf(szSegment, "?driver/msw/window%d",
22              num_window++);
23         long driver_key = HC_KOpen_Segment(szSegment);

24         char szTemp[256];
25         sprintf(szTemp,
26            "disable input, use window id = %u", hWnd);
27         HC_Set_Driver_Options(szTemp);

28         LOCALHANDLE hHoopsData = LocalAlloc(
29            LMEM_MOVEABLE | LMEM_ZEROINIT,
30            sizeof(long));
31         long * datap = (long *) LocalLock(hHoopsData);
32         *datap = driver_key;
33         LocalUnlock(hHoopsData);
34         SetWindowLong(hWnd, 0, (LONG) hHoopsData);
35         HC_Close_Segment();

36         // save the Client and Frame Window handles
37         hWndClient = GetParent(hWnd);
38         hWndFrame = GetParent(hWndClient);
39         return 0L;
40       }  // end WM_CREATE case

41     // remaining event and command cases
```

```
42      case WM_QUERYENDSESSION:
43      case WM_CLOSE: {
44          LOCALHANDLE hHoopsData =
45                  (HLOCAL) GetWindowLong(hWnd, 0);
46          long * datap = (long *) LocalLock(hHoopsData);
47          long driver_key = *datap;
48          LocalUnlock(hHoopsData);
49          HC_Delete_By_Key(driver_key);
50      } break;

51      case WM_DESTROY: {
52          LOCALHANDLE hHoopsData =
53                  (HLOCAL) GetWindowLong(hWnd, 0);
54          LocalFree(hHoopsData);
55          return 0;
56      }
```

**Program 7.10 (continued)** HOOPS with Microsoft Windows, fragments from HoopsWndProc.

For a more complete example, see the demo program in demo/win32/win32wid.

## 7.2.6 Microsoft Foundation Classes

The Microsoft Foundation Classes (MFC) are an object-oriented framework for writing windows applications. If you are writing a new application for the Windows 95 or Windows NT platforms, we recommend that you use MFC (especially in conjunction with one of the new programming environments that can generate MFC code for you automatically). It is easy to integrate HOOPS output into an MFC application.

There are two demo programs included on the CD-ROM: one in demo/mfc/simple, and a more complete example in demo/mfc/viewer. We built these examples using the Microsoft Visual C++ compiler using MFC, but other environments would be similar.

When you use an object-oriented framework, various classes are generated for your application. For example, say that your application is named "My". The application framework will generate the following classes (among others):

• CMyApp, derived from the MFC class CWinApp, represents your application.

- CMyDoc, derived from the MFC class CDocument, represents the data model of your application (see Chapter 2 for more information about models and views).

- CMyView, derived from the MFC class CView, represents your output view. In a 3D HOOPS application, this window will contain your HOOPS output.

- CMyFrm, derived from a MFC class such as CMDIChildWnd (in a Multiple Document Interface application), is the frame (border) around the view window (CMyView). When your application puts up a window, CMyFrm corresponds to the outer window, including user-interface controls, such as the close box, whereas the CMyView class corresponds to the inner window, containing only the HOOPS output. These classes are shown in Figure 7.7.

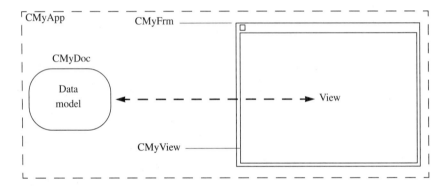

**Figure 7.7**      MFC classes.

To integrate HOOPS in with a framework-generated application, you need to modify a few of the methods of the generated classes. You can add new data members to these classes to store local variables. You can also add new methods, if you wish. For more information, see the documentation for your programming environment.

In Program 7.11, the first method that we shall modify is the InitInstance method of CMyApp. To this method, we add lines 1 and 2, which perform step 1 from Section 7.2.2.

```
1   HC_Delete_Segment("?Picture");
2   HC_UnDefine_Alias("?Picture");
```

**Program 7.11**      Lines added to CMyApp::InitInstance.

MFC will take care of step 2 — creating the window. When a window is created, MFC will call the OnCreate method of the CMyView class.

Lines 3 through 5 are generated automatically; lines 6 through 14 are the code that you need to add to perform steps 3 through 5. This code opens a new driver instance, sets the "use window id" driver option on it, and disables HOOPS input. The window handle is in the variable m_hWnd (of type HWND), which is a member of CWnd. Class CView is publicly derived from CWnd, so we can access m_hWnd directly.

```
3   int CMyView::OnCreate(LPCREATESTRUCT lpCreateStruct) {
4       if (CView::OnCreate(lpCreateStruct) == -1)
5           return -1;
6       char buf[256];
7       static int num_window = 0;
8       sprintf(buf, "?driver/msw/window%d", num_window++);
9       driver_key = HC_KOpen_Segment(buf);
10          sprintf(buf,
11              "disable input, use window id = %u", m_hWnd);
12          HC_Set_Driver_Options(buf);
13      HC_Close_Segment();
14      return 0;
15  }
```

**Program 7.11 (continued)** CMyView::OnCreate.

The key for the driver instance is stored in the variable "driver_key", which is a member that we added to CMyView. We also add a public member function to access this variable. Note that CMyView also contains quite a bit of code that was generated automatically by Visual C++.

```
16  class CMyView : public CView {
17      // (automatically generated code not shown)
18    private:
19      long driver_key;
20    public:
21      long get_driver_key() { return driver_key; }
22      // (more automatically generated code)
23  };
```

**Program 7.11 (continued)** Added member definition for class CMyView.

When the window is destroyed, we need to delete the driver instance from HOOPS. Our first guess would be to delete the driver instance in the OnDestroy method of CMyView, but that placement would cause a problem. OnDestroy is called after the output window is destroyed, and we need to detach HOOPS from this window before it is destroyed, so that HOOPS does not try to send any output to to the window. HOOPS will catch this problem and avoid sending output to the destroyed window; in the interest of good programming practice, however, we shall show you the right way to implement this step.

Instead, we delete the HOOPS driver-instance segment in the OnClose method of CMyFrm (the frame window around the HOOPS output window). This method is called when a message is received to close the window (such as the user choosing the close command) before the window is destroyed. From the frame, we can get access to the CView class, which contains the key for the driver instance, with the GetActiveView method. (Note that, in a real application, you might want to check the return value from GetActiveView() to ensure that it is not null.)

```
24  void CMyFrm::OnClose() {
25      long key = GetActiveView()->get_driver_key();
26      HC_Delete_By_Key(key);

27      CMDIChildWnd::OnClose();
28  }
```

**Program 7.11 (continued)** CMyFrm::OnClose.

Finally, it is a good idea to terminate HOOPS when the application terminates. We call HC_Reset_System inside the ExitInstance method of CMyApp.

```
29  int CMyApp::ExitInstance() {
30      HC_Reset_System();
31      return CWinApp::ExitInstance();
32  }
```

**Program 7.11 (continued)** CMyApp::ExitInstance.

There is more information about using HOOPS with MFC in the readme.txt file in demo/mfc/simple.

## 7.2.7        Clipboard and OLE Support

In Microsoft Windows (and other operating systems), you can copy information from one application to another via the clipboard. This section gives a brief

**378**

overview of how to use the clipboard support for transferring HOOPS information to another application. This section covers only Microsoft Windows (including Windows NT).

Traditionally, when you copy information from one application to another, it is just copied as static data (text or graphics). With the use of OLE, however, you can copy live data from one application to another. With live data, you can manipulate the information from inside another application. For example, using OLE, you can copy a HOOPS graphics database and paste it into a Microsoft Word application, and then manipulate the database (rotate it, change it, and so on) from inside Microsoft Word. Both possibilities are covered here.

**7.2.7.1**        **Static data.** Copying static graphics data from a HOOPS application to another application using the clipboard is similar to sending HOOPS data to a printer or to the image driver. The program w32uwid.c in the directory that is named demo/win32/win32wid on the CD-ROM shows how to do it (note that this program is written in C, rather than in C++). Program 7.12 is taken (more or less directly) from that example program.

To write to the clipboard, you need to create a Windows metafile (note that a Windows metafile is not related to a HOOPS metafile). There are two kinds of Windows metafiles: regular and enhanced. If you are running on a 16-bit version of Windows, you must use a regular metafile. Otherwise (if you are running on Windows 95 or Windows NT), you should use an enhanced metafile. The example program w32uwid.c can write either kind of metafile. See the Windows documentation for more information on metafiles.

Next, you should create a new instance of the HOOPS Windows driver (line 1 in Program 7.12). We set the "use window id" driver option to be the handle of the current window, named hWnd. This step is no different from what we would do with a normal output window to which we want to write using Microsoft Windows. In addition, we set the "use window id2" driver option to the handle of the Windows metafile that we just created, named hMfDC. It is also a good idea to disable input processing.

Finally, we include the scene to be written to the clipboard (line 7). Note that this scene is not necessarily in the include library; in fact, it will usually be under some other driver instance.

```
 1  HC_Open_Segment("?driver/msw/clipboard");
 2  char buffer[80];
 3  sprintf(buffer, "use window ID=%u, use window ID2=%u",
 4      hWnd, hMfDC);
 5  HC_Set_Driver_Options(buffer);
 6  HC_Set_Driver_Options("disable input");
 7  HC_Include_Segment("?Include Library/scene");
 8  HC_Set_Rendering_Options("hsr algorithm = painters");
 9  HC_Update_Display();
10  HC_Close_Segment();
```

**Program 7.12**     Creation of the driver instance before writing to the clipboard.

When you are creating a Windows metafile to write to the clipboard, you normally should not use the software Z-buffer hidden-surface algorithm, or specify the "technology = software frame buffer" rendering option. Either of these options causes the scene to be rendered into a memory-based frame buffer, and then sent to Windows all at once as a single image. Instead, you normally want the individual primitives to be written out to the metafile, so you should use the painter's algorithm or even the Z-sort algorithm. You should make sure that the scene that you included (on line 7) does not override the hidden-surface algorithm.

Line 9 causes the scene to be written to the Windows metafile. The scene is written out as individual Windows GDI calls. After that, all you need to do is to close the metafile and to place it in the clipboard. Again, see the w32uwid.c program for a complete example.

7.2.7.2     **Live data.** When you write out a Windows metafile to the clipboard, the metafile contains only static data that cannot be changed. Using OLE, you can paste live data into another application.

To paste live data, you need to modify your application so that it can act as an OLE server. In addition, when you write out data to the clipboard, you need to include any information that your server application needs. For example, instead of just writing out GDI data to the clipboard, you could include the HOOPS metafile. Then, you could paste this information into another application, such as Microsoft Word.

From inside Word, when you double click on the HOOPS scene, Word will invoke your server application and display its output. You can then modify the data interactively, all from inside Word (or from any other application that can act as an OLE container).

All the messy details of OLE are beyond the scope of this book. For an example of how to write a HOOPS application that can act as an OLE server, see the MFC viewer application in the directory demo/mfc/viewer on the CD-ROM. This application can act either as a stand-alone application, or as an OLE in-place server.

# 8     Interaction

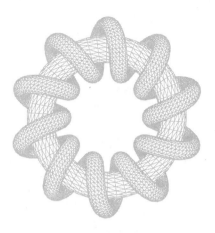

This chapter discusses how to handle input in a 3D graphics application, and explores the features of HOOPS that support graphical input. First, we discuss application architectures for handling input events. Much of this information is not specific to 3D graphics, but applies to 2D graphical applications as well. Then, we discuss aspects of graphical input that are specific to 3D graphics. Graphical input in general was discussed in Section 3.4.

## 8.1     Input Architecture

The handling of graphic input can have a profound effect on the architecture of your application. This architecture reflects the modern graphical user interface, where the user is in charge. If you have been writing applications for more than a few years, you saw the architecture of your applications change when you rewrote DOS applications to Windows applications, or UNIX command-line applications to X-Windows applications. Applications have been restructured to behave like servants that wait for commands from the user. Even while executing a user command, an application should listen for new commands from the user, and should abort what it is doing if so requested.

Nothing about this change is unique to 3D graphics, or even to 2D graphics. But it does affect how you organize your application, and how your application interacts with a 3D graphics system. HOOPS includes many features to support this kind of graphical user input.

## 8.1.1     Event Queues

Modern interactive graphics applications are organized around an *event queue*. The operating system places input events — such as mouse presses or keyboard input — into the event queue, and the application removes input from the queue, one event at a time. There is only one queue (per application), and all input goes through this queue, no matter what the input event's source. If the application requests the next input from the event queue and the queue is empty, then the application *blocks* (temporarily stops running). Blocking allows the operating system to run another application until input becomes available.

### 8.1.1.1

**Event loops and polling.** Your application must remove and process input from the event queue. The most common way is with an *event loop*, shown in Program 8.1. An event loop is just a loop that waits for events from the event queue, and then processes them one at a time.

```
1   done = FALSE;
2   while (!done) {
3       char event[32];
4       HC_Await_Event(event);
5       // determine the type of event
6       if (strcmp(event, "selection") == 0) {
7           // handle the selection event; for example,
8           // by highlighting the selected object
9       } else if (strcmp(event, "button") == 0) {
10          // quit if user pressed Q
11          char button[8];
12          HC_Show_Button(button);
13          if (strcmp(button, "Q") == 0) done = TRUE;
14      }
15  }
```

**Program 8.1**     Handling of events with an event loop.

One problem with this organization is that, while the application is processing one event, it will temporarily ignore any subsequent events. If handling an event will take a long time, we may want to check periodically to see whether any new events have arrived. Such periodic checking is called *polling*.

If you are using an operating system — such as Windows NT, Windows 95 or Sun Solaris — that supports multithreading, an excellent way to avoid having to poll is to create a separate thread to handle a time-consuming event. That way, the event loop can continue almost immediately to process any new events. If a newer event needs to interrupt an event that is being handled by a separate thread, it can kill the thread. Multithreaded programs must be careful to protect shared resources. In particular, usually only one thread can be communicating with the graphics system at any one time. Writing of multithreaded programs is beyond the scope of this book; see your operating-system documentation for more information.

**8.1.1.2**    **Centralized versus decentralized event handling.** Once your application receives an input event, it must do something with that event. If your application is going to handle only a few types of events, it can handle all events inside the event loop. For most applications, however, handling events inside the event loop turns the event loop into a huge switch statement (or an equally huge list of if–then–else statements) that is difficult to debug and even more difficult to extend or maintain.

Consider a simple example that handles selection events (Program 8.2, written in pseudo-code). If the user selects an object, we want to highlight it. If the user selects the same object again, we want to return it to its unhighlighted status. More than one object can be highlighted at the same time. How an object shows that it is highlighted depends on the object. We will highlight a polygon by changing its color to red, and highlight a line by increasing its width. Some objects, such as the window background, should do nothing if selected.

```
1   while (!done) {
2      char event[32];
3      HC_Await_Event(event);
4      if (strcmp(event, "selection") == 0) {

5         // get selected object
6         long key;
7         int o1, o2, o3;
8         HC_Show_Selection_Element(&key, &o1, &o2, &o3);

9         char type[32];
10        HC_Show_Key_Type(key, type);
```

```
11          if (strcmp(type, "polygon") == 0) {
12              if (polygon not highlighted) {
13                  save polygon color;
14                  change color to red;
15              } else {    // turn off highlighting
16                  restore saved color;
17              }

18          } else if (strcmp(type, "line") == 0) {
19              if (line not highlighted) {
20                  save line weight;
21                  increase line weight;
22              } else {    // turn off highlighting
23                  restore saved line weight;
24              }

25          } else if (strcmp(type, "mesh") == 0) {
26              // and so on
27          }  // end switch
28      }
29 }  // end event loop
```

**Program 8.2**    Handling of events inside the event loop.

There are numerous problems with this approach. First, it is not object oriented. The event loop is a single monolithic block of code that has to know about every kind of object that can be highlighted. If we add a new kind of object, or change the way that an object is highlighted, then we have to modify the event loop. In addition, this method requires a way to save polygon colors and line widths for highlighted polygons and lines — in essence, we need some sort of simple database functionality. This information must be associated with each highlighted object, so that we can restore the proper color or width when the object is deselected.

In a better organization, called *decentralized event handling*, each kind of object knows how to highlight and unhighlight itself. In addition, each object can keep track of whether it is already highlighted, and can save its own color or width for restoration when it is unhighlighted. To use this approach, we can define a C++ handler class for each kind of object that can be highlighted (lines 1 through 18 of Program 8.3).

```
 1  class Handler {    // event handler base class
 2   public:
 3     virtual void      handler_function() = 0;
 4   private:
 5     int               d_highlighted;
 6  };

 7  class Line_Handler : public Handler {
 8   public:
 9     virtual void      handler_function();
10   private:
11     float             d_saved_width;
12  };

13  class Polygon_Handler : public Handler {
14   public:
15     virtual void      handler_function();
16   private:
17     char              d_saved_color[256];
18  };

19  void Line_Handler::handler_function() {
20     if (!d_highlighted) {
21        // assumes current segment is open
22        HC_Show_Line_Weight(&d_saved_weight);
23        HC_Set_Line_Weight(d_saved_weight * 2);
24        d_highlighted = 1;
25     } else {    // turn off highlighting
26        HC_Set_Line_Weight(d_saved_weight);
27        d_highlighted = 0;
28     }
29  }
```

**Program 8.3**   Decentralized event handling — handler class.

Lines 19 to 29 define the handler function for class Line_Handler. The handler function for Polygon_Handler is similar.

We still need simple database functionality to associate these C++ objects with the graphical objects, but we can use the HOOPS graphics database. As we create each object in the graphics database, we associate the appropriate type of handler object with it, by storing the address of the handler object as a user option. We discussed user options in Section 4.5.2.1. The routine defined on lines 30 through

**387**

36 associates an instance of a handler object with a segment by storing the address of the handler object as a user option in the segment.

The event loop becomes simple. Line 39 receives events, and, if the event was a selection event, line 47 calls the handler function for the selected object.

```
30  void associate(char * segment, Handler * object);
31     HC_Open_Segment(segment);
32         char option[256];
33         sprintf(option, "handler=%x", object);
34         HC_Set_User_Option(option);
35     HC_Close_Segment();
36  }

37  while (!done) {
38     char event[32];
39     HC_Await_Event(event);
40     if (strcmp(event, "selection") == 0) {
41         char segment[256];
42         HC_Show_Selection_Pathname(segment);
43         HC_Open_Segment(segment);
44             char address[32];
45             HC_Show_Net_User_Option("handler", address);
46             Handler * handler_object = atol(address);
47             handler_object->handler_function();
48         HC_Close_Segment();
49     }
50  }
```

**Program 8.3 (continued)**   Decentralized event handling — event loop.

Note that Program 8.3 is somewhat simplified. We are assuming that each selectable object is in a segment by itself, so that it can be highlighted individually. See Section 8.3.2.2 for information on how to highlight objects when there are multiple objects in the same segment.

If you add new kinds of objects, or change the way that an object is highlighted, you will need to change only the handler function for that kind of object; you will not need to modify the event loop. Decentralized event handling uses encapsulation to associate event-handling functionality closely with the objects in the database.

### 8.1.2     User-Interface Gadgets

Decentralized event handling (rather than event handling inside the event loop) makes it much easier for us to build libraries of reusable graphical parts. These parts have a physical manifestation (the graphical objects) and a set of behaviors (the event-handler functions). We can also combine graphical objects to create *user-interface gadgets*, such as buttons, sliders, and scroll bars (in Windows, these gadgets are called *controls;* in X-Windows, they are called *widgets*). Each gadget is a C++ object that contains multiple graphical objects. There is still no change to the event loop — as before, it receives events from the event queue, and dispatches them to the handler functions.

## 8.2     Input Events

HOOPS divides input events into six categories: button, location, selection, string, wakeup, and special events. Each kind of event can be enabled or disabled individually; for example, the following command tells HOOPS to receive button events from the keyboard:

```
HC_Enable_Button_Events("?Keyboard", "anything");
```

The string "?Keyboard" is a HOOPS alias for the driver segment that controls the keyboard (most of the time, the value of this alias will be the same segment as "?Picture"). The string "anything" tells HOOPS to generate an input event when any button on the keyboard is pressed. You can also enable only selected buttons. For example, the following command tells HOOPS to generate an input event only if the user presses the "q" button or the left-arrow button. All other buttons on the keyboard are ignored.

```
HC_Enable_Button_Events("?Keyboard", "q, left arrow");
```

See the HC_Enable_Button_Events command for more information on what buttons can be enabled.

To disable button events, you can use the HC_Disable_Button_Events command, which takes the same arguments as HC_Enable_Button_Events. For example, to turn off all button events, use

```
HC_Disable_Button_Events("?Keyboard", "anything");
```

Note that you can enable the same events more than once. HOOPS keeps track of how many times events have been enabled, and requires the same number of disable commands before it actually disables those events. Thus, more than one section of your program can enable and disable events without worrying about conflicts with other sections that enable or disable the same events.

Normally, a program will handle more than one kind of event. A typical program (where HOOPS is handling input) will enable all the kinds of events that it is interested in receiving (using commands starting with the Enable verb), then will wait for events using an HC_Await_Event command in an event loop. When the HC_Await_Event command returns, the event that caused it to return is the *current event*, and you can obtain information about this event using various commands that begin with the Show verb. For example, for a button event, the application can determine which button was pressed by using the command HC_Show_Button. When the application is no longer interested in receiving a specific kind of input event, it will disable those events.

Program 8.4 waits for the user to click with the mouse, or to press the "q" button or spacebar on the keyboard. If a mouse-location event is received, a marker is drawn at that location. If the spacebar is pressed, the screen is cleared. If the "q" button is pressed, the application terminates.

```
1   #include <hc.h>
2   #include <string.h>

3   void main() {
4      HC_Enable_Location_Events(
5            "?Locater", "?Picture", "v");
6      HC_Enable_Button_Events("?Keyboard", "q, space");

7      HC_Open_Segment("?Picture");
8         HC_Set_Camera_Projection("stretched");

9         int done = 0;
10        char event[32];
11        while (!done) {
12           HC_Await_Event(event);

13           if (strcmp(event, "location") == 0) {
14              float x, y;
15              HC_Show_Location(&x, &y);
16              HC_Insert_Marker(x, y, 0);
17           }
```

```
18            else if (strcmp(event, "button") == 0) {
19                char button[32];
20                HC_Show_Button(button);
21                if (strcmp(button, "space") == 0) {
22                    HC_Flush_Contents(".", "markers");
23                } else {
24                    done = 1;
25                }
26            }
27        }
28    HC_Close_Segment();
29    HC_Disable_Location_Events(
30            "?Locater", "?Picture", "v");
31    HC_Disable_Button_Events("?Keyboard", "q, space");
32
33 }
```

**Program 8.4**     Handling of location and button events simultaneously.

The HC_Set_Camera_Projection command on line 8 is required because the HC_Show_Location command (on line 15) returns the *x* and *y* positions of the location event in screen coordinates of the output window. Because the projection is set to "stretched", these screen coordinates will exactly correspond to world coordinates. One problem with using a stretched projection, however, is that any object drawn may appear distorted (a circle may appear to be an ellipse, as discussed in Section 6.1.10).

If we want to receive a location in world coordinates (rather than in screen coordinates), one trick that we can employ is to use a selection event, rather than a location event. When the user clicks the mouse in the output window, the window itself is selected, and we can then get the coordinates inside this window using the HC_Show_Selection_Position command. That way, we do not need to use a stretched projection. Program 8.5 produces the same results as Program 8.4, except that a stretched projection is not needed.

```
1 #include <hc.h>
2 #include <string.h>
3 void main() {
4     HC_Enable_Selection_Events("?Locater", "?Picture");
5     HC_Enable_Button_Events("?Keyboard", "q, space");
```

```
 6        HC_Open_Segment("?Picture");
 7            int done = 0;
 8            char event[32];
 9            while (!done) {
10                HC_Await_Event(event);

11                if (strcmp(event, "selection") == 0) {
12                    float x, y, z, d;
13                    HC_Show_Selection_Position(&d, &d, &d,
14                            &x, &y, &z);
15                    HC_Insert_Marker(x, y, z);
16                }

17                else if (strcmp(event, "button") == 0) {
18                    char button[32];
19                    HC_Show_Button(button);
20                    if (strcmp(button, "space") == 0) {
21                        HC_Flush_Contents(".", "markers");
22                    } else {
23                        done = 1;
24                    }
25                }
26            }
27        HC_Close_Segment();
28        HC_Disable_Selection_Events(
29            "?Locater", "?Picture");
30        HC_Disable_Button_Events("?Keyboard", "q, space");
31 }
```

**Program 8.5**    Returning a location in world coordinates.

Why do we need to use a selection event to receive a location in world coordinates? Recall that each segment in the HOOPS database may have a local transformation; thus, world coordinates may be different for different segments. A selection event selects a specific segment, so it is possible to return a position in that segment's coordinate system. In Program 8.5, the selected segment is "?Picture", so the returned position is in world coordinates. A location event does not apply to a segment, so only screen coordinates can be returned.

During the execution of an application, the program can enable and disable different kinds of events. Note that, after an enable command is called, that kind of event is not actually enabled until HOOPS checks for events (typically using HC_Await_Event). This delay can cause problems. For example, if your application enables button events, and then does a lengthy computation before waiting for events, any button presses that occur while the computation is in progress will be lost. To solve this problem, your application can call HC_Check_For_Events (which checks for events, but does not block if the event queue is empty) immediately after enabling the events.

## 8.2.1    Button Events

A button event is normally generated when the user presses a key on the keyboard. Button events are "raw" keyboard events — button events are generated as each key is pressed (without waiting for the "enter" key to be pressed), and keys such as "backspace" are not treated specially. Button events, however, are not device events (device events are discussed in Section 3.4.2.2); for example, there is no event generated when the button is released, pressing the shift key does not generate an event, and uppercase and lowercase letters are treated as different buttons.

Button events are useful when you want to have your application perform a certain action when a keyboard button is pressed. Note, however, that this kind of user interface, although easy to program, is not recommended, because the user has to remember what each button does. It is generally better to generate button events by drawing buttons on the screen (which can contain a legend or descriptive icon), and using a selection event to generate an event when the user presses such a button using the mouse.

When a button event is the current event, you can determine which button was pressed to generate the event with the HC_Show_Button command. In addition, you can use the HC_Show_Button_Source command to determine which keyboard generated the event (on a system that has more than one input device that can generate button events), and what the status is of any modifier keys that can be depressed at the same time (for example, whether the "Alt" key was depressed when the key was entered).

## 8.2.2    String Events

String events are the "cooked" equivalent of button events (raw versus cooked events are discussed in Section 3.4.2.2). You can use string events when you want the user to type in the answer to a question. The string event is generated only when the user terminates the string by pressing the "enter" key. Keys such as "backspace" can be used to correct input before the event is generated.

String events have the added capability of echoing the string as it is typed in. To enable echoing, you need to insert a text string into the HOOPS database (using HC_KInsert_Text), then to create a string cursor for that text (using HC_KInsert_String_Cursor). Program 8.6 displays two strings: a question and a default answer.

```
1   #include <hc.h>
2   #include <string.h>

3   void main() {
4       HC_Open_Segment("?Picture");

5           HC_Open_Segment("question");
6               HC_Set_Text_Alignment(">v");
7               HC_Insert_Text(0.0, 0.0, 0.0, "Quit? ");
8           HC_Close_Segment();

9           HC_Open_Segment("answer");
10              HC_Set_Text_Alignment("<v");
11              long text = HC_KInsert_Text(0.0, 0.0, 0.0,
12                      "yes");
13              long cursor = HC_KInsert_String_Cursor(text,
14                      0, 3);
15          HC_Close_Segment();

16          HC_Enable_String_Events("?Keyboard", cursor);

17          int done = 0;
18          char event[32];
19          while (!done) {
20              HC_Await_Event(event);

21              if (strcmp(event, "string") == 0) {
22                  int length;
23                  HC_Show_String_Length(&length);
24                  char * answer = new char[length + 1];
25                  HC_Show_String(answer);
26                  if (strcmp(answer, "yes") == 0) done = 1;
27              }
28          }
```

```
29        HC_Close_Segment();
30        HC_Disable_String_Events("?Keyboard", cursor);
31 }
```

**Program 8.6**    String-event example.

Two separate segments are used (on lines 5 and 9), so the text alignment of the question and answer segments can be different. The right edge of the question is aligned with the left edge of the default answer.

 An alternative way to line up two text strings is to use the command HC_Compute_Text_Extent to determine the size of the strings, and then to position the strings explicitly such that they line up.

### 8.2.3    Location Events

A location event returns a location in a HOOPS output window. Location events can be generated when a mouse button is pressed, when a mouse button is released, or when the location of the mouse changes (see HC_Enable_Location_Events).

Unlike a selection event, a location event is strictly 2D. The $x$ and $y$ coordinates of the location event are returned by the HC_Show_Location command (see Program 8.4). The location is returned in device coordinates (pixels) for the output window. Normally, this location will need to be mapped into world coordinates for your output scene (via HC_Compute_Coordinates). In Program 8.4, we used a stretched projection so that the device coordinates of the output window exactly corresponded to world coordinates of the "?Picture" segment.

You can use the HC_Show_Location_Source command for determining information about a location event other than the location. For example, you can use the HC_Show_Location_Source command to determine in which application window the mouse was when the event was generated (for an application that has multiple HOOPS output windows), or to determine whether this event was generated when a mouse button was pressed, when a button was released, or when the mouse moved. HC_Show_Location_Source also returns the status of the mouse buttons (and of a few keyboard buttons), so you can differentiate between a right-button click and a left-button click (and can tell whether the shift button was pressed when the mouse button was clicked).

## 8.2.4     Selection Events

Selection events are the only events that return 3D information. Even if you are not using HOOPS for input, you will often need to generate selection events to pick objects in the HOOPS database. You can also use selection events instead of location events to generate location events in world coordinates, rather than in device coordinates (see Program 8.5).

A selection event returns a specific object in the HOOPS database. You can control which objects are selectable using the HC_Set_Selectability command. Selectability inherits like a normal attribute, so if selectability is turned on in a segment for a specific kind of object, then it is on in all subsegments, unless the selectability for that kind of object is explicitly turned off in a subsegment.

In addition to enabling selectability on all the different kinds of HOOPS geometry (lines, text, markers, edges, faces, and images), you can also enable selectability on segments that are HOOPS subwindows. For example, in an application that creates a toolbar containing a number of buttons, you would create each button as a HOOPS subwindow. When a button is pressed by the user (using the mouse), the segment containing the button (the segment on which the window attribute was explicitly set) will be returned by the selection event.

By default, selectability is enabled for HOOPS subwindows, so a selection event always returns a segment (which has the window attribute set). To enable a specific kind of geometry to be picked, you need to enable its selectability explicitly. For example, the following command allows lines (and polylines) to be selected in the database:

```
HC_QSet_Selectability("?Picture", "lines");
```

You can enable selection of all kinds of geometry by specifying "everything" in the HC_Set_Selectability command. You can also control whether an object will return a selection event when a mouse button is pressed, when a button is released, or when the mouse moves. By default, geometry is selectable only if it is visible, but this requirement too can be changed. See the HC_Set_Selectability command for more information. Note that computing selection events on geometry can take longer than computing selection events on windowed segments.

Selection events contain a large amount of information about the selected object. Consequently, there are several HOOPS commands that you can use to return information from a selection event. In addition to HC_Show_Selection, there are HC_Show_Selection_Element, HC_Show_Selection_Position, HC_Show_Selection_Pathname, HC_Show_Selection_Keys, and

HC_Show_Selection_Source. These commands are valid only when a selection event is the current event (has just been returned by HC_Await_Event).

The HC_Show_Selection command returns the name of the segment that was selected (or that contains the selected geometry, if geometry is selectable). HC_Show_Selection returns only the simple name of the selected segment, rather than the full path name. If your database has multiple segments with the same simple name, this name can be ambiguous. To identify the selected segment unambiguously, you can use HC_Show_Selection_Pathname (which returns the fully qualified path name of the segment), or HC_Show_Selection_Keys (which returns the key for the selected segment, and all its parents). Note that, because of include segments, the path to a selected segment can be complicated. See the *HOOPS Reference Manual* entries for HC_Show_Selection_Pathname and HC_Show_Selection_Keys, for more information.

The HC_Show_Selection_Source command is like HC_Show_Location_Source. It returns the name of the driver window that generated the selection event (it is useful if you have multiple HOOPS output windows), and tells you whether this event was generated when a mouse button was pressed, when a mouse button was released, or when the mouse was moved. HC_Show_Selection_Source also returns the status of the mouse buttons (and of a few keyboard buttons), so you can differentiate between a right-button click and a left-button click (and can tell, for example, whether the shift button was pressed when the mouse button was clicked).

The HC_Show_Selection_Element command returns the key of the object that was selected and further information about what was selected. If more than one kind of object is selectable, you can determine which kind was selected using the HC_Show_Key_Type command. The HC_Show_Selection_Element command also returns three integers, whose value depends on what kind of object was selected. For example, if a text string was selected, then these integers return the index of the character in the string that was selected. For a polyline, these integers return the line segment that was selected. For a shell or a mesh, these integers return the edge and face that were selected. Likewise, appropriate information is returned for polygons, markers, images, arcs, circles, and so on. See the HC_Show_Selection_Element command for more information.

The HC_Show_Selection_Position command returns cursor (mouse) coordinates in 3D. This command returns two sets of coordinates: one in the coordinate space of the application window where the pick occurred, and one in the local modeling-coordinate space of the selected segment (or of the segment containing the selected geometry). The $z$ value of the selection position gives the intersection of the picked object with the ray from the current viewpoint (defined by the camera attribute on the selected segment) through the cursor location on the screen. See the HC_Show_Selection_Position command for more information.

**8.2.4.1**        **Selection example.** Program 8.7 demonstrates selection events. This program is a simple color-picker gadget, which you can use to set colors on objects in a scene. In this case, the scene is just four subwindows. When you click in one of the subwindows, the color-picker gadget appears and allows you to set the color of the subwindow. This example also demonstrates highlighting. When a subwindow is selected, we highlight it by setting a window pattern attribute on it.

```
1   #include <hc.h>
2   #include <string.h>

3   struct Point { float x, y, z; };
```

**Program 8.7**        Initial declarations for simple color picker.

The color-picker gadget is itself a HOOPS subwindow, called "?Picture/picker", which contains a flat, rectangular mesh with eight square faces. Each face contains a different color, defined by the array mesh_colors (on line 21).

```
 4   Point mesh_points[15] = {
 5          { -1.0f,  1.0f, 0.0f },
 6          { -0.5f,  1.0f, 0.0f },
 7          {  0.0f,  1.0f, 0.0f },
 8          {  0.5f,  1.0f, 0.0f },
 9          {  1.0f,  1.0f, 0.0f },
10          { -1.0f,  0.0f, 0.0f },
11          { -0.5f,  0.0f, 0.0f },
12          {  0.0f,  0.0f, 0.0f },
13          {  0.5f,  0.0f, 0.0f },
14          {  1.0f,  0.0f, 0.0f },
15          { -1.0f, -1.0f, 0.0f },
16          { -0.5f, -1.0f, 0.0f },
17          {  0.0f, -1.0f, 0.0f },
18          {  0.5f, -1.0f, 0.0f },
19          {  1.0f, -1.0f, 0.0f }
20   };
```

```
21  char * mesh_colors[8] = {
22          "white", "cyan", "magenta", "yellow",
23          "black", "red", "green", "blue"
24  };
```

**Program 8.7 (continued)**  Mesh points and colors for simple color picker.

The compute_face_numbers routine (lines 25 through 31) is used to translate a simple face number from 0 through 7 into the HOOPS mesh face number. Because each rectangular face of a mesh is actually two triangular faces, this routine returns two face numbers.

```
25  // calculate the two face numbers for a mesh
26  void compute_face_numbers(int index, int col,
27          int &face1, int &face2) {
28      int offset = index / (col - 1);
29      face1 = index + offset;
30      face2 = - (index + col + 1 + offset);
31  }
```

**Program 8.7 (continued)**  Utility routine to compute face numbers for a mesh.

For the mesh, we turn off the visibility of markers (on line 53). We also turn on the visibility of mesh quads, to form a gray border between the color swatches. To allow one of the colored faces to be picked, we turn on the selectability of faces (line 52).

The mesh is in a separate subsegment of "?Picture/picker" called "mesh", so that we can turn on and off the visibility of the color picker without affecting the visibility of the markers and mesh quads. Initially, the color-picker gadget is invisible (line 58). Recall that an object is selectable only if it is visible.

```
32  void create_color_picker() {
33    HC_Open_Segment("?Picture/picker");
34        HC_Set_Window(-0.4, 0.4, -0.2, 0.2);
35        HC_Set_Camera_Projection("stretched");

36        HC_Open_Segment("mesh");
37            long mesh = HC_KInsert_Mesh(3, 5,
38                mesh_points);
39            HC_Open_Geometry(mesh);
```

```
40              // set face colors
41              for (int i = 0; i < 8; i++) {
42                  int f1, f2;
43                  compute_face_numbers(i, 5, f1, f2);
44                  HC_Open_Face(f1);
45                      HC_Set_Color(mesh_colors[i]);
46                  HC_Close_Face();
47                  HC_Open_Face(f2);
48                      HC_Set_Color(mesh_colors[i]);
49                  HC_Close_Face();
50              }

51          HC_Close_Geometry();

52          HC_Set_Selectability("faces");
53          HC_Set_Visibility(
54                  "markers=off, edges=mesh quads only");
55          HC_Set_Color("edges=gray");
56          HC_Set_Edge_Weight(5.0);
57      HC_Close_Segment();

58      HC_Set_Visibility("off");
59   HC_Close_Segment();
60 }
```

**Program 8.7  (continued)**   Simple color picker.

The scene consists of four subwindows.

```
61   void create_scene() {
62     HC_Open_Segment("?Picture");
63       HC_Open_Segment("upper left");
64         HC_Set_Window(-1.0, 0.0, 0.0, 1.0);
65       HC_Close_Segment();
66       HC_Open_Segment("upper right");
67         HC_Set_Window(0.0, 1.0, 0.0, 1.0);
68       HC_Close_Segment();
69       HC_Open_Segment("bottom left");
70         HC_Set_Window(-1.0, 0.0, -1.0, 0.0);
71       HC_Close_Segment();
72       HC_Open_Segment("bottom right");
73         HC_Set_Window(0.0, 1.0, -1.0, 0.0);
74       HC_Close_Segment();
75     HC_Close_Segment();
76   }
```

**Program 8.7 (continued)**   Test scene for simple color picker.

The heart of this example is the main function (line 77), which contains the event loop. Since this example is simple, we use centralized event handling — we handle all events inside of the event loop.

Two kinds of events are enabled (on lines 78 and 79): selection events, which we shall use both to select a subwindow of the scene and to select a color in the color picker; and button events, which we shall use to terminate the program when the user presses either the "q" or "Q" key on the keyboard. The color-picker gadget is created on line 81, but it is initially invisible.

Inside the event loop, we test to see whether the event is a selection event (line 89) or a button event (line 127). If it is a button event, we terminate the program. If it is a selection event, we get the key of the selected object (on line 92), and test to see what kind of object it is (line 95). If it is not a mesh, it must be a window (line 112). In this case, we turn off any previously highlighted subwindow (lines 113 to 118), save the key of the selected subwindow (line 119), and highlight it (lines 120 to 123). We highlight the subwindow by drawing a crosshatch pattern (line 122). We also turn on the visibility of the color picker (line 124), so that it appears and is selectable.

If the selected object is the mesh (line 96), it must be the color picker (and, consequently, the color picker must have been made visible previously). In this case, we open the mesh geometry, and then open the selected face (returned as off3 from the HC_Show_Selection_Element command on line 92). We then retrieve the color of the face (line 100), and set the color of the previously selected subwindow to be that color (lines 102 through 107). We also turn off the highlighting of the subwindow (line 106). Finally, since the color picker has finished its job, we turn off its visibility (line 111).

```
77  void main() {
78     HC_Enable_Selection_Events("?Locater", "?Picture");
79     HC_Enable_Button_Events("?Keyboard", "q,Q");

80     create_scene();
81     create_color_picker();

82     HC_Open_Segment("?Picture");
83        HC_Set_Color("window contrast = gray");

84        int done = 0;
85        char event[32];
86        long window = 0;
87        while (!done) {
88           HC_Await_Event(event);

89           if (strcmp(event, "selection") == 0) {
90              long key;
91              int off1, off2, off3;
92              HC_Show_Selection_Element(
93                    &key, &off1, &off2, &off3);
94              char type[32];
95              HC_Show_Key_Type(key, type);
```

```
 96                if (strcmp(type, "mesh") == 0) {
 97                    HC_Open_Geometry(key);
 98                        HC_Open_Face(off3);
 99                            float r, g, b;
100                            HC_Show_One_Color_By_Value(
101                                    "face", "RGB", &r, &g, &b);
102                            HC_Open_Segment_By_Key(window);
103                                HC_Set_Color_By_Value(
104                                        "window", "RGB",
105                                        r, g, b);
106                                HC_UnSet_Window_Pattern();
107                            HC_Close_Segment();
108                            window = 0;
109                        HC_Close_Face();
110                    HC_Close_Geometry();
111                    HC_QSet_Visibility("picker", "off");

112                } else {     // window selected
113                    // turn off highlight
114                    if (window != 0) {
115                        HC_Open_Segment_By_Key(window);
116                            HC_UnSet_Window_Pattern();
117                        HC_Close_Segment();
118                    }
119                    window = key;
120                    // highlight
121                    HC_Open_Segment_By_Key(window);
122                        HC_Set_Window_Pattern("##");
123                    HC_Close_Segment();
124                    HC_QSet_Visibility("picker", "on");
125                }

126            }
127        else if (strcmp(event, "button") == 0) {
128            done = 1;
129        }
130    }
```

```
131     HC_Close_Segment();
132     HC_Disable_Selection_Events(
133          "?Locater", "?Picture");
134     HC_Disable_Button_Events("?Keyboard", "q,Q");
135 }
```

**Program 8.7 (continued)**   Event loop for simple color picker.

---

**8.2.4.2**       **Selection of multiple objects.** You can use the "selection proximity" driver option to control how HOOPS selects objects. The selection proximity is the radius, in centimeters, of a circle around the cursor position. Any object (whose selectability is on) inside this circle is selectable. If more than one selectable object is inside this circle, the one closest to the cursor position is selected. If two objects are equidistant from the cursor position, the one closer to the viewpoint is picked. Even if the objects are the same distance from the viewpoint, HOOPS will choose one of them to be returned by the selection event. If no object falls within the selection-proximity circle, and HOOPS subwindows are selectable, then the window is returned as the selection event.

When only HOOPS subwindows are selectable, a pick event always returns the frontmost HOOPS subwindow that is under the cursor. For example, if your overall application window contains two subwindows, a regular view, and a toolbar containing buttons, and if the toolbar contains one subwindow for each button, then, if the user pushes one of the buttons, the segment containing that button is returned, even though the cursor is also inside the toolbar subwindow and the overall application window. The subwindow lowest in the database tree is returned even if that subwindow is transparent.

When geometry is selectable (in addition to windows), and more than one selectable object was within the circle defined by the selection proximity, you can access the other objects using the HC_Find_Related_Selection command. This command sets the current event to be the next-best selection, and can be called multiple times. The final object that is returned will be the containing subwindow (if windows are selectable). After that (when there are no more objects that could have been selected), HC_Find_Related_Selection returns false.

There are a few other ways to control which objects are selected. For example, an interaction technique that many applications use to select multiple objects in a scene is to have the user sweep out a rectangular area of the screen with the mouse; all objects that fall entirely or partially within this area are selected. This kind of pick is called a *marquee pick*. A variation of this technique uses an arbitrarily drawn area, rather than a rectangular one; this kind of pick is called a *lasso pick.* A third, less common variation uses a polyline drawn by the user, and selects any object that is touched by the polyline; this kind of pick is called a *fence pick.* You can perform these kinds of selections (and others) using the HOOPS commands HC_Compute_Selection_By_Area, HC_Compute_Selection_By_Polygon, HC_Compute_Selection_By_Polylin (note that the trailing "e" in *Polyline* is missing because the length of the command name exceeded C calling conventions), and HC_Compute_Selection_By_Volume. These commands take a location or some geometry as an argument, and generate a selection event. There are examples of each of these kinds of selection events in the viewer program on the CD-ROM.

## 8.2.5 Wakeup Events

A wakeup event is used to generate an event when a specific amount of time has elapsed, or to generate events that are regularly spaced out over time. The argument to HC_Enable_Wakeup_Events is a time interval, in seconds. This argument is a floating-point number, so intervals of less than 1 second are possible. The actual resolution of wakeup events is system dependent, but in no case is it greater than 0.05 seconds.

It is possible to have more than one wakeup event active at the same time, even with the same time interval. You use HC_Disable_Wakeup_Events to turn off each enable (one disable for each enable).

Program 8.8 is a variation of Program 8.6, the program that used string events to ask the user whether to terminate the program. In Program 8.8, we ask the same question, but this time we also enable a wakeup event, so that the program will terminate automatically if the user does not respond within 10 seconds. If the user does respond, and does not say "yes" to terminate the program, then the program will wait indefinitely until the user says to terminate.

The only changes to Program 8.6 are the addition of line 18 to enable wakeup events, line 29 to disable wakeup events if the user answers the question before it times out, and lines 31 through 34 to handle the wakeup event and to terminate the program.

```
1  #include <hc.h>
2  #include <string.h>

3  const float timeout = 10.0f;

4  void main() {
5     HC_Open_Segment("?Picture");
```

```
 6        HC_Open_Segment("question");
 7            HC_Set_Text_Alignment(">v");
 8            HC_Insert_Text(0.0, 0.0, 0.0, "Quit? ");
 9        HC_Close_Segment();

10        HC_Open_Segment("answer");
11            HC_Set_Text_Alignment("<v");
12            long text = HC_KInsert_Text(0.0, 0.0, 0.0,
13                    "yes");
14            long cursor = HC_KInsert_String_Cursor(text,
15                    0, 3);
16        HC_Close_Segment();

17        HC_Enable_String_Events("?Keyboard", cursor);
18        HC_Enable_Wakeup_Events(timeout);

19        int done = 0;
20        char event[32];
21        while (!done) {
22            HC_Await_Event(event);

23            if (strcmp(event, "string") == 0) {
24                int length;
25                HC_Show_String_Length(&length);
26                char * answer = new char[length + 1];
27                HC_Show_String(answer);
28                if (strcmp(answer, "yes") == 0) done = 1;
29                else HC_Disable_Wakeup_Events(timeout);
30            }

31            else if (strcmp(event, "wakeup") == 0) {
32                done = 1;
33                HC_Disable_Wakeup_Events(timeout);
34            }
35        }

36    HC_Close_Segment();
37    HC_Disable_String_Events("?Keyboard", cursor);
38 }
```

**Program 8.8**     Use of a wakeup event to time out a string request.

Program 8.9 is another example that uses wakeup events. This program is a simple arcade game that displays a moving target on the screen, and allows the user to shoot at the target using the mouse. Three kinds of events are used: wakeup events to move the target, selection events to shoot at the target, and button events to quit the game and to clear the screen.

The target is a filled-in black circle; we display it using a HOOPS marker. When a marker is hit, it is moved to the "dead" segment (lines 17 through 21), where its color is changed to red, and the marker symbol is changed to an open circle (as though the marker had a hole shot through it). You can make the game more interesting by changing how long the marker stays in one place (line 8), and how close you need to get to the marker before you hit it (line 12).

```
1   #include <hc.h>
2   #include <string.h>

3   #include <time.h>
4   #include <stdlib.h>

5   void main() {
6      HC_Enable_Selection_Events("?Locater", "?Picture");
7      HC_Enable_Button_Events("?Keyboard", "q, space");
8      HC_Enable_Wakeup_Events(2.0);

9      // seed the random-number generator
10     srand(time(0));

11     HC_Open_Segment("?Picture");
12        HC_Set_Driver_Options(
13              "selection proximity=1.0");
14        HC_Set_Camera_Projection("stretched");
15        HC_Set_Selectability("everything=off, markers");
16        HC_Set_Marker_Symbol("@");

17        HC_Open_Segment("dead");
18           HC_Set_Color("red");
19           HC_Set_Marker_Symbol("()");
20           HC_Set_Selectability("everything=off");
21        HC_Close_Segment();

22        double scale = 2.0 / RAND_MAX;
23        float xpos = (float) (-1.0 + rand() * scale);
24        float ypos = (float) (-1.0 + rand() * scale);
25        long marker = HC_KInsert_Marker(
26              xpos, ypos, 0.0);
```

```
27              int done = 0;
28              char event[32];
29              while (!done) {
30                  HC_Await_Event(event);

31                  if (strcmp(event, "wakeup") == 0) {
32                      if (marker != 0) HC_Delete_By_Key(marker);
33                      xpos = (float) (-1.0 + rand() * scale);
34                      ypos = (float) (-1.0 + rand() * scale);
35                      marker = HC_KInsert_Marker(
36                              xpos, ypos, 0.0);
37                  }

38                  else if (strcmp(event, "selection") == 0) {
39                      long key;
40                      int dummy;
41                      HC_Show_Selection_Element(&key,
42                              &dummy, &dummy, &dummy);
43                      HC_Move_By_Key(key, "dead");
44                      marker = 0;
45                  }

46                  else if (strcmp(event, "button") == 0) {
47                      char button[32];
48                      HC_Show_Button(button);
49                      if (strcmp(button, "space") == 0) {
50                          HC_Flush_Contents("dead", "markers");
51                      } else {
52                          done = 1;
53                      }
54                  }

55              }
56          HC_Close_Segment();
57          HC_Disable_Selection_Events(
58                  "?Locater", "?Picture");
59          HC_Disable_Button_Events("?Keyboard", "q, space");
60      }
```

**Program 8.9**    Arcade game that uses wakeup events.

Note that Program 8.9 uses the rand function to generate random numbers (to control the position of the target on the screen), and the time function to seed the random-number generator (so that the target does not move in the same pattern each time that the game is played). These routines may have different names and may work slightly differently on some platforms, so you may need to change lines 3, 4, 10, 22, 23, 24, 33, and 34 to port Program 8.9 to your platform.

## 8.2.6     Special Events

Special events include all events not generated by an input event. There are two main sources of special events: the HOOPS drivers, and the application itself.

### 8.2.6.1

**Driver-generated special events.** Special events were devised initially for communication between the window system and an application. In this case, the special events are generated by a HOOPS driver in response to an event generated by the window system. For example, on some platforms, the driver will generate a special event when the output window is resized. A few platforms, such as the Macintosh, generate a special event when a pull-down–menu item is selected.

Special events generated by a HOOPS driver are highly platform dependent: Different drivers will generate different kinds of special events. See the *HOOPS Installation Guide* for more information about special events on each platform.

By default, the drivers do not generate special events. To tell a HOOPS driver to generate special events, use the "special events" driver option. Note that, if you are not using HOOPS as your user interface, there is never any reason to generate special events; your application will receive these kinds of events directly from the window system.

Unlike other kinds of events, special events are always enabled, so there is no HC_Enable_Special_Events command. If you tell a driver to generate special events (using the "special events" driver option), they will be placed in the event queue and will be returned by the HC_Await_Event command. The string returned by the HC_Await_Event command will be set to "special" when a special event is encountered.

A special event contains two strings. These strings are returned by the HC_Show_Special_Event command. The first string contains two fields separated by a colon. The first field is the name of the driver that generated the event (for example, "macdriver"). The second field describes the action that generated the event (for example, "pulldown selection" or "resize"). The second string contains any data returned by the event. For example, a resize event may return the new size of the output window.

**409**

Again, special events are highly platform dependent. If you need control over window-system events, you are probably better off using the native window system for your user interface (instead of using HOOPS with special events).

You can use Program 8.10 to display special events for a platform. Line 7 turns on special events — note that, since "special events" is a driver option, this line must appear after the segment "?Picture" is opened (on line 6). Line 5 enables button events so that the user can terminate the program (by pressing the "q" key). If a special event is received (line 12), then the value of the two strings is printed out (on line 15).

```
1   #include <hc.h>
2   #include <string.h>
3   #include <stdio.h>

4   void main() {
5       HC_Enable_Button_Events("?Keyboard", "q");
6       HC_Open_Segment("?Picture");
7           HC_Set_Driver_Options("special events");

8           int done = 0;
9           char event[32];
10          while (!done) {
11              HC_Await_Event(event);

12              if (strcmp(event, "special") == 0) {
13                  char str1[80], str2[256];
14                  HC_Show_Special_Event(str1, str2);
15                  printf("'%s' '%s'\n", str1, str2);
16              }

17              else if (strcmp(event, "button") == 0) {
18                  done = 1;
19              }
20          }

21      HC_Close_Segment();
22      HC_Disable_Button_Events("?Keyboard", "q");
23  }
```

**Program 8.10**   Printing out of special events.

When you run this program, try resizing the output window, changing the window to an icon, and destroying the window, to see what (if any) special events are generated by the current HOOPS driver. The special events generated by each driver are listed in the *HOOPS Installation Guide*.

**8.2.6.2**     **User-generated special events.** When an application uses the native window system for its user interface, driver-generated special events are not needed, but user-generated special events are useful. User-generated special events are a way for a HOOPS application to send a message to itself, using the command HC_Queue_Special_Event. Special events also can interrupt HOOPS while it is updating the display. See Sections 8.2.7 and 8.2.8 for more information and examples.

## 8.2.7     User-Generated Events

Most of the time, events (of all kinds) are generated by a HOOPS driver and are received by your application using the HC_Await_Event command. It is also possible for your application to generate an event (of any kind) and to queue that event. For example, HC_Queue_Button_Event creates and queues a button event exactly as though a button had been pressed.

Consider an application that will terminate itself if the user presses the "q" key on the keyboard, or if the user selects a "quit" button that is drawn on the screen as part of a toolbar. Assume that this application uses decentralized event handling (discussed in Section 8.1.1.2), so there is a function associated with the "quit" button that is called when the button is selected. This program might have clean-up actions to perform before it terminates, and we do not want to duplicate the clean-up code in more than once place. A simple way to avoid this problem is to have the function associated with the "quit" button queue a button event, as though the "q" key had been pressed by the user.

The commands to queue events include HC_Queue_Button_Event, HC_Queue_Location_Event, HC_Queue_Selection_Event, HC_Queue_String_Event, and HC_Queue_Wakeup_Event. In addition, you can use HC_Queue_Related_Selection to queue related selection events that can be returned by the HC_Find_Related_Selection command. These commands take quite a few arguments, since they need to know all information that could be returned by any Show command on the event (such as HC_Show_Selection or HC_Show_Selection_Element). In particular, HC_Queue_Selection_Event takes 15 arguments. These commands are documented in the *HOOPS Reference Manual* under "Queue_(Fake_Event)".

Also see Section 8.2.8 for additional examples of user-generated events.

**8.2.8**          **Event Checkers and Update Interrupts**

An event checker is a user-supplied function that is called automatically by HOOPS any time that an input event is needed (by HC_Await_Event or HC_Check_For_Events), and also is called periodically during display update. You specify the event-checker routine by passing its address to the "event checker" system option (using the HC_Define_System_Options command).

The original purpose of an event checker was to allow new input devices to be added to a HOOPS application. For example, an event-checker routine could poll a tablet and generate events using the HC_Compute_Selection_Event command or the HC_Queue_Location_Event command. Of course, if you need this level of control over input devices, you probably should not be using HOOPS input events for your user interface.

An alternative use for an event checker is to write a test harness for a HOOPS application. The event checker generates a series of events — one event each time that it is called — that simulate the actions of a user. You can use this technique to stress test an interactive application.

The most common use of event checkers, however, is to solve a problem that occurs when you use the native window system to handle input events. While HOOPS is updating the display, it checks occasionally to see whether any events have occurred. For example, if HOOPS is drawing a complicated scene and the user presses the "q" key on the keyboard to terminate the application, HOOPS will not wait until it is finished drawing the scene before it processes that event. Or, if a complicated object is being moved about the screen under control of the mouse, HOOPS will interrupt drawing as new events arrive. Update interrupts make a HOOPS application more responsive to the user.

Unfortunately, when you use your platform's native window system, rather than HOOPS, for input events, there is no way for HOOPS to know that there is an input event and thus to interrupt the display update. A solution to this problem (one that uses an event checker and special events) is discussed in Section 8.5.2.

You can disable update interrupts with the "no update interrupts" driver option.

**8.2.9**          **Get Commands and HC_Pause**

HOOPS also provides six commands that can be used for simple input handling. Five of these commands begin with the Get verb. These "Get" commands combine several HOOPS commands to return a single input event. For example, the HC_Get_Button command is essentially equivalent to Program 8.11.

```
1   void HC_Get_Button(char*button){
2      HC_Enable_Button_Events("?Keyboard","anything");
3      char type[32];
4      do HC_Await_Event(type);
5         while (strcmp(type,"button")!= 0);
6      HC_Disable_Button_Events("?Keyboard","anything");
7      HC_Show_Button(button);
8   }
```

**Program 8.11**    An equivalent program to HC_Get_Button.

The main problem with the Get commands is that they wait for only one kind of input at a time. While the HC_Get_Button routine is blocked waiting for a button event, it will ignore any other kind of event. For this reason, we do not recommend that you use the Get routines.

The final convenience routine is the HC_Pause command, which waits for any kind of input event. HC_Pause is especially useful for small test programs (such as the example programs in this book), because it lets you see the output from HOOPS before the application terminates and the output window is destroyed. In a real application, HC_Pause would never be used.

Another limitation of HC_Pause is that it waits on only input events sent to the main output window ("?Picture"). If your application creates more than one output window (with more than one driver instance), you probably should not use HC_Pause. See Section 7.1.5 for a simple alternative program that can handle multiple output windows.

### 8.2.10    Multilevel Event Handling

Most applications will handle input events using a single event loop. In this architecture for handling events, your program will contain only a single instance of the HC_Await_Event command. Every kind of event in which the application is interested will be received by the event loop. The event loop will either handle the event immediately (centralized event handling) or dispatch the event to a separate function (decentralized event handling).

HOOPS also includes a command that allows an alternative application architecture for handling events, called *multilevel event handling*. Multilevel event handling is useful for processing *modal dialogs*. A modal dialog occurs when your application enters a state where it is looking for a specific kind of event. Note that many window systems use the term *dialog* to refer to a window

**413**

that pops up and asks a specific question, but a dialog can be any series of interactions between the user and the application. For example, in a drawing application, there might be a button that the user can press to insert a line into the drawing. After the user presses this button, the application expects the user to click on two points in the drawing, which become the endpoints of the new line. This dialog is "modal" because the action of pressing the button to insert a line puts the application into a mode where any following location events have a special meaning.

In multilevel event handling, there can be more than one HC_Await_Event command. For example, when the user presses the button to insert a line, that event is handled by the main event loop. The event loop then calls a function that waits for two location events (using HC_Await_Event), and inserts a line using the two locations. This program architecture is much easier to program than is one that uses flags to tell the main event loop the current mode of the application.

The only problem with this architecture is the handling of unexpected events. What do we do if a user presses the button to insert a line, then decides not to insert a line and instead presses the button to insert a circle? We cannot just ignore this event; we need to abort the current operation and to return to the main event loop, which can handle the event. Unfortunately, the line-drawing routine has already received the event, so the main event loop will not see it.

To solve this problem, HOOPS provides a command HC_Requeue_Event that pushes the current event back onto the event queue, so that the next call to HC_Await_Event will receive the event again. Using HC_Requeue_Event, the line-drawing function will requeue any events that it does not expect, and will return control to the main event loop so that it can handle the event.

Note that, once you call HC_Requeue_Event, there is no longer any current event. Thus, routines that return information about the current event (such as HC_Show_Button) will complain. In addition, you can return at most one event onto the event queue using HC_Requeue_Event (because this command requeues the current event).

## 8.3    Quick Moves and Control Update

During interactive input, we are less concerned with generating accurate images than with providing useful feedback to the user. Consider an application that lets the user select some geometry, and then move the geometry to a new location. To accomplish this interaction, we need to be able to highlight the geometry when it is selected, then to move the geometry with the mouse cursor, and finally to place the geometry into its new location. Each of these steps requires that feedback be given to the user. HOOPS contains several features that support this kind of interaction.

## 8.3.1      Quick Moves

The "quick moves" heuristic tells HOOPS that you are more concerned with rendering speed than with image accuracy. You can set this heuristic on a segment that contains geometry that you expect will be changing rapidly.

The most common use of "quick moves" is for geometry that is being modified interactively by the user. Quick moves tell HOOPS to draw this geometry such that it can be erased without the rest of the scene being disturbed.

 HOOPS is free to chose any method it knows to draw the geometry quickly. For example, HOOPS could draw the geometry using exclusive-or operations on the contents of the frame buffer. When HOOPS draws the geometry this way, it can erase the geometry by performing a second exclusive-or operation, without redrawing the rest of the scene. Alternatively, on a platform that supports separate overlay planes of memory in the frame buffer, geometry in segments with the "quick moves" heuristic could be drawn in an overlay plane. Of course, as it is with any heuristic, HOOPS is free to ignore "quick moves" and just to render the scene normally.

Program 8.12 (a version of the program in demo/common/cookbook/rubbebox.c) uses the "quick moves" heuristic to provide interactive feedback. When the user presses and holds a mouse button, HOOPS begins drawing a box from the position where the mouse button was pressed to the current mouse button. When the user releases the mouse button, the final box is drawn. The final box is solid, with a diagonal stripe pattern. The interactive rubberband box is drawn as just a red outline. Note that, depending on what your platform is (and on how the "quick moves" heuristic is implemented), the rubberband box may not be drawn in red, or it may change colors when drawn on top of other geometry.

```
1  #include "hc.h"
2  #include <string.h>
3  struct Point { float x, y, z; };
```

```
 4  void main() {
 5     HC_Open_Segment("?Picture");
 6        HC_Set_Color("edges = face contrast = white");
 7        HC_Set_Face_Pattern("//");
 8     HC_Close_Segment();

 9     HC_Enable_Selection_Events("?Locater", "?Picture");
10     HC_Enable_Button_Events("?Keyboard", "Q, q");

11     HC_Open_Segment("?Picture/rubberband box");
12        HC_Set_Heuristics("quick moves");
13        HC_Set_Color("polylines=red");

14        for (;;) {
15            char   segment[64], action[4], event[64];
16            float  x0, y0, x1, y1, junk;
17            int    status;

18            HC_Await_Event(event);

19            if (strcmp(event, "selection") == 0) {
20                HC_Show_Selection_Source(
21                        segment, segment, action, &status);

22                // mouse down, save x,y position
23                if (strcmp(action, "v") == 0) {
24                    HC_QSet_Selectability(
25                            "?Picture", "*^");
26                    HC_Show_Selection_Position(&junk,
27                            &junk, &junk, &x0, &y0, &junk);
28                }
```

```
29              // mouse move, draw rubberband box
30              else if (strcmp(action, "*") == 0) {
31                  HC_Flush_Geometry(".");
32                  HC_Show_Selection_Position(&junk,
33                          &junk, &junk, &x1, &y1, &junk);
34                  Point pts[5] = {
35                      {x0, y0, 0.0f},
36                      {x0, y1, 0.0F},
37                      {x1, y1, 0.0F},
38                      {x1, y0, 0.0F},
39                      {x0, y0, 0.0F}
40                  };
41                  HC_Insert_Polyline(5, pts);
42              }

43              // mouse up, draw final box
44              else if (strcmp(action, "^") == 0) {
45                  HC_Flush_Geometry(".");
46                  HC_QSet_Selectability("?Picture", "v");
47                  HC_Show_Selection_Position(&junk,
48                          &junk, &junk, &x1, &y1, &junk);
49                  Point pts[4] = {
50                      {x0, y0, 0.0f},
51                      {x0, y1, 0.0f},
52                      {x1, y1, 0.0f},
53                      {x1, y0, 0.0F}
54                  };
55                  HC_QInsert_Polygon("?Picture", 4, pts);
56              }

57          }

58      else if (strcmp(event, "button") == 0) break;
59  }
```

**417**

```
60      HC_Close_Segment();// ?Picture/rubberband box
61      HC_Disable_Selection_Events(
62            "?Locater", "?Picture");
63      HC_Disable_Button_Events("?Keyboard", "Q, q");
64      HC_Exit_Program();
65  }
```

**Program 8.12**   Rubberband-box example.

In Program 8.12, the final boxes are drawn directly into the "?Picture" segment (on line 55), whereas the rubberband boxes are drawn into a subsegment called "rubberband box" (created on line 11). The "rubberband box" segment has the "quick moves" heuristic (line 12).

The program enables selection events and button events (lines 9 and 10). Button events are used to terminate the program when the "Q" or "q" key is pressed on the keyboard. Selection events are used like location events: The window is selected, and we get the mouse position inside the window using the command HC_Show_Selection_Position (lines 32 and 47). When a selection event is received (line 19), we retrieve the action field (line 20) to see whether the event was caused by the mouse button being pressed (line 23). If it was, then we enable events on mouse movement and button up (line 24), so that we can track the movement of the mouse and terminate the interaction when the user releases the mouse button.

On any mouse movement (line 30), we flush out any old rubberband box (line 31) and draw a new box using a polyline (line 41). The next call to HC_Await_Event will cause the screen to be updated, but because the only objects that have changed are in a segment with the "quick moves" heuristic, HOOPS avoids repainting the entire scene, and instead simply erases any old geometry and draws the new geometry.

Note that, to erase old geometry without redrawing the entire scene, HOOPS must save any geometry drawn with the "quick moves" heuristic from one update to the next. For example, if HOOPS implements "quick moves" by drawing using exclusive-or, then, to perform the erase for the next update, HOOPS must redraw the old geometry using exclusive-or.

## 8.3.2    Control Update

*Control update* is a powerful and complicated technique that you can use to speed up user interaction. Normally, HOOPS keeps a number of flags on each segment to help it determine what needs to be redrawn during an update cycle. The HC_Control_Update command allows you to set and reset these flags explicitly, giving you precise control over what gets updated, and when.

There are two ways to use control update. The first way is to let HOOPS continue to set and reset the update flags as it normally does, but occasionally to set or reset a flag yourself explicitly. The second way is to set the "no update control" system option with the HC_Define_System_Options command. We shall focus on the second approach, because, once you understand it, you will find the first approach relatively easy to understand.

### 8.3.2.1

**Control update with the "no update control" system option.** Basically, when you set the "no update control" system option, nothing will be redrawn unless you explicitly tell HOOPS to update, using the HC_Control_Update command. The HC_Control_Update command takes two arguments: the name of the segment to be controlled, and a string specifying the control to be applied. There are many different controls that can be applied; we discuss three of them initially:

1.  The "redraw everything" control tells HOOPS to redraw everything (as in a normal HOOPS redraw). Everything in the current HOOPS subwindow will be erased and redrawn.

2.  The "redraw geometry" control tells HOOPS to draw the geometry in this segment, but not to erase or redraw any other geometry or windows. You can use this control to make a quick change to the output image, but it can lead to incorrect output. For example, if some geometry was deleted from the database, it will not be erased and thus will still appear.

3.  The "redraw partial erase" control tells HOOPS to redraw the geometry in this segment, but to use partial erase methods if possible. Partial erase is useful for moving an object around the screen quickly. HOOPS erases the object by painting the object using the window background color, rather than by redrawing everything else. Of course, if the object to be moved is in front of another object, that other object will be left with a hole in it.

There are also a few variations of the HC_Control_Update command:

- The HC_Control_Update_By_Key command takes a key instead of a segment name. The key can be used to refer to a segment, but you can also control update on individual pieces of geometry.

- The HC_Control_Update_Area command allows you to specify an area of the window to be updated. Only this area of the screen will have the control applied to it. This command is particularly useful when used with a window system, to repair damage caused by other windows. See Section 8.5.1 for more information.

- The HC_Control_Update_Area_By_Key command is similar to the HC_Control_Update_Area command, but it takes a key instead of a segment name.

Program 8.13 demonstrates control update. We shall step through this program to examine the effect that control update has on the output image.

Lines 3 through 10 define a routine that places a text message into a windowed segment, and then calls HC_Pause. We use the "redraw everything" control (on line 7) to ensure that this text string is always updated properly.

```
1   #include "hc.h"
2   typedef struct { float x, y, z; } Point;

3   void pause(const char *message) {
4      HC_Open_Segment("?Picture/text");
5         HC_Flush_Geometry(".");
6         HC_Insert_Text(0.0, 0.0, 0.0, message);
7         HC_Control_Update(".", "redraw everything");
8      HC_Close_Segment();
9      HC_Pause();
10  }
```

**Program 8.13**    Control update — the pause routine.

The main function of our program first turns off update control (line 12), and then defines our scene. The "?Picture" segment has changed the marker size to 3.0, the marker symbol to a filled in circle, and the marker color to gray (lines 14 through 16). The scene initially contains three subsegments. The "polyline" segment (line 17) contains a single polyline with a line pattern, so the line is drawn dotted (line 22). The "polygon" segment contains a single square polygon.

The "text" segment is a HOOPS subwindow (line 33), and contains a single text string (line 34). Controls applied to anything in a HOOPS subwindow affect only objects in that subwindow, and do not affect objects in any other windows (including this window's parent).

```
11  void main() {
12      HC_Define_System_Options("no update control");

13      HC_Open_Segment("?Picture");
14          HC_Set_Marker_Size(3.0);
15          HC_Set_Marker_Symbol("(*)");
16          HC_Set_Color("markers=gray");

17          HC_Open_Segment("polyline");
18              Point line[2] = {
19                      {-1.0f, -0.2f, 0.0f},
20                      {1.0f, -0.2f, 0.0f}};
21              HC_Insert_Polyline(2, line);
22              HC_Set_Line_Pattern("...");
23          HC_Close_Segment();

24          HC_Open_Segment("polygon");
25              Point p[4] = {
26                      {-0.9f, 0.0f, 0.0f},
27                      {0.0f, 0.0f, 0.0f},
28                      {0.0f, 0.9f, 0.0f},
29                      {-0.9f, 0.9f, 0.0f}};
30              HC_Insert_Polygon(4, p);
31          HC_Close_Segment();

32          HC_Open_Segment("text");
33              HC_Set_Window(-1.0, 1.0, -1.0, -0.75);
34              HC_Insert_Text(0.0, 0.0, 0.0,
35                      "line and face");
36          HC_Close_Segment();

37      HC_Close_Segment();
38      pause("line and face");
```

**Program 8.13 (continued)** Control update — initial scene.

When pause is called (on line 38), the image in Figure 8.1 will be displayed.

| line and face |
| --- |

**Figure 8.1**    Control update — initial scene.

Next, we make a number of changes to the graphics database. We change the line weight of the polyline to 4.0 (line 39), and change the face pattern of the polygon to diagonal stripes (line 41). We also insert two markers into the "polygon" segment. The first marker is placed on top of the polyline (line 42), and the second marker is placed on top of the polygon (line 43). We save a key for the second marker, and use this key to bring the marker in front of the polygon (line 45).

```
39      HC_QSet_Line_Weight("?Picture/polyline", 4.0);
40      HC_Open_Segment("?Picture/polygon");
41          HC_Set_Face_Pattern("<><>");
42          HC_Insert_Marker(0.0, -0.2, 0.0);
43          long mkey = HC_KInsert_Marker(-0.5, 0.5, 0.0);
44      HC_Close_Segment();
45      HC_Bring_To_Front_By_Key(mkey);
46      pause("No change");
```

**Program 8.13 (continued)** Control update — no change.

When we call the pause routine, what happens? Almost nothing happens. The text string changes because of the "redraw everything" control on line 7, but that control affects only objects in its subwindow. Since the text is in its own

**422**

subwindow (line 33), only the text is affected. The polyline keeps its old weight, the face of the polygon does not change pattern, and the markers do not appear. To effect these changes, we need to set controls.

Line 47 sets the "redraw geometry" control on the "polyline" segment, and that causes the polyline to be drawn with the new line weight when we call the pause routine on line 49. But the polygon does not change, and the markers still do not appear.

```
47        HC_Control_Update("?Picture/polyline",
48              "redraw geometry");
49        pause("increase polyline weight");
```

**Program 8.13 (continued)** Control update — only polyline updated.

When the pause routine is called, the line changes weight and the text updates, and the image in Figure 8.2 appears.

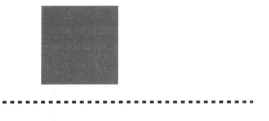

increase polyline weight

**Figure 8.2**        Control update — only polyline updated.

Note that, because we used the "redraw geometry" control, the old line was not erased. The new (thicker) line was drawn on top of the old line, obscuring the old line. If we had used the "redraw everything" control, then the old line would have been erased, but everything else in the window would have been erased and redrawn as well. So, in this case, the "redraw geometry" control allowed us to avoid a redraw of the entire scene.

Next, we use the "redraw geometry" control on the "polygon" segment (line 50).

```
50      HC_Control_Update("?Picture/polygon",
51            "redraw geometry");
52      pause("markers added, polygon turns patterned");
```

**Program 8.13 (continued)** Control update — polygon and markers updated.

When pause is called, the polygon face becomes patterned, and the markers appear. The output image now looks like Figure 8.3.

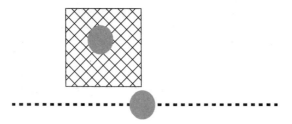

markers added, polygon turns patterned

**Figure 8.3**     Control update — polygon and markers updated.

Note that the lower marker appears on top of the polyline, because only objects in the "polygon" segment were drawn. In particular, the polyline was not redrawn.

Next, we unset the line pattern of the polyline so that the line will be solid (line 53). We unset the face pattern, so that the polygon face will be all black again (line 54). We use the HC_Control_Update_Area command to update only a part (the center third) of the output image.

```
53      HC_QUnSet_Line_Pattern("?Picture/polyline");
54      HC_QUnSet_Face_Pattern("?Picture/polygon");
55      HC_Control_Update_Area("?Picture",
56            -0.3, 0.3, -0.3, 0.3, "redraw geometry");
57      pause("update area");
```

**Program 8.13 (continued)** Control update — update area.

The HC_Control_Update_Area command was applied to the "?Picture" segment, so everything in this segment (and below it in the hierarchy) is redrawn, but only inside of the specified area. The output now looks like Figure 8.4.

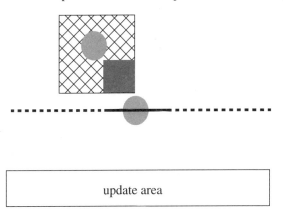

**Figure 8.4**      Control update — update area.

Note that only part of the polygon turns black, and only part of the polyline becomes solid — only those parts inside of the updated area are affected. The rest of the output is not redrawn. Also note that the polyline appears in front of the lower marker, because the markers are not redrawn.

Next, we use the "redraw everything" control on "?Picture" to update the entire image, on lines 60 and 61. Ignore lines 58 and 59 for a moment.

```
58    HC_QSet_Heuristics("?Picture/polygon",
59          "partial erase");
60    HC_Control_Update("?Picture", "redraw everything");
61    pause("update everything");
```

At this point, the image (shown in Figure 8.5) accurately displays the contents of the graphics database.

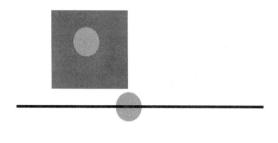

update everything

**Figure 8.5**     Control update — update everything.

Of course, HOOPS had to perform a complete redraw, including clearing the window. For a simple scene such as this one, the redraw was probably hardly visible; for a more complicated scene, however, the clear of the window followed by a redraw of all the geometry might take a noticeable amount of time.

We also set the "partial erase" heuristic on the "polygon" segment (line 58). On line 62, we delete the upper marker (using its saved key), and then use the "redraw partial erase" control on the "polygon" segment (line 63). If we want to perform a partial erase, the "partial erase" heuristic must have been set when the geometry was drawn. That is why it was set on line 58. The "partial erase" heuristic tells HOOPS to save the geometry so that HOOPS can erase the geometry by drawing it in the background color.

```
62      HC_Delete_By_Key(mkey);
63      HC_Control_Update("?Picture/polygon",
64           "redraw partial erase");
65      pause("partial erase: hole left in polygon");

66      HC_Exit_Program();
67   }
```

**Program 8.13 (continued)** Control update — partial erase.

The output image now looks like Figure 8.6.

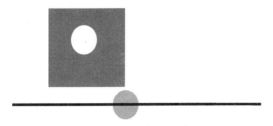

partial erase: hole left in polygon

**Figure 8.6**    Control update — partial erase.

Note that the upper marker is now drawn in the window background color (white). Of course, since we deleted the marker, the polygon should actually appear solid black, with no hole in it.

Partial erase is useful for complicated scenes, when you are moving or deleting single objects. Deleting an object by redrawing it in the window background color can be much faster than deleting it by redrawing the entire scene. In many cases, inaccuracies due to partial erase are not objectionable, especially in scenes that mainly contain lines. In addition, during interaction (such as moving an object using the mouse), minor image inaccuracies are a small price to pay for fast response and smooth interaction.

For example, if the user is allowed to pick a marker and to move it around, then it is acceptable for you to leave a hole where the marker was originally while the marker is being moved. When the user releases the marker, you can then perform a complete redraw.

Note that you can achieve the effects of partial erase without using the "partial erase" heuristic by explicitly drawing the object to be erased in the window background color. You set the color of the object to be the same color as the window background, and then explicitly paint that object (by setting the "redraw geometry" control on it).

The main disadvantage of the "partial erase" heuristic is that it causes HOOPS to save all the geometry in the affected segments, and that can increase storage requirements if you use the heuristic indiscriminately. Another problem with "partial erase" is that it is just a heuristic — HOOPS is free to ignore it. In particular, HOOPS will often ignore the "partial erase" heuristic when hidden surfaces are enabled.

The "partial erase" heuristic can be used without control update. See the HC_Set_Heuristics command in the *HOOPS Reference Manual* for more information.

**8.3.2.2**      **Control update with the "update control" system option.** In Section 8.3.2.1, we considered only the situation when the "no update control" system option was in effect. Alternatively, you can leave the "update control" system option in effect, but occasionally set or reset flags explicitly. The most useful control in this situation is the "unset redraw" control. You use this control when HOOPS has marked a segment as needing to be redrawn (because something in the segment changed), but you wish to postpone the redraw until later (presumably because you are performing an interaction). In this case, you would use the command HC_Control_Update to apply the "unset redraw" control to a segment that has changed.

Consider a drawing application that allows the user to create drawings using lines (such as a simple drafting application). A complicated drawing may contain hundreds or even thousands of lines. We now want the user to be able to select and move one line. Initially, all the lines are contained in a single segment. When the user selects a line, we want to be able to highlight it by changing its color. Because attributes apply to all geometry in a segment, to highlight the line, we need to move that line to a different segment. When we do this move, HOOPS will mark the segment containing the rest of the lines as needing to be redrawn (since some geometry was removed). During the interaction, however, we do not want this redraw to occur, because redrawing thousands of lines may take an unacceptable amount of time, so we apply the "unset redraw" control to this segment.

When we apply the "unset redraw" control, however, the old line still remains where it was, even after the user moves it. In some cases, this inaccuracy is acceptable. Alternatively, we can draw the line in the window background color (either by using partial erase, or explicitly). These alternatives leave the scene slightly damaged.

Next, the user will move the selected line around the screen. We can use the "quick moves" heuristic for faster interaction. Finally, when the user releases the line, we need to move the highlighted line back into the segment with all the other lines, to turn the highlight off. At this point, there may still be some damage where the line used to be, and we need to draw the line in its new position, unhighlighted. The easiest way to repair any damage is just to force the entire segment to be redrawn, using the "redraw everything" control.

Alternatively, we can be clever. For example, we could have saved the bounding box where the line used to be, and could redraw only the area inside this box, using the HC_Control_Update_Area command. And we could draw the line in its new position using the "redraw geometry" control. Use of the "redraw geometry" control will cause the line to be drawn on top of any other lines, without redrawing of any underlying lines.

8.3.2.3     **Control update and bounding volumes.** Another use of the command HC_Control_Update is to control when bounding volumes are computed. Normally, HOOPS recomputes bounding volumes when geometry is added to a segment. In addition, bounding volumes normally only increase in size.

If we know that we are deleting a significant amount of geometry from a segment, we can force bounding volumes to be recomputed using the "compute bounding volumes" control. Note that, even if we recompute the bounding volume of a segment, the bounding volumes of the parent segments may not get recomputed.

In addition, if we know that the computation of a bounding volume will not improve update time (for example, the bounding volume is changing for each update), we can tell HOOPS to not retain the bounding volume, using the "no bounding volume retention" control. When this flag is set, HOOPS does not compute a bounding volume for the specified segment. Thus, HOOPS will always walk this segment, and will attempt to draw the geometry in it.

# 8.4    Interaction Examples

The programs on the CD-ROM contain many examples of user-interaction techniques. See the list of example programs in Section 10.5. You should especially study the two viewer applications (written for either MFC or Motif).

One of the interaction techniques implemented in the viewer applications is a *virtual trackball*. You use a virtual trackball to rotate objects, by pretending that there is a sphere around the object, and letting the user grab this sphere and rotate it (and the object inside it).

The viewer applications (and other example programs) also contain color pickers, which are used to specify colors.

When you study these interaction techniques, be on the lookout for the following:

- How the application arranges segments to aid interaction

- How the main event loop distributes input events to the proper handler routines

- How control update, partial erase, and quick moves are used to speed up user interaction

# 8.5    Interaction with a Window System

As we discussed in Chapter 7, when you write a 3D graphics application, you have a choice of writing the user interface in HOOPS or in your target platform's native window system. In most cases, you will be writing the user interface using a window system. Chapter 7 covered how to connect HOOPS to the window system, so that HOOPS would know where to send its output, and how to disable HOOPS input processing.

You disable HOOPS input processing using the "disable input" driver option. This driver option has two variations:

```
HC_Set_Driver_Options("disable input");
HC_Set_Driver_Options("disable input = all");
```

Both variations tell HOOPS that your application will receive input events directly from the window system. Therefore, HOOPS does not attempt to read input devices such as the mouse or keyboard.

With the first variation, HOOPS does not read input devices, but it still receives paint messages (sometimes called expose or damage events) from the window system. Therefore, when your application receives a paint message (because all or part of the output window was obscured and was then made visible), HOOPS will repaint its output window automatically.

In the second variation ("disable input = all"), HOOPS receives no input messages at all. Therefore, your application will have to receive paint messages and to call HC_Update_Display explicitly.

## 8.5.1 Control Update

Normally, HOOPS updates the screen just before it waits for user input (when the HC_Await_Event command is executed). When you disable HOOPS input, you do not use the HC_Await_Input command to receive user input, so you will need to update the display explicitly using HC_Update_Display before your application waits for user input from the window system.

When HOOPS handles input events, it can be smart and repaint only those parts of the output image that were damaged. But if you handle paint messages in your application by calling HC_Update_Display, HOOPS will redraw the entire scene, even if only a small part of that scene needs redrawing. To fix this inefficiency, HOOPS provides a command called HC_Control_Update.

You can use the HC_Control_Update command to specify which parts of the HOOPS database need to be redrawn. You can specify the parts to be redrawn by segment, by key (using the HC_Control_Update_By_Key command), or by area (using the HC_Control_Update_Area or HC_Control_Update_Area_By_Key commands). For example, if a paint message from the window system specifies that only part of the output window needs to be redrawn, you can specify the area to be drawn using the HC_Control_Update_Area command.

When you use the HC_Control_Update command (or related commands) you are assuming all responsibility for choosing which parts of the HOOPS database to update. This responsibility can require serious work. See Section 8.3.2, and the entry for HC_Control_Update in the *HOOPS Reference Manual*, for more information.

## 8.5.2 Update Interrupts

When HOOPS handles input events, it can be smart and interrupt the update of the display when new events occur. When you use the native window system to handle user input, there is no way for HOOPS to know that an event has occurred. The use of the "disable input" driver option can cause your application to appear unresponsive, because, when your application calls the HC_Update_Display command, your application is unable to process new input events until HOOPS has finished updating the display. This problem was discussed in Section 8.2.8.

You can solve this problem using an event checker and special events. You can specify an event-checker routine using the "event checker" system option. While HOOPS is updating the display, it will periodically call your event-checker routine. This routine should check with the window system to see whether there are any input events pending, and, if there are, it should generate a special event (using HC_Queue_Special_Event). This event will cause HOOPS to interrupt the display update and to return from the call to HC_Update_Display. Your program can then handle the input event and call HC_Update_Display again. You should be careful to call HC_Flush_All_Events before you call HC_Update_Display again, or else the (still-queued) special event will interrupt display update continuously and will thus prevent the display from updating. There is an example of the use of an event checker for this purpose in the program w32uwid.c in the directory /demo/win32/win32wid, and in several programs in the directory demo/motif/simple on the CD-ROM.

There is a good example of a HOOPS application that handles input directly from the Motif window system, including an event checker and explicit use of HC_Control_Update, in the directory demo/motif/simple on the CD-ROM.

### 8.5.3     Selection Events

In general, most user input, including button presses and mouse events, will be handled by the window system and your application, and will not involve HOOPS at all. The main exception to this rule is 3D picking (using selection events). Because the window system has no knowledge of the 3D objects in the HOOPS database, it cannot determine which object has been picked when a selection event occurs. HOOPS provides a routine, called HC_Compute_Selection, that, given a location, returns any selected objects.

Figure 8.7 shows the path of a selection event as the input starts out as a location event from the window system. The application receives the location event and calls HC_Compute_Selection with the location; HC_Compute_Selection does a hit test against the 3D objects in the database and creates a selection event. You can then receive the selection event using HC_Await_Event.

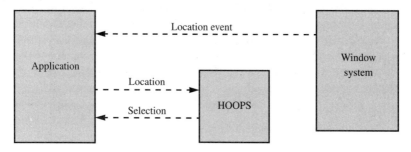

**Figure 8.7**     Performance of selection events with a window system.

# 9    Materials

*Materials* are sets of attributes that are applied to objects to give the objects color and texture. Material attributes are typically applied to surfaces such as shells and meshes, but they can also be applied to polygons, to window backgrounds, and even to other primitives, such as lines.

## 9.1    Color

As we discussed in Section 3.3.5, color has many different uses in computer graphics. For example, some applications use smooth shading to display pseudo-realistic scenes containing continuous color; other applications use a few discrete colors just to distinguish objects or for highlighting. Many applications, of course, use some amount of both.

Computer graphics hardware varies widely in how it supports color, all the way from devices (such as printers) that support only black and white (but at high resolution), through gray-scale devices, through 8-bit frame buffers that can display 256 colors at a time, all the way to full-color frame buffers that support 24 bits of color per pixel. In addition, different operating systems and window systems support different methods of color specification.

The challenge to the designers of HOOPS was to support the different uses of color, to do so in a way that was portable to widely different graphics platforms, and to make the specification of color fast and easy to use. They wanted to have reasonable defaults for color, while also giving full control to application developers who had specific requirements. This chapter explains the solution that they developed.

For a procedural graphics system, these requirements would have been almost impossible to meet. Most procedural graphics systems end up making no attempt to support device independence, and instead require the application programmer to allocate colors and color maps explicitly.

Although HOOPS provides default values for color, normally you will want to change some of the HOOPS defaults. For example, the default color for all kinds of geometry (including text, lines, polygons, meshes, and shells) is black. Although this default may be suitable for text and lines, for polygons you will normally want some color, and for meshes and shells you probably will want not only some color, but also lights illuminating the colored surfaces.

### 9.1.1     Physical Versus Logical Resources

HOOPS distinguishes between physical and logical (virtual) resources. For example, a hardware color map on an 8-bit frame buffer is a physical (in this case hardware) resource that may or may not be accessible to the programmer. HOOPS also provides color maps (through the HC_Set_Color_Map command), but it is important to realize that HOOPS color maps are completely distinct from physical color maps. In particular, it is perfectly reasonable to use a HOOPS color map on a graphics device that has no hardware color map (such as a 24-bit-per-pixel frame buffer).

Colors in HOOPS are logical resources. For example, consider an application that sets the color of an object to "dark red". The same application can be run on many different physical platforms. For example, on a platform that supports 24 bits of color per pixel, the color "dark red" will be drawn directly. On a computer that supports 8 bits of color per pixel with a hardware color map, the color "dark red" might be allocated to physical slot 42 in the color map, and the object set to color 42. Alternatively (on the same 8-bit hardware), the system might draw the color "dark red" by dithering between red and black pixels. HOOPS will even draw the color "dark red" on a black-and-white device, such as a laser printer (although it will draw the color as dark gray).

### 9.1.2     Color Specification

HOOPS supports several different methods of specifying colors. As an application writer, you can choose the method that is most appropriate to your application, or you can give the choice to the user of your application. Colors in HOOPS are specified by *name*, *value*, *index*, or *fractional index*.

Different kinds of geometry can have different color attributes, even if they are in the same segment. For example, the following command sets the text color to brown, and the line color to red:

```
HC_Set_Color("text=brown, lines=red");
```

You can set separate color attributes on edges, faces, markers, lines (including polylines), text, and lights. You can also set a face-contrast color, which is used for patterned faces of polygons (see the HC_Set_Face_Pattern command). In addition, you can set color attributes on windows (used as the background color for the window) and window contrast (used for the window frame and any window-background pattern). See the HC_Set_Color command for more information.

If you do not specify the kind of geometry, then HOOPS sets the color on all kinds of geometry. For example, the following three commands are equivalent:

```
HC_Set_Color("red");
HC_Set_Color("geometry = red");
HC_Set_Color("faces=edges=markers=lines=text=red");
```

**9.1.2.1**  **Color by name.** Possibly the most intuitive way to specify a color in HOOPS is by name. For example, the following are valid HOOPS color specifications:

```
HC_Set_Color("green");
HC_Set_Color("brownish red");
HC_Set_Color("light lavender-mulberry");
```

The set of valid color names was taken from a source of highest authority: Crayola™ Crayons. Recently, eight new colors were added to the original Crayola-64 set of colors. In addition, HOOPS added cyan to the set of colors, for a total of 73 color names. These names and their numeric definitions are specified in the chapter on system start-up in the *HOOPS Reference Manual*.

You can mix two colors by specifying their names separated by a hyphen (as in "lavender-mulberry"). Colors are mixed in hue, intensity, chromaticity (HIC) space; thus, HOOPS mixes "blue-green" by averaging 240, 0.5, 1.0 and 120, 0.5, 1.0, giving 180, 0.5, 1.0 (which is the same as cyan). The HIC color space was defined in Section 3.3.5.4.

Averaging in HIC color space is complicated by the fact that hue values are modulo 360 (the hue 360 is the same as the hue 0). The average value of two hues is found in the most reasonable way, so that the average of the hue values 10 and 350 is 0, rather than 180 (as shown in Figure 9.1).

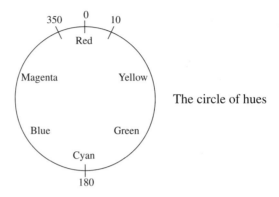

The circle of hues

**Figure 9.1**      Color mixing of hues.

Note that, if two colors to be averaged are complementary (are on opposite sides of the color circle — such as red and cyan, or blue and yellow), then there are two possible hues that are halfway in-between them; HOOPS is free to pick either one.

 HOOPS uses the HIC color space to mix colors for two reasons. First, we want to mix colors in a hue-based space (rather than RGB or CMY), so that we mix the hues by averaging their values (in degrees), rather than by averaging three primaries. Thus, when two fully saturated colors are mixed, the resulting color is also fully saturated (mixing in RGB space would tend to produce muddy colors). Second, of the possible hue-based color spaces, HIC is the only one where the maximum permissible value for saturation does not depend on either the lightness (as it does in HLS) or value (as it does in HSV).

Mixing two colors by separating them using a hyphen combines them evenly (50–50). For example, the color "black-white" is gray. HOOPS also allows you to mix colors in other proportions, by using "-er" and "-ish" forms. For example, the color "greener blue" is 35-percent green and 65-percent blue, and "greenish blue" is 20-percent green and 80-percent blue. The legal "-er" and "-ish" colors are defined in the chapter on system start-up in the *HOOPS Reference Manual*.

Use of white and black to modify other colors is so common that, in addition to the "-er" forms "whiter" and "blacker" and the "-ish" forms "whitish" and "blackish", there are several synonyms. For example, instead of "blacker" you can use "dimmer", "dim", "darker", or "dark"; instead of "whiter" you can use "brighter", "bright", "lighter", or "light".

Complex color names are parsed from right to left. Thus, the name "light lavender-mulberry" is a whiter form of lavender-mulberry (rather than light lavender mixed with mulberry). Color descriptions can be as complex as you like.

To mix two colors evenly, you separate their names with a hyphen; if you leave out the hyphen, the left color completely replaces the right color (and HOOPS issues a warning message). For example, the color "white gold" is white, and "red mahogany" is red. Mixing two colors in this way (without a hyphen) is useful when you are mixing user-defined color names that specify only certain material properties (see Section 9.1.3.2).

Note that many colors (approximately one-half of them) have two words in their names (for example, colors such as "burnt sienna", "lemon yellow", "moose brown", and "jungle green"), but there are also many colors that appear to be mixtures (for example, "blue green", "orange yellow", "red violet", and "green yellow"). These colors are considered to be single colors, rather than mixtures. These two-word color names can be confusing, because separating two color names without a hyphen will cause an error if the resulting color name is not one of the standard Crayola colors. All the legal color names are defined in the chapter on system-startup in the *HOOPS Reference Manual.*

You can add new color names to the names that HOOPS knows (including new "-er" and "-ish" forms) using the HC_Define_Color_Name command. You can also change the definitions of existing color names.

9.1.2.2    **Color by value.** Often, it is impractical to set a color using a color name. For example, if an application lets the user choose a color by moving three sliders, we would like to be able to set the resulting color by specifying three numeric values. There are two ways to specify a color numerically in HOOPS: via HC_Set_Color with a text string containing the numbers, or via HC_Set_Color_By_Value.

You can set a color by value using the HC_Set_Color command by formatting the numeric value into a string. For example, the following three commands are equivalent:

```
HC_Set_Color("red");
HC_Set_Color("R=1.0 G=0.0 B=0.0");
HC_Set_Color("H=0.0 I=0.5 C=1.0");
```

You can also set colors using HLS and HSV space in the same way (see Section 3.3.5.4 for the definitions of these color spaces).

If you want to avoid formatting the color into a string, you can use the HC_Set_Color_By_Value command:

```
HC_Set_Color_By_Value("", "HIC", 0.0, 0.5, 1.0);
```

The second argument defines the color space in which the three numeric arguments are defined. Valid spaces are RGB, HLS, HSV, and HIC.

The first argument allows you to specify on what kind of geometry the color is to be set. If it is left blank, as it is in the example of HC_Set_Color_By_Value, then the color is set on all geometry.

Alternatively, colors can be set on a single kind of geometry. For example, the following two commands are identical:

```
HC_Set_Color("lines=red");
HC_Set_Color_By_Value("lines", "RGB", 1.0, 0.0, 0.0);
```

One limitation of the HC_Set_Color_By_Value command is that you cannot set material properties such as specular color, transmission, or gloss color. To do that, you must format the color as a string and use the HC_Set_Color command — for example,

```
HC_Set_Color("specular = (R=0.8 G=0.9 B=0.5)");
```

Note that the parentheses around the color specification are optional. For more information, see the HC_Set_Color command in the *HOOPS Reference Manual.*

**9.1.2.3**     **Color by index.** A color index is an index into a HOOPS color map. To set colors by index, you first need to create a color map, using the command HC_Set_Color_Map. Note that HOOPS treats a color map as an attribute. Thus, color maps inherit (just like any attribute), and different segments can have different color-map attributes associated with them.

A color map is just an array of colors. The first color in the array has index 0. You can specify the colors in a color map by name, using the HC_Set_Color_Map command, or by value, using the HC_Set_Color_Map_By_Value command. Once a color-map attribute has been set on a segment (or inherited from a parent), you can specify colors by index — for example,

```
HC_Set_Color_Map("red, blue, green, white, black");
HC_Set_Color_By_Index("lines", 0);
```

These two commands set the line color to be the color at index 0, which is red in the color map.

Setting color by index through a color map is useful in a few situations: for setting colors by object type, for specifying images, and for sharing colors between windows.

You can use a color map to set colors by object (see Section 3.3.5.8 for more information on defining colors by object). For example, a window system could define the window frames to be color 0, the window background color to be color 1, and the text to be color 2. This arrangement allows you to change the color scheme by loading a new color map.

Note that another (and probably better) way to change the color scheme of a scene in HOOPS is to choose appropriate segment names for different types of objects, and to use the HC_QSet_Color command with a wild card to change the color attribute in multiple segments. For example, the following command changes all segments named "text" to be colored red:

HC_QSet_Color("?Picture/.../text", "red");

A more common use for color maps is for the definition of images, with the HC_Insert_Image command. Colors in an image can be specified as 8 or 16 bit numbers, which are indices into the current color map. (Images can also be specified with RGB colors, which do not use a color map). Color maps can also be used to define the colors in texture maps. See the HC_Insert_Image and HC_Define_Texture commands in the *HOOPS Reference Manual* for more information.

A more subtle use of color maps is to allow two application windows to share colors, and thus to avoid color flashing on platforms with a limited number of total colors. For example, on a system with an 8-bit frame buffer, there are only 256 colors available. In HOOPS, colors are allocated by the driver, so, if your application creates two application windows by creating two driver instances, each driver instance will try to allocate colors in the hardware color map. If each window contains a scene that uses more than 128 colors, then the window system will need to switch between color maps when the input focus changes from one window to the other. This switch will cause the colors to be wrong in the window that is out of focus. You can avoid this problem by using the same color map for both windows (by setting the color-map attribute on the driver that is the parent of both driver instances, or on the root segment), and then assigning colors to the scene from the color map (using HC_Set_Color_By_Index). See Section 9.1.8 for more information.

**9.1.2.4**     **Color by fractional index.** You need to set colors by fractional index in only a few situations. The most common use for fractional color indices is for false-color images. For example, consider a map where you want to false color the map based on elevation. The lowest elevations (between 0 and 4000 feet) will be green, gradually changing to brown (4000 to 8000 feet), then white at the highest elevations (greater than 8000 feet). To color the map, we create a color map with the desired colors:

```
HC_Set_Color_Map("green", "brown", "white");
```

In this color map, green is color 0, brown is color 1, and white is color 2. You can use a fractional index to interpolate colors between the colors in the color map. For example, the color with index 1.5 is a mixture of brown and white.

Assuming that the map is a mesh, you can set colors on the mesh vertices by opening the mesh (via HC_Open_Mesh), opening the vertex on which you want to set a color (via HC_Open_Vertex), and then setting the color on the vertex via HC_Set_Color_By_FIndex. The HC_Set_Color_By_FIndex command takes a floating-point value for the index.

```
HC_Set_Color_By_FIndex("faces", elevation / 4000.0);
```

For convenience, you can use the HC_MSet_Vertex_Colors_By_FIndex command to set multiple vertex colors with a single command.

---

To produce a contour plot — where the colors change abruptly, rather than gradually, between elevations — you can turn off the "color interpolation" rendering option. See the *HOOPS Reference Manual* entries for the "color interpolation" and "color index interpolation" rendering options, under HC_Set_Rendering_Options, and the HC_Set_Color_By_FIndex command, for more information.

---

**9.1.3**     **Material Properties**

So far in this book, we have treated color as a single quantity. As we saw in Section 3.3.4, however, the perceived color of an object is determined by a complex interaction between the object's material and one or more light sources. In HOOPS, color is made up of four *material properties,* called *diffuse, specular, gloss,* and *transmission.* When lights are present in a scene, HOOPS computes the appearance of each pixel in an object as a function of these four properties and the light sources (including the ambient light).

The diffuse color of an object is the color that the object appears to have when illuminated with a soft, diffuse light. The diffuse color of an object is what we normally think of as the object's color. The default diffuse color is black. The following command sets the diffuse color of the faces in a segment to blue:

```
HC_Set_Color("faces = (diffuse=blue)");
```

The specular color of an object is the color of any shiny reflections from a light source. The default specular color is white. The following command sets the diffuse color of the faces to red, and the specular color to pink:

```
HC_Set_Color("faces = (diffuse=red, specular=pink)");
```

The gloss of an object is a single numeric value that represents how shiny or polished the object is. Gloss affects the size and brightness of the specular reflection. Normally, gloss varies from 1.0 to 30.0, with 30.0 being an especially shiny surface with a small bright specular highlight. The default value for gloss is 5.0. The following command raises the glossiness of the faces, but lowers the intensity of the specular reflection:

```
HC_Set_Color("faces = (gloss=20, specular=gray)");
```

The transmission color is the color of the light passing through an object. The default value for transmission is black, which describes a completely opaque object; a value of white would be a completely transparent object. Other colors are possible; for example, a transmission color of red describes an object that is transparent to red light, but is opaque to green and blue light.

 Some hardware devices support transparency in hardware, but do not support colored transparent objects. In this case, the intensity of the transmission color is used, but the hue and saturation are not. A few platforms do not support transparent surfaces at all.

Material properties in HOOPS apply only to surfaces (such as meshes and shells). If a material is applied to an object other than a surface (such as lines, markers, or text), only the diffuse component is used. The only exception to this rule is that the edges and markers of a shell or a mesh are affected by the full material properties set on the shell or mesh. The edges and markers of a shell or mesh use the same material properties as the faces, however.

Also note that there are no solid objects in HOOPS (a solid object such as a cube is represented by its boundary surfaces), so the transmission color modifies the light passing through a surface, rather than through a solid object, as you might expect.

**9.1.3.1**    **Default material properties.** When you set the color of an object as a single component, you are setting the diffuse component of the color. Therefore, the following two commands are equivalent:

```
HC_Set_Color("faces=blue");
HC_Set_Color("faces = (diffuse=blue)");
```

When you set only the diffuse material property, then the other three components, since they have not been set, inherit (like any attribute) from the parent segment.

 If you execute an HC_Show_Net_Color command, you will see the values for all the color components, including a few that we have not discussed here. These extra components are *mirror*, *emission*, and *index of refraction*, which are used by the HOOPS A.I.R. rendering package (or by other renderers developed by third parties). HOOPS A.I.R. is not included on the CD-ROM (it was developed by a third party, so we could not include it without charge to you).

**9.1.3.2**    **Named materials.** The HC_Define_Color_Name command can be used to give names to colors, and, because a color can contain material properties, so can a defined color name — for example,

```
HC_Define_Color_Name("shiny brass", "", "",
    "diffuse=orange, specular=yellow, gloss=10");
HC_Set_Color("shiny brass");
```

You can also define the "-er" and "-ish" forms — for example, the following command defines the colors "plastic", "plasticer", and "plasticish":

```
HC_Define_Color_Name("plastic", "plasticer",
    "plasticish", "diffuse=white, specular=white");
```

Color names for materials can be mixed, just like any other color names. For example, if you separate two names with a hyphen, they are mixed 50–50. Mixing is done on a component-by-component basis, and only those components that the two names have in common are mixed. For example, "plasticish shiny brass" mixes the diffuse and specular colors, but leaves alone the gloss value of shiny brass.

Recall that, when you separate two color names with a space, the left color completely replaces the right color. This rule for combining colors is not particularly useful for simple colors; for materials, however, you can use this rule to replace individual components. For example, consider the following definition for the color "water":

```
HC_Define_Color_Name("water", "watery", "wet",
    "diffuse=light blue, transmission=blue");
```

The color "green water" replaces the diffuse component of water with green, but leaves the transmission component of water alone (the specular and gloss components are inherited). As another example, the following definition of "clear" has only a transmission component:

```
HC_Define_Color_Name("clear", "clearer", "clearish",
    "transmission=white");
```

The color "clear shiny brass" replaces the transmission component of "shiny brass" with the transmission component from "clear", leaving alone the diffuse, specular, and gloss components.

## 9.1.4    Mapped Color

Most of the problems that you encounter when dealing with color occur when colors are a scarce resource. When you have a 24-bit frame buffer, colors are free and plentiful, so you can set any object to any color, and you can do lighting and smooth shading with gleeful abandon. When you have an 8-bit frame buffer with a color map, however, your hardware can display only 256 colors at a time. Furthermore, window systems allow more than one application to be active at a time, so your application probably will be competing with other applications for the hardware color map. Even if yours is the only application running, the window system usually allocates a few dozen colors, so your application will typically have somewhat less than 256 colors with which to play.

A few 8-bit frame buffers perform dithering in hardware (or firmware), and behave as though they are full 24-bit frame buffers. In this case, HOOPS plays along and treats the frame buffer as though it is a full 24 bits. Note, however, that such a system might dither colors that could have been represented directly if HOOPS had control of the hardware color map.

Section 9.1.5 describes in detail how HOOPS allocates colors in the hardware color map on a mapped color system, and how you can control this allocation to suit your application. Most of the time, of course, the HOOPS defaults for allocating colors work just fine. If your application uses a large number of colors, or needs greater control over how colors are allocated, you will find valuable the information in Section 9.1.5.

### 9.1.5    Regular Colors Versus Fixed Colors

There are two ways that HOOPS allocates colors in the hardware color map in a mapped-color system. HOOPS calls these *regular-color* and *fixed-color* allocation, for historical reasons.

#### 9.1.5.1

**Regular colors.** Regular colors are colors that are created directly from a HOOPS color attribute. For example, if you set the color attribute of a segment to red, and that color is used directly to color an object in the scene, then the color red is a regular color. Regular colors are allocated dynamically in the hardware color map. Each time that HOOPS is about to update the display, it makes a pass through the graphics database and determines all the regular colors that it needs to allocate in the hardware color map.

For example, if you draw a pie chart that contains black lines and pie segments that are red, blue, orange, and green, all on a white background, then HOOPS will allocate six colors in the hardware color map. If you then add a magenta pie segment to the pie chart and update the display, HOOPS will allocate an additional slot in the hardware color map for magenta.

When regular colors are used, there is a one-to-one correspondence between each unique color in your scene and the colors allocated in the hardware color map. The allocation in the color map can change for each update of the display.

The advantage of regular color allocation is that colors are represented accurately. The disadvantage is that each unique color uses a slot in the color map. If your scene contains more regular colors than there are slots available in the hardware color map, HOOPS will signal an error.

#### 9.1.5.2

**Fixed colors.** Fixed colors are used by colors that do not correspond to specific color attributes in the graphics database. For example, if lighting is enabled (because a light was inserted into the graphics database), then the color of a face is determined both by what the face's color attribute is, and by how much light falls on the face from the light source. Thus, a scene might contain many objects that have the same color attribute, but that are rendered using different colors.

Consider a simple scene containing a red cube that is lit by a single light. If a face is lit directly by the light source (or has a specular reflection, as when Phong lighting is used), then the face will be light red in color, whereas faces that are facing away from the light will be a much darker red. If Gouraud shading (color interpolation) is enabled, then each face of the cube will be smoothly shaded, requiring hundreds or even thousands of colors.

**444**

When lighting or smooth shading is enabled, there is no way for HOOPS to know in advance what colors are needed, so, instead of allocating colors dynamically (as it does for regular colors), HOOPS allocates a fixed set of colors in the color map, with the colors spread out evenly in color space. For example, HOOPS might allocate 125 slots in the hardware color map, and assign colors to the slots to create a color cube with five shades for each of the red, green, and blue axes. See Section 3.3.5.9 for more information on fixed color maps.

For each color to be displayed, the closest color in the fixed color map is found. Of course, the closest color in the color map might not be particularly close, since we are using 125 colors to draw a palette of over 16 million colors. HOOPS uses dithering to reduce these color errors.

The advantages of fixed color allocation are that any color can be drawn, and that the color map is allocated statically (the number of colors that HOOPS allocates in the hardware color map does not depend on the number of color attributes in the database). The disadvantages are that colors are not drawn accurately, and that dithering is required.

## 9.1.6 Allocation of Fixed Color Maps

This section applies only to those platforms that use a color map (it does not apply to platforms that have a 24-bit frame buffer).

HOOPS allocates a fixed color map in the hardware color map only if the scene requires one. The situations that cause a fixed color map to be allocated include the following:

- Any visible lights in the scene

- Depth cueing (atmospheric attenuation)

- An inserted image that contains RGB colors

- Use of textures containing RGB colors

- Use of the radiosity or ray-tracing renderers in HOOPS A.I.R.

- Color attributes set on shell or mesh vertices

- Use of the software Z-buffer in 8-bit mode

 A fixed color map is allocated when a color attribute is set on any vertex in a shell or mesh, because HOOPS assumes that vertex color attributes are set only when some form of color interpolation will be performed.

When HOOPS allocates a fixed color map, it determines how many slots are available in the hardware color map, divides this number by 2 (to leave room to allocate regular colors), and then uses the largest perfect cube that is smaller than this number. For example, if there are 256 available slots in the hardware color map, HOOPS divides 256 by 2 to get 128. The largest perfect cube that is smaller than 128 is 125 (5 cubed).

If the (window or operating) system preallocates some of the slots in the hardware color map, then less than 256 slots may be available to HOOPS. For example, if the system preallocates eight slots in the hardware color map, then there will be only 248 slots available. HOOPS divides 248 by 2 to get 124. The largest perfect cube smaller than 124 is 64 (4 cubed), so HOOPS creates a fixed color map with only four shades for each of the red, green, and blue color axes.

Currently, Microsoft Windows allocates 20 colors in the hardware color map, leaving 236 available slots for HOOPS to use (of course, other applications are also trying to allocate these colors). You can use the command HC_Show_Device_Info to determine how many slots are available in the hardware color map.

```
HC_Show_Device_Info("?Picture", "colors", answer);
```

The allocation of hardware color-map slots is a tradeoff between the fixed color map and the dynamically allocated regular colors. If the fixed color map is allocated a small number of slots, then fixed colors will be inaccurate, and excessive amounts of dithering will need to be performed. But if the fixed color map is allocated a large number of slots, then HOOPS may not have enough slots left over for regular colors, and that will cause an error.

Figure 9.2 shows a typical way that the hardware color map is allocated.

**Hardware color map**

| |
|---|
| Regular colors |
| Fixed color map |
| System-allocated colors |

**Figure 9.2**    Allocation of the hardware color map.

The default algorithm for allocation of color-map slots guarantees that the fixed color map will never take up more than one-half of the available hardware slots. In many cases, however, you might want more or fewer slots allocated to the fixed color map, depending on the needs of your application. You can control how many color-map slots HOOPS uses for the fixed color map by using the "fixed colors" driver option.

The "fixed colors" driver option can take either a single argument, or three arguments. In the single-argument form, the argument must be a perfect cube; reasonable values are 8, 27, 64, 125, and 216. For example, the following command tells HOOPS to allocate a fixed color map with eight entries (the minimum).

```
HC_Set_Driver_Options("fixed colors = 8");
```

This command will create a color cube with two shades each of red, green, and blue.

Alternatively, the "fixed colors" driver option can take three arguments, which tell HOOPS how many shades of each color to allocate. The following command allocates a color map with three shades of red, four shades of green, and two shades of blue:

```
HC_Set_Driver_Options("fixed colors=(3, 4, 2)");
```

This color map will contain 24 entries (3 times 4 times 2).

 In general, the human eye is most sensitive to changes in shades of green, and least sensitive to changes in shades of blue, so the preceding color map (with three shades of red, four shades of green, and two shades of blue) will usually produce better-looking colors than will a perfect cube with three shades each of red, green, and blue (and it takes up three fewer slots).

The "no fixed colors" driver option,

```
HC_Set_Driver_Options("no fixed colors");
```

tells HOOPS to use its algorithm to determine the number of colors in the fixed color map. This option is the default.

Finally, setting the number of fixed colors to zero,

```
HC_Set_Driver_Options("fixed colors = 0");
```

prevents HOOPS from allocating a fixed color map at all. One use for this option is to deallocate a fixed color map when it is no longer needed. Normally, once

HOOPS creates a fixed color map, it never deletes that color map, even if the map is no longer needed.

For example, consider a drawing application that does not use a fixed color map. The application writer then adds a color-selector tool that draws a continuous spectrum of color and allows the user to select a color by pointing at a position in the spectrum. When the color-selector tool is drawn, HOOPS will allocate a fixed color map. When the user has finished selecting a color, however, HOOPS does not automatically free the fixed color map, even though the color map is no longer needed and may reduce the number of slots available for regular colors. You can use the driver option "fixed colors = 0" to tell HOOPS to deallocate the fixed color map. Of course, if you turn off the fixed color map and your scene needs any fixed colors, the lack of a fixed color map will cause an error.

## 9.1.7     Regular Color Allocation in the Color Map

As we stated in Section 9.1.5.1, in a mapped color system, regular colors are allocated dynamically, each time that the display is updated. Thus, the number of regular colors allocated in the color map can change from one display update to the next. If a scene contains more regular colors than there are available slots in the hardware color map, HOOPS will signal an error.

There are several ways that you can affect the number of slots available for regular colors. If your scene requires a fixed color map, then you can control the number of slots taken up using the "fixed colors" driver option (as explained in Section 9.1.6). By making the fixed color map small, you can free up more slots for regular colors.

A second way that you can control the number of slots taken up by regular colors is through the use of the "color consolidation" driver option. At update time, HOOPS makes a pass through the database to determine how many color slots to allocate in the hardware color map for regular colors. If two colors are relatively close together, then HOOPS can consolidate them into a single color. By default, HOOPS consolidates colors that differ by less than one part in 64 in red, green, and blue. You can make this number either larger or smaller. For more information, see the "color consolidation" driver option in the command HC_Set_Driver_Options.

Note that, if you turn off color consolidation (by setting the "no color consolidation" driver option), then colors will share color-map entries only when they are exactly equal. Determining whether two colors are equal can be complicated by the fact that HOOPS uses floating-point numbers to specify colors, and system color-maps entries contain integers. If you are not careful, then two colors that appear to be equal might be allocated separate slots in the color map because of the inaccuracies of floating-point arithmetic.

A third way to control the allocation of colors is through the use of the "number of colors" driver option. Normally, you use this option to restrain HOOPS to using fewer colors than it normally would. This option is useful if your application wants to allocate colors in the color map other than the ones used by HOOPS. HOOPS will signal an error if the number of fixed and regular colors exceeds the value that you set using the "number of colors" driver option.

Also useful is the "first color" driver option, which tells HOOPS not to use a specified number of slots in the color table. See the HC_Set_Driver_Options command for more information.

On a few systems, you can use the "number of colors" driver option to tell HOOPS to allocate more colors than normally would be available to it. For example, on some systems, HOOPS can reallocate slots used by the window or operating system. To see whether it can do so on your system, use the HC_Show_Device_Info command to get the values for "max colors" and "colors". The value for "colors" is the value that HOOPS normally uses for the "number of colors" driver option. If "max colors" is greater than "colors", you can set "number of colors" to the larger value. Do so only if you absolutely need the maximum number of colors, as reallocating system colors can result in the screen background or windows being drawn with incorrect colors.

HOOPS has a problem that can affect the allocation of hardware color-map slots. HOOPS determines the number of regular colors to allocate during a pass through the database at update time. HOOPS is smart about this allocation — for example, only color attributes that affect visible objects are allocated.

There is one case, however, when a color slot can get allocated for a regular color that is never actually used to draw anything. This problem occurs if a color attribute is set on a segment, and that color affects only objects that HOOPS draws using the fixed color map (such as objects that your application draws using lighting, smooth shading, or color interpolation). For example, if you draw a lit red cube, by setting the red color attribute on the segment containing the cube, a (single) slot in the hardware color map will be allocated for the color "red", even though that color is not used (because HOOPS will draw the lighted faces using the fixed color map). Currently, the only way to work around this problem is to set the colors on the individual vertices of a shell or mesh (rather than as color attributes on an entire segment).

**9.1.8**          **The "Use Color Map ID" Driver Option**

Even if the hardware color map does not run out of available slots, there is another problem that can be visually disconcerting to the users of an application. When your user is running a window system that allows more than one application to run at a time, the running applications compete for system resources, including the hardware color map. For example, say that the user is running two separate HOOPS applications. Both applications are allocating slots in the hardware color map. If the total number of colors allocated by both applications, plus any colors used by the operating (or window) system, is less than the total number of slots in the hardware color map, then both applications can share the same hardware color map. But if both applications allocate more than one-half of the available slots, the operating system will respond by swapping hardware color maps when you switch from one application to the other. Unfortunately, whichever application does not have the input focus (is not running in the foreground) will have its colors drawn incorrectly. Although this color flashing is not fatal, it can be disconcerting and annoying to the user. Thus, it is to your advantage as an application programmer to treat color-map entries as a scarce resource, and to allocate as few as possible.

Note that, even if you are running only a single HOOPS application, if that application creates more than one driver instance (output window), then these driver instances will compete for hardware color-map slots. In this case, there is another way to reduce the number of color-map slots allocated. As we discussed in Section 9.1.2.3, you can set a HOOPS color map above the two driver instances in the segment tree, and then use HC_Set_Color_By_Index to set regular colors. This trick enables the two driver instances to share colors, and avoids competition for hardware color-map slots.

Alternatively, for applications that create more than one output window containing HOOPS output, you can use the "use colormap ID" driver option to share color maps between the windows. Normally, separate driver instances allocate their own color maps, and compete with each other for color-map slots. When you use the "use colormap ID" driver option, you take total control of and responsibility for the color map. Details of how to allocate color maps vary from platform to platform. The *HOOPS Installation Guide* contains more information about the use of the "use colormap ID" driver option.

When you allocate regular colors out of a shared HOOPS color map in two separate driver instances, the operating system switches the hardware color map when you change focus from one window to another, but, since both windows use the same colors, allocated in the same positions in the hardware color map, the user will not notice the switch.

### 9.1.9   16-Bit Frame Buffers

So far, we have discussed only 8-bit frame buffers, which use a hardware color map, and 24-bit frame buffers, which represent all colors directly without the use of a color map. HOOPS also works with 16-bit frame buffers. On most platforms, a 16-bit frame buffer does not have a hardware color map. HOOPS treats a 16-bit frame buffer like a 24-bit frame buffer, and represents colors directly (using dithering, if necessary). Unfortunately, on some platforms (in particular, Microsoft Windows), the conversion from 24-bit to 16-bit color can introduce a significant speed penalty. For maximum rendering speed, setting the system to either 8 or 24 bits is recommended.

Note that some platforms support frame buffers with other color depths. For example, on the HP platform, HOOPS will work with 4-bit and 6-bit frame buffers. On many platforms, HOOPS will work with 12-bit frame buffers. Any platform with less than 16 bits per pixel is typically used in mapped-color mode.

### 9.1.10   Color Tweaking

HOOPS has several defaults that it uses to display colors. In some cases, however, these defaults do not result in the best color rendition. Sections 9.1.10.1 to 9.1.10.4 cover defaults that you might want to override to get better looking color output.

### 9.1.10.1

**Gamma correction.** As we discussed in Section 3.3.5.10, gamma correction is the process of correcting for nonlinearities in CRT displays. Without gamma correction, colors can look too dark. HOOPS, by default, does gamma correction on the colors in a scene before it displays them. Recently, however, many graphics cards have begun doing gamma correction in hardware, so gamma correction might be applied twice, which would make the colors look washed out. You can turn off HOOPS gamma correction using the driver option named "no gamma correction." See the HC_Set_Driver_Options command for more information.

To determine whether your graphics card does gamma correction, look for a system utility routine that allows you to adjust the gamma correction of the monitor. Lacking that, look in the documentation for the graphics card. If all else fails, draw a scene using HOOPS, and then draw it with HOOPS gamma correction off, and see which looks better.

For an excellent discussion of monitor gamma and a test image that you can use to determine the gamma of your monitor, see the following World Wide Web page written by Robert Berger:

http://www.cs.cmu.edu/afs/cs.cmu.edu/user/rwb/www/gamma.html

**9.1.10.2**     **Ambient light.** As we discussed in Section 3.3.4.2, ambient light is a constant amount of light that illuminates everything in a scene. Its main purpose is make sure that objects that are facing away from any light source are not completely dark. The default value for the ambient light is "dark gray" (R = 0.325, G = 0.325, B = 0.325). This value is fairly light, but it was chosen such that scenes would not be overly dark when a single light source is used. Unfortunately, this value can result in washed-out colors. If you are lighting a scene using multiple light sources or want a darker look, you will want to reduce the amount of ambient light in your scene.

Ambient light is normally set at the window level, with the HC_Set_Color command. The following command reduces the amount of ambient light:

```
HC_QSet_Color("?Picture",
        "ambient light = (H=0, S=0, V=0.1)");
```

Note that ambient lighting applies only when there is at least one light source in your scene.

**9.1.10.3**     **Light scaling.** When a scene contains lights, the color of each object in the scene is a function of the light falling on that object from each light source. The light from each light source is additive, which can cause a problem if there is more than one light source in a scene. Consider a scene containing a single gray polygon. If this polygon is illuminated by a single white light source that is directly in front of it, it will be rendered correctly as medium gray. If an additional white light source is added that also illuminates the polygon, the two light sources add, and the polygon will be rendered as white (or close to white). If a third light source is added (which also illuminates the polygon), then the polygon will have an intensity of 1.5, which will get clipped down to 1.0.

To avoid this problem, HOOPS scales the color values in a scene depending on the number of light sources. For example, if a scene contains three light sources, HOOPS would scale all colors by one-third. Thus, our polygon, which had an intensity value of 1.5 when illuminated by three lights, will be scaled to 0.5 (which is medium gray).

The algorithm that HOOPS uses for light scaling is slightly more complicated, because it takes into account the color of the lights. The RGB values of all lights in a scene are added together, and whichever of R, G, or B is greater is used as the scale value. Thus, if you have three lights — one red, one blue, and one green — the scale factor will only be 1.0, instead of 3.0. In addition, HOOPS treats the value for ambient light as a light source in this calculation.

Light scaling in HOOPS minimizes the clipping of color values, even in worst-case scenes. In most scenes that contain multiple light sources, however, objects are not illuminated by all light sources in the scene. Consider a scene containing a cube and six distant lights, each light shining directly at one face of the cube. Even though there are six lights, no face of the cube will be illuminated by more than one light at the same time. In this case, the HOOPS value for light scaling will be excessive, and the scene will appear too dark.

Or consider a scene with 20 narrow-beam spot lights, each of which is aimed at a separate object (like those in an art gallery). In this case, the colors in the scene will be scaled by 0.05, and, since no object is illuminated by more than one light, no object can be brighter than 0.05, resulting in an almost completely black scene.

The only way to avoid this problem is to set the value for light scaling explicitly, using the "light scaling" driver option. For example, the following command sets the light scaling to 1.0:

```
HC_Set_Driver_Options("light scaling = 1.0");
```

Remember that driver options must be set on a driver instance (such as "?Picture").

When you set light scaling explicitly, you need to take into account the lights' number, colors, positions, and types (distant, local, or spot). Also note that you can purposely set the light scaling too low, which will cause color values greater than 1.0 to be clamped at 1.0. This clamping is not an error; if done excessively, however, it can cause scenes to appear washed out.

9.1.10.4    **Multiple color problems.** Excessive gamma correction and ambient light can make a scene too bright, whereas light scaling can make a scene too dark. Do these problems cancel out each other? Unfortunately, they do not. In fact, they do not always apply at the same time. In a scene that does not contain any light sources, only gamma correction can be a problem (and only if your graphics card also does gamma correction). Even in a scene with multiple light sources, which suffers from both too much ambient light and excessive light scaling, these problems do not cancel each other out. Instead, the result is muddy, washed-out colors, with no deep blacks or bright whites. You will be able to see everything in the scene, but it might not be a pretty sight! If you care about accurate and pleasing colors, the only solution is to correct each problem separately.

## 9.1.11      Edge Lighting

Normally, HOOPS calculates lighting on both faces and edges of shells and meshes (it will even calculate lighting on markers associated with shells and meshes, if markers are visible). When there are lights in a scene, and faces are visible, it is normally to your advantage to turn off the visibility of edges, so that lighting calculations are not done on them. Assuming that the edges are the same color as the faces, turning off edge visibility will not make any difference in the resulting output image. On many systems — especially systems with special hardware for performing lighting calculations on faces — turning off edge visibility can result in dramatically faster rendering times.

If there are no lights in a scene, and the faces of a shell or mesh are all the same color, then it will be difficult to see the boundaries between faces unless you leave on the visibility of edges, and set the edges to a color different from that of the faces. For example, when displaying a red geodesic dome, you can set the edge color to black to make the structure of the dome visible. In this case, you want the edges to be visible, but you probably do not want lighting calculations to be done on them, so you can turn off lighting calculations on the edges with the following command:

```
HC_Set_Visibility("lights = (edges=off)");
```

Another technique to make individual faces visible is to apply a pattern, or a texture map, to the faces. In this case, you would probably will want to turn off edge visibility, whether or not you have any lights in the scene.

## 9.1.12      Color-Map Animation

Color-map animation is a trick that is sometimes used to do simple animation. The most common example of this kind of animation is a marquee selection tool, which draws a two-color dashed rectangle around a selected area and animates edges of the rectangle such that the boundary appears similar to the marching lights on a movie marquee. Rather than redraw the rectangle over and over to animate it, a faster approach is to draw a single rectangle made up of segments of four different colors. Each color has a different index in the hardware color map, as shown in Figure 9.3.

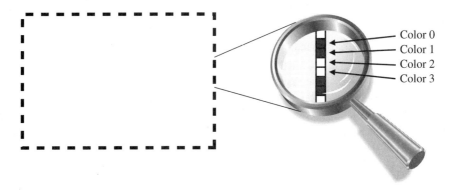

**Figure 9.3**   Color-map animation of a marquee.

We can then animate the rectangle simply by changing the values in the color map. First, we assign the color black to the colors with indices 0 and 1, and white to the colors with indices 2 and 3. We wait a short time, then change the color map so that color indices 1 and 2 are black, whereas 0 and 3 are white. We change the color map twice more, until the colors are back to their original configuration. The rectangle will then appear to be made up of segments that move around the rectangle clockwise, with no redrawing required.

Even though HOOPS is device independent, and so does not provide direct access to the hardware color map, you can perform color-map animation using the HC_Modify_Color_Map command in HOOPS. You create a HOOPS color map, using the HC_Set_Color_Map command, containing four colors. Recall that a HOOPS color map is not the same as the hardware color map. You then draw the rectangle, setting the colors of each segment using the command HC_Set_Color_By_Index. For each step of the animation, you modify the color map as follows:

```
1  HC_Modify_Color_Map(0, "black, black, white, white");
2  HC_Get_Wakeup(0.25);
3  HC_Modify_Color_Map(0, "white, black, black, white");
4  HC_Get_Wakeup(0.25);
5  HC_Modify_Color_Map(0, "white, white, black, black");
6  HC_Get_Wakeup(0.25);
7  HC_Modify_Color_Map(0, "black, white, white, black");
8  HC_Get_Wakeup(0.25);
```

This cycle repeats itself.

Note that this technique will work on any platform — even a platform that does not have a hardware color map (such as a 24-bit frame buffer). Of course, without a hardware color map, HOOPS will have to redraw the rectangle for each step of the animation, but that will look fine on a platform that supports double buffering. You can determine whether your platform has a hardware color map, and whether it is capable of double buffering, by using the HC_Show_Device_Info command.

 For images that are defined with mapped (non-RGB) colors, you can use the HC_Modify_Color_Map command to create psychedelic effects.

## 9.2      Texture

As we discussed in Section 3.3.4.8, it is possible to paint a texture onto a surface. In HOOPS, you paint surfaces by using an image as a color.

### 9.2.1      Creation of an Image for a Texture

A texture map is created from a HOOPS image. Consequently, the first step in defining a texture map is to create a HOOPS image using the HC_Insert_Image (or HC_Insert_Image_By_Ref) command. The HC_Insert_Image command was discussed in Section 5.2.13. To use an image as a texture map, however, you must name the image.

The HC_Insert_Image command takes seven arguments:

```
HC_Insert_Image(x, y, z, format, width, height, data);
```

The first three arguments are the coordinates where the image is to be inserted, and the final three arguments are the image's width and height, and the actual image data. The fourth argument — format — normally gives information to HOOPS, such as whether the image data contain RGB triples or indices into a color map.

You can also use the format argument to give a name to the image — for example,

```
HC_Insert_Image(0, 0, 0, "RGB, name=my_image",
      width, height, data);
```

This image has been given the name "my_image".

An image can be created from raw data created by your application, or it can be read in from a file. In Section 5.2.13, we showed how to create a HOOPS image by reading in an image file in GIF format using the routine gif_to_hoops that is supplied on the HOOPS CD-ROM. The gif_to_hoops routine takes four arguments:

```
long image_key = gif_to_hoops(
      "/hoops/demo/common/txtruniv/stop2.gif",
      ".", "rgb", "stop_sign");
```

The first argument is the file name containing the GIF image. The second argument is the name of the HOOPS segment in which to place the image. The third argument is the format to use for the resulting image. The fourth argument is a name to give to the image. This name is passed through to the command HC_Insert_Image.

If we plan to use an image as a texture, then we normally do not want the image itself to be visible. Either the image will be placed into the HOOPS database in a segment that is not under a driver, or else we can put it into an arbitrary segment and turn off the visibility of the segment. In either case, the actual values of the $x$, $y$, and $z$ coordinates supplied to the HC_Insert_Image command are irrelevant.

## 9.2.2    Use of an Image as a Backdrop

The simplest way to use a named image is as a window backdrop. You can use an image as a backdrop by using the image name as the window color. Program 9.1 reads in an image from a GIF file and places it into a segment named "/image" (the second argument to the gif_to_hoops function, on line 7). Because this segment is directly under the root segment, rather than under a driver segment (such as "?Picture"), the image will not be visible. The image is named "stop_sign" (the final argument to gif_to_hoops, on line 7). This image name is then used (in line 9) as the window color of "?Picture". Note that, if the image is smaller than the window, then the image is repeated as many times as necessary to fill the window.

```
1   #include <hc.h>
2   extern "C" long gif_to_hoops(
3          char *, char *, char *, char *);

4   void main() {

5      long image_key = gif_to_hoops(
6                  "/hoops/demo/common/txtruniv/stop2.gif",
7                  "/image", "rgb", "stop_sign");

8      HC_Open_Segment("?Picture");
9          HC_Set_Color("window = stop_sign");
10     HC_Close_Segment();

11     HC_Pause();
12  }
```

**Program 9.1**   Use of a named image as a window backdrop.

The HOOPS demo/common/txtruniv directory contains several sample texture maps taken from the Autodesk texture universe CD-ROM. Program 9.2 displays these textures one at a time as the backdrop of the window. It also displays the name of the image in the title bar of the window (lines 18 and 19).

```
1   #include <hc.h>
2   #include <stdio.h>
3   extern "C" long gif_to_hoops(
4          char *, char *, char *, char *);

5   void main() {
6      char fname[] =
7              "/hoops/demo/common/txtruniv/%s.gif";
8      char * txtrnames[18] = {"asphalt1", "bluepad",
9              "cedfence", "dotplate", "drymud3", "gray",
10             "grayfab", "grycon3", "limesto3", "marble2",
11             "oakply1", "pinkgra2", "redglas", "stucco4",
12             "tanleath", "treebrk4", "water1", "ysponge"};
13     char buff[80];
```

**458**

```
14      for (int i = 0; i<18; i++) {
15          sprintf(buff, fname, txtrnames[i]);
16          gif_to_hoops(buff, "/image", "rgb", "texture");
17          HC_QSet_Color("?Picture", "window = texture");

18          sprintf(buff, "title = \'%s\'", txtrnames[i]);
19          HC_QSet_Driver_Options("?Picture", buff);

20          HC_Pause();
21      }
22  }
```

**Program 9.2**    Display of several textures.

Note that you will probably need to change the directory name (line 6 in Program 9.1, and line 7 in Program 9.2), depending on where you installed the HOOPS software. Of course, you can use any GIF-format image files, as well as the ones in the texture universe directory.

## 9.2.3    Use of an Image as a Texture

Using an image as a texture on an object is only slightly more complicated than is using it as a window backdrop. A texture map can be applied to a shell or a mesh, but using a texture map with a mesh is slightly easier (and more common). To use a texture map, you must perform four steps:

**1.** Insert an image and give it a name (as we did in Section 9.2.2).

**2.** Make sure that the "texture interpolation" rendering option is enabled (it is enabled by default).

**3.** Assign texture-coordinate parameters to the shell or mesh, to control the mapping between points on the surface of the object and points in the texture.

**4.** Use the image as the color of the object.

### 9.2.3.1

**Texture-coordinate parameters.** The main new operation that you need to do is to assign texture-coordinate parameters to the shell or mesh. To apply a 2D texture to a 3D surface, you must define how points on the 3D surface map onto points in the texture. For example, if you want to apply a striped texture to a cylinder, you can apply it such that the stripes run around the cylinder, or such that they run up and down the cylinder (or diagonally, and so on). You make that determination by assigning a texture-coordinate parameter to each vertex in the shell or mesh.

You can apply texture-coordinate parameters to an individual vertex in a shell or mesh by opening the shell or mesh (using HC_Open_Geometry), then opening a vertex (using HC_Open_Vertex), and then setting the texture-coordinate parameter using the HC_Set_Parameter command. The use of HC_Set_Parameter is identical to the way that colors are set on individual vertices in a shell or mesh. Alternatively, you can use the command HC_MSet_Vertex_Parameters to set texture-coordinate parameters on multiple vertices.

A texture coordinate specifies a pixel location in the texture to use as the color of the object. Regardless of the size (in pixels) of an image used as a texture, the texture coordinates are assumed to go from 0.0 to 1.0 in both $x$ and $y$. In addition, texture coordinates are 3D points, but the $z$ coordinate is ignored. If a vertex has a texture-coordinate parameter of (0.0, 0.0), then the color at that vertex is taken from the pixel at the lower-left corner of the texture image. Likewise, if a vertex has a texture-coordinate parameter of (1.0, 1.0), then the color at that vertex is taken from the pixel at the upper-right corner of the texture image.

**9.2.3.2**    **Textures in driver segments.** Because of the way that HOOPS handles colors, you can sometimes get incorrect images if you apply a texture to a shell or mesh that is contained in a driver-instance segment (such as "?Picture"). The easiest way to avoid this problem is to put the geometry into a subsegment.

**9.2.3.3**    **Example program with a texture.** Program 9.3 defines a cylinder using a mesh, and applies a texture (read in from a GIF file) to that cylinder. This program uses the gif_to_hoops routine (that is included in the directory demo/common/gifrdr) to read in a GIF file, and to convert that file into a HOOPS image (this routine was discussed in Section 5.2.13).

Most of the code in Program 9.3 defines the mesh for the cylinder. The parts that are extra for applying the texture map are lines 35 through 42, which define the array of texture coordinate parameters for the points in the mesh; line 46, which applies the texture coordinate parameters to the mesh; and line 50, which uses the image as a texture for the faces of the mesh. The texture-coordinate parameters are defined such that the texture wraps around the cylinder.

Note that line 11 (which turns on texture interpolation) also turns off color interpolation and color-index interpolation. We often turn off interpolation when we are using texture mapping, since we want the colors to be taken from the texture, rather than interpolated from the vertex colors. Also note line 48, which turns off the visibility of edges and markers. HOOPS will happily apply a texture to the edges of a shell or mesh, but that texture application takes time to compute.

Applying the texture to only the faces results in exactly the same picture as would applying the texture to faces and edges, and is much faster.

```
1   #include <hc.h>
2   #include <math.h>

3   extern "C" long gif_to_hoops(
4           char *, char *, char *, char * );

5   struct Point { float x, y, z; };

6   void main() {
7       gif_to_hoops(
8               "/hoops/demo/common/txtruniv/limesto3.gif",
9               "/image", "rgb", "image");

10      HC_Open_Segment("?Picture");
11          HC_Set_Rendering_Options(
12                  "no color interpolation, "
13                  "no color index interpolation, "
14                  "texture interpolation");
15          HC_Set_Color("windows = black");

16          // tessellate a cylinder
17          HC_Open_Segment("cylinder");
18              static Point point_list[42];
19              static Point params[42];
20              const double angle = 3.1415926535 / 10.0;

21              // create two circles in x,z plane
22              for (int loop = 0; loop <= 20; loop++) {

23                  // circle at top of cylinder
24                  point_list[loop].x =
25                          (float) cos(loop * angle);
26                  point_list[loop].y = 1.0f;
27                  point_list[loop].z =
28                          (float) sin(loop * angle);

29                  // circle at bottom of cylinder
30                  point_list[loop + 21].x =
31                          point_list[loop].x;
32                  point_list[loop + 21].y = -1.0f;
33                  point_list[loop + 21].z =
34                          point_list[loop].z;
```

```
35              // texture map coordinates for top
36              params[loop].x = (float) loop / 10.0f;
37              params[loop].y = 1.0f;
38              params[loop].z = 0.0f;

39              // texture map coordinates for bottom
40              params[loop + 21].x = params[loop].x;
41              params[loop + 21].y = 0.0f;
42              params[loop + 21].z = 0.0f;
43          }

44          long key = HC_KInsert_Mesh(
45                  2, 21, point_list);
46          HC_MSet_Vertex_Parameters(key, 0, 42, 3,
47                  (float *) params);

48          HC_Set_Visibility("no edges, no markers");
49          HC_Scale_Object(0.8, 0.8, 0.8);

50          HC_Set_Color("faces = image");

51      HC_Close_Segment();
52    HC_Close_Segment();

53    HC_Pause();
54 }
```

**Program 9.3**    Using an image as a texture.

Figure 9.4 shows the output from Program 9.3; a cylinder made of limestone blocks.

Notice that a texture map can do only so much, because it is a flat image. In particular, the silhouette edges of the cylinder in Figure 9.4 are completely

**Figure 9.4**     A cylinder made of limestone blocks.

smooth. If the cylinder were really made of limestone blocks, the edges would be rough. Also remember that a texture map will usually have its own lighting and shadows. If the texture map's lighting does not agree with the lighting in your scene, the resulting image will likely be disconcerting to view.

If our texture-mapped cylinder will be used in a scene with any lights, we will probably want to set the vertex normals (particularly on the seam), so that the lighting is done properly (appears smooth across the seam).

**9.2.3.4**     **Texture-coordinate parameters on shells.** When you apply a texture to a shell, you may encounter problems, because you often need a vertex to have more than one texture-coordinate parameter. For example, if you used a shell for the cylinder in Program 9.3, then the seam where the surface connects with itself will need to have two texture-coordinate parameters — one for the left side of the texture and one for the right side, as shown in Figure 9.5.

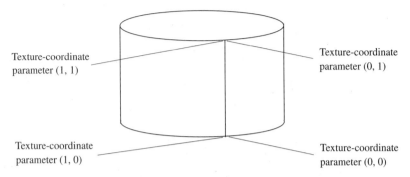

Texture-coordinate
parameter (1, 1)

Texture-coordinate
parameter (0, 1)

Texture-coordinate
parameter (1, 0)

Texture-coordinate
parameter (0, 0)

**Figure 9.5**          Vertices with more than one texture-coordinate parameter.

The solution to this problem is simply to duplicate the vertices in the shell's point list. That way, even though two points may have the same geometric coordinates, they can have different texture-coordinate parameters. Note that, when you duplicate vertices, you will probably want to set the normals on duplicated vertices explicitly.

### 9.2.4          Other Texture Attributes

Although applying textures to surfaces can be relatively easy in HOOPS, there are numerous options and attributes that you can use to exercise a fine level of control over the texture maps in your application.

9.2.4.1          **Use of textures as material properties.** In Program 9.3, we used the image as the entire color specification for the faces of the mesh (on line 50). It is also possible to use a texture map as one component of the color. For example, we can use one texture for the diffuse color, and another texture for the specular color. See the HC_Set_Color command for more information.

9.2.4.2          **Transformation of texture-coordinate parameters.** Normally, texture coordinates are fixed. When you move an object that has a texture applied to it, the texture moves with the object. You can also apply transformations to the texture coordinates. Normally, you transform texture coordinates with the commands HC_Translate_Texture, HC_Scale_Texture, HC_Rotate_Texture, and HC_Rotate_Texture_Offaxis. For example, you could use the command HC_Rotate_Texture to rotate the limestone texture in Program 9.3, so that the limestone blocks run up and down the cylinder, rather than around it (alternatively, you could specify different texture-coordinate parameters).

You can also use HC_Scale_Texture to make the limestone blocks larger or smaller in Program 9.3. If you apply the command

```
HC_Scale_Texture(0.25, 0.5, 1.0);
```

to the texture coordinates (by inserting it after line 47 in Program 9.3), you will create a more realistic-looking limestone-block cylinder, as shown in Figure 9.6.

**Figure 9.6**     Scaled texture.

Note that, unlike modeling-transformation matrices, and like most attributes, texture transformations in separate segments are not concatenated. Texture matrices act like normal attributes — a local one overrides an inherited one. Multiple rotate, scale, and translate texture commands in a single segment do accumulate, however.

You can set the texture-transformation matrix explicitly using the command HC_Set_Texture_Matrix, and can remove any texture-transformation matrix using HC_UnSet_Texture_Matrix. You can also concatenate a transformation matrix onto the texture-transformation matrix using the command HC_Append_Texture_Matrix. See the *HOOPS Reference Manual* for details.

**9.2.4.3**     **Perspective correction.** Because texture coordinates are normally linearly interpolated in screen space, viewing objects that are texture mapped in perspective can cause the texture map to appear distorted. You can correct for this problem using the "perspective correction" rendering option (which is on by default). This perspective correction was discussed in Section 3.3.4.5.

9.2.4.4      **HC_Define_Texture.** The general use of textures can be complicated. HOOPS gives you full access to all the complexities of texture mapping via the HC_Define_Texture command. Using HC_Define_Texture, you can manipulate texture maps in almost any way imaginable. You can specify which coordinates of the texture-coordinate parameters to use, and you can even tell HOOPS to ignore the texture-coordinates parameter and to use the world coordinates of the vertex as the texture coordinate.

Note that, even if you use world coordinates as the texture coordinates, HOOPS still requires you to set a texture-coordinate parameter on a shell or mesh before it will perform texture mapping. Luckily, you can set a texture-coordinate parameter using the HC_MSet_Vertex_Parameters command. Just set the pcount (third) argument to 0.

HC_Define_Texture has many different options. One of the most useful is the "tiling" option, which specifies what to do if a texture coordinate is outside the 0.0 to 1.0 range. The default is for the texture to repeat itself over and over, *tiling* itself onto the surface to be textured. You can also set tiling to off, which clamps the texture coordinates, so only a single copy of the texture image appears on the surface. You can also set tiling to "mirror", which causes every other copy of the texture image to be reversed. This option can sometimes help to hide the seams where copies of the texture image meet (however, most images in the texture-universe directory are designed to be seamless).

Another useful option is "interpolation filter", which allows you to specify a filter to reduce aliasing artifacts. Because a texture is just an array of pixels, when you zoom in close to a textured object, you will see individual pixels of the image. You can use an interpolation filter to interpolate between pixel values in the texture image, and thus to smooth out the texture.

The HC_Define_Texture command takes a named image and creates a named texture. The named texture is then used as the face color for a shell or mesh. For more information, see the *HOOPS Reference Manual* entry for the command HC_Define_Texture.

### 9.2.5      The Texture Demo

The directory demo/common/feature contains a program called texture.c (it is written in C, not C++) that demonstrates almost all the various options that can be applied to texture maps. If you plan to make significant use of texture maps, you should run this program, and read the code.

This same directory contains several textures that are stored in HOOPS metafiles. When you run this program, you should set the environment variable HOOP_METAFILE_DIRECTORY to include both the directory hoops/demo/common/hmf and hoops/demo/common/feature, so that this program can find all the metafiles that it needs. Of course, the directory names may be different, depending on where you installed the software from the CD-ROM.

# 10    Tips and Techniques

This chapter covers various techniques and tricks that you can use to make your application run faster and to avoid problems that people commonly encounter when they write 3D graphics applications. For additional tips and techniques, you should also look at Sections 5.3 and 9.1.10.

In Section 10.5, there is a catalog of the demo programs that are included with the HOOPS distribution on the CD-ROM. These demo programs are typically implemented more fully than are the simple example programs that are presented in this book.

Finally, there is a complete application program on the CD-ROM called the *viewer* (also called the *hoopster*). The viewer allows you to view 3D models and to make changes to them. This application is useful for three reasons. First, as a debugging tool, it can help you to examine your models and to track down problems. Second, it is useful as a example program, to help you see how to organize a 3D graphics application and to integrate HOOPS with a window system. The viewer application is available in two versions: one written for MFC, and one written for Motif. Third, the viewer application is useful in its own right, or as a basis for other applications. For example, you could modify the viewer to read in DXF (AutoCAD exchange format) or 3DS (3D Studio) files and to view them.

## 10.1     Common Problems

Reading this section can help you to avoid common problems that people encounter when they write 3D graphics applications.

### 10.1.1     Segment Organization

Segments are the primary organizational principle in HOOPS. In HOOPS, however, segments primarily organize *attributes*, rather than geometry. It is a common mistake for programmers to structure their segments to mimic the organization of the geometry in a scene. Although this structure works, it can slow rendering and can even make your program more difficult to write.

For example, imagine that you are drawing a checkerboard with white and black squares (ignore for a moment that the best way to draw a checkerboard would be with a mesh). The squares cannot all be in a single segment, because they do not all share the same color-attribute value. One way to organize the database is to put each square of the board in its own segment, but that requires 64 different segments. A more efficient organization is to use two segments, and to put all the black squares in one segment, and all the white squares in the other. This structure uses fewer segments, is faster to render, and can make it easier to change attributes (for example, to change all the white squares to red).

The best way to design a HOOPS database is to structure it based on like attributes. Organizing the database is a two-step process. The first step is to put into the same segment all geometry that has the same color, transformation, and other attributes. Some attributes, such as transformations, will naturally tend to follow the organization of the geometry in a scene; if they do, then your segment organization might follow the organization of your geometry, but it will not be dictated by that organization. In addition, if you have a group of geometries that will be deleted together, you can put them in their own segment to make deleting them easier.

The second step is to build an inheritance hierarchy for segments with similar attribute settings. For example, if, in the resulting database, there are two segments with nearly identical attribute values, then you should give them a common parent segment and should set the common attributes in the parent. Notice that organizing an attribute hierarchy is just like designing a good class hierarchy in C++. Continue until your attributes are well organized — the goal is to structure your database so that you can change any attribute that affects a group of geometry by changing it in only one place. For example, if a group of objects will normally move together, give the group a common parent so that you can change the transformation in one place. If two attributes conflict on how they want the database to be organized, consider putting one of the attributes into a style segment.

Good segment organization is a primary differentiator of good HOOPS programs from bad ones.

## 10.1.2 Precision Errors

Since HOOPS uses single-precision floating-point numbers to store coordinates, your application needs to be careful that it does not inadvertently create incorrect images because of precision errors. One common problematic situation is using a camera that is extremely far away from the objects to be viewed, and then zooming the camera until the image fills the screen. The problem is caused by the distance from the camera to the objects. When the hidden-surface algorithm compares two objects to see which one is in front, it will be comparing two relatively large numbers that differ by only a small amount. Numerical-accuracy problems can cause these two objects to trade places.

You should aim to keep the distance from the camera to the camera target no more than 10 times the size of the camera field (taking into account that a camera zoom reduces the size of the camera field).

## 10.1.3 Z-buffer Quantization

The Z-buffer hidden-surface-removal algorithm was described in Section 3.3.3.5. One problem with the Z-buffer algorithm is that the floating-point distance from the camera to the object is mapped into a (typically 16-bit) integer value in the Z-buffer. This reduction in precision can cause quantization errors.

To reduce quantization errors, you can control how object distance is mapped into the Z-buffer values by making sure that your camera target lies approximately in the geometric center of the objects that are being displayed. See the Section 6.1.7 for two routines that set up an appropriate camera automatically.

When the camera uses a perspective view, the object distance is mapped onto the Z-buffer values logarithmically, so that one-half of the Z-buffer values lie between the camera and the camera target, and the other half from the camera target to positive infinity. Thus you can control the Z-buffer quantization by moving the camera target closer or farther away (and adjusting the camera view to compensate for the change)

When an orthographic camera is used, and if *d* is the distance from the camera to the camera target, then the object distances from –3*d* to 5*d* (4*d* in front and behind the camera target) are mapped linearly onto the Z-buffer values. Again, you can control Z-buffer quantization by moving the camera target.

### 10.1.4     Edge Stitching and Edge Shinethrough

A common hidden-surface error is called *edge stitching*. When both the edges and faces of a polygon are visible, they are almost exactly the same distance from the camera. Due to numerical-accuracy problems, an edge can appear dashed as it pops in and out from behind one or more faces, as shown in Figure 10.1.

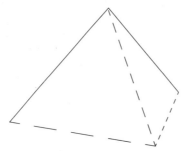

**Figure 10.1**     Edge stitching.

To avoid the edge-stitching problem, you can use the "face displacement" rendering option. This rendering option renders the faces of polygons, shells, and meshes as though they were slightly farther away than the edges, so that the edges appear in front of the faces. The "face displacement" rendering option takes an argument, whose units are Z-buffer units. Thus, the proper value for face displacement is dependent on the camera view. If the face-displacement value is too small, edge stitching will not be eliminated.

If the face-displacement value is too large, then another problem can occur, called *edge shinethrough*. Shinethrough occurs when faces are pushed so far back that an edge that should be hidden appears (at least partially). In Figure 10.2, a hidden interior edge shines through partially at the top of the pyramid, because the face that should have hidden it has a face-displacement value that is too large.

See the *HOOPS Reference Manual* entry for the HC_Set_Rendering_Options command for more information.

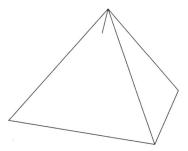

**Figure 10.2**     Edge shinethrough.

 Hardware Z-buffers sometimes suffer from more severe edge stitching than that caused by the HOOPS software Z-buffer. You can also try setting the "debug = 4" rendering option, which can alleviate edge stitching at the expense of speed.

### 10.1.5     Color Flashing

Color flashing occurs when there are multiple applications (or a single application with multiple windows) that use more colors than are available in the hardware color map (color flashing occurs on only platforms that use mapped color). When you switch between windows, the system must swap color maps, so the colors in the window that is not in focus will be displayed incorrectly. The easiest way to avoid color flashing is to avoid allocation of too many colors.

Alternatively, you can allocate a single HOOPS color map, and share it among windows. Sharing of color maps is discussed in Section 9.1.2.3. You can also completely take over the allocation of the hardware color map, as discussed in Section 9.1.8. Also, look at the viewer applications on the CD-ROM.

### 10.1.6     Smooth Shading and PostScript

If you produce a hardcopy image on a PostScript device of a scene that contains color-interpolated objects (such as Gouraud-shaded polygons), you may run into PostScript problems. The problem is that PostScript supports only flat shading, where all pixels in an object have the same color. If you try to use PostScript to draw an object where the color changes smoothly across the object, HOOPS must send the object pixel by pixel (as a PostScript image).

Large PostScript images can cause your printer to run out of memory. For example, an scene sent to the printer as a single 8.5- by 11-inch (full-page) 300–dot-per-inch image will consume over 50 megabytes of data (PostScript stores color data in ASCII form). Currently, HOOPS tries to solve this problem by reducing the resolution of smoothly shaded objects. Although it greatly reduces memory requirements, this reduction of resolution causes increased aliasing (also called jaggies — see Section 3.3.3.8 for more information). You can control this reduction in resolution using the "hardcopy resolution" driver option on the PostScript driver. The use of this option is demonstrated by the example program found in the file demo/common/feature/gouhard.c.

Another solution is to use the image driver to create a lower-resolution image, and then to send this image to the PostScript driver. You can even use different resolutions for different objects in a scene, using this technique. See Section 6.2.3 for more information on the image driver.

### 10.1.7    Z-Buffering and PostScript

Another PostScript problem is caused by using the software Z-buffer algorithm or the software frame buffer on a scene that is being printed by a PostScript printer (or other hardcopy driver). Because the Z-buffer algorithm and the software frame buffer send all objects to the printer as pixels (even if they are not smoothly shaded), the use of these options with hardcopy drivers will either consume enormous amounts of memory or cause aliasing problems. To avoid sending geometry to the printer as pixels, you should use the painter's algorithm for hidden-surface removal when printing (using the HC_Set_Rendering_Options command).

## 10.2    Optimization

This section presents a few guidelines to make sure that you are getting maximum performance from HOOPS for your application.

### 10.2.1    2D Scenes

When you are using HOOPS to display 2D data, make sure that your $z$ values are all set to zero. In other words, resist the temptation to use the $z$ value to control which objects appear in front of other objects. Instead, use the commands HC_Bring_To_Front or HC_Set_Priority. When the *z* values of your geometry are all zero, HOOPS recognizes the scene as 2D and switches to a faster mode.

## 10.2.2 Heuristics

There are several options that you can set with the HC_Set_Heuristics command that can greatly speed up display for certain kinds of scenes. For example, when you are displaying a scene that contains only lines, markers, and text, you should turn off hidden surfaces with the "no hidden surfaces" heuristic. If you are sure that your scene contains only convex polygons, you should set the "no concave polygons" heuristic. You can also let HOOPS do backplane culling on polygons if you set the "polygon handedness" heuristic. If you are absolutely sure that every object in your scene is onscreen, you can turn off clipping with the "no clipping" heuristic.

## 10.2.3 Control Update

You can use the HC_Control_Update command to optimize what parts of the output image are redrawn when the graphics database changes. Unfortunately, the use of the HC_Control_Update command can be complicated, since you are assuming all control over what gets redrawn, and when. See Section 8.3.2 for more information.

## 10.2.4 Segment Names

If your application creates data structures that refer to HOOPS segments, it is more efficient to refer to the HOOPS segments by key (using, for example, HC_Open_Segment_By_Key) than to do so by name. Also, if you are creating numerous segments, remember that unnamed segments are generally faster to access than are named segments.

There are a few commands that take a segment name, and that cannot be used with a key. In these few cases, you have two alternatives: you can open the segment using HC_Open_Segment_By_Key and then refer to the current segment as ".", or you can manufacture a segment name from the key. To manufacture a segment name from a key, you create a string of the form "@hex-value" — an at sign followed by the ASCII representation of the hexadecimal value of the key. See Section 4.2.5.4 for more information.

## 10.2.5        Pipeline Stalls

The arrangement of subsegments can affect rendering speed dramatically because of *pipeline stalls*. Most high-performance graphics hardware is arranged in a pipeline — drawing commands enter one end of the pipeline and pop out the other, with multiple commands being processed at the same time. Some graphics commands need to reconfigure the pipeline, and so require the pipeline to empty, reconfigure, and then fill back up. The commands that cause a pipeline stall depend on the graphics hardware, of course. In general, it is best to group geometry with like attributes as close together as possible.

There is one common, but subtle, pipeline stall that is caused by an optimization that HOOPS performs. HOOPS keeps bounding volumes for segments; when it determines that all the geometry inside a segment lies completely on the screen, it turns off clipping. If your platform does clipping in hardware, turning off clipping can cause a pipeline stall. Sometimes, unfortunately, a pipeline stall can happen even when all the geometry in a scene is completely onscreen.

The problem is caused by geometry that is *transform dependent*, such as text, images, and grids. HOOPS cannot compute an accurate bounding volume for transform-dependent geometry, because that geometry's size in object space is dependent on the complete object-to-screen transformation, which HOOPS does not know when the geometry is inserted. Because HOOPS cannot compute an accurate bounding volume for a segment containing such geometry, it also cannot compute an accurate bounding volume for that segment's parent, or for any other segment above the geometry in the segment tree. HOOPS will draw any segment that has an inaccurate bounding volume with clipping turned on (because it does not know whether clipping is required).

One way to avoid excessive pipeline stalls in a scene that contains transform-dependent geometry is to put all the transform-dependent geometry in the tree first. Consider the segment hierarchy in Figure 10.3.

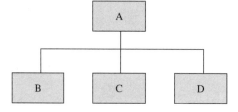

**Figure 10.3**        Graphics database that contains transform-dependent geometry.

If segment B contains transform-dependent geometry and segments C and D contain geometry that is completely onscreen, then segments A and B will be drawn with clipping turned on, and C and D will be drawn with clipping turned off. Turning off clipping will cause a pipeline stall between segments B and C. If, instead, the transform-dependent geometry is in segment C, then you will have a pipeline stall between segments A and B, between segments B and C, and between segments C and D. Thus, by creating segments that contain transform dependent-geometry first, you can avoid extra pipeline stalls.

### 10.2.6 Rendering Algorithms

If your platform has a hardware Z-buffer, then "hardware Z-buffer" will normally be the fastest hidden-surface algorithm. If your platform does not have special hardware, however, the default rendering algorithm is the painter's algorithm. In most cases, the software Z-buffer will be much faster. The only problems with the software Z-buffer algorithm is that it uses more memory, and the scene appears all at once after HOOPS is done drawing, rather than appearing one polygon at a time (as it does with the painter's algorithm). The pause before display with the Z-buffer algorithm can be disconcerting, unless your application displays an activity indicator to the user while the scene is being rendered.

If your application does not need to use a hidden-surface algorithm, you can still gain performance by enabling the "technology = software frame buffer" rendering option. This option tells HOOPS to render everything into a frame buffer in main memory, and then to transfer the image to the display frame buffer all at once. This option can speed up rendering considerably, especially on systems such Microsoft Windows and X11, where calls to display each primitive are relatively expensive. Note that you would normally use the "technology = software frame buffer" rendering option only when the "no hidden surfaces" heuristic also is specified. See Section 4.4.2.4 for more information.

### 10.2.7 Tri-Strip Length

Shells and meshes are converted by HOOPS into strips of connected triangles, called *tri-strips*. Some hardware platforms can render tri-strips directly. On these platforms, rendering time is directly affected by the length of the tri-strips formed by HOOPS. For example, in a shell containing a dozen triangular faces, in the worst case, each tri-strip contains a single triangle, resulting in 12 tri-strips. In the best case, HOOPS will be able to create a single tri-strip containing all 12 triangles. The latter case is usually much faster to render.

Note that, on some platforms — especially those without hardware acceleration — tri-strips are turned into individual triangles before they are rendered, so tri-strip length is irrelevant.

The simplest way to optimize tri-strip length is to use a mesh, instead of a shell. If you must use a shell, you can affect what the tri-strip length is by how you specify the shell. A simple reorganization of your shell data can result in a significant speedup in rendering time. The problems to avoid in defining shells are redundant vertices, nonuniform face orientation, and bad face–vertex ordering.

**10.2.7.1**　**Redundant vertices.** A shell consists of a list of vertices and a list of faces. The face list consists of a list of indices into the vertex list. If two faces share a common edge (which is common in shells), then these two faces should share some of their vertices in the vertex list. For example, a shell representing a cube should be defined with a vertex list containing eight vertices and a face list containing six faces, with each vertex shared by three different faces.

Of course, sharing of vertices is not required. It is perfectly legal to define a cube by specifying the four vertices for each face separately. In such a definition for a cube, the vertex list would contain four vertices for each face, or 24 vertices instead of eight. In addition to wasting space, failing to share vertices makes it much harder for HOOPS to form long triangle strips, and thus can slow down rendering significantly.

Thus, you should share vertices whenever possible. HOOPS also provides a command, HC_Compute_Minimized_Shell, that removes redundant vertices from the vertex list. There is an example of how to use the command HC_Compute_Minimized_Shell in Section 6.7.

**10.2.7.2**　**Face orientation.** A shell consists of a vertex list and a face list, where the face list is a list of indices into the vertex list. For any face in the face list, the vertices can be listed either in clockwise or in counterclockwise order, as viewed from the front of the face (Figure 10.4).

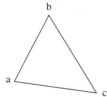

Clockwise: a, b, c

Counterclockwise: a, c, b

**Figure 10.4**   Face orientation.

The orientation in which you choose to enter the faces is not important; however, the faces in a single shell should all have the same orientation. The main reason for this requirement is performance — HOOPS can create much longer tri-strips if all faces in a shell have the same orientation.

A second reason that all faces should have the same orientation is so that HOOPS can use backplane culling to throw away back-facing faces, using the "backplane cull" heuristic, which is on by default (see the HC_Set_Heuristics command for more information).

If the faces in a shell do not all have the same orientation, HOOPS will issue a warning. Note that some applications that produce tri-strips generate the tri-strips with alternate faces oriented in opposite directions — and that is the absolutely worst case with respect to maximizing tri-strip length.

There is a program called fixshell.c in the demo/common/hmf directory of the HOOPS distribution that shows how to reorient the faces of a shell. This program was written because earlier versions of HOOPS did not require faces to be oriented uniformly; consequently, many HOOPS metafiles were produced with bad shell-face orientations. The fixshell.c program reads in a metafile, fixes all the shells, and writes out a new metafile. That is why this program is located in the hmf (HOOPS metafile) directory.

**10.2.7.3**   **Face–vertex orientation.** Even if you have no redundant vertices and use correct face orientation, the order in which you specify the vertices in the face list can affect the length of the tri-strips that HOOPS will generate from a shell. Consider the shell in Figure 10.5, which consists of two quadrilateral faces.

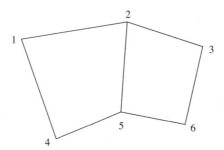

**Figure 10.5**    Face–vertex orientation.

The vertex numbering in Figure 10.5 follows the order in which the vertices appear in the vertex list for the shell. In the face list, the first face is defined as 4, 1, 2, 5, and the second face is defined as 2, 3, 6, 5. Unfortunately, when the second face is defined in this manner, HOOPS creates two tri-strips, instead of one, for this shell (even though there are no redundant vertices and both faces have the same orientation). If, instead, the second face is specified as 5, 2, 3, 6, then HOOPS can generate a single tri-strip for the entire shell.

HOOPS first splits the faces in a shell into triangles, and then attempts to piece them together into tri-strips. The problem when the second face is specified as 2, 3, 6, 5 is that the second face is split between vertices 3 and 5, and the first face is split between vertices 1 and 5. These faces must be split in the same way so they can be joined into a single tri-strip. HOOPS performs triangulation of a convex polygon by taking the points in the following order: first, second, final, third, next-to-final, fourth, and so on.

If your platform has special hardware for drawing tri-strips and you are concerned about speed, then it might be worthwhile to use the printf driver (which prints out what would be drawn, instead of drawing it) to draw your shells, so that you can manually control the length of the generated tri-strips. See Sections 4.3 and 6.2 for more information on how to use the printf driver.

Of course, for the particular shell in Figure 10.5, the easiest way to maximize tri-strip length is to use a mesh instead of a shell.

**10.2.8    Edge and Marker Lighting**

When shells and meshes are drawn, three different parts get drawn: the faces of the shell or mesh, the edges between the faces, and a marker for each vertex in the shell or mesh. When lighting is enabled (whenever a light is included in your scene), lighting calculations such as highlights and smooth shading are done on all three parts. These extra computations can slow down rendering speed significantly.

One solution is to turn off the rendering of markers and edges (using HC_Set_Visibility). People often turn off markers because they do not want markers displayed for shells or meshes.

If you do want markers to be visible, you can turn off the lighting calculation for the markers (which calculation is expensive and rarely useful), with the following command:

```
HC_Set_Visibility("lighting = (markers=off)");
```

This command leaves the markers themselves visible, but makes them invisible to any lights. Thus, the lighting calculations are not done on the markers.

Unlike markers, unless edges are explicitly set to a color different from that of faces, it impossible to tell whether edges are on or off. Thus, you might be paying to render edges that make no visible difference in your final rendered image. In this case, you should turn off the visibility of edges with the command

```
HC_Set_Visibility("markers=edges=off");
```

You can also turn off the lighting calculation for edges. This setting is especially useful when you want the edges of a polygon to be a single color (for example, black), but still want to do a lighting calculation on the faces:

```
HC_Set_Visibility("lighting = (edges=off)");
```

In other cases, you might want edges to be lit, but you can save time by avoiding lighting interpolation across the edge with the following command:

```
HC_Set_Rendering_Options(
    "lighting interpolation = (edges=off)");
```

Likewise, you can turn off color interpolation and color-index interpolation with the following commands:

```
HC_Set_Rendering_Options(
    "color interpolation = (edges=off)");
HC_Set_Rendering_Options(
    "color index interpolation = (edges=off)");
```

In general, when you are drawing lit shells or meshes, you can always save time by turning off unnecessary or unwanted lighting calculations. See the commands

HC_Set_Visibility and HC_Set_Rendering_Options in the *HOOPS Reference Manual* for more information.

### 10.2.9    Bounding Volumes

By default, HOOPS computes and retains bounding volumes for all segments in the graphics database. Bounding volumes allow HOOPS to avoid drawing geometry that lies entirely offscreen, and to avoid performing clipping on geometry that lies entirely onscreen.

In HOOPS, bounding volumes only grow. As you add new geometry to a segment, the bounding volume grows automatically. But when you delete geometry from a segment, the bounding volume does not shrink. This behavior can cause geometry to be drawn unnecessarily (even when the geometry lies entirely offscreen). You can force HOOPS to recompute a bounding volume with the HC_Control_Update command. For example, to force the bounding volume to be recomputed on the current segment, use the following command:

```
HC_Control_Update(".", "compute bounding volume");
```

A second problem can occur because bounding volumes cannot be computed accurately for segments that contain transform-dependent geometry, such as text, images, or grids. *Transform-dependent* geometry is discussed in Section 10.2.5. Any segment containing transform-dependent geometry always will be rendered, even if it lies entirely offscreen, and always will have clipping done, even if it lies entirely onscreen.

HOOPS computes only a single bounding volume per segment, so, if a segment that contains transform-dependent geometry also contains other kinds of geometry, such as polygons, then the other geometry will suffer the same problem as the one that plagues the transform-dependent geometry. As a result, if the polygons lie entirely offscreen, they will be rendered anyway; if they lie entirely onscreen, they will be clipped unnecessarily. Thus, it can be to your advantage to separate into two separate sibling segments transform-dependent geometry and other kinds of geometry.

## 10.3    Debugging

HOOPS metafiles are useful for tracking down bugs. If you have an application that produces an incorrect image, you can write out a metafile to examine the exact state of the HOOPS database. If your application has not put the correct data into the database, then you can use the metafile to help find the problem. If the database is correct, but the image is wrong, then you must have found a bug in HOOPS (oh dear!). In that case, you can submit the metafile along with your bug report (rather than sending your entire application) to help Autodesk track down and fix the bug. See Section 6.3 for more information.

As an alternative to writing out a metafile, you can use the "code generation" system option. This option causes HOOPS to generate a C program containing every HOOPS call that your program makes. You can send this C program to Autodesk to help track down a bug in HOOPS. See the command HC_Define_System_Options for more information.

Another system option that is useful for debugging is "continuous updates". This option causes HOOPS to update the display after every HOOPS command that could have changed the output image. It is particularly useful when you are running a graphics application under a debugger, because it ensures that, when the debugger stops at a breakpoint, the displayed HOOPS image will reflect accurately the current state of the graphics database.

## 10.4      Error Handling

When HOOPS encounters an error, it prints an error message by calling the HC_Report_Error command. In a real application, you normally do not want HOOPS error messages to be sent to the user. Instead, you should install your own error-handler routine, using the HC_Define_Error_Handler command. See the HC_Define_Error_Handler command in the *HOOPS Reference Manual* for more information.

Sometimes, you can use a HOOPS error handler to gain efficiency. For example, the fixshell.c program in the demo/common/hmf directory finds shells that do not have a consistent face orientation. Rather than explicitly check each shell for face orientation, this program sets an error handler. When HOOPS finds a shell with inconsistent face orientation, it signals an error. This error is caught by a routine installed using the HC_Define_Error_Handler command; the installed error handler fixes the face orientation of the offending shell, and proceeds.

Another (dangerous) alternative is to turn off HOOPS error reporting entirely using the HC_Define_System_Options command. You can turn off different classes of error warnings (fatal errors, errors, warnings, and info) separately. You can also (to gain a small amount of performance) turn off the sanity checking that HOOPS does using the "no sanity checking" system option.

## 10.5    Demo Programs

The HOOPS CD-ROM contains programs that demonstrate various features of HOOPS. These programs are all written in C, but they can be easily adapted to C++. This section describes each program.

### 10.5.1    Directory demo/common/air

The demo/common/air directory contains programs that demonstrate the radiosity and ray-tracing capabilities of the HOOPS advanced interactive renderer (A.I.R.) product. Note that A.I.R. is a third-party renderer, and is not included with this book (or with the version of HOOPS on the CD-ROM).

### 10.5.2    Directory demo/common/cookbook

The demo/common/cookbook directory contains the example programs from the HOOPS cookbook. The text for the cookbook is included on the CD-ROM in PostScript format.

**10.5.2.1**    **Assodata.** The assodata program demonstrates how to associate application data with HOOPS segments. An outline map of the United States is displayed, with selected cities represented by markers. Each marker is in its own segment and has an associated pointer that refers to data that are specific to the city. When the user selects a marker, the data for the city are displayed.

**10.5.2.2**    **Camcoord.** The camcoord program demonstrates how to set camera coordinates. Four perspective views of a Volkswagen Beetle are displayed, each in a separate HOOPS window. Each HOOPS window has a different physical size on the display screen. The mapping of camera–world space to window space and the notion of preserving aspect ratio of world space are illustrated.

**10.5.2.3**    **Camproje.** The camproje program demonstrates the different camera projections. It shows three different views of a champagne glass, each in a separate HOOPS window. The windows each have the same size, but each uses a different camera projection: perspective, orthographic, and stretched.

**10.5.2.4**    **Dialobox.** The dialobox program demonstrates the use of HOOPS windows and geometry to create a user-interface dialog gadget — in this case, a color selector. This example is written entirely in HOOPS, without any calls to a window system (such as Motif or MFC).

**10.5.2.5**     **Highligh.** The highligh program demonstrates the use of the "quick moves" heuristic to eliminate screen redraws when selected geometry is highlighted. It also shows the use of information returned by a selection event to retrieve data for the selected geometric primitive.

**10.5.2.6**     **Interpol.** The interpol program demonstrates how to display data as color on the surface of shells and meshes for a visualization application. The "color interpolation" and "color index interpolation" rendering options are used to map user data to geometry, and to display information as color gradients across the geometry's surface.

**10.5.2.7**     **Perbench.** The perbench program is a performance benchmark. It orbits the camera around an object multiple times, and computes the update rate.

**10.5.2.8**     **Posthard.** The posthard program demonstrates how to use PostScript hardcopy. It creates some geometry, and then generates PostScript hardcopy output.

**10.5.2.9**     **Rubbebox.** The rubbebox program demonstrates a common technique called a *rubberband box*. When the mouse button is pressed and held down, an initial point is set. Further mouse movement results in a box being drawn from the initial point to the current mouse position. When the mouse button is released, the program uses the initial and final mouse positions to draw a polygon. This program shows the use of the "quick moves" heuristic to provide interactive feedback to the user without redrawing the entire screen. This program also demonstrates the HOOPS event queue, and shows how to branch on the state of the pointer device (mouse down, mouse moved, and mouse up).

**10.5.2.10**     **Shadows.** The shadows program demonstrates the radiosity and ray-tracing rendering options. This program will work only if you have the optional HOOPS A.I.R. rendering package.

**10.5.2.11**     **Simulati.** The simulati program demonstrates how to give real-time visual feedback on the state of a graphically represented system. A map of the United States is displayed, with lines representing a computer network connecting cities. The color of the lines changes over time to show changing network traffic.

**10.5.2.12**     **Sixurns.** The sixurns program uses rendering options and heuristics to demonstrate wireframe display, Gouraud shading, Phong shading, flat shading, hidden-line elimination, and color interpolation.

**10.5.2.13**    **Stretcam.** The stretcam program demonstrates the use of stretched camera projections. A double-ended arrow spanning $-1.0$ to $1.0$ in the $x$ direction is created, and is stored in the include library. The arrow is then included in three different views, in three HOOPS subwindows. One view is not modified. The second view has a scale operation applied to it. The third view uses a stretched camera projection.

**10.5.2.14**    **Surffunc.** The surffunc program demonstrates how to display a parametrically generated surface with a quadrilateral mesh.

**10.5.2.15**    **Trangeom.** The trangeom program demonstrates the use of database queries to transform geometry. Given a collection of polygons (taken from the champagn.hmf metafile), this program searches the collection, computes the scale factor needed to transform the geometry to fit into a unit cube, and adds a rotation to produce a modeling matrix. The program then searches the database and transforms each point in any geometry by multiplying by the computed modeling matrix.

This example is pedagogical, as you would never apply a scale and rotate in this fashion. The program is a good example of database query and geometric transformation. It is not intended to be an viable approach for transforming geometry.

**10.5.2.16**    **Twoshell.** The twoshell program demonstrates two methods that take an arbitrary set of points and fit a shell to them. The first method passes the points to the HC_Compute_Convex_Hull command, and then takes the returned information and creates a shell. The second method computes the shell manually so that it can leave an open face (HC_Compute_Convex_Hull generates only closed polyhedra).

**10.5.2.17**    **ViHilite.** The ViHilite program demonstrates multiple views and highlighting. Four views of an object are displayed in four HOOPS subwindows. As the user moves the mouse cursor into each window, the object in the window is high-lighted, and the previously highlighted object is returned to normal. This program shows the use of HOOPS windows, events (mouse up and moved), highlighting, and attribute lock.

**10.5.2.18**    **X11WinID.** The X11WinID program demonstrates how to create an X11 window with the Xlib library, and then to pass the object handle for this window into HOOPS via the "use window id" driver option. HOOPS then displays all output in the X11 window, rather than creating one of its own windows. This program is a good example for UNIX applications that are being written at the Xlib level, rather than with Xt (the X toolkit) or Motif.

### 10.5.3      Directory demo/common/feature

The demo/common/feature directory contains simple programs that demonstrate one or more of the features of HOOPS. Similar programs are found in the demo/common/misc directory.

**10.5.3.1**      **Capjoin.** The capjoin program demonstrates the different kinds of end treatments and line joins (beveled, rounded, squared, mitered, and so on) available for polylines and lines in HOOPS.

**10.5.3.2**      **Diffview.** The diffview program demonstrates how to use HOOPS I.M. to set a callback on a segment. This callback checks a user-index value during database traversal, sets a color based on this index, then draws the segment. In particular, the notion of view-dependent attributes is illustrated.

**10.5.3.3**      **Flylogo.** The flylogo program shows how to use the HOOPS text commands to convert a text string with a particular font into a HOOPS shell, to add material properties, and to animate the resulting geometry. The result is a flying logo.

**10.5.3.4**      **Fonteng.** The fonteng program demonstrates the abilities of the BitStream outline font engine embedded in HOOPS 4.1. It displays various text strings in different states of 3D transformations. Pressing the mouse button or a key on the keyboard causes the text font to change.

**10.5.3.5**      **Gouhard.** The gouhard program demonstrates use of the "hardcopy resolution" driver option to control the resolution of hardcopy output. This driver option is used to help solve a problem with hardcopy of Gouraud shaded images (this problem was discussed in Section 10.1.6). Note that this HOOPS driver option applies to only certain drivers — namely, hardcopy drivers for raster devices (such as laser printers), and some file-output drivers (such as the CGM driver)

**10.5.3.6**      **Texture.** The texture program demonstrates texture maps and the rendering options that apply to texture-mapped surfaces. It also implements a completely HOOPS-based user interface, with radio buttons and other gadgets.

## 10.5.4    Directory demo/common/gifrdr

The demo/common/gifrdr directory contains source code for a routine that reads image files in GIF format and converts them into HOOPS images. This routine enables the display of GIF images with HOOPS, as well as their use for texture mapping HOOPS shells and meshes. This routine is used by several of the example programs in Chapters 5, 6, and 9.

## 10.5.5    Directory demo/common/hmf

The demo/common/hmf directory mainly contains HOOPS metafiles. It also contains two programs: fixshell and setmeta.

### 10.5.5.1    **Fixshell.** In HOOPS, all the faces in a shell are required to have the same orientation (either right-handed or left-handed). The orientation of a polygon is defined in Section 3.3.3.6. The fixshell program reads a HOOPS metafile and displays it. If the metafile contains any shells that have nonuniform orientation, the program corrects the problem and outputs a new metafile. This program also demonstrates how to write an error handler.

### 10.5.5.2    **Setmeta.** The setmeta program reads in a HOOPS metafile and finds the appropriate type of bounding volume to use when you are setting a camera to view the entire contents of the file.

## 10.5.6    Directory demo/common/im

The demo/common/im directory contains several programs that illustrate how to use the HOOPS intermediate mode (I.M.) commands. HOOPS I.M. allows the user to associate callback routines with either a segment or a specific type of primitive within a segment (using the HC_Set_Callback command). During traversal of the graphics database, when a callback routine is encountered, the callback routine is invoked.

Although HOOPS I.M. is enabled in the version of HOOPS contained on the CD-ROM, it is not specifically covered in this book. For more information, refer to the section on HOOPS I.M. in the *HOOPS Reference Manual,* or examine these example programs.

### 10.5.6.1    **Clip.** The clip program demonstrates how to set a callback at the "draw dc" (drawing-device-coordinates) level, to query a user index value, and to set clipping limits based on the value found.

**10.5.6.2**     **Doily.** The doily program demonstrates how the user can create arbitrary face patterns using the HOOPS I.M. callback "draw dc face". It inserts a polygon, and defines a callback routine that will create a face pattern on the polygon.

**10.5.6.3**     **Lines.** The lines program demonstrates how the user can create arbitrary marker symbols and line patterns using the HOOPS I.M. callbacks "draw dc marker" and "draw dc lines".

**10.5.6.4**     **Objclip.** The objclip program demonstrates how the user can dynamically modify the clip limits that HOOPS uses to render a segment.

**10.5.6.5**     **Tracks.** The tracks program demonstrates how the user can define new kinds of geometry. In this case, the user defines a railroad-track primitive. The mechanisms used are similar to the ones used to define new line styles.

**10.5.6.6**     **Tristrip.** The tristrip program demonstrates the "draw 3D tristrip" callback for shells and meshes. The urn metafile is read into the program, and several views created. In each view, a different draw 3D tri-strip callback is set. Each produces different renderings of the urn's geometry.

**10.5.7**     **Directory demo/motif/simple**

The demo/motif/simple directory contains a simple version of the viewer application, using a Motif user interface. The main purpose of this example is to demonstrate the HOOPS Motif widget, which creates a window for HOOPS output. The program creates an instance of the widget within a Motif-based user interface (widget hierarchy), and associates callback routines with the HOOPS widget to process mouse actions.

**10.5.8**     **Directory demo/motif/viewer**

The demo/motif/viewer directory contains the source code for a complete viewer application, written with a Motif user interface. The program uses the principles demonstrated in the demo/motif/simple application to implement a HOOPS segment-tree browser and attribute editor. This example is useful as a standalone application for viewing HOOPS models, or as the basis of other applications.

### 10.5.9    Directory demo/mfc/simple

The demo/mfc/simple directory contains a simple version of the viewer application, written in MFC. The program creates an output window using MFC, and passes the window's handle to HOOPS. HOOPS then uses this window to display its output. The program also shows how to integrate graphics routines into the event loop.

### 10.5.10    Directory demo/mfc/viewer

The demo/mfc/viewer directory contains the source code for a complete viewer application, written with an MFC user interface. The program uses the principles demonstrated in the demo/mfc/simple application to implement a HOOPS segment-tree browser and attribute editor. This example is useful as a standalone application for viewing HOOPS models, or as the basis of other applications.

### 10.5.11    Directory demo/win32/win32wid

The demo/win32/win32wid directory contains a simple version of the viewer application, written with a Microsoft Windows user interface (but without MFC). The program shows how to create a Windows output window, and to pass the window's handle to HOOPS. HOOPS then uses this window to display its output. The program also shows how to integrate graphics routines into the event loop and to associate them with pull-down menus.

### 10.5.12    Directory demo/win32/fortran

The demo/win32/fortran directory contains FORTRAN versions of the HOOPS tutorial examples.

### 10.5.13    Directory demo/win32/misc

The demo/win32/misc directory contains programs that demonstrate how to use HOOPS with 32-bit Windows applications.

#### 10.5.13.1

**Sharepal.** The sharepal program demonstrates how to share a color palette between a HOOPS window and a regular Windows window. The first window is a Windows window, which displays the color map. As each HOOPS window is opened, it allocates 16 colors out of the same color map. These entries appear in the first window as the system updates them. The user can open up to seven

HOOPS windows, in addition to the Windows window. Note that, because only 16 colors are allocated per window, metafiles that contain lights or perform smooth shading will not work with this demo.

**10.5.13.2**      **Twowins.** This program demonstrates how to have two Microsoft Windows windows display two HOOPS pictures using the same palette with the software frame buffer.

## 10.5.14      Directory demo/win32/unixport

The demo/win32/unixport directory contains utility routines to help you port UNIX (and many DOS) C and C++ programs to Microsoft Windows.

**10.5.14.1**      **W32cmain.** The w32cmain file contains routines that allow programs that were developed under UNIX or DOS to run under Microsoft Windows. UNIX and DOS programs define a function called "main" that is called by the operating system, but Windows programs require a function called "WinMain" to be defined instead. This file defines a WinMain function that performs initialization, and then calls your application's main function. It also defines a simple printf function, which displays its output in a dialog box.

If you want to run the example programs in this book under Windows or Windows NT, you must compile this file and link it in with them.

## 10.5.15      Directory demo/common/install

The demo/common/install directory is so named because the UNIX installation script automatically installs and runs the example programs in this directory (to verify that HOOPS was installed properly). For other platforms, you can compile and run the programs manually.

**10.5.15.1**      **3dselect.** The 3dselect program demonstrates how to build a HOOPS-based user interface, how to use the HC_Set_User_Value command, and how to perform picking (3D selection). The user interface includes push buttons that invoke action routines and move the camera.

**10.5.15.2**      **Crayola.** The crayola program builds a model of a box of Crayola crayons. This example (graphically) demonstrates how colors can be set in HOOPS by name. The crayon box and 64 crayons, each with its own color, are modeled in this program.

**10.5.15.3**    **Lookat.** The lookat program demonstrates different lighting and modeling attributes and their visual effect on a mesh. The user does all input by pressing keys on the keyboard. To see what the different possibilities are, examine the switch statement in the main event loop.

**10.5.15.4**    **Popup.** The popup program demonstrates how to create a popup menu using a HOOPS-based user interface.

**10.5.15.5**    **Text.** The text program demonstrates different text attributes and their effect on a text string.

**10.5.15.6**    **Track.** The track program accepts successive mousedown events and draws a polyline connecting them.

**10.5.16**    **Directory demo/common/misc**

The demo/common/misc directory contains programs that demonstrate specific features of HOOPS. The difference between the misc directory and the feature directory is that the feature directory normally contains programs that demonstrate features of HOOPS that are new in the current release. The misc directory contains programs that were previously in the feature directory, but were moved here because they now apply to a previous release.

**10.5.16.1**    **Bvolume.** The bvolume program demonstrates how bounding volumes optimize display speed when you have a large database but display only a part of it. The program displays a grid of boxes, with each box in its own segment. The user can zoom in or out on the grid by pressing the "i" (for in) or "o" (for out) keys on the keyboard. Holding a mouse button down and dragging dollies the camera.

HOOPS stores bounding-volume information for each segment and can test a segment's bounding volume against the clip region for the screen and decide whether or not an object needs to be drawn. As a result, when the camera is zoomed in on the grid, the dolly speed becomes faster, because less geometry requires drawing.

**10.5.16.2**    **Depthcue.** The depthcue program demonstrates the "atmospheric attenuation" rendering option and this option's effect on text, lines, markers, and shells. You can use atmospheric attenuation to provide depth cues on geometry, and to simulate fog.

**10.5.16.3**     **Minshell.** The minshell program demonstrates how to take a collection of polygons, to turn them into a shell, and then to optimize the shell. The program reads in a HOOPS metafile and searches it for polygons. Any polygons that are found are inserted into a HOOPS shell; then, the shell is optimized with the HC_Compute_Minimized_Shell command. The resulting optimized shell is written to a new HOOPS metafile. A similar program (written in C++) is discussed in Section 6.7.

**10.5.16.4**     **Picking.** The picking program demonstrates two common variations on hit testing (object selection), and shows how to implement them using HOOPS. A polygonal aperture selection (also called a lasso pick) selects everything inside of a polygon. A polyline crossing selection (also called a fence pick) selects everything that intersects a polyline. This program uses the HC_Compute_Selection command.

**10.5.16.5**     **Rings.** The rings program demonstrates how to map a parametrically generated surface (in this program, a torus) into a HOOPS shell. It also shows the use of inclusion to produce three instances of the same data.

**10.5.16.6**     **Userfpat.** The userfpat program demonstrates user-defined face and window patterns. The HOOPS I.M. "draw dc face", "draw dc colorized face", and "draw window" callbacks are demonstrated.

**10.5.16.7**     **Xpimage.** The xpimage program demonstrates the use of alpha blending to display nonrectangular images. You can display an image with an arbitrary shape by placing it into a rectangular image, and then using alpha blending to let the background scene show through.

**10.5.17**     **Directory demo/common/test**

The demo/common/test directory contains programs used by the HOOPS Q-A team. These programs are not meant to be examples of how to use HOOPS in an application; they are included because they are useful when you are debugging applications or are trying to gather information on the graphics services available on a particular hardware platform. They will also be of use to developers who are writing HDI drivers.

**10.5.17.1**     **Allfonts.** The allfonts program searches for and displays all the available system-level fonts on a particular hardware platform.

**10.5.17.2**     **Attrtest.** The attrtest program test various combinations of attributes for each kind of HOOPS primitive.

**10.5.17.3**     **Bug.** The bug file is a template for submitting HOOPS bugs to the Autodesk OEM Technical Support staff.

**10.5.17.4**     **Line.** The line program is used for driver testing. It inserts a line and displays that line. This program is usually the first one that HDI driver writers execute when they try out their newly written HOOPS driver.

**10.5.17.5**     **Nmesh.** The nmesh program demonstrates various attribute settings on a mesh, including lighting, visibility, color interpolation, and color-index interpolation. This program displays a parametrically generated surface mapped to a quadri-lateral mesh. The user can turn on and off the various attributes by pressing keys on the keyboard. To see what is possible, you should examine the switch state-ment in the main event loop.

**10.5.17.6**     **Perftest.** The perftest program contains a performance-testing suite for HOOPS. You can use it to determine the raw drawing speed of HOOPS primitives on various platforms. The HOOPS developers used this program extensively to optimize the performance of HOOPS 4.1.

**10.5.17.7**     **Qmoves.** The qmoves program tests the "quick moves" heuristic on each HOOPS primitive.

**10.5.17.8**     **Rendtest.** The rendtest program tests various rendering options.

**10.5.17.9**     **Stdtest.** The stdtest program is the standard test suite for HOOPS primitives and attributes.

**10.5.17.10**     **Waytest.** The waytest program tests the interaction between the "technology = software frame buffer" rendering option and the "hidden surface removal algorithm = software z-buffer" rendering option. All combinations are tested.

**10.5.18**     **Directory demo/common/tutorial**

The demo/common/tutorial directory contains C language source code for the programs that appear in the HOOPS Tutorial. The Tutorial is available on the CD-ROM in PostScript form.

**10.5.19**   **Directory demo/common/textuniv**

The demo/common/textuniv directory contains selected GIF image files from the Autodesk "Texture Universe" CD-ROM. They are provided with HOOPS to demonstrate the use of images for texture mapping. Use of images in GIF format in a HOOPS program requires use of the GIF reader routine found in demo/common/gifrdr (or of a similar routine). The use of these images for texture mapping is demonstrated in Section 9.2.

# A Short History of HOOPS

In 1980, at the Cornell Engineering School, Donald Greenberg and John Dill start one of the first undergraduate computer-graphics laboratories in the United States. The Computer Aided Design Instructional Facility (CADIF) is funded by the National Science Foundation. The charter of the laboratory is novel: to build software that students and other researchers will use to solve real-world engineering problems.

Garry Wiegand is hired as the first manager of CADIF. These are the early days of computer graphics. The group buys Grinnell equipment because the Vice President of Software for Grinnell is a student at Cornell.

Meanwhile, Gary Wayne graduates from Cornell and is hired by the university to teach engineering design. He starts using CADIF's graphics equipment. Gary Wayne hires Carl Bass to put together software to demonstrate drawing techniques (such as perspective projection) using computer graphics.

Progress is hampered by the poor state of graphics software. Existing software is a hodge-podge of libraries supplied by the hardware manufacturers. CADIF has many different kinds of donated equipment, so portability is a big problem.

In 1982, Garry Wiegand forms a consulting company and obtains a contract to write a graphics library. It runs on graphics equipment manufactured by Sanders, and is called Sanders Kernel. The company is called Flying Moose Systems and Graphics (which is why there is a color called *moose brown* in the HOOPS color set). Carl Bass joins Wiegand soon thereafter.

In May 1985, Wiegand and Bass incorporate Flying Moose Systems and Graphics with $155 in cash. They begin writing the HOOPS reference manual; in a break from normal software-development practice, they design the library before they start coding it. They design HOOPS to be easy to use and portable, so that it will run on a variety of graphics hardware. They choose the name *HOOPS* because Bass is a basketball fan, and they fit an acronym to it (Hierarchical Object-Oriented Picture System). Other names they consider include Lighthouse and Exegesis (which means "wherein what is obscure is made plain").

In April 1986, Gary Wayne joins Wiegand and Bass as Executive Vice President (in charge of everything other than writing software).

In July 1986, Flying Moose takes HOOPS to SIGGRAPH. The reference manual is finished, but the software is "demoware". They demonstrate hidden-surface removal, but it will be another six months before they finish writing the code. The software already runs on four different platforms, including VMS and UNIX.

HOOPS is competing against a rash of standards, including the SIGGRAPH Core standard, GKS (an international standard), and PHIGS (not yet a standard, but being developed). No one else is foolish enough to compete against all these standards, but existing standards are hard to use and are inadequate for writing real applications.

In reality, most companies have been writing their own graphics libraries from scratch. This situation is like the old days when companies wrote their own compilers. It will be over six months before the first real sale of HOOPS.

If this fledgling company had stopped to analyze the market (or had tried to get outside funding), they probably would not have gone forward. PHIGS soon becomes a standard, and over $150 million will be spent to promote it. PHIGS is adopted by ISO, ANSI, all major hardware companies, and many software vendors, and will be specified as a requirement for use in graphics applications by the U.S. government. What hope do three guys with $155 have against that? You might have a better mousetrap, but the world has to find your door before it can beat a path to you.

What Flying Moose does have is the knowledge that PHIGS does not meet customer needs, and HOOPS does. PHIGS suffers from being designed by committee — even worse, a committee made up primarily of hardware manufacturers, rather than of the software developers who will be using the end result. Because no manufacturer wants PHIGS to run faster on someone else's system than on its own, PHIGS is not allowed to take advantage of any specialized hardware, and so is designed for the lowest-common-denominator graphics hardware. As a result, it does not run particularly well on any platform. Even with all the money spent promoting PHIGS, few applications will ever be released that use it.

In midwinter, someone's car skids on the ice and runs into Wiegand's car. The insurance money keeps the moose flying.

In November 1986, Famotik signs up as the Japanese distributor of HOOPS.

In February 1987, HOOPS has its first customer, DuPont.

In March 1987, on a bet by a graduate student at Cornell, Bass ports HOOPS to a PC running DOS with 640 kilobytes of memory and a 16-color display. At the time, 3D graphics on a PC is mainly a curiosity.

By now, HOOPS runs on almost a dozen platforms, including an IBM mainframe, and is in use by various groups at Cornell.

In July 1987, Flying Moose attends its second SIGGRAPH conference. HOOPS is demonstrated running on a PC with graphics-acceleration hardware by Nth Graphics.

In September 1987, Wiegand, Bass, and Wayne change the name of the company to Ithaca Software (Cornell is located in Ithaca, New York), because they are advised that "a company such as General Motors would have trouble writing a check to any company with such a name." Sure enough, 1 month later, they get a check from Corning Glass, whose purchasing department had held up the payment because of the old name.

As the price of graphics hardware starts to fall, sales start to pick up. The company starts to grow, funded entirely by sales. Its first major customer is VersaCAD, but the honor of being the first software product to be shipped using HOOPS as its graphics engine goes to Solutions 3000, a mechanical CAD product sold by Micro Engineering Solutions.

In May 1990, Ithaca Software moves to California and grows by more than five times in terms of sales (over the previous year). Unlike those of some companies, Ithaca Software's founders realize that they need professional management. They hire Eric Wagner to manage engineering and Glen Vondrick to manage sales — positions that these men still hold as this book is written. Many CADIF engineers, who happen to be graduating from Cornell this spring, join Ithaca Software as the company grows.

A decisive battle in the war against PHIGS also occurs during the fall of 1990, when ComputerVision decides to replace PHIGS with HOOPS in an already-shipping product. When HOOPS 3.0 (the version that replaces PHIGS in the ComputerVision product) ships in 1991, the entire HOOPS engineering team celebrates by going to Hawaii.

In 1992, Ithaca Software is number 170 on the Inc. 500 list of the fastest-growing small companies.

Ithaca Software forms a Technical Advisory Board, which includes Andries van Dam (one of the authors of the standard textbook on computer graphics and of the PHIGS and PHIGS+ standards), Joel Orr (graphics author), and Thomas Atwood (founder of several object-oriented database companies).

By now, most of the original members of the PHIGS committee have stopped using PHIGS, and several have even become HOOPS users.

HOOPS Advanced Interactive Rendering (A.I.R.) adds advanced rendering capabilities to HOOPS, including ray tracing and radiosity. HOOPS Intermediate Mode (I.M.) adds the ability to add new geometric types and low-level control to HOOPS.

In August 1993, Ithaca Software is purchased by Autodesk (at the time, the fifth largest seller of personal-computer software, and the largest vendor of computer-aided–design software) in preparation for the incorporation of HOOPS technology into AutoCAD and other Autodesk products. Ithaca Software remains an independent company, and continues to sell HOOPS on the open market (including selling to competitors of Autodesk). The goal is to establish HOOPS as the de facto standard for writing 3D graphics software.

Even though HOOPS was ported to a personal computer early in its life, because of the performance required for 3D graphics, it has been used mainly on UNIX workstations. By late 1994, this situation has changed. With the possibility of doing real interactive 3D graphics on personal computers, HOOPS is reengineered to be optimized for those platforms, and to run faster in general. Release 4.1 (shipped in October 1995) is an order of magnitude faster than Release 4.0. With Release 4.1, HOOPS on a PC is faster than are many low-level graphics languages on workstations, including OpenGL.

The ability that people now have to run real interactive 3D graphics on a personal computer means that many of them will need a good 3D graphics library to write their applications. This book will help to make HOOPS available to this new audience.

# B   Software Installation

This appendix contains step-by-step directions for installing HOOPS for each of the available platforms. There is one section per platform; it will tell you how to retrieve HOOPS from the supplied media. Once you have installed HOOPS using these notes, you can get further information from the *HOOPS Reference Manual,* which is supplied in an HTML form. The browseable version of the *Reference Manual* is located in the html subdirectory of the HOOPS CD-ROM.

Each HOOPS library comes compiled with the drivers necessary for the particular platform. Inappropriate drivers are not available. For example, attempting to use the Sun XGL driver on Microsoft Windows NT is inappropriate. A mapping of the appropriate drivers to platforms follows:

| Platform | CGM | GL | HPGL | image | MSW | OpenGL | PICT | Post Script | SBX | X11 | XGL |
|----------|-----|-----|------|-------|-----|--------|------|-------------|-----|-----|-----|
| AIX | x | x | x | x | | x | x | x | | x | |
| HP-UX | x | | x | x | | | x | x | x | x | |
| IRIX | x | x | x | x | | x | x | x | | x | |
| Microsoft Windows | x | | x | x | x | x | x | x | | | |
| OpenVMS | x | | x | x | | | x | x | | x | |
| OSF/1 | x | | x | x | | x | x | x | | x | |
| Solaris | x | | x | x | | | x | x | | x | x |
| Sun | x | | x | x | | | x | x | | x | x |

An "x" indicates that the driver is appropriate for the platform. Using a driver with HOOPS is simple. In most cases, all you do is set HOOPS_PICTURE.

# AIX

HOOPS support for AIX systems has been verified on an IBM RISC System/ 6000 POWERstation 550e running Version 3.2.5 of AIX. HOOPS should run on all IBM RISC System/6000 POWERstations running AIX Version 3.2.5 and higher (e.g., AIX 4.1). HOOPS has been verified on the 601 PowerPC microprocessor, with GXT150 2D single-buffered graphics adapter, running AIX 4.1.

To install HOOPS from CD-ROM, you must create a file system where you can mount a CD-ROM.

- If you are using an external CD-ROM drive, be sure the power switch is set to ON.
- Remove the CD-ROM from its plastic case, and place it in the disk caddy.
- Insert the disk caddy into the CD-ROM drive.
- Log in as root.
- Create the CD-ROM file system by entering the following SMIT command:
  ```
  smit cdrfs
  ```
  The screen appears with the following options:
  1. Add a CD-ROM file system
  2. Change/Show characteristics of a file system
  3. Remove a CD-ROM file system

  Select item 1. The Add a CD-ROM File System screen then appears. Then go to first field, DEVICE name. Press F4 to list all available devices. The DEVICE name overlay pops up over the previous screen. Highlight the device name that you wish to use, and press ENTER. Go to second field, Mount Point. Enter the name that you wish to use—for example, /cdrom. Go to the third field, Mount Automatically at System Restart. If you prefer to mount manually, you need to press the Tab Key to indicate "No." For the fourth field, Start Disc Accounting, leave the default choice "No." When you have finished making all changes, click the Do button.
- Press F12 to exit Smit and to revert to a normal, nonroot, login.

Once you have established a file system (e.g., /cdrom), you can use it to access the HOOPS CD-ROM, and to install HOOPS:

```
mount /cdrom
cd /cdrom/install/unix
setup
```

Follow the instructions that you see on the display. The Unix installation script automatically extracts the AIX version of HOOPS, and installs it in a subdirectory of your home directory called hoops-<version>. As installed, the instance of HOOPS in $HOME/hoops-<version> can be used as a personal library. If you wish to use HOOPS as a system library, the installation script allows you to install HOOPS into /usr/lib and /usr/include.

# HP-UX

HOOPS support for HP-UX systems has been verified on HP 9000/735, HP 9000/730, HP 9000/720, HP 9000/715, HP 9000/712, and HP 9000/710 workstations running HP-UX Version 9.05. HOOPS should run on all HP 9000/700 or /800 series workstations running HP-UX 9.05. The file tested.hw (which is included with HOOPS distributions) contains information on the latest status of OS versions. The HP 9000/700 series systems have been tested with and without PowerShade software.

The HP-UX distribution comes on the HOOPS CD-ROM with the rest of the platforms. To install HOOPS on HP-UX, you must have a CD-ROM device on the system. To add a CD-ROM device, use

```
su root
sam
```

- Open the "Disks and File Systems->" menu.

- Open the "CD-ROM, Floppy, and Hard Disks" option. A list of SCSI devices should be displayed, one of which is your CD-ROM drive. Identify your CD-ROM drive by the "Hardware Path" field, which will be in the format "2.0.1.X.0", and by the "Use" field, which will indicate "unused". The "X" represents the SCSI-ID for your CD-ROM drive, and will be different on every system.

- Select (highlight with the mouse) your CD-ROM drive from the list. Select "Add a hard disk drive..." from the "Actions" pull-down menu.

- Select "Set Disk Usage and Options..." from the pop-up menu. Type in the mount directory "/cdrom," and select "OK".

- Select "Modify Defaults..." from the pop-up menu. Select the "Read Only" button; then, select "OK".

- Select Exit SAM.[1]

---

1. You may want to check your /etc/checklist file. It should have a line of the form: /dev/dsk/c201d2s0/cdrom cdfs ro,suid.... If hfs appears in place of cdfs, you should change it to cdfs.

To install HOOPS on HP-UX, you insert the HOOPS CD-ROM into your CD-ROM device and enter

```
su root
mount /cdrom
<revert back to normal login>
cd /cdrom/INSTALL/UNIX²
SETUP.\;1
```

Note: You must cd to where the install script resides on the CD. Once you have invoked the script, you follow its instructions. The Unix installation script automatically extracts the HP-UX version of HOOPS, and installs the latter in a subdirectory of your home directory called hoops-<version>. As installed, the instance of HOOPS in $HOME/hoops-<version> can be used as a personal library. If you wish to use HOOPS as a system library, the installation script allows you to install HOOPS into /usr/lib and /usr/include.

To run the HOOPS demo programs, you must to be running the X11 windowing system. You will also need the unbundled C compiler from HP. (The bundled C compiler is the one that comes free with the machine. The unbundled one costs extra, but you will need it if you want to do any serious program development.)

## IRIX

The Silicon Graphics system support has been verified on Irises running version 5.3 of the IRIX operating system. To determine what version of your operating system you are running, use the following command:

```
uname -a
```

The IRIX distribution comes on the HOOPS CD-ROM with the rest of the platforms. To install on IRIX, you insert the HOOPS CD-ROM into your CD-ROM device and follow these steps. If a CD-ROM drive is connected to your own system, the CD-ROM drive icon on your desktop shows an inserted CD. Otherwise, if the CD-ROM drive is on another system, use the Remote Directory tool in your DeskTop menu bar to locate the /cdrom directory. Once you have

---

2. Currently, HP-UX 9.05 does not support the Rock Ridge extensions for handling CD-ROMs. As such, the directories names and file names appear in uppercase characters (with files having ;1 extensions) on the CD itself; however, once the install script is invoked, it translates the directory and file to conventional Unix names, before copying the data to the user's $HOME directory.

located the /cdrom directory, you simply change to the unix install directory and run the setup shell from that directory:

```
cd/cdrom/install/unix
setup
```

You then follow the instructions. The Unix installation script automatically extracts the IRIX version of HOOPS, and installs the latter in a subdirectory of your home directory called hoops-<version>. As installed, the instance of HOOPS in $HOME/hoops-<version> can be used as a personal library. If you wish to use HOOPS as a system library, the installation script allows you to install HOOPS into /usr/lib and /usr/include.

## Microsoft Windows NT Systems

You will need a system compatible with the Microsoft Windows NT 3.5 operating system that has sufficient memory for program development, as specified by Microsoft. As a rule of thumb, HOOPS development is done on personal computers with any one of Intel Pentium, DEC Alpha, or PowerPC processors; with 32 megabytes of RAM; and with a 1-gigabyte hard disk. HOOPS is compiled such that a floating-point math coprocessor (built in to the CPU or separate) is required.

HOOPS for Microsoft Windows NT is available for the following operating systems and hardware:

| CPU | C | Fortran | Notes |
|---|---|---|---|
| Intel 386 or better | Intel version of Microsoft Visual C++ 4.0 for NT, or Watcom C 10.1 for NT | Microsoft Fortran PowerStation 4.0 for NT | Run under Windows 3.1 using Win32s Version 1.25.124 |
| Alpha AXP | Alpha AXP version of Microsoft Visual C++ 2.0 | | |
| PowerPC 601 | Motorola compiler and SDK supplied by IBM | | |

To install HOOPS on your hard disk, put the CD in the appropriate CD-ROM drive. Choose File-Run from the menu. Specify <drive>:install\nt_<cpu>/setup, and press Enter. Another way to install HOOPS is to run setup.exe using the File

Manager. The installation is menu driven from this point on. Assuming that you have chosen default values for the install options, setup creates a directory structure containing various components of the HOOPS product:

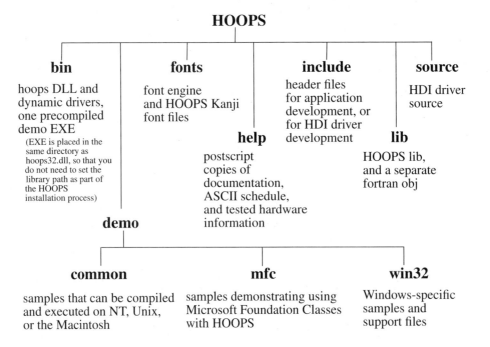

---

## OpenVMS

The OpenVMS VAX system support has been verified on a large variety of color and black-and-white devices using OpenVMS AXP Version 6.1.

Before mounting your HOOPS CD-ROM, you must first know the device name of your CD-ROM drive, and you must have access (authorization) to use the device (see your system manager for assistance). The device name will look something like the "DKA400:" used in the following example, but may be different on every system. The OpenVMS distribution comes on the HOOPS

CD-ROM with the other platforms. To install on OpenVMS, you insert the HOOPS CD-ROM into your CD-ROM device and enter

```
$ mount dka400/over=id/media=cd-rom
   /undefined=stream_lf:2048
$ set default dka400:[install.vms]
$ install
```

The install.com will then lead you through further steps.

If you install HOOPS as a system resource, about 2500 nontemporary blocks will be required on the system disk.

## OSF/1

HOOPS support for DEC Alpha OSF/1 systems has been verified on DEC Alpha 3000 running OSF/1 V3.2. HOOPS also runs on all other DEC Alpha OSF/1 machines.

The OSF/1 distribution comes on the HOOPS CD-ROM with the other platforms. To install on OSF/1, insert the HOOPS CD-ROM into your CD-ROM device, and enter

```
su root
mkdir /cdrom
mount -t cdfs -o noversion /dev/r24c /cdrom3
<revert to normal login>
cd /cdrom/install/unix4
setup
```

Follow the instructions. The Unix installation script automatically extracts the OSF/1 version of HOOPS, and installs the latter in a subdirectory of your home directory called hoops-<version>. As installed, the instance of HOOPS in $HOME/hoops-<version> can be used as a personal library. If you wish to use HOOPS as a system library, the installation script allows you to install HOOPS into /usr/lib and /usr/include.

---

3. The device name for the CD-ROM may differ from "r24c." Please ask your system administrator for the specific device name for your CD-ROM.

4. If you have not built your operating system with the proper CD-ROM utilities, you will see the directory names in uppercase characters and the script will be named SETUP\;1. The script will handle this situation.

To run the HOOPS demo programs, you must be running the X11 windowing system.

## Solaris

This release of HOOPS is compatible with Sun Solaris 2.4, which is OS Version 5.4 with XGL Version 3.1. Sun OS 4.1.x users should obtain a different release of HOOPS. The Solaris and Sun OS releases of HOOPS cannot be interchanged.

HOOPS support for Sun systems has been verified on Sun 4 (SPARC architecture) workstations running Solaris 5.4 with Sun XGL 3.1. HOOPS support with XGL has been verified for the SX and ZX Sun hardware graphics accelerators. The HOOPS X11 Driver supports GX, SX, GS, GT, and ZX hardware.

This HOOPS distribution is built for Solaris 5.4 only. Older versions, such as Solaris 2.0, are not supported. The Solaris distribution comes on the HOOPS CD-ROM with the rest of the platforms. To install HOOPS on Solaris, you insert the HOOPS CD-ROM into your CD-ROM device, and enter

```
su root
mount -F hsfs -o ro /dev/sr0 /cdrom⁵
<revert to normal login>
cd /cdrom/<volume>/install/unix
setup
```

The <volume> on the CD-ROM embodies the release of HOOPS—for example, H41018B, for HOOPS 4.10-18 BETA. You may or may not see the <volume> directory on your CD-ROM, depending on whether or not your workstation is running the Sun volume-manager software. Follow the instructions. The Unix installation script automatically extracts the Solaris version of HOOPS, and installs the latter in a subdirectory of your home directory called hoops-<version>. As installed, the instance of HOOPS in $HOME/hoops-<version> can be used as a personal library. If you wish to use HOOPS as a system library, the installation script allows you to install HOOPS into /usr/lib and /usr/include.

---

5. The HOOPS CD-ROM must be mounted as a High Sierra File System. The device name for the Solaris CD-ROM drive may be different from "sr0." Please ask your system administrator for your specific device name.

To run the HOOPS demo programs, you must be running the X11 windowing system.

# SunOS

This release of HOOPS is compatible with Sun OS 4.1.3. Sun Solaris 2.3 users should obtain a different release of HOOPS. The Solaris and Sun OS releases of HOOPS cannot be interchanged.

HOOPS support for Sun systems has been verified on Sun 4 (SPARC architecture) workstations running Sun OS 4.1.3. HOOPS should run on all Sun 4 (SPARC architecture) workstations running Sun OS Version 4.0.3 or higher. Note that Sun Microsystems no longer supports SunView. Thus, the HOOPS SunView Driver is no longer supplied in HOOPS distributions.

This HOOPS distribution is built for Sun OS Versions 4.0.3 to 4.1.3.

The Sun OS distribution is on the HOOPS CD-ROM with the other platforms. To install on Sun OS, insert the HOOPS CD-ROM into your CD-ROM device, and enter

```
su root
mkdir /cdrom
mount -r -t /hsfs /dev/sr0 /cdrom⁶
<revert back to normal login>
cd /cdrom/<volume>/install/unix
setup
```

The <volume> reflects the release of HOOPS—for example, H41018B, for HOOPS 4.10-18 BETA. You may or may not see the <volume> directory on your CD-ROM, depending on whether or not your workstation is running the Sun volume manager software. Follow the instructions. The Unix installation script automatically extracts the Sun OS version of HOOPS and installs the latter in a subdirectory of your home directory called hoops-<version>. As installed, the instance of HOOPS in $HOME/hoops-<version> can be used as a personal library. If you wish to use HOOPS as a system library, the installation script allows you to install HOOPS into /usr/lib and /usr/include.

---

6. The HOOPS CD-ROM must be mounted as a High Sierra File System. The device name for the Sun's CD-ROM drive may differ from "sr0." Please ask your system administrator for your system's CD-ROM drive device name.

To run the HOOPS demo programs, you must be running either the X11 (OpenWindows) or SunView windowing system. You may encounter permissions problems if you run the HOOPS demo programs and display graphics using the relevant windowing-system environment, if you are not the person who logged in and started that windowing-system environment on your workstation.

# Index

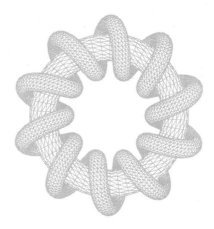

Page numbers shown in boldface indicate primary entries.

HOOPS commands are listed under H.

# About the Authors

**Wm Leler** and **Jim Merry** have written this book for **Autodesk, Inc.,** one of the world's largest PC software companies. Wm holds a Ph.D. from the University of North Carolina at Chapel Hill, and has done extensive work and published numerous articles on computer graphics, constraint languages, virtual reality, and parallel programming. His previous book, *Constraint Programming Languages,* also was published by Addison-Wesley. Jim holds a degree in operations research and industrial engineering from Cornell University, where he concentrated in system design and optimization. His introduction to computer graphics and to HOOPS came when he met the founders of Ithaca Software (now a division of Autodesk) in a laboratory at Cornell set up by Don Greenberg. Jim became product manager for HOOPS during the development of this book.